THE LIBERALIZATION OF CAPITAL MOVEMENTS IN EUROPE

FINANCIAL AND MONETARY POLICY STUDIES

Volume 29

The titles published in this series are listed at the end of this volume.

THE LIBERALIZATION OF CAPITAL MOVEMENTS IN EUROPE

THE MONETARY COMMITTEE AND FINANCIAL INTEGRATION 1958–1994

by

AGE F. P. BAKKER

Free University, Amsterdam
Deputy Director of De Nederlandsche Bank

SPRINGER-SCIENCE+BUSINESS, MEDIA, B.V.

Library of Congress Cataloging in Publication Data

Bakker, Age.
The liberalization of capital movements in Europe : the Monetary Committee and financial integration, 1958-1994 / by Age F.P. Bakker.
p. cm. -- (Financial and monetary policy studies ; 29)
Includes index.
ISBN 978-94-010-4059-4 ISBN 978-94-011-0123-3 (eBook)
DOI 10.1007/978-94-011-0123-3
1. Capital movements--Europe. 2. Monetary policy--Europe.
3. Commission of the European Communities. Monetary Committee.
4. European Economic Community. Monetary Committee. I. Title.
II. Series.
HG3942.B35 1995
332'.042--dc20 95-20404

ISBN 978-94-010-4059-4

Printed on acid-free paper

C'est alors que je me suis demandé comment établir une règle, puisque je n'acceptais pas de vivre sans règle, et que cette règle je ne l'acceptais pas d'autrui.

André Gide, Les faux-monnayeurs

In the longing that starts one on the path is a kind of homesickness, and some way, on this journey, I have started home.

Peter Matthiessen, The snow leopard

For my parents

Contents

Figures

Tables

Acknowledgements

This book is based on a dissertation which I defended in December 1994 at the University of Amsterdam. But its origins lie much further back in time. On an early morning in the spring of 1981 my then-mentor J.J. Polak, who at this time was Executive Director at the International Monetary Fund, handed me four pages of scribbled notes, jotted down in a wakeful night, with a complete scheme for a dissertation on an IMF-related subject. I took up the challenge and started some research. Back in Europe, however, when my work focused on European monetary cooperation, the project was abandoned. This book, albeit on a different subject, testifies to the chord Dr Polak then touched. The choice of the subject matter originates from the intellectual curiosity which I felt when the process of liberalization of capital movements gained momentum in the 1980s and eventually succeeded in overcoming the authorities' attachment to exchange controls and regulations. This liberalization sparked off discussions on the form and modalities of monetary cooperation in Europe and its ultimate goals. What seemed to be a merely technical, rather esoteric subject apparently contained ingredients which were able to revitalize Europe's quest for integration and, eventually, unification.

I would like to thank many colleagues and friends who have contributed with their support and comments to bringing this project to a close. Nout Wellink encouraged me to start working on this book. André Szász provided thoughtful comments with respect to the leitmotiv. Henk Jager has stimulated me throughout my research with his pointed questions and suggestions. Although we may not have finished our debates on the respective roles of the monetarist and economist camps in the drive towards capital liberalization, his comments have helped to keep me on track. Finally, I owe a large debt of gratitude to Henk Boot who has commented on various drafts of the study. His sharp analytic mind and his sense of purpose have helped me greatly in sorting out the main themes from the overwhelming amount of detailed information on capital liberalization.

A number of experts have provided useful material or have commented on drafts or chapters. I would like to thank in particular Günter Grosche, Wolfgang Kiemel, Emile van Lennep, Philippe Moutot, Jean-Jacques Rey, Wolfgang Rieke, Carlo Santini, Mario Sarcinelli, Jan Schuijer and René Smits for their valuable suggestions. Ken Lennan of the Directorate General for Economic and Financial Affairs of the European Commission read the entire manuscript and provided me with some interesting thoughts on the respective roles of the Commission and the Monetary Committee in the process of capital liberalization. On the same subject, albeit viewed from a different angle, Andreas Kees, the former secretary of the Monetary Committee, commented in his habitual lucid manner. It goes without saying that the author, while having been receptive to some of the comments, is solely responsible for the present text. I also thank my colleagues at the Nederlandsche Bank who assisted me in finding documentation. In naming Raymond Moonen, Olaf Sleijpen and Wim Vanthoor I thank them all. I am grateful to the Governing Board of the Nederlandsche Bank for granting me access to the archives. Part of the research, especially with respect to the proceedings of the Monetary Committee, is based on internal memoranda. Positions of individual member states have in most cases been double-checked with other material which is available in the public domain.

Coen Collee has been so kind as to proofread the entire manuscript and remove the gravest grammatical errors in the English text. Harmen Warris provided useful research assistance in the early stages. Cobie Hogewoning, Kees de Boer and Kasper van Veen have contributed in assembling the statistical material for the figures and tables. The typescript has been prepared by Imelda Drubbel, Katja Groeneweg, Martine Hijstek-Weeling and Nicolette Ligtenberg with much care and dedication. Last but not least, I thank Klara for her love and understanding. Without her cheerfulness and her unwavering support this book would not have been finished. And I apologize to Barbara and Feite who have been deprived of so many hours which could have been spent so much better playing games, but who one day may understand the temptations of the quiet seclusion of one's own study.

I dedicate this book to my parents, who have taught me to combine freedom of thought with consideration for other opinions.

Introduction

> *The member states are facing the choice between either reaping the benefits of increasing integration in a certain area – in this case the capital markets – attended by a significant reduction in national powers of autonomous decision-making and independence, or retaining this national independence enabling them to pursue their own policy objectives with the aid of instruments selected at their discretion. To this question, there is no generally valid answer. The solution is determined by the weight assigned to the benefits, on the one hand, and that assigned to the reduction in national sovereignty, on the other. This, however, is a subjective matter, which is assessed differently in the various countries.*
>
> *Onno Ruding, 1969*

1.1 CAPITAL LIBERALIZATION AND MONETARY UNIFICATION

In the 1980s Europe made a leap forward towards the liberalization of capital movements. EEC directives were accepted by all member states obliging them to abolish all remaining exchange controls. This common objective of freedom of capital movements has been consolidated in the Treaty on European Union. Nowadays virtually all restrictions have been lifted. This stands in striking contrast to the state of affairs only a decade ago, when many countries still operated a tight regime. Although the Treaty of Rome provided for the freedom of capital movements, this objective was circumscribed by the clause that such liberalization should only be carried through to the extent necessary to ensure the proper functioning of the Common Market. In practice, for a long time trade liberalization took precedence over capital liberalization. It is only since the publication of the White Book on the completion of the Internal Market in 1985 that freedom of capital movements generally has been accepted as a common goal. Apparently there has been a major shift in the appreciation of the pros and cons of free capital flows over time.

The move towards free capital movements in the EEC came at a time of significant progress in the process towards European *integration*. In the Single European Act, signed in 1986 and ratified one year later, principles and procedures were adopted facilitating the removal of the obstacles to the establishment of the Internal Market. The European Commission considered the capital restrictions applied in the majority of member states to be such an obstacle which needed to be removed. The dynamism displayed by the Commission in this respect contrasted sharply with the consideration it had shown earlier for restrictive regimes, which were often in contravention of agreed Community obligations.

The turnaround in the attitude towards capital liberalization, both on the side of member states and of the Commission, was boosted by the stabilizing influence exerted by the operation of the *European Monetary System* on both economic policies and financial markets. The protective shield of exchange control was ever less needed since convergence of economic performance improved gradually. Controls moreover were losing their efficacy in the changed international financial environment, characterized by financial deregulation and globalization. The negotiations on capital liberalization in Europe were accompanied by discussions on a strengthening of monetary cooperation, lest the coherence of the EMS would be sacrificed on the altar of enhanced capital mobility. These were aimed at creating conditions to ensure that freedom of capital movements would not jeopardize exchange rate stability in Europe.

The reorientation of the Commission was motivated by wider-reaching strategic considerations as well. Freedom of capital movements is a sine qua non for *monetary unification*. The objective of a European economic and monetary union (EMU) had been a recurrent theme ever since the establishment of the European Community. A number of reports on European union – the Werner report, the Tindemans report, the Spadolini report – had been published in the course of the years. All had been shelved due to the lack of political consensus and economic convergence, and their precondition, abolition of exchange control, had not been fulfilled. With the growth of consensus on capital liberalization the chances for a breakthrough on EMU would increase as well. In 1988, when the negotiations on capital liberalization were wound up, France took the initiative to put the issue of economic and monetary union again on the agenda. Not much later, on 1 July 1990 the start of the first stage of EMU was proclaimed with full freedom of capital movements well established in the core of the Community and with firm commitments of the lagging member states to bring such freedom about soon. Eventually, the political will to forge ahead proved to be so forceful that, against all historical odds, in December 1991 in Maastricht a new Treaty on European Union was agreed. The traditional inhibitions against the implicit surrender of national sovereignty had finally been overcome.

Capital liberalization	–	The easing or abolition of restrictions and administrative controls on financial cross-border transactions.
Financial deregulation	–	The easing or abolition of rules with respect to domestic financial markets and institutions.

1.2 CAPITAL LIBERALIZATION AND MONETARY POLICY

The abolition of exchange controls in Europe prior to the Maastricht Treaty constituted a tangible expression of member states' willingness to conduct policies in an open, market-oriented environment. This fitted in well with a world-wide movement towards increased attention on the part of economic policy makers for the functioning of markets. Capital liberalization has been attended by an increased use of market-oriented monetary instruments by the central banks. Previously, capital restrictions typically went hand in hand with *direct instruments* of monetary policy, which imposed limitations on the growth of commercial banks' assets and, in some cases, liabilities. Direct control mechanisms were aimed at achieving monetary objectives at a lower interest rate level than would otherwise have been the case. Capital restrictions provided the protection needed to conduct relatively autonomous monetary policies and at the same time maintain exchange rate stability by preventing capital outflows seeking higher yields. Conversely, such restrictions sometimes were needed as a complement to avoid the circumvention of domestic credit ceilings through capital inflows. Direct monetary instruments and capital restrictions were considered as two sides of the same coin.

The costs associated with direct monetary instruments, in terms of distorted allocation and risks of bureaucratic manipulation, began to weigh more heavily in the course of the years. They stifled competition between financial institutions, gave rise to disintermediation, tended to favour the privileged financing of governments to the detriment of private enterprise, and were perceived as standing in the way of the development of an internationally competitive financial centre. Market participants demonstrated increasing ingenuity in finding ways to circumvent credit and exchange controls. The transition to the use of *indirect instruments* of monetary policy, which seek to influence credit expansion through price mechanisms (i.e. changes in interest rates), and the deregulation of financial markets gathered momentum, first in Anglo-Saxon countries, later on the Continent. This process can also be understood in the historical perspective of the gradual return to market-oriented systems in the post-war period, when the immediate focus on reconstruction and industrialization, necessitating active government involvement, lost force.

The release of market forces has shifted attention to other policy domains, notably to the *task and position of the central banks*. Freely functioning markets only perform well if price and volume signals are distorted as little as possible by uncertainty about the future policy actions of the budgetary and monetary authorities. This is all the more important with respect to the financial markets, which by their very nature are more prone to vicissitudes than the commodity markets. In the 'incompatible triangle' of freedom of capital movements, stable exchange rates and autonomy for domestic monetary policy, a phrase coined in the literature on optimum currency areas in the 1960s, theory suggests that one of the three angular points has to give in.

The discussions on liberalization of capital movements in the framework of the EMS therefore have focused attention on the goals of monetary policy. If autonomy of monetary policy is perceived as supporting government policies in achieving domestic economic goals, which can shift over time and may differ among countries, the triangle will remain incompatible. If, on the other hand, domestic price stability is the primary common goal of monetary policy an important element of divergence will have been removed. The chances of combining free capital movements with stable exchange rates will be increased. Over time, disillusionment with stimulatory monetary policies and the apparent success of German policies predicated on stability-oriented policies have fostered the acceptance of price stability as the primary goal of monetary policy.

A measure of *independence* of the national central banks is required in order to enable them to strive for domestic price stability unhampered by short-term domestic political considerations. After the ratification of the Treaty on European Union, which provides for independence to be established before the start of the final stage of EMU, important steps have been taken in this respect in several member states. Comparable institutional positions of the central banks in the member states encourage cooperation and facilitate the coordination of monetary policies. This important shift towards institutional independence of the central banks reflects the increased attention given to the need to preserve price stability in economies characterized by freedom of capital movements. It also reflects the exemplary role of the independent Deutsche Bundesbank as the central bank which has been most successful in the fight against inflation.

The *case of Europe* is an interesting one. Its combined drive for liberalization of capital movements and for strengthening the position of national central banks has inspired many countries outside the European Community to follow suit. Although capital liberalization has been a global phenomenon in the past ten years or so, affecting a number of developing countries as well, many of these countries practise a relatively high degree of exchange rate flexibility. EC member states, however, have firm exchange rate objectives in the framework of the European Monetary System and have even higher aspirations in pursuing monetary unification. They therefore have to deal with the allegedly incompatible triangle. In the wake of the EMS crises of 1992 and 1993 a division has become visible, with some countries abandoning exchange rate fixity and other countries continuing to align monetary policies. After a brief interlude of experimentation, eventually none has reverted to exchange controls, despite calls for their reintroduction.

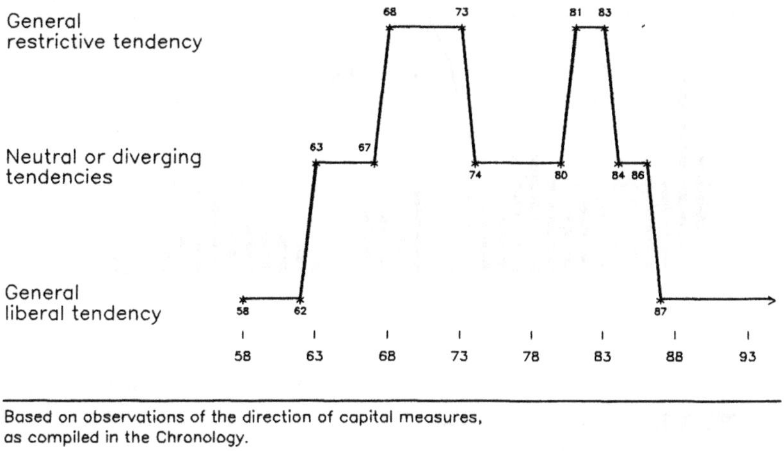

Fig. 1. Trends in capital regimes in the EEC.

1.3 THE TIDAL MOVEMENT OF EXCHANGE CONTROL

The process of the imposition of capital restrictions and their subsequent liberalization has been a constant ebb and flow in economic history. After the liberalism of the nineteenth century, the inter-war period was characterized by severe restrictions on capital and ultimately on trade. The post-World War II period in Europe can be divided into three distinct periods. In the years immediately following the war there was an important move towards liberalization. As shown in Figure 1, towards the end of the 1960s this trend was reversed and restrictions were reimposed in a spectacular manner in European countries, on outward as well as on inward capital flows. This was followed in the 1980s by a dramatic reversal, eventually leading towards the full liberalization of capital movements in all European countries for the first time since the Treaty of Rome had been signed. One important question addressed by this study concerns the causes which lay behind these regime shifts and the eventual complete abolition of exchange control in the member states of the European Community. Another question is whether this state of full freedom of capital movements in Europe will be maintained or whether there is a chance that the ebb and flow of economic history will re-take its due course, opening the perspective of yet another tide of restrictive policies.

The tidal movements of the regime with respect to capital movements run partly parallel to the *cyclical situation* of the world economy. In times of cyclical downturn the authorities tended to avoid through restrictive measures that the stimulatory effect of lower interest rates on domestic demand would get thwarted by capital outflows. Exchange controls were particular-

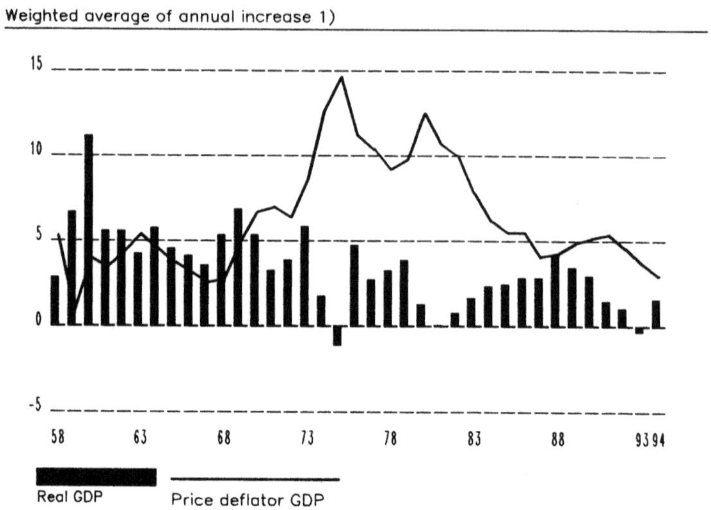

1 Average of actual EEC member states.
Source: European Economy no 58 1994, European Commission.

Fig. 2. Cyclical movements in the EEC.

ly favoured if economic downturn went hand in hand with high inflation, so-called stagflation. In general higher rates of price increases tend to coincide with larger *inflation differentials* among countries, which in turn spark off exchange rate tensions. Countries tried to counteract these tensions by imposing capital restrictions. Indeed, Figure 2 provides prima facie evidence of a degree of correlation between the direction of price movements and the general tendency with respect to capital regimes in the EEC. When domestic stability was endangered – in the final years of the Bretton Woods System – and policies diverged – the first years of the European Monetary System – restrictive tendencies manifested themselves most forcefully. In times of cyclical upturn liberalizing measures were in general taken more easily, especially if inflationary pressures were contained. In those circumstances pressure groups seeking protection became less vocal. Such groups could include financial institutions wishing to protect their home market, industrial sectors wishing to preserve privileged financing arrangements, but also monetary authorities were inclined to maintain the status quo. International cooperation, which implies give-and-take in negotiations, flourishes during cyclical upturns, because then authorities are more willing to make concessions involving potential short-term costs but long-term benefits.

The lifting of capital restrictions formed part of *negotiations*, conferring obligations upon member states of the European Community. Like trade negotiations, the abolition of restrictions was made conditional on the fulfilment of demands in other areas, notably as regards the strengthening of monetary cooperation mechanisms. Liberalization measures thus could be presented as a compromise deal, with other countries taking measures as well. Capital restrictions were seen as the lesser evil as compared to *trade restrictions*. In fact, it will be argued in this study that capital restrictions by implied agreement for a long time were tolerated by the Commission and by other liberally-oriented member states because their abandonment was regarded as potentially endangering the Common Market for goods and services. There was another distinguishing characteristic: some member states maintained an open exchange regime regardless of the practice in other countries. Capital controls were rarely utilized in order to discriminate between countries. Such discrimination was circumvented easily anyway. But there was one thing which trade and capital restrictions had in common: once imposed they were not easily removed. In this sense capital restrictions shared the ratchet effect typically associated with trade restrictions.

1.4 THE ROLE OF THE MONETARY COMMITTEE

The involvement of the Monetary Committee of the European Community runs through this book as a continuous thread. In this rather secretive body the highest civil servants of the national Treasuries convene monthly with their counterparts of the national central banks and representatives of the European Commission. One of the main assignments of this body has been the promotion of the liberalization of capital movements. All proposals of the Commission for directives with respect to capital movements have been discussed at length in this committee. Because of its unique composition it was well placed to oversee the implications for economic and monetary policies. At times the committee has played a stimulating role, at other times the political obstacles in this field became manifest in the committee's deliberations. The committee's role was not in the nature of a supporting act. In practice the Commission proposals with respect to capital movements would not be presented to the Council of Ministers as long as the committee had not given its seal of approval.

The main motives for maintaining capital controls were considerations regarding the exchange rate and monetary policy. All decisions concerning the EMS, and in particular exchange rate realignments, were prepared in the Monetary Committee. As the name of the committee implies, it is in this forum that the institutional checks and balances concerning monetary policy decisions come together as well. Thus the link which was all along placed by some member states between the dossier on capital liberalization and the dossier on monetary cooperation was ideally dealt with in the committee. In the Monetary Committee the controversies between the 'economist' school, which proclaimed that monetary integration was dependent on economic convergence, and the 'monetarist' school, which held that monetary integration could move in parallel with progress towards economic convergence, came to the fore. The monetary cooperation dossiers culminated in the discussions on economic and monetary union.

1.5 THE PURPOSE OF THIS BOOK

This study takes as its starting point the provisions in the Treaty of Rome with respect to the liberalization of capital movements. It then follows the ups and downs in this liberalization process ending with the Treaty of Maastricht. On the way the study picks up the thread which Onno Ruding, the later Minister of Finance of the Netherlands, had to leave in 1969 in his magnum opus 'Towards one integrated European capital market?' The question mark he wisely put in the title could only be removed much later than could be foreseen at the time. This book does not seek to describe in detail the precise form of the liberalization of capital transactions, e.g. by distinguishing between types of instruments, and the micro-economic impact on market participants. Neither does it deal with detailed descriptions of liberalization codes of other international organizations, such as the OECD. Others have done this exhaustively and also the organizations themselves publish heavily. What this book is about is the apparent shift in the balance between the pros and cons of capital restrictions in the course of the years, the economic and political forces which were behind this changing perception, and the implications this has had for monetary policy cooperation in Europe, in particular for the use of monetary instruments and the position of central banks. In analysing the discussions on capital liberalization attention focuses in particular on the attitude of the European Commission vis-à-vis the freedom of capital movements and the involvement of the Monetary Committee. Throughout the attitude of individual member states is analysed, starting with the six founding members and including new members as they joined the Community. Following the analysis of these factors, tentative answers are formulated with respect to the question whether the capital liberalization which has taken place in Europe will prove to be of an irreversible character.

The book is organized as follows. In *Chapter 2* capital controls are defined and categorized and the different motives for imposing restrictions and abolishing them are analysed. Particular attention is paid to the sequencing of liberalization measures. *Chapter 3* deals with the provisions in the Treaty of Rome with respect to capital and briefly comments on the involvement of the OECD and the IMF in capital liberalization. In *Chapter 4* the Monetary Committee is introduced and its main tasks, apart from liberalization of capital movements, are examined. Many related tasks of the committee concern areas which were dealt with in parallel in the negotiations on capital liberalization. Annex 2 contains a complete list of the members of the Monetary Committee since its establishment.

Chapters 5 through 9 constitute the core of this study. In a largely chronological order the attitudes of member states and the Commission with respect to capital liberalization are analysed. The first successful steps towards liberalization in a common EEC framework are dealt with in *Chapter 5*. Gradually momentum was lost and towards the end of the 1960s restrictions were reintroduced. In *Chapter 6* the failed attempt towards economic and monetary union along the lines of the Werner report is examined. In the wake of the collapse of the Bretton Woods system and the oil crisis member states went their own separate ways and European integration came to a stand-still. The decade of the 1970s, however, ends on an optimistic note with the establishment of the European Monetary System and the abolition of exchange control in the United Kingdom. *Chapters 7 and 8* examine the negotiations in the 1980s leading up to the acceptance of the common obligation to fully liberalize capital movements. Just as for earlier years, related dossiers, such as taxation and supervisory issues, are touched upon, and the discussions are documented on the erga omnes principle which demands that capital liberalization be applied to third countries as well. In *Chapter 9* the actual implementation of the liberalization directives is described, as well as the incorporation of the principle of full freedom of capital movements into the Treaty on European Union. The chapter ends with a discussion of the crises in the EMS which for a time seemed likely to reopen the debate on freedom of capital movements. In a final *Chapter 10* some conclusions are drawn, and some tentative answers are formulated with respect to the questions phrased in this introduction.

For a survey of major measures with respect to capital movements the reader is referred to the chronology at the end of the book. In annexes the main relevant Community texts are reproduced.

CHAPTER 2

Capital Restrictions: Classification and General Observations

Private financial markets have become internationalized much more rapidly and completely than other economic and political institutions. That is why we are in trouble.

James Tobin, 1978

There may have been some cases of unwarranted speculative attacks on some currencies, although I find it difficult to think of conspicuous examples, while it would be easy to cite many examples where the speculators were right and the authorities dead wrong.

Gottfried Haberler, 1976

2.1 INTRODUCTION

Although capital controls have formed a major instrument for the monetary authorities in the conduct of economic policy, they have not received the same degree of intellectual attention as many of the other policy instruments. There is a substantial range of *academic literature* on capital controls. Still it is a mere trifle in comparison to the vast bulk of literature on specialized subjects such as trade restrictions or tax incentives. One of the explanations may be that the use of capital restrictions, while having redistributional effects, generally has not been regarded as having negative allocation and growth effects of a magnitude in any way comparable to trade restrictions or tax incentives.[1] Another explanation may be that capital controls have not been a generalized phenomenon in industrial countries in the post-World War II period. Moreover, shaped by tradition and the country-specific institutional set-up of the financial system, restrictions have taken manifold forms and were often camouflaged in complex administrative rules.

The two major *reserve currency countries*, the United States and Germany, have traditionally followed liberal economic policies. The United States, as the dominant economy with the major world reserve currency, has generally not availed itself of outright restrictions on capital flows. Nevertheless, it has in the final years of the Bretton Woods system taken measures with the aim of discouraging capital outflows.[2] Another reserve currency nation like Germany, apart from a brief albeit intensive experiment in the immediate post-Bretton Woods period to curtail capital inflows through exchange control, likewise has not used capital restrictions to the same extent as the other industrial countries have done. Switzerland and Canada, too, in general have adhered to a well-established liberal regime.[3] But in most *non-reserve currency countries* capital controls have been a major economic tool, although varying in intensity and taking widely diverging forms.[4] Academic attention thus mainly focused on the analysis of the merits of specific forms of exchange regulations in individual countries. In economic models capital controls have been utilized as constraining variables, enabling the authorities to fix their exchange rate and to shield domestic interest rates from external influences.

For the purpose of this study, this introductory chapter briefly discusses the various types of controls utilized and their implications. The motives to introduce or maintain capital controls are examined. These are of an economic but sometimes also of a wider-ranging political nature. In the discussion of these motives it becomes clear that there is a significant difference between the application of controls on outflows of capital as opposed to controls on inflows of capital. The drawbacks of controls are commented upon; these drawbacks have led to liberalization being perceived as preferable to the 'second best' solution of capital controls. One of the major theories with respect to the utilization and subsequent dismantling of capital controls is briefly treated: the theory of sequencing. This theory takes as its starting point the general axiom that the unhampered functioning of markets yields the best economic results, but that economic or political circumstances may justify the temporary utilization of controls. Policies should strive for the abolition of controls in steps, depending on the attainment of economic equilibrium conditions.

2.2 TYPES OF CAPITAL CONTROLS

The general label of capital controls encompasses a wide range of diversified and often country-specific measures. These restrictions on and impediments to capital movements have manifested themselves mainly in four distinct general forms.[5]

a) *Administrative controls on cross-border capital movements*. These controls usually involve an approval procedure by a governmental agency or the national central bank for cross-border transfers of capital. Approval can be based on a judgement as to the character of the underlying transaction or, alternatively, on rules regarding limits on the permitted amounts of capital transferred. The responsibility for operating exchange control regulations has often been delegated to commercial banks.[6] Controls generally have covered the whole spectrum of capital movements, from long-term direct investment flows and foreign equity transactions to short-term external positions of commercial banks and foreign exchange transactions by residents. By restricting forward cover operations or regulating the settlement of exports or imports, shifts in leads and lags have been restricted. Administrative controls thus influenced greatly the room for manoeuvre for cross-border financial transactions, portfolio decisions of non-bank residents and the internationalization of companies. Citizens were affected in their freedom to travel abroad by limits on the amount of foreign currency they could take with them. In one way or another administrative controls were applied at times in all European countries, least in Belgium and Luxembourg which relied on a dual exchange market.[7] Common features of administrative controls are that they imply legislation and regulations, and impose administrative obligations on the banking system in order to control flows. They also necessitate compliance and enforcement procedures. The judicial treatment of offences differed among European countries, with Italy's treatment of violations as criminal offences outranging other more lenient regimes.[8]

b) *Dual or multiple exchange rate systems.* In such systems different exchange rates apply to certain types of commercial and financial transactions. Typically all or a significant part of current account transactions are settled at a uniform fixed or managed exchange rate, capital account transactions and sometimes selected current account transactions being settled at another exchange rate. Usually the latter so-called financial rate is allowed to float and thus is entirely determined by supply and demand on the 'financial' exchange market, normally without any official intervention. In most cases the financial exchange rate stands at a discount (i.e. foreign currencies carry a premium) because the room to buy foreign exchange for cross-border capital transactions is limited by foreign demand for the national currency related to capital transactions. The latter is likely to be negatively influenced by the existence of a dual exchange market as long as foreign investors favour portfolio investment in countries with a liberal exchange regime. Two-tier exchange markets typically have been established to insulate current account transactions from speculative outward capital movements which could call for undesired interest rate adjustments or lead to reserve losses. They can, however, also accommodate excessive inflows and thus prevent an overshooting of the exchange rate for current transactions.

Belgium and Luxembourg, tied together in a monetary union since 1922, were the only countries to consistently operate a dual exchange rate system. France and Italy briefly operated a dual market in the currency turmoil of the early 1970s. Some countries experimented at times with specific currency markets, mainly in the form of a closed-circuit type, where the funds involved in purchases by residents of securities denominated in foreign currency had to be matched by the proceeds from sales of such securities by residents (see Table 1). Like administrative controls multiple currency systems need to be enforced by compliance procedures and thus imply the administration of foreign exchange transactions of residents and domestic currency transactions of non-residents, in order to separate the current (commercial) and capital transactions.

TABLE 1

Multiple currency practices in the EEC.

Dual markets		
Belgium-Luxembourg	financial franc market	1955–1990
France	financial franc market	1971–1974
Italy	financial lira market	1973–1974
Specific currency markets		
France	devises-titres market	1955–1962
	devises-titres market	1969–1971
	devises-titres market	1981–1986
Ireland	investment currency market	1947–1978
The Netherlands	foreign security market	1959–1966
	closed bond 'O-circuit'	1971–1974
United Kingdom	investment currency market	1947–1979

c) *Specific taxation of cross-border financial flows or of income resulting from external portfolios.* Under such a system taxes are levied on external financial transactions, thus limiting their attractiveness, or on income resulting from the holding by residents of foreign financial assets or the holding by non-residents of domestic assets. In principle such taxation only impedes cross-border flows if it discriminates between domestic and external assets or between residents and non-residents. In this sense a generalized withholding tax, which treats residents and non-residents alike, cannot strictly speaking be considered an impediment to cross-border flows. However, in practice differences in tax regimes have given rise to substantial capital movements and, from the standpoint of the authorities, changes in taxation regimes have been considered as an alternative to direct capital controls. A specific type, only applied in the United States in the 1960s, is interest equalization taxation which seeks to eliminate yield differentials, mainly because of diverging interest rates, between domestic and foreign assets.

Apart from these three types of direct restrictions there is d) a *residual group of indirect restrictions or regulations*. This category includes measures such as limitations on interest payments on deposit accounts of non-residents, reserve requirements which discriminate between residents and non-residents, provisions for the net external position of commercial banks, and other measures which are intended to limit cross-border capital flows, although not explicitly outlawing them. Some of these provisions at times have not been intended primarily to regulate cross-border capital flows, but were rather motivated by domestic monetary policy considerations or supervisory concerns.

TABLE 2

Introduction of a positive exchange control regime.

1961	September	Germany
1977	September	The Netherlands
1979	October	United Kingdom
1988	October	Denmark
1988	October	Italy
1989	June	France
1992	February	Spain

Note: Other member states introduced a positive regime when they abolished all restrictions in 1992 to 1994. France briefly introduced a positive regime in 1967, which was repealed in the wake of the 1968 crisis.

More in general, a distinction must be made between restrictions taken in the framework of *exchange control*, which only relates to the import and export of capital, and those restrictions which are based on *national regulations* with respect to the domestic flow of capital. Initially EEC provisions were only applicable to direct exchange control measures. When in the course of the years the EEC took a gradually less permissive attitude towards discriminatory national regulations indirect capital restrictions were outlawed as well, especially after the Brugnoni and Ruffinengo ruling of the European Court of Justice in 1986. The distinction between exchange controls and discriminatory national regulations is an important one in connection with the *erga omnes* principle. In the case of exchange control it is technically difficult to discriminate between countries, as opposed to national regulations where discrimination is easier to administer, i.e. in the case of establishment or of issues of securities.

Another important distinction can be made with respect to positive and negative regimes of exchange control. Under a *positive exchange regime* all cross-border capital transactions are permitted unless explicitly restricted. Germany was the first European country to adopt such legislation in 1961. On the contrary, under a *negative exchange regime* all cross-border capital transactions are restricted unless explicitly permitted. Most European countries operated negative systems well into the 1980s (see Table 2).

2.3 THE IMPACT ON CAPITAL FLOWS

Views have differed as to the merits and demerits of these respective types of capital controls, and as to whether they impinged in a comparable way on the activities of economic agents. *Administrative controls* influence the volume of flows, either by forbidding them altogether or by capping them off by limiting the amounts allowed. Administrative controls have been applied as a structural economic policy instrument, but they have also been utilized on a temporary basis. Frequently they were meant to last for a limited time. *Taxation*, on the other hand, has a direct impact on the price of capital flows. The taxation of financial transactions or external portfolios most often has been utilized with the specific aim of limiting short-term speculative flows. Because these flows were considered to be a temporary phenomenon, the relevant taxes were also considered to be temporary and thus could be withdrawn. In this respect authorities could keep alive the fiction of free financial flows.[9] Promises, both as to taxation and to administrative controls, were, needless to say, not always kept. As Alworth (1993) has said: 'The taxation of cross-border flows is a stepchild of conflicting objectives (i.e. raising government revenues as well as domestic savings) being generally an outgrowth, if not an afterthought, of the domestic tax system.'

Domestic *regulations* can constitute an indirect barrier to cross-border capital flows. An important example is provided by administrative rules with respect to the investment policies of pension funds and other institutional investors. They typically were required to invest a substantial proportion of their assets in domestic (government) bonds. Regulations with respect to the allowed share of foreign assets in their portfolio effectively dampened cross-border flows. Regulations with respect to foreign ownership of domestic companies, too, can limit inward investment without formally restricting it. Apart from the formal restrictions there are thus many hidden ways of limiting outflows. It is only recently that these hidden barriers have received more attention once formal restrictions were lifted.

Dual exchange rate systems often have been considered by the authorities concerned as being of a less restrictive character than the other types considered above. It was argued that cross-border flows were uninhibited and that the price for the conversion of national into foreign currency and vice versa was solely determined by economic forces in a freely functioning market. This view was contested by others who saw in the separation of exchange markets for current and financial transactions an infringement of the free play of supply and demand. Nevertheless, a dual system, because of its market-oriented approach, probably can be considered as the lesser evil. In practice it was likely to be the least effective as well, because large differentials between the financial and the commercial rate were not likely to persist for very long. The larger the differential, the greater the incentive there is for private market operators to try to circumvent the regulations separating the two markets.[10]

Dornbusch (1986), in a discussion of the appropriateness of a dual exchange system for developing countries, has concluded that such a system works well if the commercial rate is maintained close to its equilibrium level, i.e. in a range close to the free rate. The managed rate therefore should be allowed to shift in response to fundamental macro-economic changes.

This leads to the conclusion that the different types of control more or less have the same *economic impact.* Administrative controls primarily influence the volume of transactions, taxation the price of such transactions. Dual exchange systems influence both the price and volume of transactions. In all instances therefore capital flows are affected, either directly (volume) or indirectly (price). In this respect Adams and Greenwood (1985) have rightly noted that dual exchange rate systems and capital controls can be thought of as having equivalent effects to the same extent as the standard trade literature views tariffs and quotas to have. The discriminatory character of exchange control systems makes it necessary in all cases to have procedures for compliance and enforcement, requiring complex sets of rules and administrative red-tape. In an economic sense all types of capital controls lead to a separation between the domestic financial market and the external financial markets. This segmentation of markets through capital controls, if effective, makes domestic interest rates less dependent on international interest rates.

The types of capital control reviewed here stand in the way of truly liberal international financial markets because they imply *segmentation* and *discrimination.* If liberalization of capital movements is to be pursued, from a policy viewpoint, therefore, there is no need to distinguish between the types of control discussed here. In the European context, the policy conclusion has been drawn that all three types of direct capital controls as well as the indirect restrictions stood in the way of the creation of the Internal Market and thus had to be eliminated. But, as we will see, it has been a lengthy process to overcome ingrained habits. Liberalization has not come overnight.

2.4 TYPES OF TRANSACTIONS AFFECTED BY CAPITAL CONTROLS

In the application of capital restrictions generally a distinction has been made according to the type of financial instruments or transactions involved. Typically distinctions have been made between long-term and short-term capital flows and between incoming and outgoing capital flows.

2.4.1 Long-Term and Short-Term Capital Flows

Long-term capital flows are more closely related to the real economy, so it is generally felt, because they involve investment flows and the building-up of external portfolio positions. In general it has been considered desirable to obstruct as little as possible such capital movements which respond to long-term considerations with respect to portfolio preferences or investment and

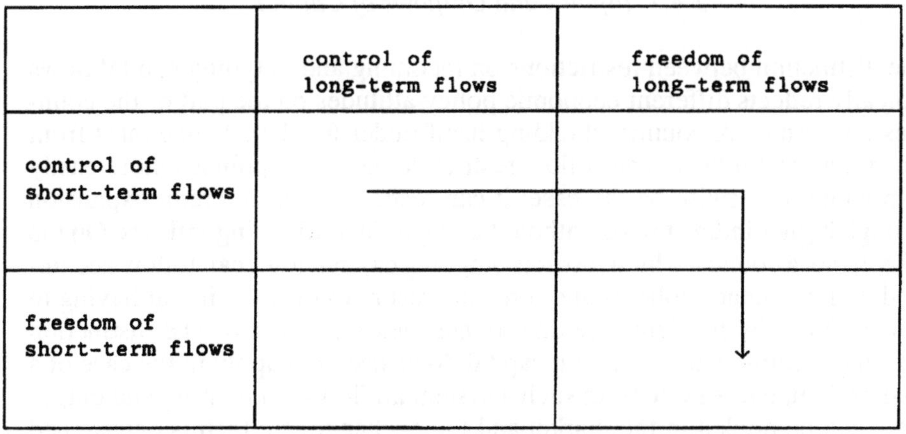

Fig. 3. Typical sequencing of capital liberalization.

profit opportunities. Typical examples are direct investment flows, the buying and selling of securities, the admission of issues of foreign securities on the domestic capital market, as well as transactions in real estate. Although these transactions often have received priority when direct exchange restrictions were abolished, they frequently remained subject to domestic regulations because of political sensitivities concerning foreign ownership.

Short-term capital flows are regarded as financial flows and provide the most common channel for speculative capital movements. Although such flows can have a macro-economic impact through their effect on interest and exchange rates, they are easily reversible by their very nature. In the absence of financial disturbances the influence of short-term capital flows on the real economy is deemed to be small, because they are only distantly related to the financing of real activity and trade. Short-term flows typically have been restricted more frequently because the benefits of freedom were not deemed to be commensurate with the possible costs associated with speculative flows, bringing pressure on the exchange rate or complicating domestic monetary control.[11] Typical examples are short-term non-trade related loans, deposits by residents (non-residents) in foreign (domestic) currencies and the buying and selling of money market instruments or short-term unquoted securities. Generally the demarcation line between short and long-term flows is drawn at a maturity of one to two years. Because *travel allowances* provided a notable loophole, foreign exchange entitlements for tourists, while formally being an invisible transaction, were frequently tightened at the same time as short-term capital flows were curtailed.

2.4.2 *Inflows and Outflows of Capital*

The distinction between restrictions on incoming and outgoing capital flows typically reflects different economic policy attitudes on the part of the countries concerned. A country shielding itself under fixed exchange rates from incoming capital flows can follow restrictive monetary policies more easily than would otherwise be the case: it can restrict domestic credit expansion through higher interest rates without having to fear offsetting inflows. On the other hand, a country which restricts outgoing capital flows can follow accommodating monetary policies and force interest rates down, without having to fear outflows by residents seeking higher yields elsewhere. The distinction between incoming and outgoing capital flows need not apply in the case of a dual exchange rate system. In such a system all flows – incoming and outgoing – can be pooled in the market and the exchange rate then is determined by supply and demand. Nevertheless, some countries have combined such a system with administrative controls, thus indirectly influencing the balance between supply and demand, and hence the price. Others, such as Belgium and Luxembourg, initially targeted the dual market to outflows only, while capital inflows could be settled in the official market. Only in the beginning of the 1970s inflows were led through the dual market as well.

From a policy standpoint, the distinction between restrictions on outflows and those on inflows is a significative one. Restrictions on *outflows* typically were used by weak-currency countries. This weakness of the currency in turn was the outcome of economic policies, which favoured low interest rates and accepted higher inflation rates in order to reach in the short run a better point on the Phillips curve, the negatively sloped curve depicting the relationship between the levels of inflation and unemployment. Such policies typically resulted in a weak position on the current account of the balance of payments, which provoked confidence crises. Controls on capital outflows for exchange rate considerations thus could be considered a sign of weakness on the part of the countries concerned.

On the other hand, restrictions on *inflows* were utilized to avoid that stability-oriented domestic policies in strong-currency countries were thwarted by capital inflows out of countries with more lax policies. Such inflows would enlarge the money supply and thus would frustrate restrictive monetary policies. In the beginning of the 1970s such inward capital controls were imposed to avert so-called hot money, speculative flows in the final days of the Bretton Woods System and thereafter.

These distinctions between types of capital control demonstrate the wide array of choices open to the authorities. The particular constellation chosen has been usually inspired by the motives the authorities had for imposing capital restrictions.

TABLE 3

Official objectives of exchange control.

France	to protect the currency, to preserve the autonomy of monetary policy, and to control the participation of foreign capital in sensitive sectors of the economy
Germany	to counter adverse effects on the purchasing power of the Deutsche mark and to secure equilibrium on the balance of payments
Ireland	to help to safeguard the national external reserves and to regulate the effects of capital movements on the exchange rate of the Irish pound
The Netherlands	to prevent the capital market from being disrupted, to prevent a large outflow of capital which (threatens to) considerably reduce the gold and foreign exchange holdings, or to prevent a large inflow of capital which (threatens to) seriously thwart financial and economic policies
United Kingdom	to conserve the United Kingdom's gold and foreign currency resources and to assist the balance of payments

Sources: France: Galy (1986); Germany; Aussenwirtschaftsgesetz (1961), Article 23.2; Ireland: Memorandum of Irish delegation to OECD (1983); the Netherlands: External Financial Relations Act (1980), based on Articles 4, 7 and 8; United Kingdom: A guide to United Kingdom Exchange Control (1977).

2.5 THE MOTIVES FOR CAPITAL RESTRICTIONS

Capital restrictions have been a critical ingredient of the set of economic control instruments of the authorities in the post-World War II period. They have lain close to the heart of politicians and have frequently been part of the agenda of political parties. It is only quite recently that these restrictions have been dismantled in a number of countries under the influence of economic and political forces. A gradually accelerating process of erosion of the effectiveness of capital controls has precipitated this process. We will dwell on this process of financial liberalization later. First, it is important to understand why in the past the authorities were so attracted to capital restrictions and thus for a long time were extremely reluctant to give up this instrument to control financial transactions.

Many arguments to justify capital controls have been advanced in the economic literature.[12] In Table 3 some of the official objectives are brought together. But there were other motives as well and policy makers have been quite vocal in their advocacy of control mechanisms. The main arguments can be grouped in four thematic categories, related to exchange rate policy, monetary policy, savings and investment, and taxation, respectively.

2.5.1 *Exchange Rate Considerations*

Without any doubt the foremost motive to impose restrictions has been the wish of the authorities to limit downward or – more rarely – upward pressure on the exchange rate. These restrictions have mainly been applied to short-term capital transactions. They were frequently maintained or strengthened to counter volatile *speculative flows* which threatened to undermine the stability of the exchange rate and to deplete a country's foreign exchange reserves, especially in times of a balance-of-payments crisis. In many countries residents have long been forbidden to hold deposits denominated in foreign currencies, in order to prevent them from quickly converting domestic currency into foreign currency in case of a crisis of confidence in the economic policies of the national authorities. Sometimes these restrictions functioned as an alternative to the adjustment of economic policies and thus helped to 'buy time' for the authorities. At other times they were taken to avoid the effects of foreign disturbances on the domestic economy. Particularly the excessive exchange rate volatility, caused by the unstable short-term behaviour of financial markets, has formed a justification for restrictions in order to insulate the real economy from 'markets dominated by traders in the game of guessing what other traders are going to think'.[13] Once restrictions were imposed, however, there was a reluctance to abolish them out of fear that policies would immediately be put to the test again by the financial markets.

Capital controls on short-term inflows became a particular feature of the late 1960s in Europe, when the earlier process of liberalization was reversed. This was caused by the underlying strains in the Bretton Woods system of *fixed exchange rates*. The loss of confidence in the US dollar resulted in capital outflows towards low-inflation countries like Germany, the Netherlands and Switzerland. They either had the choice to revalue their exchange rate and thus take the pressure off or to accept the inflationary consequences of the liquidity inflows on their monetary aggregates. Initially, both roads were considered unattractive. Restrictions on inward capital flows were imposed, while after the first oil crisis other countries experiencing downward pressure on their exchange rate imposed restrictions on outward capital flows. Although most controls on inward flows were lifted in the course of the 1970s and an appreciation of the currency vis-à-vis the US dollar was accepted, the controls on outward flows were more sticky. At the time of the establishment of the EMS it was taken for granted that these controls would remain in place and would help to beat off speculative attacks. In fact, it was widely believed that this was the only feasible way to maintain a system of fixed, but adjustable exchange rates among economies with diverging economic performances.[14]

2.5.2 *Monetary Policy Considerations*

A motive closely related to the exchange rate policy considerations has been the wish on the part of the authorities to increase the room to manoeuvre for monetary policy. Capital controls enabled monetary policy to be directed towards *domestic objectives*, while maintaining the exchange rate irrespective of external developments, because a wedge was driven between domestic and international interest rates. In the 'incompatible triangle' of simultaneous autonomy over monetary policy, freedom of capital movements and stability of the exchange rate, the freedom of capital movements was generally considered to be the intermediate variable which could be dispensed with at the least costs. Pressures exerted on the exchange rate could be countered by introducing or tightening capital restrictions instead of relieving such pressures by adjusting interest rates. Interest rate adjustments could be considered inappropriate in the light of domestic policy goals and exchange restrictions formed a commensurate substitute for monetary policy action.[15]

More in general capital restrictions were considered necessary in order to close loopholes under regimes of direct credit control. Such restrictions were aimed at avoiding that credit taking abroad was substituted for domestic credit which was subject to ceilings or penal reserve requirements. Typically, therefore, as discussed in chapter 1.2, the use of direct monetary instruments went hand in hand with exchange controls.

2.5.3 *Saving and Investment Considerations*

Another rationale for the imposition of restrictions has been the wish to use scarce domestic savings to finance investment at home rather than abroad. The popular paraphrase of this argument was that national thrift should be put at work to generate jobs at home. The controls often were disguised in the form of *rules on investments* in foreign assets by pension funds and insurance companies.[16] More outright controls were aimed at limiting access of non-resident borrowers to domestic capital markets. But there were less noble afterthoughts in operating exchange control: governments frequently adopted a negative stance against *foreign ownership* of domestic industry and thus subjected inward direct investment flows to cumbersome authorization procedures. Especially countries conducting active government-led industrial policies availed themselves of such controls. A prime example is France where considerations concerning national industrial development inspired a complicated set of permits for the establishment of foreign controlled companies.[17]

2.5.4 *Tax Considerations*

A fourth motive for capital restrictions has been the wish on the part of the fiscal authorities to be able to tax financial transactions, interest and dividend

	short-term	long-term
outflows	- preserve low interest rates - avoid downward pressure on exchange rate	- protect domestic savings - protect domestic capital market
inflows	- preserve domestic price stability - avoid upward pressure on exchange rate	- protect domestic control of key industries

Fig. 4. Main motives for capital restrictions.

income, as well as wealth. Capital is a highly mobile factor of production. Controls have been imposed to avoid the erosion of the tax base and to limit the possibility for residents to shift their financial portfolios abroad to countries with lower tax rates in order to avoid domestic taxes. It was hoped that capital controls would insulate the domestic tax base from such *tax arbitrage* and would prevent the movement of assets to off-shore centres.[18]

2.6 DRAWBACKS OF CAPITAL CONTROLS

Although all countries have experimented with capital controls, be it in a direct manner or indirectly in a disguised manner, there always has been a strong undercurrent in favour of abolishing them. The arguments of the proponents of liberalization were related to doubts as to the effectiveness of controls with respect to the objectives they were supposed to achieve, as well as to the costs of capital controls.

2.6.1 Low Degree of Effectiveness

Capital controls are most likely to form especially a hindrance for legitimate capital transactions. The latter are easier to restrict than speculative or other unwanted transactions, which by their very nature will tend to be diverted through unrestricted channels or be camouflaged as other transactions, e.g. in the current sphere. Controls will induce market participants to find ways of *circumventing* them. Bhagwati's study (1978) of exchange control regimes in developing countries provides sometimes amusing but mostly sad evidence of the incentives for illegal outflows under control regimes in cases of an overvalued currency. If controls lead to an artificially low interest rate and an overvalued currency, there are particularly strong incentives to find loopholes in the regulations in order to place funds in higher-yielding external assets. In its turn this will provoke the authorities to impose new controls. There is thus an inherent tendency for an extension and *cumulation of controls*, leading to increased restrictiveness. In fact, there has been a distinct tendency for control measures, once taken, to remain in effect. Controls cannot be easily switched on and off according to the needs of the moment.[19] The *technical apparatus* needed for the implementation and control of the capital restrictions tends to grow all along.

In the economic literature the effectiveness of capital restrictions frequently has been measured by comparing *differentials* between domestic and Euro interest rates. Also the effects on *capital flows* have been assessed. This empirical work, which generally observes a certain degree of effectiveness, will not be redone here. What interests us primarily is the perception from the side of the policymakers of the effectiveness of capital restrictions to reach predetermined goals, such as the preservation of the exchange rate or of domestic monetary stability. In general, experience shows that capital controls may be effective in warding off speculative attacks in the short run, but that in the long run the exchange rate has to be adjusted anyway. There is evidence that the effectiveness of capital controls in this respect has eroded over time because of the technological and structural changes which have taken place in the financial markets, making it harder for the authorities to monitor compliance with restrictions.

2.6.2 Undermining Economic Discipline

The *macro-economic costs* of capital controls are found in the distortions in asset prices and interest rates which can lead to a suboptimal allocation of capital resources. From a policy viewpoint, however, the disturbing *effects on economic and monetary policy* have been a more important consideration. By shielding domestic financial markets from external influences, governments were enabled to direct policies to suit their own priorities and keep domestic interest rates artificially low. This may have had temporary economic and political advantages, especially if the external shock was a temporary one. However, it led to suboptimal economic solutions if the necessary adjustment of policies by governments or adaptation of strategies by private economic agents to changed international circumstances was postponed. The shielding of domestic financial markets has made it easier for the authorities to follow stimulatory monetary policies, and capital controls typically have been associated with a relative poor inflation performance, as discussed in chapter 1.3. The combination of low interest rates and high inflation, often leading to negative real interest rates, has induced countries to pursue less sound fiscal policies as well. In sum, controls on capital outflows enabled the authorities to follow less disciplined policies, leading to divergence with the performance of other, more stability-oriented countries. It was especially this aspect which would became a primary focus of attention in the discussions in the European context.

2.6.3 Hampering the Domestic Financial Centre

Other costs are associated with the position of the country concerned as a financial centre. The banks and other financial institutions in countries with extensive capital restrictions are handicapped in international financial transactions. Industry and investment companies are likewise restricted in the management of their assets and liabilities.

2.6.4 Costs of Controls

Gottfried Haberler has summed up his objections to capital controls in a rather blunt manner: 'The controls give rise to expensive and wasteful efforts of circumvention and evasion by legal or illegal means to which the authorities react with equally expensive and wasteful measures to tighten and expand the controls.'[20] And expensive the administrative apparatus was. The Belgian National Bank, over the years an outspoken proponent of the dual exchange market, later stated that 'the administrative costs entailed by the two-tier system were admittedly fairly substantial'. In defence of these costs, however, it argued that the controls also permitted the compilation of statistics.[21] The French technical apparatus was notoriously formidable. France had developed a technique of controls, which rightly could be called 'pointilliste' in style,[22] consisting of checking the balance of payments section by section. The complexity of the French regulations is illustrated by the fact that in 1985 the total of official texts, instructions and advisory notes made up a voluminous book, 8 centimetres (3 inches) thick.[23]

factors which have been important motives for keeping capital controls in place. Liberalization therefore often has been conditioned by changes in the perception of these risks or of the possibilities to raise taxes on capital. It is generally felt that governments should not undertake all liberalizing measures simultaneously. In practice, this has meant that countries typically strive for gradualism in the liberalization of capital movements. However, there are important exceptions. The United Kingdom (1979), Australia (1983) and New Zealand (1984) opted for a shock therapy by crossing out all capital restrictions at one stroke.

Much attention in the literature on economic development has been devoted to the optimal sequencing of liberalization and deregulation in commodity and financial markets. The judgment on optimal sequencing depends partly on the initial macro-economic framework of government policies. If the reigning ideology is market-oriented, steps towards liberalization can be taken more easily than in the case of a long-standing history of interventionist policies.

The literature suggests that *fiscal control* should precede financial liberalization.[24] Nowadays strict budgetary policies are more necessary than may have been the case in the 1960s, because of the much less favourable expectations on the part of governments' creditors, either foreign or domestic, in view of the major fiscal derailments in the past two decades which resulted in high government debt ratios. Furthermore domestic capital markets should be liberalized, so that depositors receive, and borrowers pay, substantial real (inflation-adjusted) interest rates. The pace of *deregulation* of banks and domestic financial markets should be carefully geared to the government's success in achieving macro-economic stability. Only after such successful domestic liberalization and stabilization will there be appropriate scope for the liberalization of the foreign exchange markets. Otherwise, the premature abolition of exchange controls could lead to an unwarranted capital flight or an unwarranted build-up of foreign indebtedness, or both. If, on the other hand the fiscal deficit is under control and the domestic financial market is liberalized, the opening up of the capital market may result in large capital inflows. Such inflows may be triggered by inflation differentials and, therefore, interest differentials, but also by portfolio adjustments, inspired by increased confidence because fiscal balance is restored and capital controls are abolished. The *credibility* of the continuation of sound macro-economic policies and the free movement of capital is crucial. The inflows initially cause a real appreciation. The inflows, however, may have a temporary character insofar as they reflect once-and-for-all portfolio adjustments. And they may send the wrong signal to the authorities, who feel official reserve ease and may be tempted to relax fiscal and monetary policies. Sometimes this cannot be avoided, because forced interventions lead to a growth of the money supply. Inflationary capital inflows triggered by the credibility gained through anti-inflationary policies – the so-called Walters effect[25] – would play an important role from 1988 to 1991 when countries like Italy, Portugal and Spain liberalized capital movements.

2.8 CONCLUSION

The foregoing analysis shows a wide variety of arguments pro and contra the use of restrictions of capital movements. This has been reflected in an even greater diversity of practices in individual countries, both with respect to the advisability of using restrictions in principle and to the type and form of restrictions actually employed. The analysis further shows that there is a close interconnection between capital restrictions and a number of important issues which are at the heart of economic policy-making. Theoretical considerations would suggest that quite a number of conditions need to be fulfilled before capital restrictions can be abolished without unduly risking undue pressures on the exchange rate. In particular, domestic macro-economic stability has been singled out as an important condition. Domestic price stability, a balanced budgetary position and equilibrium of the balance of payments are fundamental constituent parts of such macro-economic stability. The deregulation of domestic markets, or at least the abolition of financial repression, is another condition for liberalization as is the use of market-oriented indirect monetary instruments. In practice, as will become clear in this study, these conditions will not always be fulfilled. At the same time, the authorities have been aware of these conditions. As was hinted at in Chapter 1.3, and will be discussed more in detail in the following chapters, the case of Europe shows a rather well-established correlation between macro-economic instability and diverging developments on the one hand and the existence of controls on the other hand. Conversely generalized convergence towards stable macro-economic conditions goes hand in hand with the abolition or absence of controls. Therefore, successful policy coordination among countries is conducive to the process of capital liberalization.

Whatever the theoretical merits of free capital movements, experience shows that countries could not and did not take a detached attitude towards exchange controls. Disregard for the external constraints would provoke instantaneous reactions by the international financial markets. This called for a quick policy response because either the official reserves of the national central bank would be depleted or the exchange rate would be devalued. These were always politically sensitive issues. The imposition of capital restrictions was a highly visible response. At the same time, their effectiveness always has been in doubt and has probably decreased in the course of the years. In Europe this has caused increased political sympathy for the route towards a common currency. In this study we will follow this hazardous route from the viewpoint of the governments involved. High stakes were involved. The issue of capital liberalization never was viewed in isolation because of its implications for monetary and fiscal policies. All in all, it would seem that the policy implications have carried a greater weight in the balancing of the pros and cons of liberalization than the theoretical arguments in favour of optimal resource allocation.

NOTES

1. Alesina *et al.* (1993) reject rather strongly the hypothesis that capital controls reduce growth. Their analysis is based on a dummy variable assuming a value of one when capital controls are in place and zero otherwise. The simplification, however, notably ignores the fact that the macro-economic effects of controls differ greatly depending on the types of transactions affected.
2. In July 1963 the Interest Equalization Tax was introduced with the aim of forcing Europe to develop its own capital market and find there the capital which hitherto it had raised in the United States. This measure was followed by 'voluntary' programs aimed at restraining direct investment abroad and the establishment of a reserve requirement on Eurodollar borrowing by commercial banks. Eventually these arrangements were not successful in curbing speculative outflows and they were abolished after the move to floating exchange rates. For a discussion of the US regulations see Cairncross in Swoboda (1976).
3. Switzerland, which frequently was a magnet for capital flows seeking refuge from currency turmoil, at times deemed it necessary to take temporary measures to curb such inflows. Particularly in the aftermath of the collapse of the Bretton Woods system, like other European countries, it had recourse to banning interest payments on deposits of non-residents and introducing other disincentives and penalties for increasing such deposits. This was at a time when the vagaries of the exchange rate of the Swiss franc were comparable, as Tobin (1978) argued, to those of the prices of 'rare coins, precious metals and baseball cards.' After intensive experiences with different sorts of administrative measures, the Swiss authorities seem to have come to the conclusion that they never produced more than a very temporary brake on the appreciation of the Swiss franc (OECD, 1982).
4. The United Kingdom tried to maintain its reserve currency status in the post-war period while preserving exchange control. However, when the pound sterling came under repeated pressure the subsequent tightening of exchange controls in the 1960s and 1970s heralded the final demise of its reserve currency status.
5. The IMF classification is followed here, see IMF, Exchange arrangements and exchange restrictions, Annual report, various issues; see also Matthieson and Rojas-Suárez (1993), page 4. This listing is not exhaustive but covers the main types. The OECD (1982) uses a distinct classification of categories of controls, i.e. (a) *individual authorization requirements* on the basis of legal or regulatory prohibitions involving direct controls on quantities of certain cross-border flows; (b) *general administrative regulations* which are designed to limit the volume of certain cross-border flows by indirect means; such regulations can comprise conditions with respect to operations (eg timing, costs, composition etc); dual exchange markets, surrender requirements and interest rate controls are also included in this category; (c) *other control measures* which at the same time try to achieve other policy objectives (protection of investors, supervisory considerations) but indirectly influence the incentives for cross-border flows; such measures may include taxation measures, minimum reserve requirements on external assets and liabilities, and limits on domestic credit expansion.
6. Payments with non-residents typically have been centralized with authorized banks ('intermédiaires agréés').

7. At times of severe strains, particularly in the early 1970s, the dual market system in Belgium had to be supplemented with administrative controls (see Chapter 6.11).
8. Italy practised its criminal offence regime from 1976 through 1988.
9. Taxation redirects market forces. Cairncross (1976) has argued that the main effect of the US Interest Equalization Tax, by shifting the financing of outward direct investment by US companies to foreign sources, has contributed to the rise of the Eurodollar market.
10. Gros (1988), discussing the dual exchange rate system of Belgium, argues that '... dual exchange rates (as well as capital controls) could succeed only temporarily in dampening the effects (...) of shocks to financial or other markets (...) a steadily increasing differential would also lead to a steadily increasing incentive for private operators to circumvent the regulations that separate the two markets by buying foreign exchange at the lower rate (usually the controlled or commercial rate) and selling it at the higher rate (usually the free or financial rate).' He concludes that 'the use of dual exchange rate regimes to offset permanently the effects of permanent shocks should therefore not be attempted'. See also Marion (1994).
11. See OECD (1982) for an elaborate survey of the merits and demerits of restricting certain types of short-term capital movements.
12. Cairncross (in Swoboda, 1976) distinguishes four main purposes: (a) to influence the direction taken by inward or outward capital flows, (b) to operate on the long-term balance between domestic and foreign investment, e.g. in order to increase the proportion of domestic savings invested at home, (c) to reduce the pressure on the balance of payments, and (d) to extend the freedom of manoeuvre of the monetary authorities. Matthieson and Rojas-Suarez (1992) identify four partly overlapping main purposes: (a) to limit volatile short-run capital flows and avoid balance-of-payments crises, (b) to maintain the domestic tax base, (c) to retain domestic savings and (d) to help stabilization and structural reform programs.
13. Tobin (1978), who ascribes such behaviour to the absence of any consensus on fundamentals.
14. Eichengreen and Wyplosz (1993) are still of the opinion that the European Monetary System will not survive without capital controls and advocate throwing sand in the wheels of international finance (see for discussion chapter 9.9.2). Gros and Thygesen (1992, p. 114–126) discuss extensively the use and effectiveness of capital controls in the EMS. They reach the opposite conclusion that the elimination of capital controls need not threaten the stability of the EMS.
15. For a further discussion of monetary policy considerations under various exchange regimes see OECD (1990), p. 24–26, and Gruijters (1992), p. 5–8.
16. Many countries use sector-specific regulations with respect to the investment of assets abroad by banks and other financial institutions. They are normally not intended to restrict capital exports, but are designed for creditor protection or for sound, prudent banking principles. Admittedly, there is a grey area here and there is a tendency, in the framework of the liberalization of the insurance market in the EC, to relax such regulations.
17. Rather surprisingly, few complaints have been made. A case went to the European Court of Justice in the 1960s, but judgement was not delivered since the restriction subsequently was abolished. Other countries, too, have erected obstacles to foreign investment in key sectors deemed of national interest, such as the airline industry or the maritime sector.
18. The importance of off-shore centres is demonstrated by BIS statistics on international banking and financial market developments (August 1993), which show that as of the end of 1992 the external assets of reporting banks vis-à-vis the off-shore centres Bahamas, Bahrain, Cayman Islands, Hong Kong, the Netherlands Antilles and Singapore amounted to nearly $ 1,000 billion, representing approximately 20% of total external assets.
19. Szász (in Swoboda, 1976) mentions three reasons for the stickiness of exchange restrictions: (a) the authorities and the public get used to the measures, (b) the authorities do not want to take the risk of having to reintroduce restrictions a short while after having

abolished them, and (c) the expanded technical apparatus to administer controls cannot be easily shrunk.

20. See Haberler's essay on The case against capital controls for balance of payments reasons in Swoboda (1976).
21. The operation of the two-tier foreign exchange market, The experience and its lessons. Internal memorandum of the National Bank of Belgium (1992).
22. Jean Peyrelevade quoted in Neme (1986).
23. Neme (1986) enumerates 129 published texts in the Official Journal, 12 general instructions to the Intermédiaires agréés, 57 letters of the Banque de France still in force (out of a total of 262) and 29 advisory notes, compiled in a collection of the Association Française des Banques.
24. Edwards (1984) and McKinnon (1991) provide good overviews of the existing literature. Although their considerations are applied mainly to the context of developing countries, they may have a more universal application.
25. Walters (1986) argues in his critique of the European Monetary System that a credible exchange rate commitment leads to a fall in nominal interest rates and an increase in domestic demand, and hence to upward pressure on prices.

CHAPTER 3

The Treaty of Rome and Capital Movements

I learned that there is no solution to economic problems without growth and that growth cannot come from bureaucratic manipulations, but only from the individual efforts of all, working in freedom that is as near complete as possible.

Robert Marjolin, 1989

3.1 INTRODUCTION

In the first few years after World War II the attention of policymakers in Europe was focused entirely on reconstruction and rehabilitation. Foreign exchange scarcity, in practice a shortage of US dollars, imposed, however, severe constraints on the pace of economic recovery. Due to a lack of creditworthiness European governments had no easy access to private funding from US commercial banks. Official assistance from the newly founded Bretton Woods institutions was slow in forthcoming. In these circumstances the US Administration took the initiative to put the necessary financial resources at the disposal of the war-torn European countries in order to revitalize their economies. Behind this Marshall aid was a well thought-out political concept. The European states were asked to design themselves a common recovery plan and thus were forced to get organized and cooperate. To this end the *Organisation for European Economic Cooperation* (OEEC) was established on 16 April 1948. As a complement to its coordinating functions, the organization was mandated to pursue the liberalization of trade flows and current payments. Under its aegis the *European Payments Union* was established in 1950 with a view to gradually restoring external convertibility of the European currencies for the settlement of trade in goods and services. This goal was achieved at the end of 1958. By that time important steps had been taken with respect to the dismantlement of trade barriers as well.[1] In most countries, however, barriers to non-trade related capital flows remained in place.

In the meantime the countries cooperating in the framework of the OEEC held intensive discussions on the future shape of a more united Europe. As an initial step, at the instigation of Jean Monnet and Robert Schuman, the *European Coal and Steel Community* (ECSC) was established in 1952 by France, Germany, Italy and the Benelux countries, marking the first break with the tradition of national sovereignty of European states. A year later J.W. Beyen, the Dutch Minister of Foreign Affairs, launched a plan to expand the existing cooperation to a common market and a customs union. The plan was targeted towards the free flow of goods and services. It did not yet address the issue of capital flows, understandably so at a time when external convertibility had not yet been restored. Actually not many advocated a rapid return to capital account convertibility with still vivid memories of the destabilizing speculation in the interwar period, apart from a circle of advisors around Ludwig Erhard in Germany.[2] Beyen had a reputable economic and financial background, unique among his counterparts, which he had acquired during his tenure at the BIS and the IMF. His plan, which was to be the first blueprint of the later EEC, was designed to complement the existing ideas among the other ECSC member states to form a European Political Community. All along views differed about the form and intensity of cooperation between European countries. For the Dutch government political integration was only acceptable if it were accompanied by economic integration.[3] Discussions on political integration broke down after the echec of the European Defence Community, which was postponed sine die in the French Assemblée on 30 August 1954.

After this set-back in the political field the Benelux ministers attempted to initiate a European 'relance'. Among themselves the Benelux countries had made substantial progress in liberalizing bilateral trade, and proposals were submitted to extend this into other areas, including capital. For the European relance the original plan for a common market was unshelved. Its practical goals seemed more likely to be attained. At the *Conference of Messina* on 1 and 2 June 1955 an intergovernmental committee was established under the chairmanship of the Belgian Minister of Foreign Affairs Paul-Henri Spaak in which experts participated from the six ECSC member states. This committee was asked to examine the methods for the development and progressive integration of their markets. In the resolution adopted in Messina it was stated that the integration of the six member states should also encompass the movement of capital. The Spaak report indeed included freedom of capital flows as an important element of a common market, because this would facilitate the efficient deployment of savings for investment purposes in the member states. But the report was prudent in its recommendations in this respect. The Spaak report was to serve as the basis for the negotiations on the Treaty of Rome, which were successfully concluded in the course of 1957. Various attempts to pull the United Kingdom on board all failed because of diverging views on the extent of cooperation, particularly between France and the United Kingdom. Under British leadership a separate organization was to be formed, the *European Free Trade Association,* with less far-reaching goals. Among them, freedom of capital flows did not figure. EFTA's less ambitious concept of pulling down trade barriers did not require, unlike the EEC's integration ideal, common undertakings and obligations in the field of capital movements.

The establishment of the *European Economic Community* coincided with the collapse of the IVth Republic and the reappearance of General Charles de Gaulle at the head of the French government. This rekindled fears that France would not live up to its European commitments. It had not been forgotten that it was de Gaulle who had opposed the further integration aspirations and had greatly contributed to the shelving of the plans for a European Defence Community. De Gaulle had opposed the supranational ideas of his compatriots Robert Schuman and Jean Monnet. These fears, however, did not come true. France was preoccupied with solving the Algerian question and was interested in 'buying time' on other fronts. The impending decolonization process would necessitate a restructuring of the European economies, for which the EEC with its social and investment funds could provide an attractive vehicle. At the same time it was considered useful to retain the OEEC as an umbrella organization in which the other European countries participated. Membership of the organization was opened to non-European industrial countries as well and in 1961 it was rechristened the *Organisation for Economic Cooperation and Development* (OECD). The liberalization of capital movements, which had advanced considerably since the establishment of the EEC, was to be an explicit goal of the organization, to the extent that it enhanced economic cooperation among its member states.

3.2 THE SPAAK REPORT

In the Spaak report the free movement of the main production factors – capital and people – was considered to be part and parcel of the establishment of a common market. But they were to be the very last to be achieved – actually the liberalization of capital made up the concluding chapter of the Spaak report. The free movement of people and capital was to be conditional upon progress in three main policy areas: the coordination of economic policies, the realization of basic investment in the underdeveloped regions of the Community and the suppression of large-scale unemployment. Therefore, precise obligations, particularly in the field of capital movements, could not be written beforehand into the Treaty. Rather, capital liberalization was to depend on the circumstances and the interaction within the Community institutions, which could weigh the implications with respect to other common targets.

The members of the Spaak committee were aware of the reservations of the member states towards liberalization, which they grouped under four headings: (a) the fear of speculative movements in case of divergent monetary policies; (b) the fear of outflows to third countries through member states with a liberal regime; (c) the risk of capital flows motivated by tax evasion; and (d) the risk that capital would flow mainly to developed areas. As a practical solution certain types of capital transactions were selected where liberalization should have priority. Particularly direct investment flows and transactions in securities were singled out as promising areas. Lastly, the Spaak report accepted that even in the final stage of the common market recourse to safeguard clauses should remain possible. Although their effectiveness was doubtful, given the possibilities to camouflage capital transfers in the form of goods or services, temporary restrictions should remain possible as long as member states retained autonomy over budgetary and monetary policies.[4]

Beyond this cautious and pragmatic attitude the Spaak committee firmly held that full freedom of capital movements should be the ultimate goal. Many experts in the committee were convinced that behind the existing exchange controls a certain measure of illusion was apparent. It was not self-evident, so it was argued, that a member state by enforcing exchange controls would have more capital at its disposal for investment purposes; by restricting the outflow of domestic capital, foreign capital was discouraged from entering its territory as well. In short, the issue of exchange controls was deemed to be an area of considerable prejudices, in which national sensitivities were hardly disguised.

3.3 THE ATTITUDES AMONG THE FOUNDING MEMBER STATES

The Spaak report was adopted by the Ministers of Foreign Affairs at their meeting in May 1956 in Venice, although its reception by the French government at best could be considered lukewarm. The latter presented its own memorandum on the establishment of a common market, which in essence contained an endless list of French demands and reservations.[5] Nevertheless, the momentum was maintained and an intergovernmental conference of representatives was established which used the Spaak report as a basis for the design of the Treaty establishing the European Economic Community. French political support for the European common market idea increased appreciably after the ill-fated Suez affair, as a means to divert public opinion. On 25 March 1957, less than two years after the go-ahead had been given at the Conference of Messina, the Treaty was signed by the Ministers of Foreign Affairs in the Campodiglio, the proud city hall of Rome. In the course of the year it was ratified in all member states. The Treaty came into effect on 1 January 1958.

The negotiations on the provisions of the Treaty had been held in the context of the impending restoration of *current account convertibility* and the abolition of the European Payments Union. However, some countries still experienced a shortage of official reserves and monetary equilibrium had not yet been generally restored. Consequently, the exchange control regimes with respect to capital movements varied considerably among the six prospective EEC members. Given the diversity of national positions it was clear that the relevant Treaty provisions would have to constitute a compromise.

Under the influence of the liberal policies of Ludwig Erhard, Adenauer's Minister of Economic Affairs since 1949, *Germany* had opened up its borders at a rapid pace. Erhard's thinking was influenced by the writings of Wilhelm Röpke on the soziale Marktwirtschaft, in which government interventions should be aimed at reaching as large as possible free competition of market forces. Since 1952 Germany had registered surpluses on its current account, enabling a replenishment of its official reserves. From this healthy external position the government actively encouraged capital outflows. In line with its policy of giving free reins to market forces in September 1957 all remaining controls on outflows were abolished, whereas only a small number of inward capital controls was retained. The latter were, however, of limited economic significance. Germany, traditionally liberally-oriented, thus was in a strong position to favour the inclusion of the free movement of capital as a common goal in the Treaty. There were no great sacrifices involved either because Germany's domestic capital market was relatively underdeveloped. Although non-residents in principle had gained free access to the German capital market, in practice its use remained limited because of the prevailing relatively high interest rates in Germany.[6] Nevertheless Germany did not push very hard for its preference of freedom of capital movements. Being a net capital exporter, it had no great interest in gaining access to the domestic capital markets in other European countries. Nor did it wish to see its high-interest rate policy undermined by large capital inflows from third countries. Therefore, the German negotiators did not attach overriding importance to the promotion of their own ideology of free capital movements.

In the course of the negotiations, when it became increasingly clear that the establishment of a European Economic Community was to be a real proposition, there was considerable preparedness on the German side to make concessions to the French on a broad front of issues. One of the striking examples was the common agricultural policy, which would imply that Germany was to be a net payer to the Community in the years to come. Another plausible area for compromise was formed by capital movements, where Germany stood more or less alone in its advocacy of full freedom and the interventionist attitude of France with respect to capital movements was backed by Italy and the Netherlands. Against this crowd Germany was ready to compromise and no longer postulated the free movement of capital. This open attitude reflected in large part the political agreement Chancellor Konrad Adenauer had reached with his French counterpart, premier Guy Mollet. Germany, eager to align itself with its former adversaries, stood ready to back specific French demands as long as they did not go against vital German interests. The free flow of capital movements was not deemed to be vitally important, neither for Germany, nor for the Common Market.

France still was in a weak external position in the mid–1950s. As shown in Table 4 it had only a limited amount of official exchange reserves at its disposal. France operated an extensive exchange control system, including

TABLE 4

Financial indicators at the eve of the Treaty of Rome.

1957	Official reserves	Current account	Fiscal deficit	Government debt	Long-term interest rate
	% imports	% of gdp			%
Belgium	33.7	2.0	–0.4	63.6	6.0
France	11.9	–2.4	–4.9	33.2	5.9
Germany	68.5	2.7	–2.3	9.1	7.5
Italy	40.3	0.1	–1.5	45.0	6.8
Netherlands	25.6	–1.7	0.6	50.8	4.6

approval procedures for direct investment flows. For the French government it was imperative that the Treaty provisions on the movement of capital would not obstruct the national economic plans. The dirigistic economic approach, apparent in the portioning and subventioning of credit to specific sectors of the economy, stood in the way of allowing complete freedom of capital movements. The French therefore insisted on safeguard clauses. In their view these should also imply that governments in case of need autonomously could take restrictive measures with ex post approval by the Commission (the so-called clause d'urgence). In his memoirs Marjolin reports that the French Minister of Economic and Financial Affairs, Paul Ramadier, sent memo after memo to Guy Mollet to put him on his guard against what he, Ramadier, regarded as a surrender to Mammon. To introduce freedom of capital movements would in the French eyes be playing into the hands of the speculators, who would take advantage of it to attack the franc.[7] The latter position did not, however, deter the French administration, while operating a full-fledged exchange control system, from devaluing the French franc twice in 1958, in June by 20% and in December by 17.5%. These devaluations, which were accompanied by a substantive financial and monetary reform, gave the French economy an excellent competitive starting position in the Community.

Italy operated a mixed system: there was a free market for cross-border capital transactions, but residents had only limited access. Italy generally favoured the liberalization of capital movements during the Treaty negotiations because it wished to attract capital for the development of Southern Italy. It wished, however, to retain the right to control issues on its own capital market through domestic regulations. *Belgium* and *Luxembourg* were in a special position. Their relatively favourable economic situation enabled them to liberalize capital movements earlier than most other European countries.

With that consideration in mind a dual exchange market was introduced in 1955, consisting of a free financial market, which was separated from the official exchange market for current payments. The dual market's advantage, so it was argued, lay in its steering a middle course between full freedom of capital movements, which was not yet attainable, and the more cumbersome 'formalities' of a direct control system. The Belgian negotiators generally adopted a liberal attitude with respect to capital movements.[8] Among the European countries *the Netherlands* held a position in the middle. Capital transactions were subject to permissions, which, however, especially with respect to trade in shares, were granted liberally. Although its general attitude towards controling capital movements was close to the French dirigistic position, in the application of its control system the Dutch authorities were much more liberally-oriented. Their attitude in the negotiations therefore proved to be important in determining the extent of the Treaty obligations.

3.4 THE DUTCH ATTITUDE TOWARDS CAPITAL LIBERALIZATION

The attitude of the Netherlands deserves further consideration. Its intermediate position could tip the scales in determining the scope of the Treaty obligations and drawing the line between those capital movements which would be necessary for the proper functioning of the Common Market, and those which would not. The Netherlands was opposed to the full liberalization of capital movements, both on policy and ideological grounds. The Netherlands had two main policy motives for a rather restrictive attitude: it wished to protect its domestic capital market and it wished to control domestic monetary expansion. As far as the first motive – *protection of the domestic capital market* – was concerned, there were three arguments in favour of restrictions on capital outflows:

(a) *Capital outflows would force up domestic interest rates* in countries, such as the Netherlands, where they were low because of sound fiscal policies. Holtrop, the central bank's president, argued that the lifting of restrictions in itself would not guarantee the rational distribution of saving surpluses in Europe. He essentially took a static viewpoint: '... economic integration by itself does not generate new savings and thus no new capital; therefore the advantages of free capital movements can only be the displacement of the utilization of capital from one area to another'.[9] Therefore, foreign demand for credit on domestic markets would crowd out national credit-takers.

(b) Free capital movements would *facilitate the financing of free-spending governments and undermine budgetary discipline*. The Dutch concern that spendthrift governments would borrow in the capital markets of thrifty governments had been eloquently voiced by Holtrop.[10] 'Should the ant from La Fontaine's fable open up its store-room to the cricket?', he asked himself. Would it really be wise policy for the government, which as a good father has taken care to keep his own house in order, to open up his capital market and give free access to other members of the Community who take their financing problems more easily and spare their own taxpayers? Holtrop's answer was straightforward: this would be irresponsible policy. It might force the domestic government to monetary financing, it might drain the official reserves and it could put upward pressure on interest rates. Against these drawbacks he saw no obvious advantages.

(c) Freedom of capital movements could lead to *flows from the poor areas to the rich areas* of the Community. Posthuma, the Dutch delegate from the side of the central bank, when elaborating on this argument which had also figured in the Spaak report, held that both the speed and the substance of capital liberalization should be subordinated to the fulfilment of wider-ranging objectives of the Treaty, such as economic harmonization and a high degree of employment. Complete freedom of capital movements could only become mandatory if the economic climate in which entrepreneurs had to work, as well as the social and economic policies were sufficiently equalized. His main fear was that the prevailing differences might induce capital movements from underdeveloped countries to more developed regions, whereas the aim of balanced growth in the Community and a high level of employment would require the very opposite. He wrote: 'The liberal economic doctrines of the 19th century, influenced by natural philosophy, took it that with free capital movements flows would go in a direction which would optimalize welfare. Nowadays no economist of reputation shares this notion'.[11] Here economic ideology was at stake: the Dutch authorities, contrary to their German counterparts, did not have faith in the free play of market forces, which could lead to undesirable outcomes in terms of welfare. The latter apparently was defined in terms of equalization of income, production and employment across the Community.

The second motive – the *control of domestic monetary expansion* – was closely related to the influential monetary doctrine which Holtrop had developed during his presidency of the Nederlandsche Bank. Short-term capital inflows were regarded as liquidity creation from external sources. There was no economic reason why this source of liquidity creation, which would come on top of domestic liquidity creation and thus could have inflationary consequences, would have to be allowed to flow uninhibitedly. Monetary policy should be able to be geared exclusively to price stability: '... only a government which accepts stability of the currency as an absolute rule of policy has the moral right to attract at the lowest possible interest rate savings running into thousands of millions of guilders'.[12] Monetary control was exercised by direct means, mainly in the form of credit ceilings for commercial banks. Exchange controls were deemed necessary in order to prevent credit ceilings from being circumvented by the taking up of credit in third countries. In theory, sterilization of such flows could of course dampen the direct monetary consequences, but it would leave the source of credit expansion uncapped.

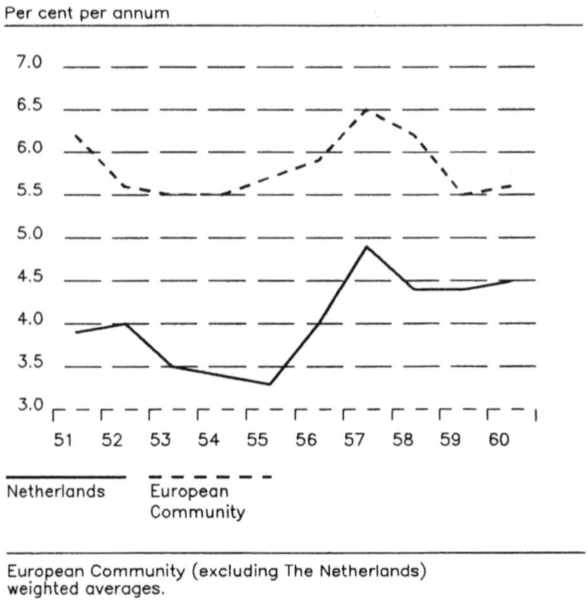

Fig. 5. Dutch long-term interest rates in the 1950s.

These two motives for a restrictive attitude were founded in the practical situation of the day, in which forced savings were generated through cautious fiscal policies. From the Dutch standpoint the Netherlands, which in the post-World War II years followed a *cheap money policy*, stood to lose from complete liberalization of capital movements. At the time it had one of the best-developed domestic capital markets, its financial community was outward-looking and interest rates were relatively low. Therefore, it was feared that for the foreseeable future the Dutch capital market would be one of the few sources of capital for the other member states. The serious implications this would have for the Dutch interest rate level and indirectly for the level of wages and housing rents explain the dissuasive, cautious Dutch attitude. Because the Dutch relied solely on exchange controls to regulate the access to the domestic capital market, their liberalization would leave the Dutch authorities empty-handed, whereas all other EEC member states had domestic regulations in place through which they de facto could restrict foreign issues. The Dutch authorities wished to preclude foreign credit-takers from financing themselves at low interest rates on the capital market. This could thwart the cheap money policy.

There was also a *systemic vision* – with an ideologic Calvinistic undertone – in the Dutch attitude: a government which behaves badly should be punished for its sins and not be provided with easy escape routes or granted indulgences. In his advocacy of disciplinary incentives for governments,

Holtrop took up a theme which would come back incessantly over the next decades. The full freedom of capital movements would not satisfy the monetary desiderata that the Nederlandsche Bank under Holtrop cherished. It was a time in which the Dutch authorities still believed in their ability to determine their own economic policies. Fiscal policy and monetary policy were both directed towards internal stability. The rewards in the form of a low interest rate should not be jeopardized by failing policies elsewhere. Therefore the Netherlands did not shy away from dirigistic measures in the sphere of capital flows. Apparently the authorities did not share the German ideology of free functioning of markets.

Interestingly, the Dutch argument that capital liberalization undermines fiscal discipline in other countries by allowing easy access to foreign capital markets, would be contradicted much later, in the 1980s, by the German argument that capital liberalization on the contrary fosters *fiscal discipline.* In the latter view, which would gain widespread acceptance at a time when international financial markets had expanded in a spectacular manner, the judgement of market operators on the soundness of pursued policies played a major role in expectations concerning exchange rates and interest rates, and therewith in the availability and cost of external finance for fiscal deficits.

The two Dutch motives – to protect the domestic capital market and to control domestic monetary expansion – fitted in comfortably with the emphasis in Dutch monetary thinking on the strict separation of liquidity and capital. This reasoning had as a practical implication that walls of defence were raised from two sides: restrictions were imposed both on long-term outflows – to protect the domestic capital market – and on short-term inflows – to control domestic monetary expansion.

The Dutch preoccupations implied that the Netherlands wished to restrict the freedom of capital movements through a number of provisions in the Treaty. In particular the Netherlands demanded: (a) decisions with respect to capital movements should be taken with *unanimity* during the entire transitional period; (b) there should be no obligation to liberalize loans of *foreign governments*, including parastatal entities, on the domestic capital market; (c) there should be a *safeguard clause* which could be invoked for all capital transactions not only in case of balance-of-payments problems, but also in case of a threat to domestic employment or the functioning of the domestic capital market; and (d) a *clause d'urgence* should enable member states to take restrictive measures in case of sudden disturbances which should be authorized ex post by the Commission.[13] On page 44 we will see in how far these Dutch demands were fulfilled.

3.5 THE TREATY PROVISIONS

In one of the first drafts of the Treaty only three relatively simple articles with respect to capital were provided for, namely (a) a general definition of the freedom of capital movement as the right to freely take up, transfer and invest capital within the Community, (b) the time frame and modalities according to which this freedom should be realized in the transitional phase, and (c) a general safeguard clause. The Treaty text on capital movements, which eventually was agreed, was a considerably more complicated one. The final text has to be regarded as a compromise between the conflicting views of the member states. Although free movement of capital was intended to be one of the foundations of the Community, the Treaty provisions in this respect could not bind the member states to a specific and immediate result because member states wished to retain their room for manoeuvre.

The Treaty of Rome is based on the principle of the four freedoms: the free movement of goods, of persons, of services and of capital. The structure of the text of the Treaty suggests that the founding fathers saw a hierarchical order in the accomplishment of these freedoms. After the treatment of the Principles of the European Economic Community (Part I, containing Articles 1 to 8) the Foundations of the Community are dealt with under 4 separate titles: 1) free movement of goods, 2) agriculture, 3) free movement of persons, services and capital and 4) transport. Indeed, for a long time the Community has rightly been associated with the first two foundations: the free trade of goods and the common agricultural policy. The accomplishment of the remaining three freedoms, the free movement of persons, of services and of capital, has been a more arduous task. As regards the free movement of persons the Community advanced rather well through the adoption of secondary legislation, but in the field of services, where progress primarily was based on case-law, domestic regulations protecting home markets continued for quite some time to stand in the way of progress in all sectors.

In the following paragraphs the original text of the Treaty of Rome with respect to the free movement of capital will be dealt with. In Annex 1, the full text of the relevant Treaty provisions is reprinted. Subsequent important modifications of these texts in the Single European Act and the Treaty on European Union will be discussed in chapter 7 and chapter 9 respectively.

In the Title on the free movement of persons, services and capital, the chapter on *Capital,* covering Articles 67 to 73, is the last. Specific provisions with respect to capital movements in the context of balance-of-payments disturbances are not spelled out in this chapter of the Treaty, but are dealt with later in a special chapter on the *Balance of Payments* (Articles 104 to 109) in the part of the Treaty which deals with economic policy. There, member states were authorized to impose or tighten capital controls in a crisis situation. In the same chapter the Monetary Committee was set up which, among other things, was entrusted with the surveillance of capital movements. Apparently, there was a serious concern that balance-of-payments disturbances on account of swings in capital movements could hinder the free movement of goods, the raison d'être of the Common Market. Such impediment could either follow indirectly from forced exchange rate adjustments, which would give an unwarranted competitive edge to goods traded at the depreciated exchange rate, or directly through the reintroduction of restrictions in the trade area.[14] At the time capital restrictions were by and large considered to be the lesser evil, in line with the implicit hierarchical order of freedoms.

The tenet of the Treaty provisions concerning capital is *Article 67*. The article deals explicitly with the lifting of impediments to the free flow of capital within the Community, thus forming the legal principle for all subsequent secondary legislation dealing with the liberalization of capital flows. The text of Article 67.1 is: *'During the transitional period and to the extent necessary to ensure the proper functioning of the Common Market, Member States shall progressively abolish between themselves all restrictions on the movement of capital belonging to persons resident in Member States and any discrimination based on the nationality or on the place of residence of the parties or on the place were such capital is invested'*.

The Treaty obligations concerning the movement of capital did not seek to consolidate the liberalization which had already taken place in some member states. There was merely the firm obligation in Article 67.2 to bring about current account convertibility, i.e. free settlement of cross-border current payments, by the end of the first four-year stage of the transitional period.[15] In fact, such convertibility was already largely reached by the end of 1958 when the European Payments Union was dismantled. As regards non-trade related capital movements, member states in essence committed themselves to endeavour not to introduce new exchange restrictions (Article 71) and to abolish as much as possible existing restrictions. In practice this weak *standstill clause* meant that the Treaty started with a clean sheet and that directives would have to be issued with a view to obliging member states to liberalize capital movements in the transitional period, provided that this was necessary for the proper functioning of the Common Market. Obviously, a measure of good will on the part of the member states, each operating different exchange control systems, was needed to bring this about.

Procedures for *secondary legislation*, which would give legal content to the Treaty obligations, were provided for in Articles 69 and 70. In Article 69 the legal basis was provided for the Council to issue directives for the implementation of Article 67 on a proposal of the Commission and after consultation of the Monetary Committee. Article 70 concerned the movement of capital between the Community and third countries. The Commission could come forward with proposals to progressively coordinate the policies in this area vis-à-vis non-EEC countries. Measures could also be taken to prevent residents from utilizing the more liberal exchange regime of other EEC countries to evade national restrictions. These provisions were clearly inspired by the desire to prevent long-term capital outflows, which were regarded as a drain on domestic resources. In the same vein, with a view to protecting the domestic capital market, in Article 68.3, loans of other member state authorities were explicitly excluded from the obligation to liberalize.

The Treaty established a link with the freedom of *financial services* in Article 61.2, where it was provided that the liberalization of banking and insurance services should be effected in step with the progressive liberalization of movement of capital. Real progress in this area could only be made in the late 1980s in the framework of the Internal Market exercise.

In the Treaty exemptions were formulated with respect to certain categories or circumstances. In case of disturbances on the domestic capital market (Article 73) and balance-of-payments problems (Articles 108 and 109) a member could call for derogation from the liberalization obligations. These *safeguard clauses* gave assurances to member states that they could take protective measures in crisis situations. Under the *clause d'urgence* (in Article 109) a member state could on its own take measures. The Commission and other member states had to be informed immediately, and the Council, after having heard the opinions of the Commission and the Monetary Committee, could by qualified majority decide that the measures should be amended or abolished. But in practice the Community could not do much about it once a member state had taken protective measures, beyond exercising peer pressure. The safeguard clauses confirmed that in the final analysis the regulation of capital movements remained primarily in the national domain.

The *transitional period* for the establishment of the Common Market, foreseen in the Treaty, was 12 years (or at the most 15 years), reflecting the explicit hope of the drafters of the Treaty – and the commitment of the governments which had signed the Treaty – that by the year 1970 the Common Market would be established. The EEC Treaty in essence had the character of an enabling law, which needed to be given content later. For this purpose the Commission, as guardian of the Treaty, was given the right of initiative to see to it that the intentions of the Treaty were fulfilled. With respect to capital movements the Commission could put forward proposals which went beyond the explicit, rather minimalistic Treaty obligations. The capital provisions of the Treaty provided the EEC with real decision-making powers. But this required, at least initially, the consent of all member states.[16]

3.6 SUBORDINATION TO THE FREEDOM OF TRADE

A crucial clause in Article 67 is that the obligation for countries to lift capital restrictions was limited '*to the extent necessary to ensure the proper functioning of the Common Market*'. Article 67 thus does not contain an unconditional obligation to liberalize capital movements. There is, however, an apparent inconsistency with the Principles of the Treaty. In Article 3 it is stated that for the purposes of the Community 'the abolition, as between Member States, of obstacles to freedom of movement for persons, services and capital' shall be included in the activities of the Community. Ruding (1969, p.199) explains this inconsistency on the ground that the definitive text of the chapter on Capital was decided upon at a late stage of the negotiations (February 1957), when agreement had already been reached on the general principles of the Community. It is only in respect of the freedom of movement of capital that such an escape clause exists; the other three freedoms are not subject to any comparable restrictive conditions.[17]

The insertion of the clause has to do with the fact that member states were not prepared to surrender economic and monetary competences to the supranational level. In Article 104 the drafters of the Treaty entrusted each member state with taking care of its own internal and external equilibrium. Elsewhere in the Treaty the obligation to *coordinate economic policies*[18] – to the extent necessary to attain the Treaty objectives – was circumscribed by the provision that the internal and external financial stability of the member states should not be jeopardized by the Community institutions (Article 6). These provisions make clear that maintenance of domestic economic and monetary equilibrium remained in the realm of national authorities. The obvious conclusion was drawn that the possibility to impose capital restrictions in case of need should be left open. If the authorities of member states felt that undesirable capital flows threatened domestic equilibrium, they could feel vindicated by the Treaty in taking countervailing measures. The inconsistency, or rather ambiguity in the Treaty with respect to the freedom of capital movements therefore underlines the close link between policy autonomy and capital restrictions. This connection with the question of national sovereignty would make it difficult to reach agreement on common obligations with respect to capital liberalization, or to enforce compliance with these obligations once they had been agreed upon.

In practice the escape clause has given member states considerable *leeway* in the application of capital restrictions. Through this clause the freedom of capital movements actually is subordinated to the freedom of trade movements as the more immediate objective of the Common Market. The vague phrasing of the escape clause has left room, as we will see, for various interpretations, which could be advanced by national governments as they saw fit to suit their own preoccupations. One such typical restrictive interpretation of the clause was that the drafters of the Treaty only had in mind the free flow of goods and factors of production. In this view the basic intention was to free investment flows in the real economic sphere and not other financial flows of a more short-term character.[19]

The reserved, cautious attitude of the Treaty drafters which was revealed in this clause has to be seen in the context of the time the Treaty was written. Europe was on the brink of restoring full convertibility of domestic currencies for current account transactions. The prevailing capital scarcity, especially in the form of foreign currency (in this particular case US dollars), of the post-World War II period was just coming to an end. For the rebuilding of Europe all attention was directed towards the restoration of open markets for goods and services. The opening up of financial markets was seen as far less important.

The provisions with respect to capital movements were the result of a *compromise*. The Dutch attitude was important because by aligning itself to the French dirigistic position it tipped the balance towards an ambiguous text. The escape clause – to the extent necessary to ensure the proper functioning of the Common Market – was proposed by the Netherlands delegation and after having received support from France and Belgium was accepted despite German protests.[20] It was a formula which succeeded in allaying the French fears in respect of full freedom of capital movements. Each country was free to choose its own interpretation and France's interpretation would be more restrictive than that of other countries.[21] The list of Dutch desiderata, as discussed on page 39, was more or less fulfilled. The Dutch and the French had advocated decision-making by unanimity during the entire transitional period, and had only accepted such unanimity for only the first two stages after other member states had reluctantly agreed to the inclusion of the clause d'urgence. At a Dutch initiative Article 68.3 was inserted at a rather late stage, in which it was provided that there would be no obligation to liberalize loans of other EEC governments on the domestic capital market.[22] This article was regarded by the Dutch delegation as an example of a movement of capital which was not necessary for the proper functioning of the Common Market. Finally the Dutch had succeeded in introducing a safeguard clause for disturbances on the domestic capital market, although the employment motive was not accepted. In its explanatory memorandum to parliament the Dutch government, rather than espousing the goal of free movement of capital, elaborated lenghtily on those categories of capital transactions which in the Treaty were not deemed necessary to ensure the proper functioning of the Common Market, including categories for which safeguard clauses could be invoked. Such a broad interpretation of the general escape clause was a far cry from the goal of freedom of capital movements.

3.7 PUBLIC REACTIONS

The public reactions to the Treaty on the topic of capital liberalization were mixed. To the observers of the day it was apparent that in the sphere of capital liberalization the Treaty mainly consisted of good intentions. Not all official arguments for maintaining capital restrictions in one way or another were accepted by commentators. Two examples of such reactions from the financial and commercial community are the comments of the European Banking Association and of the International Chamber of Commerce.

The *European Banking Association*, in a memorandum submitted in July 1958, considered that the European Community would only become a full success if there would be freedom of capital movements. The right of establishment in the Community would be an illusion if the transfer of capital, needed to bring this about, would not be allowed.[23] The bankers did not deny that disturbing capital flows could occur, but they pointed out that capital movements, even speculative ones, generally were a consequence rather than the cause of balance-of-payments imbalances. Nevertheless, they admitted that diverging policies between member states might continue to call for some capital restrictions. They concluded that effective coordination of economic, monetary and financial policies was essential for the total liberalization of capital movements.

Another interesting comment on the Treaty was given by the *International Chamber of Commerce.*[24] This organization had asked a committee under the chairmanship of Maurice Frère, the President of the Bank for International Settlements and former Governor of the National Bank of Belgium, to comment on the monetary provisions of the Treaty, including those on capital movements. The committee did not accept the lack of coordination of monetary policies, which was used as an excuse for the maintenance of exchange restrictions, as a given fact. It sought actively to restrain policy autonomy for member states and so to impose a degree of discipline which would make the freedom of capital movements a less risky affair. The committee argued that one of the first measures of harmonization under the Treaty should apply to the conditions under which the national central banks could provide credit. It noted that in this respect there were important differences among member states, which also extended to the relationship between the central bank and the government. It was of course realized that any change in this relationship would have serious political implications. Therefore, it confined itself to a concrete operational proposal: governments should renounce the taking up of new credits with their central banks, except in exceptional circumstances to be judged by a third party. Such renunciation would have disciplinary effects on the public sector. Governments would have to balance receipts and expenditures in such a manner as not to overburden the domestic money and capital markets. At the same time it would strengthen the position of the central banks and provide them with the independence needed for a satisfactory operation of the monetary policies of the Community. In this way a truly 'monetary' Community could evolve, which one day, political circumstances permitting, could have a single currency. Both these public reactions show that there were genuine pressures in society to force upon the authorities a greater commitment to free capital movements. The banking community took issue with the official argument that capital controls were needed to contain speculation, the commercial community wished to introduce mechanisms to enforce greater fiscal and monetary discipline as a condition for freedom of capital movements. The latter gave a visionary advice, which did not go down well in political circles. Only in the framework of the Treaty of Maastricht was a prohibition against monetary financing of governments by central banks agreed upon, effective 1 January 1994, 35 years after the recommendation.

TABLE 5

Selected judgements of the European Court of Justice.

November 1978 *Thompson* Case 7/78

The term movement of capital is roughly delineated by distinguishing between financial, real and monetary capital.

November 1981 *Casati* Case 203/80

Article 67 regarding capital movements does not have the same direct effect as the other fundamental freedoms of movement of goods (Article 30), persons (Articles 48 and 52) and services (Article 59).

January 1984 *Luisi & Carbone* Case 286/82 and 26/83

Further definition of movement of capital as financial operations directed towards depositing or investing, to be distinguished from current payments as settlement for goods or services rendered. Safeguard measures under Articles 108 and 109 only to be applied in periods of crisis. Freedom of payments (Article 106) declared directly effective.

June 1986 *Brugnoni & Ruffinengo* Case 157/85

Administrative restrictions must be abolished with respect to fully liberalized capital movements under the EC directives.

3.8 INTERPRETATIONS BY THE COURT OF JUSTICE

In the course of the years the European Court of Justice has given a number of judgements on the purport of the Treaty provisions concerning capital movements. The most important ones have been recapitulated in Table 5. Some judgements were directed towards defining a dividing line between current account and capital account transactions, the Treaty itself lacking a proper definition of capital movements. In the *Luise and Carbone case* (1984) the Court ruled that capital movements were to be defined as financial operations directed towards depositing or investing of means of payment and not as the settlement of an underlying real transaction. Two years later, in the *Brugnoni and Ruffinengo case*, the Court ruled that discriminatory national regulations concerning liberated capital transactions should be eliminated as well.

Some judgements elaborated on the philosophy of the drafters of the Treaty with respect to the freedom of capital movements. Interestingly the Court gave a rather restrictive interpretation of the Treaty provisions as late as 1981 in the *Casati case*.[25] The Court ruled that the freedom of capital movements did not directly follow from the Treaty and therefore indeed was on a different footing than the other three freedoms. In its interpretation of the escape clause the Court stated: 'At present, it cannot be denied that complete freedom of movement of capital may undermine the economic policy of one of the Member States or create an imbalance in its balance of payments, thereby impairing the proper functioning of the Common Market.' Consequently, the scope of the restriction 'varies in time and depends on an assessment of the requirements of the Common Market and on an appraisal of both the advantages and risks which liberalization might entail'. The Court noted that there were close links between the movement of capital and the economic and monetary policies in the member states. Apparently it judged that the extent of liberalization of capital movements should depend on the degree of equilibrium in economic and monetary policies among member states. Thus the Court implicitly argued that satisfactory policy coordination, to which Article 105 of the Treaty obliges the member states, should precede full capital liberalization.

The Court's cautious attitude can be understood against the background of the currency unrest in the beginning of the 1980s. It shied off from reasoning away the escape clause in Article 67, but the Court reserved the right to come back to the issue if it felt that the Council backed off from the Treaty obligations. In later years the Court in practice would merely follow the political agreement reached elsewhere on the pace of capital liberalization in the Community. With respect to the freedom of capital movements the Court of Justice did not play an independent, initiating role.

3.9 THE INVOLVEMENT OF THE IMF AND THE OECD IN CAPITAL LIBERALIZATION

This study deals with the manner in which the articles of the Treaty were given content in later years by the secondary legislation adopted by the member states. This emphasis on the role of the European Community in the process of capital liberalization has been chosen as it best permits the linkages with the other policy domains to be illustrated. In the deliberations within the Community institutions the political and economic quid pro quos prominently came to the fore, because capital liberalization was part and parcel of a wider-ranging drive towards integration. This focus on the European Community, however, is not in any way intended to detract from the contributions made by other international organizations with respect to the liberalization of capital movements. In particular the Organisation for Economic Cooperation and Development has played an important role. Lately also the International Monetary Fund is showing a keen interest. As an aside, it is therefore appropriate to deal briefly with the relevant provisions of these international institutions.

Although the Treaty is not ambitious in its aims for capital liberalization, it goes far beyond the detached attitude taken in the Articles of Agreement of the *International Monetary Fund,* which had been drafted 13 years earlier, in 1944. Article VI, Section 3, explicitly condones the imposition of capital restrictions 'as are necessary to regulate international capital movements'. This was seen by the founding fathers as a necessary instrument in the context of the Bretton Woods system of fixed parities. In the original proposal of *Keynes* for a *Clearing Union* there was even an outright plea for control of all capital movements: '... control of capital movements, both inward and outward, should be a permanent feature of the post-war system'.[26] Of course it could be objected that '... control, if it is to be effective, probably requires the machinery of exchange control for all transactions, even though a general permission is given to all remittances in respect of current trade', but Keynes argued that effective control of capital movements necessitated controls at both ends and thus a multilateral control system. The main purpose was that countries should be able to protect themselves against short-term speculative movements. International investment flows for legitimate purposes of course should not be hindered. To this end the control system should distinguish between investment loans from surplus countries, which should be facilitated, and flows out of deficit countries, which should not be encouraged if the country was lacking the necessary financial means.

White in his plan for a *Stabilization Fund*, in accordance with the official United States view that trade and capital flows should be interfered with as little as possible, took a more liberal stance, contemplating the abolition of exchange control, except when approved by the Fund. At the constituent meeting the view of other countries prevailed that the postwar world would require the use of exchange controls. Apparently, memories of the disturbing role of speculative capital movements in the Interbellum, *hot money* as these flows were then called, were still all too vivid. It was believed that authorities could follow more effectively stimulative policies, aimed at full employment, behind restrictive walls. In this way fixed exchange parities and a certain measure of autonomy over domestic monetary policy could be maintained. Moreover, on the hypothesis that the United States was to remain the most important surplus country and thus the main financier of the IMF, the drafters wanted to avoid that Fund resources taken up by deficit countries would be used to finance capital flows out of Europe into the United States.

Article VI has given rise to controversies in the Executive Board of the IMF. As early as in 1946 the US Director asked for an *interpretation* of the article. It was then decided that Fund resources could only be used to finance a deficit on the current account.[27] In practice, a more generous attitude was taken and in 1961 the Board formally reversed this interpretation to the effect that Fund resources could also be used to finance capital flows, as long as they were not big and continuous. The IMF never has requested a member country to impose capital restrictions, neither on outflows nor on inflows, although it was empowered to do so in case of use of Fund resources. Gold (1977) asserts that by adopting such attitude the Fund has acknowledged an almost completely unfettered discretion of members to impose or to refrain from imposing capital

Article VI of the IMF's Articles of Agreement

Capital Transfers

Section 1. *Use of the Fund's general resources for capital transfers*

(a) A member may not use the Fund's general resources to meet a large or sustained outflow of capital except as provided in Section 2 of this Article, and the Fund may request a member to exercise controls to prevent such use of the general resources of the Fund. If, after receiving such a request, a member fails to exercise appropriate controls, the Fund may declare the member ineligible to use the general resourses of the Fund.

(b) Nothing in this Section shall be deemed:
  (i) to prevent the use of the general resources of the Fund for capital transactions of reasonable amount required for the expansion of exports or in the ordinary course of trade, banking or other business; or
  (ii) to affect capital movements which are met out of a member's own resources, but members undertake that such capital movements will be in accordance with the purposes of the Fund.

Section 2. *Special provisions for capital transfers*
A member shall be entitled to make reserve tranche purchases to meet capital transfers.

Section 3. *Controls of capital transfers*
Members may exercise such controls as are necessary to regulate international capital movements, but no member may exercise these controls in a manner which will restrict payments for current transactions or which will unduly delay transfers of funds in settlement of commitments, except as provided in Article VII, Section 3(b) and in Article XIV, Section 2.

TABLE 6

Acceptance of the Article VIII obligation.

15 February 1961	Belgium
	France
	Germany
	Ireland
	Italy
	Luxembourg
	The Netherlands
	United Kingdom
1 May 1967	Denmark
15 July 1986	Spain
12 September 1988	Portugal
7 July 1992	Greece

controls. Nowadays the article, which in essence remained unchanged in the subsequent amendments of the IMF's Articles of Agreement,[28] does not play a major role. The IMF has concentrated its efforts on bringing about *current account convertibility* among its members. On 15 February 1961 all six EEC member states accepted, together with some other industrial countries, Article VIII of the Fund's Articles of Agreement (see Table 6). Under this article countries assume the obligation to maintain currency convertibility for current transactions and to abstain from applying any restrictions on current payments or discriminating vis-à-vis other countries. It was only in 1992 that Greece as the last EEC member state was to acquire Article VIII status. Presently a little over one half of the IMF membership has accepted the Article VIII obligations.

Despite the focus of the Fund's Articles of Agreement on current account convertibility the IMF has in the course of the years taken a more active stance in the promotion of free capital movements. It was particularly active in the fight against *multiple exchange rate regimes*, although it was lenient with respect to the Belgian dual exchange market type where a distinction was only made between current and capital transactions. Nowadays, in some of its programs capital liberalization measures are supported by Fund resources, since it increasingly has been realized that capital controls are not only ineffective in avoiding capital flight – Latin America in the 1980s constituting a prime example of the powerlessness of comprehensive exchange control systems – but that they may discourage direct investment and long-term portfolio inflows. At the Interim Committee meeting in Madrid in October 1994 member states were encouraged to remove impediments to the free flow of capital. The time seems to be ripe to extend the responsibilities of the IMF to the overview of capital controls in view of the fact that most members now have eliminated exchange restrictions on most current transactions. This would fill an institutional gap because presently there is no international agency which exercises jurisdiction on a global scale on capital transactions.

Right from its start in 1961 the *Organisation for Economic Cooperation and Development*, which has mainly industrialized countries among its membership, has added the progressive freedom of capital movements to the continued vocation of promoting the liberalization of international trade in goods and services taken over from its predecessor the OEEC. In this respect the OECD has established a separate policy role which distinguishes the organization from the IMF and the GATT, despite the considerable overlap in their respective general mission statements (see Table 7). In the OECD Convention member states have agreed that they will endeavour to extend the liberalization of capital movements.[29] To this end they can voluntarily undertake obligations resulting from decisions of the OECD Council. These obligations, once they are accepted, have a binding character. Over time these obligations have been regularly updated in the *Code of Liberalization of Capital Movements*, which was first drafted in 1961, the year of foundation of the

TABLE 7

The distinctive roles of international institutions.

Institution (year of foundation)		Primary policy area	Provisions with respect to capital movements
IMF	1946	international monetary system, adjustment process	members may exercise such capital controls as are necessary to regulate international capital movements
GATT[1]	1947	trade liberalization	nil
EEC	1958	common market, economic integration	progressive abolition of capital controls to the extent necessary to ensure the proper functioning of the Common Market
OECD	1961	economic cooperation	progressive abolition of capital controls to the extent necessary for effective economic cooperation

[1] The World Trade Organization will be mandated to pursue the liberalization of financial services.

OECD.[30] Interestingly, the OECD Code, too, contains a conditional clause for such liberalization. Article 1 spells out that its member countries shall progressively abolish between one another restrictions on movements of capital 'to the extent necessary for effective economic co-operation'. Whereas in the Treaty of Rome the proper functioning of the Common Market is the leading principle for the extent to which countries undertake liberalization obligations, in the framework of the OECD, a cooperative organization par excellence, it is the effectiveness of international cooperation. Admittedly as vague a notion as the escape clause in the EEC Treaty, but with a different emphasis. The EEC provisions, as interpreted by the Court of Justice in the Casati case, postulate cooperation between member states as a preliminary condition for capital liberalization. The OECD provisions consider capital liberalization useful in so far as it contributes to, or at the least does not harm, policy cooperation. However, this difference of degree did not have a great practical impact as to the manner in which capital restrictions were treated by the organizations.

Like the safeguard measures contained in the Treaty of Rome the OECD Code provides for exemptions under similar circumstances. The clauses of derogation may be invoked if a country's economic and financial situation justifies the taking of measures, if there are serious economic and financial disturbances, or if the overall balance of payments and the country's official reserves deteriorate seriously.[31] An important element of the Code is

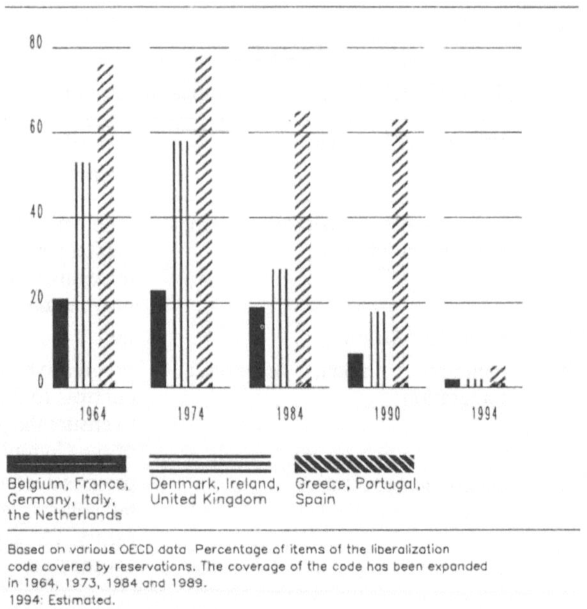

Fig. 6. Position of EEC member states under the OECD liberalization code.

that member states cannot retract from liberalization measures unless they ask for a derogation from their obligations. There thus is a 'ratchet mechanism' which is designed to consolidate the liberalization gains, once they are achieved. This mechanism is similar to the standstill undertaking in Article 71 in the Treaty, which provides that member states endeavour to avoid introducing new restrictions or making existing rules more restrictive.[32] The peer pressure exerted in the regular examinations can positively influence the member states. The Code also sees to it that restrictions are applied in a non-discriminatory manner. On the other hand, there is no mechanism or sanction to enforce obligations on the OECD membership. On the whole, the Code has not been a very powerful liberalization instrument.

Just as the application of controls within the framework of the European Community has been regularly examined in the Monetary Committee, the OECD member states have been regularly examined in the OECD *Committee on Capital Movements and Invisible Transactions* (CMIT). In this examination countries have had to justify any retained restrictions. Apart from the EEC directives, the OECD Code has been the only multilateral instrument promoting the liberalization of capital movements. Its content and scope in general have kept pace with the current state of liberalization, although, of course, it has been attempted to be somewhat ahead of the common denominator in order to prevent the pace from being dictated by the most restrictive countries.

3.10 CONCLUSION

The drafters of the Treaty of Rome had shown vision in their design of a Common Market. Although the Treaty was less ambitious in its operational design than the earlier European Coal and Steel Community, the fact that the six countries could reach agreement on such a goal with far-reaching implications as to cooperation and coordination was significant. However, in the field of capital movements it is obvious that *caution* prevailed. Progressive liberalization and non-discrimination are guiding principles. But the subordination of the goal of free capital movements to the higher-ranking goal of the free movement of goods in the Common Market shows that the Treaty was indeed primarily designed to achieve a customs union, albeit with a wider-reaching institutional and cooperative design, and that there were fears that free trade could be imperilled by destabilizing capital flows. The main motives for retaining capital restrictions were: the maintenance of a certain degree of autonomy for economic and monetary policy, the wish to raise obstacles to speculative short-term capital movements, and the desire to protect domestic capital markets.

In the prevailing situation of fixed exchange rates under the Bretton Woods system – which implicitly was taken for granted by the drafters of the Treaty – the wish to maintain a measure of *autonomy* in the conduct of monetary policies seemed to justify for most countries the maintenance of capital controls. Exchange rate coordination had been one of the weak spots in the Treaty, where Article 107 stipulated merely that policies with regard to exchange rates should be a matter of common concern.[33] More in general, the Treaty follows a minimalistic approach in the monetary area. Monetary coordination could not properly come off as long as there were no forceful Treaty provisions with respect to coordination of national budgetary policies, the most conspicuous hiatus in the Treaty. In essence member states were not prepared to surrender competences in the financial field. It is therefore not surprising that in the area of capital movements, where potentially supranational powers are assigned to the Community, with close links to both internal and external monetary policy, the drafters have been cautious. The majority view was that short-term, monetary capital flows, which more often than not were associated with speculation, did not contribute to economic integration and could hinder monetary policy.

Long-term capital outflows were regarded as a drain on domestic resources. Allowing non-residents on the domestic capital markets often ran counter to the desired regulation of those markets. Moralistic arguments were used to defend this position, such as the fear that productive capital would flow from poor to rich areas of the Community. Understandable as this fear may have been at a time of capital scarcity, the Treaty had provided the very instruments to counter deprivation of underdeveloped areas, such as the social funds and the European Investment Bank.

The overriding desire to ensure freedom of trade, stability of exchange rates as well as autonomy of monetary policy made it imperative that any obligation to liberalize capital movements was *circumscribed*. The more liberal, market-oriented economies of Germany and Belgium willingly accepted that the more dirigistic policies – albeit in varying shades – followed in France, Italy and the Netherlands called for exchange regulations for capital movements. For Belgium and Luxembourg, the dual market functioned as a shock absorber if inconsistencies arose between domestic monetary policies and the fixity of the exchange rate. Germany in principle did not avail itself of market regulation – although for a long time it would discourage the internationalization of the Deutsche mark – but it did not press for such liberalization in other countries, because it did not need foreign capital and its stability-oriented policies could be undermined if premature liberalization would facilitate speculative capital fleeing other member states.

All in all the Treaty provisions on capital liberalization, as well as their later political and legal interpretation, show that in the *sequencing* of the whole process of liberalization the freedom of capital movements was given relatively low priority. Characteristics of sequencing, such as a ranking order, a time framework, the fulfilment of conditions and linkages with other policy domains, show up in the relevant Treaty provisions:

- hierarchy – trade liberalization is put first and foremost, before capital liberalization (Article 3);
- gradualism – a progressive step-by-step approach is to be followed (Article 67);
- conditionality – capital liberalization is confined to the need to ensure the proper functioning of the Common Market (escape clause, Article 67);
- interlinkages – the freeing of financial services, connected with the movement of capital, shall be effected in step with capital liberalization (Article 61.2).[34]

These characteristics of sequencing incorporated in the Treaty implied that actual obligations with respect to capital movements would be phased in, depending on progress in other areas. In practice the lack of policy coordination and, consequently the divergence of economic performance, would prove to stand more in the way of capital liberalization than the lack of progress in other domains, including the remaining three freedoms.

Notwithstanding the fact that the actual state of capital liberalization differed considerably among the six members states, the Treaty made no attempt to impose a minimum regime of liberalization. In practice, this would mean that further obligations to liberalize would have to be worked out and would form the subject of *negotiations*. The lack of a Treaty provision for a minimum regime put the countries with a restrictive regime in a stronger negotiating position: they were the ones who had to give up national control instruments which the countries with a liberal regime already had abandoned. The position of the latter was already weakened by the standstill provision in Article 71 which stipulated that countries would endeavour not to introduce new restrictions nor make existing rules more restrictive, although admittedly the frequent and continued recourse by the restrictive countries to safeguard measures had undermined this provision.

Although the liberalization of capital movements within the European Community is the subject matter of this book, important work in this area has been done in the framework of the OECD as well. At times this has resulted in cross-fertilization, each of the organizations taking the lead in turns. The important liberalization drive in the 1980s, however, primarily had its roots in intra-EC discussions, in part resulting from a fresh analysis of the effectiveness of controls in view of the globalization of international financial markets. Here the European Community took the lead. After European liberalization directives had been adopted, the OECD Code could be significantly extended as well. The role of the IMF in the process of capital liberalization has been a much more modest one, in particular because in its Articles of Agreement the primary principle with respect to capital is that member countries are free to control international capital movements. The IMF, however, has been actively involved in the liberalization of current account payments – at the foot of the pyramid of capital movements – and in the pursuit of unification of multiple exchange rate systems. It would be worthwile to explore whether the IMF's responsibilities could be extended to cover capital liberalization as well. This would fill a global institutional gap.

NOTES

1. Eichengreen (1993) argues that the EPU had important positive spill-over effects for the European countries by actively encouraging intra-European trade liberalization.
2. Compare Eichengreen (1993), p. 40. On further consideration Eichengreen argues that in the post-war years a surge of inward foreign investment would not have materialized anyway because US private lenders were still demoralized about the interwar defaults (p. 116 et seq.).
3. In its explanatory memorandum addressed to parliament, attached to the EEC Treaty proposals, the Dutch government takes this principle as a point of departure (Memorie van Toelichting, zitting 1956–57, no. 4725.3, p. 3 et seq.). The argument had been elaborated earlier by Beyen in a speech in 1955, reproduced in Hommes (1980), p. 170–182, in which he concluded: 'economic strength is the necessary foundation for maintaining European political unity'.
4. In the subcommittee which prepared this part of the report, headed by Verrijn-Stuart, the question whether the safeguard clauses would remain possible in the final stage had not yet been decided. Two conflicting views were presented, one arguing the total demise of capital controls without fall-back postition, and the other arguing the need for an escape clause in case of balance-of-payments difficulties (Rapport de la Commission du Marché Commun, des investissements et des problèmes sociaux, 17 October 1955, Brussels, p. 52 et seq.). Apparently the latter view prevailed (see also note 8).
5. Marjolin (1989), p.288.

6. In the Dutch eyes the German interest level was 'extremely' high (Ministry of Finance memorandum, 15 February 1958). This could in part probably be ascribed to the Bundesbank's restrictive monetary policy, but the relatively underdeveloped capital market – 'badly organized' – may also have been a factor.
7. Marjolin (1989), p.300–301
8. The view of the Belgian experts in the Spaak Committee that in the final stage no safeguard clauses with respect to freedom of capital movements should apply prompted a missive of the Dutch authorities to their Belgian counterparts, calling on them to display Benelux solidarity and accept the maintenance of safeguard clauses (letter Ministry of Finance, dated 10 October 1955).
9. Holtrop (1956), p. 819. For a more general description of Holtrop's line of thought see Vanthoor (1993).
10. Holtrop (1956), p. 821.
11. Memorandum of 16 May 1959, De Nederlandsche Bank.
12. De Nederlandsche Bank, Annual Report 1957, p. 18.
13. Listing based on various internal memoranda of the Ministries of Finance and Foreign Affairs and the Nederlandsche Bank, 1956 and 1957.
14. In Article 107, which requires member states to treat their exchange rate policies as a matter of common concern, member states may be authorized to take countervailing measures if one of the member states carries through a competitive devaluation. In practice this provision has not been applied by the Commission.
15. Kapteyn et al. (1987) consider the freedom of payments, as laid down in Articles 67.2 and 106, the fifth freedom.
16. Article 69 provides for unanimity during the two first stages and for decision-making by a qualified majority thereafter. In the Single European Act, which became effective on 1 July 1987, the provisions with respect to capital movements between member states and third countries were amended to the effect that decisions in this sphere would be taken by qualified majority as well (Article 70.1).
17. Articles 30 (free movements of goods), 48 and 52 (free movement of persons and right of establishment), and 59 (free movement of services). These articles, other than Article 67, are directly applicable and thus extend rights which EEC citizens may invoke against contrary provisions of national law.
18. Article 2 provides that the progressive 'approximation' of economic policies, together with the establishment of a common market, is one of two means to attain the goals of the Treaty; Article 103 provides that member states regard their conjunctural policies as a matter of common concern; and Article 145, first indent, provides for the general coordination of economic policies of member states by the Council.
19. Ruding (1969, p. 200) makes a distinction between capital in the real economic sphere and in the financial sphere. In the latter sense 'financial capital' is closely related to money (op. cit., p. 7). He concludes that the Treaty contains the obligation that a common market for 'real capital', such as direct investment or transactions in securities, is established, but not one for 'financial capital'. In his view capital liberalization is not to be regarded as an independent obligation under the Treaty itself, but as a complementary obligation with respect to the Common Market for goods (op. cit., p. 477). There is a certain parallel with the subdivision given by the Court of Justice in its judgement in the Thompson case (case 7/78), where a distinction was made between financial, real and monetary capital.
20. Presentation of country positions based on internal memoranda, De Nederlandsche Bank, January 1957.
21. Marjolin (1969), p. 301, in describing the French fears, seems to suggest that France was the auctor intellectualis of the escape clause.
22. See Kapteyn et al. (1987), p. 297.
23. Article 221 provided that as from 1961 all EEC nationals should be accorded equal treatment as regards participation in the capital of companies. In practice, however, this

article did not play a large role because of its subordination to other provisions in the Treaty.

24. Declaration of the International Chamber of Commerce on Monetary issues in the European Economic Community, Paris, 6 May 1958.
25. Judgement of the European Court of Justice on 11 November 1981, case 203/80. Casati, an Italian citizen resident in Germany, had been arrested for exporting bank notes out of Italy. He argued that he had taken the bank notes with him out of Germany to buy inventory in Italy, but that he had to return empty-handed because the factory was closed. This he could not prove and the Court decided that the EEC provisions would not invalidate the imposition of a fine on Casati because the export of bank notes did not fall under the liberalization obligations of the Community.
26. Proposals for an International Clearing Union (April 1943), reproduced in Horsefield (1969), Vol. III Documents, p. 32.
27. See Gold (1977), p. 23–26.
28. Only Article VI(2), concerning specific IMF-related provisions, has been amended.
29. Article 2 of the OECD Convention stipulates that member states will '... pursue their efforts to reduce or abolish obstacles to the exchange of goods and services and current payments and maintain and extend the liberalization of capital movements ...'.
30. The Capital Movements Code was expanded in 1964; there were two additions in 1973 and 1984, which dealt with operations in collective investment securities and with direct investment respectively. Up till the mid–1980s the Code, as a reflection of current practice in most member states, was confined mainly to long-term capital flows and did not apply to short-term financial transactions, such as money-market activities. In May 1989 a major revision of the Code was agreed upon. All capital movements, including cross-border financial services, money-market activities and financial innovations, such as swaps and options, were included in the coverage of the Code. See for an exhaustive description Liberalization of capital movements and financial services in the OECD area, OECD (1990).
31. Article 7 of the Code of liberalization of capital movements. Articles 13 to 15 provide for the notification and examination procedures of derogations.
32. The 'standstill' provision has been strengthened through the amendment in the Single European Act in Article 70.1, where it was provided that measures which constitute a step back as regards the liberalization of capital movements could only be taken by unanimous consent.
33. This weakness was demonstrated already on the first occasion of a major readjustment of exchange rates, in 1961, when the Deutsche mark and the Netherlands guilder were revalued. In its Annual Report on 1961 the Monetary Committee notes disapprovingly that these decisions were taken without full ex ante coordination within the EEC.
34. In practice for the liberally-oriented countries, as Germany, the Netherlands and the United Kingdom, the actual liberalization of capital movements, and not the minimum obligatory liberalization regime, determined the liberalization of services of banks and insurance companies.

CHAPTER 4

The Role of the Monetary Committee

I have always felt that the Monetary Committee has made an immense contribution to international cooperation by demonstrating how a small group of people who know each other well can easily break through the barriers of rigid national positions and develop new orientations, which are accepted and welcomed by governments.

Emile van Lennep, 1978

4.1 INTRODUCTION

In the process of capital liberalization in Europe the Monetary Committee of the European Community has played an influential role. The committee, where high-ranking officials regularly meet, provides a unique forum for frank and open policy discussions on issues of common concern and where its members do not immediately bind their countries' positions. In this committee the policy aspects of liberalization came to the fore in a dialogue between the Commission, as the guardian of the Treaty, and the member states. Both the imposition of exchange controls as well as their abolition having significant implications for other policy areas, the Monetary Committee provided the natural forum for a thorough discussion of these wide-ranging consequences. In order to put these discussions into the proper perspective we will investigate in this chapter the role of the Monetary Committee in its different aspects. We will allow ourselves a few asides which may be useful in throwing some light on this rather uncharted terrain.

4.2 THE TREATY STATUS OF THE MONETARY COMMITTEE

The Monetary Committee is the only committee of officials, presently functioning in the Community in the economic area, which is mentioned explicitly in the Treaty of Rome.[1] Other committees, like the Committee of Governors of the Central Banks or the Economic Policy Committee, have been established by the Council pursuant to relevant provisions in the Treaty.[2] In Article 105(2) the *legal basis* for the Monetary Committee can be found:

'In order to promote coordination of the policies of Member States in the monetary field to the full extent needed for the functioning of the common market, a Monetary Committee with advisory status is hereby set up. It shall have the following tasks:

– to keep under review the monetary and financial situation of the Member States and of the Community and the general payments system of the Member States and to report regularly thereon to the Council and to the Commission;

– to deliver opinions at the request of the Council or of the Commission or on its own initiative, for submission to these institutions.

The Member States and the Commission shall each appoint two members of the Monetary Committee.'

The special Treaty status of the Monetary Committee gives this body an added significance, which had been the outcome of intense discussions on the content of economic and monetary cooperation. The burial of the European Defence Community in the French Assemblée in 1954 had made it clear that supranational solutions with respect to European integration would be unattainable. The result was that the Treaty, as enabling legislation, had a *dualistic character:* the Treaty declared various policy areas as matters of common concern, but fell short of declaring those areas as matters of common competences. Therefore, in practice the coordination of policies between member states in the areas of common concern was of a non-committal character. There were no ways for the Community to enforce decisions in the areas of common concern because it lacked the powers to do so. All depended therefore on the good-will of the member states to coordinate voluntarily or on the adoption of secondary legislation, which would provide for such cooperation to be enforceable.

This dualistic design of the Treaty was particularly visible in the phrasing of the provisions relating to *exchange rate policy.* In Article 107.1 each member state is called upon to 'treat its policy with regard to rates of exchange as a matter of common concern.' But the Treaty does not provide for Community competences in the area of exchange rates. The latter is hardly surprising given the feeble provisions regarding economic policy coordination. The Commission, being denied concrete powers in the field of economic let alone monetary policies, could not be given competences in the area of exchange rates, which are the very outcome of economic and monetary policies.

The caution exercised in the Treaty concerning the *coordination in the monetary field* and the abolition of exchange restrictions reflected the prevailing preference at the time for trying to isolate domestic money and capital markets from international developments. At the same time, this isolation made it possible to conduct domestic monetary policy in a relatively autonomous manner. Moreover, the national competences with respect to monetary policy varied greatly. The newly created Deutsche Bundesbank[3] was independent in the conduct of monetary policy, whereas, at the other side of the spectrum, the Banque de France in the post-war nationalization had surrendered many of its powers. The Treaty of Rome thus could not provide for any imperative mechanism for the coordination of monetary policies.

The dualistic approach of the Treaty as regards economic and financial policies – yes to the *coordination* of areas of common concern, no to the surrender of national *sovereignty* to the Community level –, taken together with the purpose of the Treaty – 'to the extent necessary for the proper functioning of the Common market' – made it imperative that mechanisms were established to ensure that these areas of common concern would be treated properly and that coordination would not prove to be a dead letter. Yet, in the economic field, where the need to coordinate figures prominently in the Treaty, the drafters saw no need to explicitly establish the institutional framework for this coordination at the level below the Council. Apparently, it was supposed that the appropriate mechanisms would work out themselves. Conversely, in the monetary field and as regards exchange rate policy no explicit powers were formulated in the Treaty.

Nevertheless, there was a wish to fill this void in the monetary policy area. The drafters of the Treaty chose to set up a committee, with coordinating powers and, in the interest of the Community, independent expert members and its own statute. The Monetary Committee thus introduces a Community element and is shaped to further the goals of the Community.[4] At the same time the committee has an independent institutional position sui generis within the Community. It acts independently of the national states, the Commission and the preparatory bodies of the Council, i.e. the General Secretariat of the Council and the Coreper.[5] This *position sui generis* is the natural reflection of the dualistic character of the Treaty in the economic and monetary field and of the distinct institutional position of the national central banks in the member states. In its first Annual Report the Monetary Committee addresses this dualistic character and describes in passing its raison d'être in a crystal-clear manner: 'In Articles 104 and 107 of the Treaty the responsibility of each member state in determining its own economic and monetary policies is affirmed. However, in their policy execution member states have to take into account the objectives of the Treaty; therefore Article 105 provides for the coordination of economic and monetary policies, because, if such policies were to diverge too much, they could lead to the application of safeguard clauses, which would endanger the establishment of the Common Market.'

The progress achieved in restoring external convertibility and liberalizing trade should not be put at risk. Indeed, it is significant that the article establishing the Monetary Committee is inserted in the Treaty in the chapter on the *Balance of Payments*. Apparently, there must have been strong fears that exchange rate or balance-of-payments disturbances could lead to a deceleration in the process of trade liberalization or even to the reintroduction of trade barriers. This may be one major explanation of the Treaty status of the Monetary Committee: it was of overriding importance that the work of this committee would create conditions in the monetary and financial field which would not jeopardize the attainment of the goal of the Common Market. The further-reaching objective of monetary and financial integration, which would later come to the fore in the committee, was not yet an issue in a world which lived in the relative calm of the Bretton Woods system.

However, the creation of the Monetary Committee was *not undisputed.* In the Brussels preparatory conference on the Common Market[6] the German delegation unexpectedly opposed the creation of the Monetary Committee. It considered that the European Commission would suffice. In the background there was the fear on the German side that the Monetary Committee would be invested with more than advisory powers and thus would undermine the position of the Commission. The German delegation stood alone in this respect and at a later stage joined the majority. As we will see in this study, the relationship between the Monetary Committee and the Commission indeed would not always be an easy one. Theirs would be a love-hate relationship, each quarrel being ended with the confirmation that they needed each other.

4.3 THE TASKS OF THE MONETARY COMMITTEE

The powers of the committee are carefully *circumscribed,* in line with the dualistic character of the Treaty in the monetary and economic sphere. The committee can only 'keep under review', 'report' and 'deliver opinions'. The promotion of the coordination of monetary policies in the framework of the committee is limited to the extent needed for the functioning of the Common Market. From this description of competences it cannot easily be gauged that in fact this committee has evolved into one of the most influential policy-making bodies in the Community. The latter can be ascribed to the wide-ranging areas in which the committee would be called upon to advise in the years to come, where it acted as the main preparatory forum for the meetings of the Council of Ministers. Its strength is in part precisely based on the lack of a supranational common authority in these areas. Kees (1984) writes that 'throughout the committee's history there has been no example of the Council taking a decision that went against an orientation expressed by the committee.' What was true before 1984, remains true until this very day.

Apart from the more general coordinating task mentioned in Article 105, the committee has a separate task in specific areas where the Community has some, albeit restricted powers. These tasks are of an *advisory* nature, but in the course of time they have expanded and acquired a *preparatory* status. Three closely related areas in particular are referred to in the Treaty, where the committee needs to be consulted by the Commission before decisions or action can be taken: (a) the liberalization of capital movements (Articles 69 to 73) and (b) the exchange rate policies of member states (Article 107) and (c) the mutual assistance of member states in case of balance-of-payments problems (Articles 108 and 109). These articles are reproduced in Annex 1.

4.3.1 Liberalization of Capital Movements

Article 69 of the Treaty of Rome specifies that the Monetary Committee is consulted on directives aimed at the implementation of the provisions of Article 67 concerning the progressive liberalization of capital movements. These directives are issued by the Council of Ministers on a proposal from the Commission after consultation of the Monetary Committee. This three-pronged *procedure* – initiative of the Commission, opinion of the Monetary Committee, decision by the Council of Ministers (EcoFin) – in fact has become the standard procedure for a number of issues which the Treaty has assigned to the sphere of competence of the ministries of finance and the central banks. By means of this provision the Monetary Committee thus was given an important task in preparing policy decisions concerning the gradual dismantling of obstacles to the free movement of capital in Europe. In the Chapter on Capital the committee is given a consultative task in the *monitoring* of the regime of exchange controls in the member states. It is to be consulted if the Commission is to give recommendations concerning the exchange regime of a particular member state in the framework of Article 71. And it is to be consulted as well if derogations are asked for by member states which are experiencing disturbances in their national capital markets because of capital movements (Article 73).

The tasks of the Monetary Committee in the field of capital movements, extensive as they are, have been broadened in the course of the years by means of *secondary legislation.* Of particular importance has been the provision in the first Directive for the implementation of Article 67 that the Monetary Committee shall examine at least once a year the existing restrictions on capital movements with a view to advising the Commission on the possible abolition of certain restrictions.[7] Although this obligation fell into abeyance in the late 1960s when many member states tightened their controls, the provision could be used as an important stepping-stone at a later stage in order to prompt the Commission to enforce the Treaty obligations.

4.3.2 Exchange Rate Policies

In Article 107 member states have undertaken the obligation to treat their exchange rate policies as a matter of *common concern.* If certain member states nevertheless follow an exchange rate policy which would jeopardize the goals of economic policy in the Community – equilibrium on the balance-of-payments, high level of employment and a stable level of prices (Article 104) – and would distort competitive relations within the Community, the other member states would be allowed, after consultation of the Monetary Committee, to take countervailing measures. The article apparently was included in the Treaty for fear of competitive devaluations in case of balance-of-payments disturbances, as witnessed in the 1930s. Apart from this article, the Treaty,

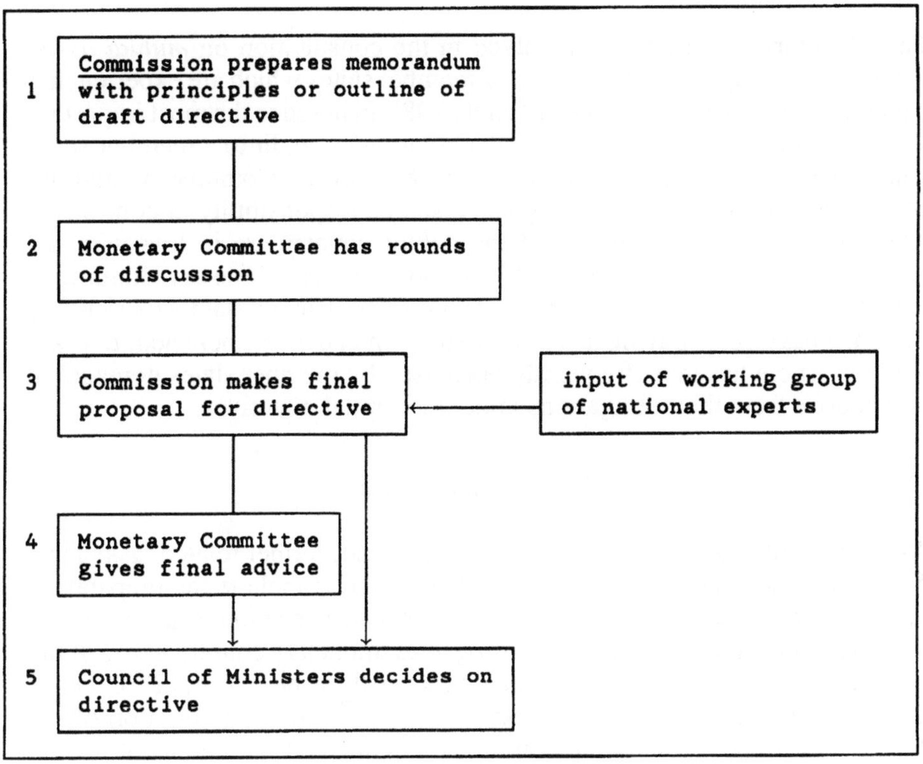

Fig. 7. Preparation of EEC directives.

written in the context of the Bretton Woods system of fixed exchange rates, confiries itself to the general obligation of Article 104 that each member state shall 'pursue the economic policy needed to ensure the equilibrium of its overall balance of payments and to maintain confidence in its currency'.[8]

The role of the Monetary Committee in the field of exchange rates has culminated in its active involvement in the functioning of the *European Monetary System* and the *development of the ECU*. One of the tasks conferred upon the committee – some would argue the most important task – has been the preparation of the decisions by ministers and central bank governors on realignments of exchange parities within the EMS.[9] The negotiations on exchange rate adjustments largely are conducted in the Monetary Committee and often Ministers do not separately meet but merely confirm the outcome of the committee's deliberations. This helps to dedramatize the realignment negotiations.[10]

4.3.3 Balance-of-Payments Assistance

The Monetary Committee is involved in the consultation on *mutual assistance* and accompanying measures for member states which are experiencing balance-of-payments difficulties (Article 108). In practice the most important form of mutual assistance has been the granting of credit to a member state. Under the new Community financing mechanism the Commission and the Monetary Committee have been given a shared responsibility in controlling whether the economic policies of the debtor country are in line with the agreed policy conditions. Article 109 provides that the Monetary Committee advises whether protective measures taken by a member state experiencing a sudden balance-of payments crisis shall be amended or abolished. In practice this article has most frequently been used by member states demanding derogations from their obligations under the capital directives.

4.3.4 Further Tasks

As Community secondary legislation was enacted, further related tasks have been assigned to the Monetary Committee.[11] These include the preparation of the *multilateral surveillance* of member states' economic policies; the oversight of economic *convergence programs*; monetary consequences of the EEC *agricultural* policy; surveillance tasks with respect to the EEC *credit facilities;* and *international monetary relations*.[12] After the adoption of the Treaty on European Union the committee assumed an important role in the *excessive deficit procedure*. The listing of subjects the Monetary Committee deals with is not exhaustive. In the course of the years the committee has become more actively involved in the preparation of the EcoFin Council meetings, especially the policy-oriented informal meetings which are attended by the central bank governors as well. As Kees (1984) has said '... it is not the legal framework but the political weight of the committee ... which results in and provokes the manifold requests for action.'

Through these provisions in the Treaty of Rome and the later secondary legislation the role of the Monetary Committee in the field of monetary and economic cooperation has been specified and gradually expanded. They form the legitimation of the important *intermediary role* in the decision-making process between the Commission and the Council. The provisions have been written in the historical context of the 1950s in which the problem of foreign exchange scarcity had just been overcome, convertibility of national currencies for external current transactions had been restored and the Bretton Woods system of fixed exchange rates was in its hey-day. However, the institutional set-up has proved to be flexible enough to accommodate the changing circumstances of the post-Bretton Woods area. The Monetary Committee has played an important role in shaping the monetary identity of Europe, culminating in its important contribution to the Treaty on European Union. This Treaty

TABLE 8

The regular tasks of the Monetary Committee

(a)	At each monthly meeting in the *tour d'horizon* recent policy measures and economic developments are reviewed, as well as recent exchange rate and interest rate developments.
(b)	Twice a year the *monetary policy in the Community* is reviewed. The end-year exercise includes a discussion of monetary targets for the following year.
(c)	Two or three times a year the *economic and monetary situation of one member country* is examined in depth. In addition the extent to which a country respects the policy conditions attached to Community loans is reviewed regularly.
(d)	Twice a year the *statement to the Interim Committee* on behalf of the Community is prepared.
(e)	Once a year *bilateral consultations* are held by the chairman with the prospective member states Norway, Austria, Sweden and Finland.
(f)	Once a year the existing *exchange restrictions* and derogations are examined with a view to recommending possible abolition.
(g)	Twice a year a *multilateral surveillance* exercise of economic policies in member states is conducted with a view to promoting convergence.

Source: Partly based on the 29th Activity Report of the Monetary Committee, Brussels, September 1988.

provides that the task and the composition of the committee will change in the final stage of Economic and Monetary Union. We will come back to this issue in Chapter 9.

4.4 THE COMPOSITION OF THE MONETARY COMMITTEE

The member countries and the Commission each have the right to appoint two members to the committee. In turn these members can each appoint one alternate who can replace them at meetings. Members are chosen from *high-ranking government officials* and from the *national central banks,* normally the executive director who deals with international affairs.[13]

The government officials usually are the Treasurers-General or the Permanent Secretaries at the Ministries of Finance, the exception being Denmark where the Ministry of Economic Affairs is charged with international policy coordination. In the case of Germany, where powers are shared between the two departments the alternate member presently comes from the Ministry of Economic Affairs. In this way a unique blend of expertise is obtained. The same officials usually meet also in other international fora, like the IMF Interim Committee, the meetings of the G7 and G10-Deputies and the meetings of Working Party 3 of the OECD, the body which deals with international policy coordination, balance-of-payments adjustment and the exchange markets. The central bank members regularly meet in their own circle in the framework of the Basle weekends on the premises of the BIS and in the context of Council meetings of the European Monetary Institute in Frankfurt.

The members of the committee act in a *personal capacity* and in the interest of the Community. At times they can adopt positions beyond national interests and take responsibility for defending concessions at home. The value of their advice is determined by their knowledge of facts, based on domestic responsibilities and tasks. Although formally their *mandate* lasts two years, in practice renewal follows automatically. In fact many members, particularly those from central banks, serve very long terms on the Monetary Committee.[14] Thus an influential network of long-standing acquaintances is established.

The *Statutes* of the committee, reproduced in Annex 3, provide for general arrangements and procedures as well as for voting procedures. Since their adoption in 1958 only minor changes have been made to the Statutes, but in 1994 an overhaul of the Statutes, which had increasingly become outdated, especially after the coming into effect of the Treaty on European Union, was being contemplated.[15] According to the Statutes each member has one vote, but in practice voting is rare, the decision-making process in the Monetary Committee being driven by the desire to reach consensus. Insofar as the committee prepares decisions to be taken by the EcoFin Council which require unanimity, there is a strong urge to agree on compromises which will be carried in the meeting of the ministers. If conclusions cannot be reached, deliberations normally are deferred to future committee meetings and no formal vote is taken.

4.5 THE CHAIRMAN OF THE MONETARY COMMITTEE

The committee chooses from among its members a chairman who serves for a period of two years. The role of the chairman of the committee is a momentous one. He has an important say in the items to be put on the agenda of the committee meetings and he can set the tone of the discussion. He also takes the initiative in summing up discussions and advancing compromise proposals. In the course of the years, the '*chairman's reports*' have become more and more important. In these reports the chairman on his own responsibility outlines the stance of the meeting for ministers. These reports have frequently taken the place of the formal advice the committee is asked to deliver. The reports and opinions of the Monetary Committee are explained by the chairman at the ministerial EcoFin meetings, in which he has a separate seat.

Although the Statutes provided that the chairman's two-year *term of office* could be extended only once, after a Council amendment in 1962 this provision was dropped and in the first years of the committee the chairman was routinely reappointed. The first chairman Emile van Lennep, Treasurer-General of the Dutch Ministry of Finance, served for nearly twelve years, from 1958 till October 1969, when he was appointed Secretary-General of

TABLE 9

Chairmen of the Monetary Committee.

1958–69	Emile van Lennep	The Netherlands	MoF
1970–73	Bernard Clappier	France	Bank
1974–76	Coen Oort	The Netherlands	MoF
1976–77	Karl-Otto Pöhl	Germany	MoF/Bank
1978–79	Jean van Ypersele	Belgium	MoF
1980–82	Jean-Yves Haberer	France	MoF
1982	Horst Schulmann	Germany	MoF
1983–84	Michel Camdessus	France	MoF/Bank
1985–87	Hans Tietmeyer	Germany	MoF
1987–88	Geoffrey Littler	United Kingdom	MoF
1989–90	Mario Sarcinelli	Italy	MoF
1991–92	Cees Maas	The Netherlands	MoF
1992–93	Jean-Claude Trichet	France	MoF
1993–(present)	Nigel Wicks	United Kingdom	MoF

MoF – Ministry of Finance

the OECD.[16] Thereafter the terms of the chairman approached the two-year period. Over the years 1958–94, 4 Frenchmen served as chairman, 3 Germans and 3 Dutchmen, 2 Britons, whereas Belgium and Italy provided the chairman once.

With a few exceptions all chairmen have come from the *ministries of finance* (see Table 9). This underlines the important political role the Monetary Committee performs, which calls for a chairman who is in close contact with the responsible elected authorities. Nevertheless, many chairmen have also served for the central bank, viz. Karl-Otto Pöhl who left the Finanzministerium for the Bundesbank, Michel Camdessus who left the Trésor to become Governor of the Banque de France before taking the lead at the International Monetary Fund and, recently, Hans Tietmeyer who also left for the Bundesbank to become eventually its Governor.

The Statutes provide for the appointment of three vice-chairmen,[17] one of whom can replace the chairman in his absence. In practice, however, this rule is liberally applied. The chairman and vice-chairmen convene together with other invited members in meetings of the *Bureau* of the Monetary Committee. This Bureau is not mentioned in the Statutes and therefore has no official status nor fixed participation. As a rule the Bureau convenes in informal luncheon meetings after the morning sessions of the committee. Members of the four larger countries, in particular those representing the ministries of finance, seem to be always present. The Bureau meetings are meant to informally sound out members on the positions taken with respect to agenda items of

TABLE 10

Chairmen of the Alternates of the Monetary Committee.

1958–68	A.W.R. baron Mackay	The Netherlands	Bank
1968–74	J. Mertens de Wilmars	Belgium	Bank
1974–77	Geoffrey Littler	United Kingdom	MoF
1977–79	Henry Baquiast	France	MoF
1980–82	Werner Flandorffer	Germany	MoEA
1982–84	Jean-Jacques Rey	Belgium	Bank
1985–88	Stefano Micossi	Italy	Bank
1988–90	Pieter Stek	The Netherlands	MoF
1991–92	Henrik Fugmann	Denmark	MoEA
1993–94	Michael Tutty	Ireland	MoF
1994–(present)	Vitor Gaspar	Portugal	Bank

MoF – Ministry of Finance; MoEA – Ministry of Economic Affairs

the committee or on other matters of mutual interest (e.g. appointments for international institutions).

4.6 THE ALTERNATES OF THE MONETARY COMMITTEE

The alternate members of the Monetary Committee frequently convene among themselves at the request of the Monetary Committee to discuss technical or administrative details and thus prepare the deliberations in the full committee. The Alternates have played an important role in the field of *capital liberalization* by preparing the yearly examinations and discussing the technical details of Commission proposals for directives. In recent years country examinations are routinely prepared by the alternates. Whereas the attendance of meetings of the Monetary Committee normally is strictly limited to members and alternates, admission to the meetings of the alternates is more liberal and thus provides an opportunity for junior civil servants and central bankers to observe or participate in the decision-making process in the Community. On technical matters specialists, e.g. tax experts, are called in to provide advice to the alternates. The alternates normally report to the full committee by way of a written report or a 'chairman's report'. They also prepare each year the statement which the country chairing the EC makes for the annual meeting of the International Monetary Fund on behalf of the Community.

As can be seen from Table 10 the choice of the *chairmen* of the Alternates of the Monetary Committee shows a much larger diversity both with respect to national background as well as to professional background. Only Belgium has held the chair twice and the chairmanship has been more or less equally divided between the ministries of finance and of economic affairs and the central banks. Obviously the office of chairman of the Alternates has been regarded as being of minor political importance and as a means to provide satisfaction to countries which have felt underrepresented.

4.7 THE PROCEEDINGS OF THE MONETARY COMMITTEE

The committee meets generally *every month* in Brussels. Since its inception the committee has held over 400 meetings. Each year another EC country acts as host to the committee members. In the beginning two-day meetings werd held, but this practice was discontinued in the course of the years. In case of need meetings can be called at short notice. Preferably the committee does not meet on Fridays in order to dispel any market expectations that a realignment in the Exchange Rate Mechanism of the EMS might be imminent. Such realignments normally take place over the weekend and speculation is fuelled by rumours of meetings of the Monetary Committee.[18]

The Statutes of the Monetary Committee provide that the discussions of the committee and of its working groups are confidential. The committee reported on its activities in *annual reports* up till 1988, when this practice was discontinued by tacit consent. The principal reason forwarded for this discontinuation was the lack of resources within the secretariat, the Commission having tightened the purse strings. These annual reports provided one of the few published documents of the committee which were easily available to the general public. In annexes to the report opinions and reports of the committee were published as well.

The need for *confidentiality* apparently sometimes has been called into question and in one of its annual reports some explanations were given.[19] The committee pointed in particular to the character of the tasks conferred upon it which called for limited attendance (only members and their alternates) and confidentiality of its deliberations and reports. The need for confidentiality reflected the sensitivity of the issues under consideration and the impact the decisions in these areas have on the financial markets. The discussions on exchange rate questions, and in later years in particular on realignments within the EMS, form a particularly sensitive area. The secrecy surrounding meetings is resented by journalists who, sometimes in a pack, have to wait outside the Centre Borschette where the meetings usually are held. The International Herald Tribune said sneeringly that 'Since its founding in 1958, the ... committee has taken on the trappings of a clandestine organization.'[20]

Confidentiality has been relatively well assured and it has been a major contributing factor to the effective functioning of the committee. There have been four other factors which have enabled the committee to proceed in a pragmatic manner and generally to arrive at *consensus:* (a) strict attendance rules, (b) opinions and reports under the responsibility of the chairman, (c) preparations of the meetings in the Bureau, and (d) an independent position of the secretary.

The strict *attendance rules,* under which no officials other than the Alternates can attend the committee's meetings, have contributed to the development of a 'club of like-minded personalities'.[21] In this club understanding for each other's problems grows and there is no need to play to the gallery. The instrument of *chairman's reports* makes it easier for committee members to depart from their national standpoint because a committee member cannot be held responsible at home for the chairman's report. In the *Bureau meetings* representatives of the four major member states are always present. In an informal manner they can already explore each other's positions and concoct possible compromises. The independent position of the *secretary,* who attends these meetings, enables him to act as a bridge between the Commission and member states. All these organizational procedures, which have proved their value over the years, have contributed to reaching agreement among the members.

4.8 RELATIONSHIP WITH THE COMMISSION

The relationship of the Monetary Committee vis-à-vis the Commission, as guardian of the Treaty, is a complex one. The Monetary Committee has a *dual role:* it prepares not only the Ecofin Council meetings but also advises the Commission. At the same time two Commission representatives are members of the committee. In practice the deliberations in the committee provide the Commission with an impression of how its proposals will be received. After having sounded out the member states the Commission can choose to amend its definite initiative proposals in order to reach agreement. The attendance of Commission representatives at the meetings of the committee ensures that the Commission's standpoint and the considerations behind it can be well explained. The practical set-up of the Monetary Committee forms the expression of an intricate set of checks and balances in the interinstitutional relations between the Commission and the member states. There never has been any urge for a fundamental change in this set-up, and with good reason. The efficient proceedings of the committee have proved its worth over time. Outside the direct context of the Treaty the Monetary Committee has taken many initiatives and submitted proposals to the Ministers.[22] The committee then provides a platform for intergovernmental consultation and coordination. This is especially true for the operation of the EMS which is based not only on a Council Decision but also on an agreement among the national central banks.

The committee is assisted by a *Secretariat,* which is financed through the budget of the European Community. The secretary of the Monetary Committee, who also participates in the Bureau meetings, traditionally takes an independent position and is considered to be a servant of a committee of independent national experts. The secretary and his staff are responsible to the committee and, therefore, they work under the instructions of the committee and not the Commission. At times this has led to strained relations between the Secretariat and the Commission; the latter has been less than forthcoming at times in providing the necessary personal assistance for the secretary, even after an exhortation to this effect by the Council.

There have been repeated attempts on the part of the Commission to nibble away at the authority of the Monetary Committee. In its initial proposals on capital liberalization, presented in December 1985, the Commission had proposed that the Monetary Committee henceforth would only be involved in a discussion of those restrictions which did not yet fall under a liberalization obligation. This would give the Commission a free hand in applying and extending derogations for restrictions, falling under the liberalization regime. The committee protested, feeling that the Commission had been too lax in the application of the derogation clauses. The Commission quickly announced that it would withdraw this part of the proposal.

4.9 RELATIONSHIP WITH THE COMMITTEE OF GOVERNORS

The Monetary Committee provides a unique blend of central bankers and treasury officials. The Ministers of Finance meet in their regular EcoFin Council meetings. On the side of the *central banks,* however, it was only several years after the signing of the Treaty that the Committee of Governors of the Central Banks of the EEC was established in 1964.[23] As early as in January 1958 in the framework of their regular monthly meetings at the BIS in Basle the five governors of the EEC central banks had discussed the necessity of closer cooperation. They agreed to seize the opportunity of their monthly BIS meetings for this purpose. Dutch central bank governor and BIS president Holtrop advanced proposals to formally set up a committee,[24] but apparently there was a certain hesitancy among the Commission services to institutionalize the central bank cooperation. Had not the Monetary Committee just been set up '... in order to promote coordination of the policies of the Member States in the monetary field ...'?

The decision to establish the Committee of Governors was taken among a number of other institutional measures.[25] Some of these were designed to *circumscribe* the sphere of operation of the newly created committee. In particular it was provided that the Monetary Committee was to be the body which would deliberate on all important decisions and positions of member states in the realm of international monetary relations.[26] Accordingly the Committee of Governors started on a modest scale and its main purpose was to set in motion a process of mutual information.[27]

In the course of the years the role of the Committee of Governors was broadened. In 1971 a new Council decision mandated the committee to coordinate

TABLE 11

Tasks of the Committee of Governors and the EMI Council.

Committee of Governors[1]

- hold consultations concerning the general principles and the broad lines of monetary policy, in particular as regards credit, the money and foreign exchange markets as well as issues falling within the competence of the central banks and affecting the stability of financial institutions and markets;
- exchange information regularly about the most important measures that fall within the competence of the central banks, and to examine those measures;
- normally be consulted before the national authorities take decisions on the course of monetary policy, such as the setting of annual money supply and credit targets;
- to promote the coordination of the monetary policies of the Member States with the aim of achieving price stability as a necessary condition for the proper functioning of the European Monetary System and the realization of its objective of monetary stability;
- to formulate opinions on the overall orientation of monetary and exchange rate policy as well as on the respective measures introduced in individual Member States;
- to express opinions to individual governments and the Council of Ministers on policies which might affect the internal and external monetary situation in the Community and, in particular, the functioning of the European Monetary System.

EMI Council[2]

- strengthen cooperation between the national central banks;
- strengthen the coordination of the monetary policies of the Member States with the aim of ensuring price stability;
- monitor the functioning of the European Monetary System;
- hold consultations concerning issues falling within the competence of the national central banks and affecting the stability of financial institutions and markets;
- take over the tasks of the European Monetary Cooperation Fund;
- facilitate the use of the ecu and oversee its development, including the smooth functioning of the ecu clearing system;
- hold regular consultations concerning the course of monetary policies and the use of monetary policy instruments;
- normally be consulted by the national monetary authorities before they take decisions on the course of monetary policy in the context of the common framework for ex ante coordination;
- at the latest by 31 December 1996, specify the regulatory, organizational and logistical framework necessary for the ESCB to perform its tasks in the third stage.

[1] Based on Article 3 of the Council Decision of 12 March 1990 (90/142/EEC).
[2] Based on Article 4 of the Statutes of the European Monetary Institute.

monetary policies and to study the harmonization of monetary instruments. From this time both the Committee of Governors and the Monetary Committee had a *mandate* to coordinate monetary policies, a reflection of the different institutional arrangements concerning monetary policy in the member states.

In practice this shared responsibility did not give rise to frictions because the monetary coordination in practice retained a noncommittal character.

When in the run-up to the Treaty of Maastricht the coordination decisions of the Committee of Governors were rewritten, at the start of the first stage of EMU in 1990, a *division of tasks* between the two committees was realized.[28] The Committee of Governors was accorded prime responsibility with respect to the coordination of monetary policies. This gradual shift in the division of monetary responsibilities between the Monetary Committee and the Committee of Governors is illustrative of the change over time in the position of the national central banks. Increasingly their powers to define and execute monetary policy, independent of government instructions, have been expanded. The role of the Monetary Committee in the monetary area consequently diminished.

At the same time there have been suggestions to transfer certain responsibilities with respect to external monetary policies to the Committee of Governors as well. It was suggested in particular that so-called *technical realignments* of central rates within the EMS, meaning small adjustments which would not need to have an impact on market rates, could be dealt with in the Committee of Governors in the hope that thus the political suspense which normally surrounds them could be avoided. But even small realignments carried a political dimension, and therefore there was no follow-up to this suggestion.[29] Instead, in order to dedramatize exchange rate adjustments, the committee advised that the usual practice should be for the decision to be prepared by the Monetary Committee, and be given the approval of Ministers by telephone, whenever possible. Public statements should be avoided and a ministerial meeting should be called only if needed. For this procedure to be workable it would be necessary that negotiating mandates given to the committee members should not be too narrowly drawn.

In the *preparation of the Treaty of Maastricht* there has been a sensible division of tasks between the Monetary Committee and the Committee of Governors.[30] In the framework of the Delors Committee the governors under the chairmanship of the President of the Commission presented a blueprint for Economic and Monetary Union, which would form the basis for the intergovernmental negotiations. Whereas subsequently the governors prepared the Statutes of the future European Central Bank and its precursor the European Monetary Institute, the Monetary Committee concentrated on the economic part of the Union. In particular it was involved in the design of the convergence criteria and the excessive deficit procedure.

4.10 CONCLUSION

The unique *institutional set-up* of the Monetary Committee and its pragmatic proceedings have enabled the committee to live up to the high expectations the drafters of the Treaty had. The committee was left with much room for manoeuvre with respect to the choice of the policy issues it wished to address. It had the freedom to give advice or present proposals of its own accord. In practice this meant that it shifted the focus of its attention in line with the major economic and political developments of the day. In this respect its members were affected as much as anybody else by the fits and starts of European integration. Although its members could not overcome the major political obstacles which at times have hampered the European integration process, they have kept the spirit of cooperation alive and have greatly contributed to a better mutual understanding. What set the committee apart from anybody else was the institutional continuity, firmly embedded in the Treaty, and the direct contact which the members had with their political masters at home.

Its influence has increased in the course of the years as it was called upon to assume *other duties,* apart from genuine monetary matters, frequently with a political dimension. After a flying start in the beginning of the 1960s, when important measures with respect to capital liberalization could be taken, attention was diverted to the increasing cracks in the international monetary system. The committee did not have a comparative advantage over other international fora, such as Working Party 3 of the OECD and the Group of 10 where the major discussions were held, and its influence on the systemic debate was limited. In the beginning of the 1970s European countries drifted apart and the proceedings of the Monetary Committee had above all the character of crisis management.

The Monetary Committee assumed high responsibilities in the preparation of the *European Monetary System.* It became much more inward-looking and the attention given to international developments decreased. The composition of the committee was upgraded when the EMS started in 1979. The common procedures for realignment decisions assigned to the committee a central role in the operation of the system. The participation of central bank members in the committee assured that the day-to-day management of the system by the central banks was coordinated. At the same time the Committee of Governors and its subcommittees had an important role to play as well. After repeated attempts in the first years to strengthen the institutional structure of the EMS, which all failed, and to which the committee had a rather skeptical approach, it redirected its attention to the liberalization of capital movements. Here the Monetary Committee would play a stimulatory role, as will be extensively dealt with in the following chapters.

For the purpose of this study, the *liberalization of capital movements*, the role of the Monetary Committee has been a central one. It provided the forum where all interrelated policy areas were discussed as well. There were simultaneous discussions on capital liberalization in the Committee of Governors which proved to be a helpful input. The power of the Monetary Committee was based on the Treaty provisions and subsequent secondary legislation. Particularly important in this respect was that the committee needed to be consulted with respect to directives on capital liberalization and that it annually had to examine existing restrictions. In the next chapters we will examine how the committee performed this task.

It is deplorable that over the years the *accountability* of the committee has decreased. The listing of the membership of the committee was discontinued in 1986, whereas the last annual activity report was published in 1988. As a corollary, the valuable recommendations of the committee, which were frequently annexed to the annual reports, are no longer published and therefore are not easily available to the interested general public. At a time when it is generally felt that policy makers distance themselves too much from the general public, as demonstrated by the cool reception of the Treaty of Maastricht, it would be useful to resume publication of progress reports. Powers wielded without informing the outside world evoke counterforces.

With the coming into effect of the *Treaty on European Union* the coordination of monetary policy as well as its eventual unification has been enshrined into Treaty texts. Therewith, one of the raisons d'être of the committee – to fill the void in the monetary policy area in the Treaty of Rome – has disappeared. In the course of the years many related tasks have been taken up in the committee, to the effect that the present set-up of the committee will continue to be useful for the foreseeable future. However, when the final stage of EMU will materialize, there will be a need to overhaul the committee's role. The Treaty on European Union provides a framework for this new role which will be discussed in Chapter 9.

NOTES

1. The Treaty provides for the establishment of two other committees, the *Transport Committee* (Article 83) and the *Economic and Social Committee* (Article 193 et seq.). The latter committee differs in character from the Monetary Committee because of its divergent composition, comprising professionals from various categories of social and economic activities. The committee, which has an advisory capacity, was to act as a bridge between the Community and interest groups from trade and industry. Irreverently put, the committee was designed to be an institutionalized pressure group. However, in practice its opinions have not carried much weight.
2. The *Committee of Governors* of the Central Banks has been established pursuant to Article 105(1), which provides for the cooperation between the administrative departments and the central banks in order to attain the objectives of the Community. In the framework of the Single European Act the Committee of Governors explicitly was included in the new Article 102 A, where it is stipulated that both the Monetary Committee and the Committee of Governors shall be consulted regarding institutional changes in the monetary area. On 1 January 1994, at the start of the second stage of EMU, the committee was superseded by the European Monetary Institute, established pursuant to the Treaty on European Union. The *Economic Policy Committee* was established in 1974 (Council Decision of 18 February 1974), merging several committees on economic and fiscal policies.
3. The Bundesbank was established in 1957 as the successor to the Bank Deutscher Länder, which had been set up in 1948 by the Allied forces as an independent central bank system in West Germany.

4. The once-secretary of the Monetary Committee Kees (1984) describes this Treaty provision as the setting-up of a 'coordinating body which was expected to achieve future monetary cooperation. The Monetary Committee was left to develop its own momentum and was given responsibility for preparing the way for the different steps of monetary integration.'
5. Coreper is the customary French abbreviation of the Committee of the Permanent Representatives of the member states. The Coreper, assisted by the General Secretariat, prepares the meetings of the Council. The Permanent Representatives have the status of ambassador and report to and are recruited from the national Ministries of Foreign Affairs.
6. Meeting on 27 November 1956.
7. First Council Directive of 11 May 1960 for the implementation of Article 67 of the Treaty, Article 4.
8. The general obligation of Article 104 was complemented by the proviso that governments should at the same time take 'care to ensure a high level of employment and a stable level of prices'. Comparable goals with respect to general equilibrium are formulated in the statutes of the IMF and the OECD.
9. The Council Decision of 21 April 1980 provides that preparatory consultations regarding the adjustment percentages and the accompanying policy measures take place in the Monetary Committee, where its members do not act as independent experts, but as representatives of their country. The chairman advises the ministers and central bank governors (i.e. not the Council). If the committee does not reach agreement, the chairman formulates a compromise proposal.
10. There is a trade-off between on the one hand the danger of overexposure of the Monetary Committee, which should not take political decisions by proxy, and on the other hand the additional theatrical drama of a ministers' meeting on Sunday. When following the September 1992 devaluation of the Italian lira, which in a matter of days was followed by the withdrawal from the EMS of the pound sterling and the Italian lira, there was some criticism on the handling of the matter by the committee's chairman, ministers in unison declaring that next time they would have to convene and take the decisions. Of course, they would not have done any better. On the next occasion, the September 1992 devaluation of the Spanish peseta, they already had forgotten their intentions and left the matter to the committee.
11. The EcoFin Council in its meeting on 25 February 1958, in which it approved the committee's Statutes, added further items (see Annex 3).
12. The Council Decision of 8 May 1964 (64/301/EEC) provides that 'consultations shall take place within the Monetary Committee in respect of any important decision or position taken by Member States in the field of international monetary relations.'
13. In general high-ranking officials are nominated, although initially Germany and France nominated Treasury officials from the second echelon (director's level). After the establishment of the European Monetary System in 1979, in which the Monetary Committee had an important role to play, several countries, including Germany and France, upgraded their representative from the Ministry of Finance. Kees (1994) reports that this move met with resistance from the Commission services, since it would strengthen the position of the committee with respect to policy formulation.
14. In Annex 2 a list of the members of the Monetary Committee is reproduced. From this list it appears that generally central bank members stay longer on the committee than their counterparts from the Ministries of Finance who more frequently seem to change career. Among long-serving members are Otmar Emminger, who as vice-governor of the Bundesbank was a member of the committee from its start in 1958 up till his appointment as President of the Bundesbank in 1976, and André Szász of the Nederlandsche Bank who served a record 21-year span as a member of the committee (1973–94).
15. Since 1976 the Statutes were left unchanged, even when new countries joined the Community and some operating procedures of the committee were changed. In part this illustrates

the pragmatic manner in which the committee operates. But there was also a politically inspired preference for leaving things as they were, because amendment of the Statutes requires the heavy procedure of a decision of the Council.

16. The fact that Emile van Lennep was chosen chairman, apart from his personal qualities, may have been related to the fact that he was one of the highest-ranking Treasury officials in the committee (see Note 13). The level of representation had been intensively discussed in the Netherlands. The Nederlandsche Bank already at an early stage (May 1957) had decided that it would nominate an Executive Director, prof Posthuma, in view of the hierarchical level of the central bank nominees of other countries. Governor Holtrop let it be known to the Minister that the Bank would prefer the Finance representative to be of equal level so that they could freely confer and take decisions. If the Finance representative were to be chosen from a lower hierarchical level, this would imply that he automatically would carry less weight and influence. Then the Bank representative would have a certain preponderance and would need to have direct access to the Minister. This argument of Holtrop apparently carried the day. Eventually the Ministry would nominate Treasurer-General Emile van Lennep.
17. In 1983 it was decided to add a vice-chairman, but there was no formal Council decision. In later years, the position of vice-chairman has been tacitly dropped; what mattered more was attendance at the Bureau meetings.
18. Sometimes the agendas of the experts are filled so much that a meeting on Friday has to be accepted. This was the case when a meeting was planned for Friday, 11 September, 1992. In that week the traditional Basle weekend meetings were followed by meetings of Working Group 3 of the OECD and the Deputies of the G10, to the effect that only Friday was left for a Monetary Committee meeting. This was only one week before the French referendum on the Treaty on European Union was to be held and the exchange markets had become more and more nervous about the outcome and the possible implications of a negative vote. A Friday meeting of the Monetary Committee might get on the nerves of the markets and fuel speculation. Eventually the meeting was called off. In the end it proved to be of no avail. The markets had smelt blood and on Friday evening the German members of the committee took the initiative to call for a realignment in the ERM.
19. Annual Report of the Monetary Committee, 1961.
20. 'At EC, gnomes in shadows; who sets monetary policy? Try to find out', International Herald Tribune, 24 October 1992.
21. Oort in Twenty years of the Monetary Committee (1978), p. 11.
22. Kees (1994) enumerates a number of proposals presented by the Monetary Committee to the Ministers and the Council.
23. Council Decision of 8 May 1964 (64/300/EEC).
24. Letter from Holtrop of 25 January 1958 to the Dutch Minister of Finance. In his letter Holtrop suggests to bring about, possibly through the good services of Sicco Mansholt, the Dutch Commissioner, that the European Commission would make a proposal to set up a committee of governors of the EEC central banks.
25. At the same date the Committee for Fiscal Policy was established, one of the predecessors of the Economic Policy Committee (see Note 2).
26. This decision (see also Note 12) confirmed that external monetary policies, in particular exchange rates, remained in the realm of governments. Through the involvement of the Monetary Committee a linkage was created with Working Party 3 of the OECD, which was likewise chaired by Emile van Lennep.
27. Baer (1994) provides a detailed description of the functioning of the Committee of Governors till its merger into the European Monetary Institute.
28. Council Decision of 12 March 1990 (90/142/EEC).
29. In its 29th Activity Report (1988, p.19) it was concluded: 'The Monetary Committee is of the view that there is no such thing as a technical realignment'.

30. Less wise decisions were also taken. In 1990 in an attempt to assert the independent position of the Committee of Governors, its chairman Karl-Otto Pöhl kicked out the secretary of the Monetary Committee who up till then had been allowed to attend the meetings. In retaliation the secretary of the Committee of Governors no longer was allowed to attend the meetings of the Monetary Committee. A pacification took place in 1994 when the Director-General of the newly-founded European Monetary Institute was invited to participate in the meetings of the Monetary Committee.

CHAPTER 5

The 1960s: Lost Momentum

Large movements of money have been induced by exchange rate uncertainties because of the need of private business and financial institutions to protect themselves and even because of pure speculation. We must face the fact that more often than not the judgement of the market has correctly evaluated the underlying situation and that the fault lay with official indecision with respect to the adjustment process. Direct controls are less effective in these cases because of the huge shifts of funds that can come about by changes in leads and lags under present-day business conditions.

Jelle Zijlstra, 1972

5.1 INTRODUCTION

After the Monetary Committee had started its work it was some time before the issue of capital liberalization was taken up. This was largely due to two factors, a practical one and a political one. The *practical* factor was that both the Commission and the committee had to get organized. Priorities had to be set. They had to take stock of the prevailing situation, make an inventory of existing restrictions and design a framework for giving content to the Treaty obligations.

But there was also an important *political* factor: the *change of government in France*. The Algerian question had caused the socialist government under the IVth Republic to collapse and had cleared the way for a re-entry of General de Gaulle in government. A new constitution, giving greater powers to the president, was adopted and in December 1958 de Gaulle was elected as the first president of the Vth Republic. His attitude vis-à-vis European integration remained unknown for some time, until in an accord with the German Chancellor Konrad Adenauer a definitive choice was made for the EEC.

Thus the first year of the EEC was marked by a certain wait-and-see attitude. The *economic and financial situation in France* gave cause for concern and figured prominently on the agenda of the six meetings held by the committee in 1958. France had been forced to suspend trade liberalization for some time. There were fiscal and monetary imbalances; inflationary pressures ran high. In the course of 1958 stabilizing measures were taken, the exchange rate was devalued and a *New Franc* was introduced at the end of 1959 (equal to 100 'old' francs). In its last meeting in December 1958 the committee for the first time discussed the issue of capital liberalization in the context of a secretariat's paper on the competences and working methods of the committee. It was agreed that the committee's role should be interpreted widely. In particular it was the Commission's intention to involve the committee continuously in the formulation of proposals to liberalize capital movements. The Commission thus renounced its right to ask the committee's advice only when it had drawn up a concrete proposal. As a first step the Commission would prepare an inventory of the existing regulations in domestic capital markets and the restrictions to cross-border capital flows in the member states for discussion in the Monetary Committee.

In the course of 1959 the deliberations on the liberalization of capital movements gained considerable momentum. The *economic climate* was propitious for liberalizing initiatives: the EEC economies enjoyed a cyclical upswing unhampered, thanks to improved productivity and competitiveness, by external constraints. All EEC countries registered surpluses on the current account of their balances of payments. The two least liberal countries, France and Italy, recorded sizeable capital inflows which swelled their official exchange reserves. These favourable developments made it easier to restore external convertibility for current account transactions and to undertake gradual liberalization of capital movements. In 1960 and 1962 two directives were to be adopted which gave practical content to the provisions of the relevant Article 67 of the Treaty by imposing binding obligations on member states.

5.2 THE INITIAL ATTITUDE OF MEMBER STATES

The preparation of the first directive was preceded by a fundamental debate in a string of meetings of the Monetary Committee on the merits of the liberalization of capital movements. This discussion was provoked by a voluminous document of the EEC Directorate General for Economic and Financial Affairs, which came under Robert Marjolin. The report advocated the greatest possible liberalization, and considered this to be as urgent as the free movement of goods, services and persons in the Community.[1]

Full liberalization should be the *ultimate objective*, notwithstanding the escape clause – 'to the extent necessary to ensure the proper functioning of the Common Market' – in the Treaty. The crux of the argument of the Commission was that the eventual freedom of goods, services and persons provided for in the Treaty would prove to be a dead letter if free capital movements would continue to be curtailed by stringent restrictions. At the same time it was acknowledged that full liberalization could not be carried through at one stroke and therefore an order of *priorities* was set. The Commission proposed to confine liberalization in a first round to (1) direct investment, (2) issues of securities and (3) certain capital flows in the personal sphere. These types of transactions roughly corresponded to the capital movements marked out earlier as priorities in the Spaak report. This would have practical consequences only for France, Italy and the Netherlands. Germany had already liberalized these capital transactions, whereas under the dual exchange rate system of the Belgium-Luxembourg Economic Union all capital transactions could be freely settled in the financial market.

5.2.1. Germany in Favour of Full Liberalization

The Commission received unequivocal support from the German members of the committee in its advocacy of full liberalization of capital movements as the ultimate goal. The representative from the Ministry of Economic Affairs took an orthodox position in the discussions, arguing that there was no reason to treat capital flows in a different manner than movements of goods and services. In line with Erhard's laissez-faire thinking, capital restrictions were considered as an *anomaly* in the context of the increasing freedom of international trade. Although the Bundesbank representatives usually took a more thoughtful approach to the issues, they too were a firm supporter of free capital flows. Such freedom should also extend to informal exchange restrictions such as discriminatory fiscal provisions and regulations concerning foreign ownership. These should be harmonized and, if possible, eliminated.

Right from the start Germany insisted that liberalization of capital movements within the Community should not discriminate vis-à-vis *third countries*. The Alternates of the Monetary Committee, who had been asked to study this matter further, indeed came out strongly against discriminatory treatment. They concluded that a European discriminatory exchange regime would impair the pull of the Common Market in attracting foreign capital. Actual investments in the EEC from third countries (especially those from the United States, the United Kingdom, Canada and Switzerland) at the time far outweighed those originating from within the EEC. Furthermore, it was considered that, technically, effective control of a discriminatory regime was simply not feasible. Germany throughout the years would remain a staunch supporter of what later came to be known as the 'erga omnes principle', i.e. capital liberalization agreed within the European Community should extend to all countries.

5.2.2 France in Favour of Monetary Policy Coordination

The starting point of the Commission that the EEC territory eventually would form a unified economic area ('espace économique unifiée') in which all factors of production, including capital, would flow freely, was instantly contested by the French members of the committee, supported to a certain point by the Dutch and Italians. It could not be helped, the French argued, that the Treaty had a dualistic character, blending binding obligations on member states in some policy areas with national autonomy as regards economic and monetary policies. But such was reality. Capital liberalization would have to be dependent on and should go hand in hand with improved *coordination of monetary policies*. Such coordination should primarily aim at preventing speculative capital flows. Despite its tight exchange regime France had been plagued by speculative outflows, which in 1958 had twice forced large devaluations. After the monetary reform, culminating in the introduction of the new franc, the authorities wished to restore confidence and err on the safe side. Therefore, the strength of the balance of payments would be the decisive factor in the relative tightness of the exchange control system. Moreover, France was concerned about capital outflows inspired by tax evasion.

Although France acknowledged that liberalization should be of a non-discriminatory nature, it preferred to leave the door open to *'differentiation'*. This was a subtle distinction: the legal exchange regime should be based on the principle of non-discrimination, but a certain favouritism through administrative and other domestic regulations was considered acceptable to create a 'zone de préférence' for the circulation of capital for investment purposes within the Common Market.

5.2.3 Italy Fears Speculation

The Italian position was close to the French one. Traditionally Italy was fearful of speculative capital movements, which it felt did not exert an equilibrating influence. The banking system had been prevented from becoming a channel through which hot money could easily flow into or out of the country, because of its disturbing effects on the official foreign exchange reserves or on domestic monetary conditions.[2] The Italians thus were doubtful whether the complete liberalization of capital movements was advisable. In any case it was felt that this could not be achieved without prior cooperative arrangements among the monetary authorities. Among such desired arrangements *cross-holdings* of each other's currencies in the official reserves figured prominently. This would enable the national central banks to undertake timely interventions which might counteract undesired capital movements before they assumed unduly large proportions.[3]

As shown in Figure 8, Italy in the first years of the EEC was confronted with a much higher expansion of economic activity than expected. At the same time, its current account position was satisfactory. But Italy did not contemplate becoming a structural capital exporter. It maintained a restrictive and complicated exchange control system, which, however, was notorious for its many loopholes. Nevertheless, liberalization of capital movements did not carry much political priority. It was feared that the public at large, which did not hold shares, would not comprehend liberalization measures. They would simply be conceived as favouring the interests of the rich and as a vehicle for tax evasion. For Italy liberalization of capital movements already had progressed far beyond anything envisaged in the early post-war years.

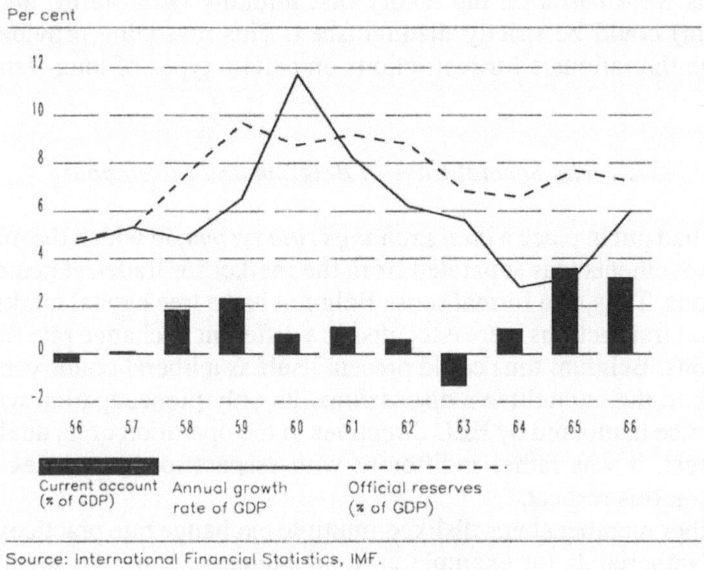

Fig. 8. Italy's economic miracle.

5.2.4 Dutch Misgivings

Although the Dutch authorities were not unfavourably disposed towards further liberalization, they maintained the misgivings with respect to the *final objective* of full liberalization which had been manifest during the negotiations on the Treaty. In their view the Common Market would not become equivalent to the 'ideal' type of a freely functioning domestic market within a country. The main difference was that the Community lacked a coordinated economic and monetary policy. Therefore, interest rates would differ between countries, but these differentials need not reflect differences in the productivity of capital. It could not yet be taken for granted that capital utilized in countries with higher interest rates would bear more fruit than in countries with lower rates as long as there were differences in policy priorities. Of course, a less ambitious concept of a Common Market would make a lesser contribution to the optimal allocation of resources. But such was reality: 'an evolution of centuries which had made Europe a split continent could not be undone within a few decades'.[4]

Like France and Italy, the Netherlands was opposed to the liberalization of *short-term capital movements*. But there was a fine distinction in motivation: the Netherlands argued on principle that short-term flows did not fall under the obligations of Article 67. As discussed in Chapter 3, its main objection concerned short-term *inflows* which were considered as unwelcome sources of liquidity creation and thus could obstruct domestic monetary policy. These objections were based on the theory that liquidity (short-term) and capital (long-term) could be strictly distinguished. This reasoning provided at the same time the rationale for restrictions on certain types of long-term capital outflows.

5.2.5 The Special Case of Belgium and Luxembourg

Belgium had put in place a *dual exchange rate system,* in which the market for capital movements was separated from the market for trade-related currency transactions. Thus, in a formal sense Belgium had a free capital market, albeit that capital transactions were executed at a different exchange rate than other transactions. Belgium thus could present itself as a liberal country and could lean back in the committee's discussions. Its only preoccupation was that it would not be hampered by EEC directives in the operation of its dual market. For the rest, it was rather indifferent with respect to the policies in other countries in this respect.

The other member states disliked multiple exchange rate practices. France and the Netherlands for example used an exchange control system of individual permits, with foreign currency available at the fixed exchange rate. They felt that the degree of liberalization depended not only on the *formal* exchange control system utilized, but also on the *material* content of the system. If the actual free market under a dual market system was not very deep, the execution of capital transactions might be hindered even more than under an exchange control regime of permits, so it was argued. For them further capital liberalization was regarded as a sacrifice because it could complicate the pursuit of domestic monetary or economic objectives. Such sacrifices would be only acceptable if other countries would take steps as well and would not hide behind techniques which had the same economic effect,[5] but could be presented to the outside world as liberal because of their form. This explains the irritation which other member states felt with respect to the Belgian position that its dual market should be kept outside the liberalization obligations pursuant to the Treaty.

5.2.6 Assessment

The positions taken in these first discussions by the six founding members of the EEC with regard to the full liberalization of capital movements were to be constant themes, albeit in varying shades, in the discussion in the coming years. *Germany* stood alone in advocating full liberalization. As a structural capital exporter it did not fear speculative movements as much as the other countries. Instead it concentrated on pursuing stability-oriented policies at home which would gain the confidence of the international financial markets. Such self-confidence was lacking in *France* and *Italy.* Although their economies and external positions were developing much better than expected, they were fearful of sudden speculative capital outflows. In their view monetary cooperation should be strengthened in order to prevent such speculation. Italy went as far as proclaiming that as long as institutional arrangements between the central banks were lacking which could provide ammunition to frighten off speculators, it was not willing to contemplate the full liberalization of capital flows. The *Dutch,* in a balancing act between their traditional liberally-oriented policies as a major trading country and their reluctance in principle to ease the channels for undesirable capital flows, were inclined to adopt a rather restrictive attitude as well. In the course of the years the balance between pros and cons in the positions of individual member states would change. But at the time, it was clear that a large majority of the member states was not willing to consider the unconditional freeing of all capital flows.

A number of other themes came up as well which would surface more prominently in later years. Germany made it clear that liberalization obligations agreed upon in the framework of the EEC should be applied to third countries as well: the so-called *erga omnes principle*. Although this formally was not contested, France and the Commission were instinctively inclined to allow a certain favouritism towards member states, possibly in the form of *indirect regulations*. These positions betrayed the more outward-looking attitude of Germany versus the increasingly European-oriented attitude of France. Other themes concerned the link to related policy areas, above all that of *monetary policy*, but *tax considerations* also played a role. This linkage to other areas would later contribute to the emergence of an attitude that countries which would liberalize would expect a quid pro quo from other member states.

5.3 PREPARATION OF THE FIRST DIRECTIVE

In July 1959 the *Dutch* members presented a *memorandum* to the Monetary Committee, in which they elaborated on their hesitations with respect to the full liberalization of capital movements. Countries should have the possibility to impose restrictions in good time, before balance-of-payments difficulties would emerge. Unconditional liberalization in their view should only apply to direct investment. Private issues and loans, as well as trade in securities could only be conditionally liberalized.[6] More fundamentally, the Dutch once again tried to substantiate their claim that short-term 'money' movements did not fall under the provisions of Article 67, which only dealt with 'capital' movements. Moreover, in their view countries should retain the possibility, over and above the safeguard clauses of the Treaty, to deliberalize certain categories of capital transactions if economic and monetary policy goals were endangered. This was an outright departure from the principle of irreversibility contained in Article 71. All in all it was a rather ponderous document which dampened the high hopes of Marjolin's paper.

Although the committee shared the Dutch interpretation that Article 67 did not require full liberalization of capital movements, the majority rejected the view that *short-term money movements* were not part and parcel of capital movements. Although the Dutch members thus did not win their case on principle, from a practical standpoint this did not matter very much. Other countries, like France and Italy, were likewise not favourably disposed to the freeing of short-term flows. Their fear mainly concerned the effects of speculative outflows on exchange rates, whereas the Dutch feared the inflationary effects of inflows on domestic monetary policy. So much for the ideological debate. But as far as the acceptance of concrete liberalization obligations of other capital transactions was concerned, only Germany and the Netherlands were prepared to go rather far. The French and Italians hesitated to liberalize direct investment unconditionally and the Belgians would channel such flows only through the free exchange market. Others did not consider the latter to constitute real liberalization because exchange rate fluctuations on this market might prove to be a hindrance.

In its meeting in September 1959 the committee finalized its report to the ministers, prepared by the Alternates, on the liberalization of capital movements. In this report a distinction was made between three categories of capital movements: (1) transactions which were to be liberalized *immediately* and *unconditionally,* (2) transactions which also were to be liberalized *immediately* but *under certain conditions,* and (3) transactions for which there was *no obligation* to liberalize. Category (1) comprised short and medium-term trade-related credits and direct investment, category (2) comprised public issues, long-term trade-related credits, long and medium-term non-trade related credits and transactions in securities, and category (3) comprised short-term capital movements. Liberalized capital transactions in the first category could only be deliberalized by having resort to the safeguard clauses, the so-called *'régime sévère'*. The transactions of the second category fell under the *'régime conditionnel'*, and were not deemed to be indispensable for the functioning of the Common Market. This regime implied that countries which did not liberalize these transactions or wished to deliberalize them had to provide an explanation to the Commission. The Commission, after having consulted the Monetary Committee, then could give recommendations to abolish or relax these restrictions, but these were non-binding. For transactions in the third category countries were completely autonomous, but there would be a regular monitoring in the Monetary Committee. The system opened up the possibility that certain categories of capital movements could move up the list to the unconditional liberalization obligation. In a meeting in January 1960 the Monetary Committee was formally asked for advice on the *proposal for a directive* which the Commission had formulated on the basis of the previous discussions.[7] In broad outline the Commission had followed the position taken by the committee. On some points the Commission tried to go a little further, notably with respect to transactions in listed shares which the Commission wanted to place under the unconditional liberalization regime.[8] The committee agreed to this, but there were two reservations. Italy was opposed to the unconditional liberalization of medium-term trade-related credits, fearing a loophole. And France was opposed to the unconditional liberalization of transactions in shares of undertakings for collective investment in securities. These investment trusts had nothing to do with the proper functioning of the Common Market because they mainly invested in blue chip funds, preponderantly of US companies, so it was argued. The real reason could be found closer to home. As part of the French dirigistic financial system the Trésor actively attracted funds from small investors in order to finance the public sector deficit. It did not wish to encourage competitors to fish in the same waters.

The final proposal for a directive was introduced in the EcoFin Council meeting on 10 March 1960 by Robert Marjolin, vice-chairman of the Commission. It was finalized in the May meeting of the Council after Italy had dropped its reservation against the unconditional liberalization of medium-term trade credits. France, however, held on to its opposition to the unconditional liberalization of transactions in shares of undertakings for collective investment in securities. At the time it could not be foreseen that it would last more than two decades before these transactions finally were liberalized in 1985.[9] France got its way and the Commission moved this category to the *régime conditionnel.*

5.4 THE FIRST DIRECTIVE OF 1960

This first directive, adopted by the Council in May 1960, could be seen as giving body to the Treaty obligations, although it fell far short of any call for full liberalization. Member countries were obliged to liberalize unconditionally short and medium-term trade-related credits, direct investment flows and transactions in listed shares. These were the financial transactions which could be considered as having the most direct influence on the *physical* creation of the Common Market and thus were most directly linked to the clause of Article 67, ‘to ensure the proper functioning of the Common Market’. Trade in goods and services had to move unhampered by restrictions concerning trade credit. And the freeing of direct investment would enable companies to gain a foothold in other EEC markets through the operation of subsidiaries and thus stimulate competition, both through cross-border trade and through intra-EEC production. Finally, cross-border transactions in listed shares, i.e. securities quoted on official stock exchanges, would enable investors to acquire an interest in other European companies.

Short-term financial transactions, however, did not fall under any obligation to liberalize. The preparedness of member states to abolish capital restrictions had generally decreased as the categories had a more short-term character.[10] The discussions held in the Monetary Committee brought out clearly that a major reason was the wish to retain control over domestic monetary policies, and especially for France and Italy, the fear of capital flight.

The provisions of the First Directive only applied to *intra-Community* flows. There was no attempt to coordinate policies in respect of capital movements between member states and third countries, as provided for in Article 70. However, the wish was expressed that liberalized categories would apply to third countries as well. In practice this erga omnes principle generally was adhered to.[11] The directive *consolidated* to a large extent liberalizations which had already been undertaken or were in the process of being undertaken in some countries. Now it would become more difficult to go back on these liberalization measures. In the course of 1960 all member states had adjusted their exchange regime in order to be in compliance with the new directive.[12]

As regards the *dual exchange market* of Belgium, the directive allowed transactions which had to be unconditionally liberalized to be channelled through the free financial market, as long as the exchange rates did not appreciably and lastingly diverge from the rates on the official market.[13] The Monetary Committee would monitor this and report to the Commission. There were further tasks for the committee. The Commission would consult the Monetary Committee when making recommendations to member countries with respect to their exchange regime. More importantly, the committee was required to hold *annual examinations* with a view to exploring whether further progress could be made in abolishing capital restrictions, in line with the preamble of the directive which stated that the attainment of the Treaty objectives required '... the greatest possible freedom of capital ... and therefore the widest and most speedy liberalization of capital movements.' Whether this was only a matter of harmonious presentation or of hard commitments of the member states would become clear in the coming years.

The adoption of the directive showed that good results could be reached through *cooperation* between the Monetary Committee and the Commission. Although the Commission had wished to go further with respect to capital liberalization, it was slowed down in its drive for action by the committee members who took the interests of their country into account as well. The supranational interest of full capital liberalization, defended by the Commission, had not yet found sympathy in the intergovernmental forum of the Monetary Committee. The committee members rather tended to espouse the views of their political masters at home. In general the opinion of the committee members was the decisive factor, but there was a certain give and take. In this way the Commission got a good impression of what was politically and economically feasible. Subsequently, in its final proposal it pushed a little harder on specific components, and all in all was not dissatisfied with the end-result. So, a common understanding and sense of direction had grown. In a note to the Council on its consultation of the Monetary Committee, the

TABLE 12

Official reserves of EEC member states 1956–1965 in billions of US dollars.

	1956	1957	1958	1959	1960	1961	1962	1963	1964	1965
Belgium	1.2	1.2	1.6	1.3	1.5	1.8	1.8	2.0	2.2	2.3
France	1.3	0.6	1.1	1.7	2.3	3.4	4.0	4.9	5.7	6.3
Germany	4.2	5.2	5.9	4.8	7.0	7.2	7.0	7.7	7.9	7.4
Italy	1.3	1.5	2.3	3.1	3.3	3.8	4.1	3.6	3.8	4.8
The Netherlands	1.1	1.1	1.6	1.4	1.9	2.0	1.9	2.1	2.3	2.4

Note: Gold valued at US dollar 35 per ounce, end of period figures.
Source: International Financial Statistics, IMF.

Commission wrote: 'Now that the proceedings with respect to the first directive concerning capital movements have been concluded, the Commission considers itself fortunate to have involved the Monetary Committee already at an early stage in the proceedings without having waited until the formal consultation. The Commission is convinced that this cooperation has led to a good result.'[14] A good result it was and some member states might have wished to stop there. The directive provided a good basis for ensuring the proper functioning of the Common Market. But the Commission wanted more. It wished to maintain the momentum. Soon the Commission would come forward with new proposals.

5.5 MAINTAINING THE MOMENTUM

In 1960 the economies of the EEC prospered: there was a strong economic expansion, prices remained stable and there were no balance-of-payments problems. The Common Market was off to a good start and had fostered an accelerated pace of expansion of intra-EEC trade. France had experienced a favourable evolution of the balance of payments and a large rise in its official reserves (see Table 12). This provided room to slowly, but with determination, relax its remaining exchange controls.[15] Italy, which was lagging behind as far as its exchange regime was concerned, had succeeded in combining strong economic growth with monetary stability and liberal external relations. Thus it was well-placed to take further capital liberalization measures as well.

Yet, there were some *warning signals*. The relaxation of exchange controls, even though mainly limited to long-term capital flows, had facilitated speculation, which was directed at the strong economies of Germany and the Netherlands. Monetary tightening by the Bundesbank, matched in a 'tragic coincidence' by an easing of American monetary policy, led to sharply increased interest rate differentials, which fueled 'hot money' flows. In March

1961 the Deutsche mark and the Dutch guilder were revalued. This development was viewed with concern. The Banca d'Italia, noting the enormous transfers of funds, commented: "These displacements put the spotlight on the perils to which all currencies are exposed in a world from which administrative controls have gone, one after another. This situation is full of dangers for the orderly functioning of international payments.'[16] They had led Germany, whose members of the Monetary Committee had advocated the merits of full capital liberalization, to reimpose in June 1960 restrictions on the purchase by non-residents of money market paper and to prohibit the payment of interest on Deutsche mark deposits held by non-residents. Both measures would remain in place until 1969 when the Deutsche mark again was revalued. The near-complete freedom of capital flows in Germany, established in 1959, had lasted only one year! Emminger in his memoirs vividly describes this dramatic episode: 'the spell was broken.'[17] The German economy had soon left the 'magic triangle."

In May 1961 the Monetary Committee held its *first annual examination* of the state of affairs concerning capital liberalization, as provided for in the 1960 Directive. The Commission had prepared a memorandum for this meeting in which it advanced suggestions for further liberalization beyond the 1960 Directive in three areas: direct investment flows should be excluded from the free financial market (in practice only existent in Belgium) and transferred to the official exchange market for current payments; individual permits for capital transactions under the unconditional regime should be replaced by general permits; and transactions in shares of undertakings for collective investment in securities (unit trusts) should be placed under the unconditional regime. Furthermore, it advocated that further progress should be made towards the admission of foreign issuers of shares and bonds on domestic capital markets. Mindful of the exchange rate tensions earlier in the year the Commission refrained from advocating the liberalization of those (short-term) channels which were preferably used for speculation.

The Commission's suggestion to transfer direct investment flows to the official market in *Belgium* led to heated discussions in the committee. The Belgian members did not wish to give in, because they felt that making a hierarchical order in capital movements would undermine the fundamental concept underlying the dual market. The Commission was supported by chairman van Lennep who pointed to the fact that exchange rate differentials had been of such a size (between 2.2 and 3.6%) and so sticky that one could not escape the conclusion that they were both 'appreciable and lasting'. Against this the Belgian members argued that the exchange rate differential was due to the political upheavals in Belgian Congo (later Zaire) and that actual direct investment flows did not seem to be much affected by the differential. The French and Italian members of the committee, apparently fearing that they would also be put under pressure to liberalize, came to the support of the Belgians. Later in the year, they were saved by the bell, when the tensions in Belgian Congo subsided and the differential quickly diminished to less than 1%. The Belgian delegation promised to examine the possibility of transferring certain categories of capital movements to the current exchange market, without committing themselves to any fixed time schedule. In its report to the Council the Monetary Committee left the issue open.[18]

As to the suggestion of the Commission to bring all unconditionally liberalized transactions under a *system of general permits,* there was opposition from France and the Netherlands which still practised a system of individual permits. The Dutch system, so it was argued, was only meant to permit a check whether the transaction in fact was a liberalized one. In practice authorizations were granted generously. The French used the system for preliminary control reasons as well as for statistical purposes in order to ascertain the origin or destination of capital flows. Both countries would go no further than examining whether authorization could be facilitated by simplifying and shortening procedures.

The French continued to oppose the liberalization of transactions in *shares of undertakings for collective investment in securities.* They had not allowed such institutions in France because the Treasury, which drew heavily on the savings of small investors, feared the competition for funds. France was equally reluctant to allow the issuance of shares by third countries on its domestic capital market. In this respect it was lagging considerably behind other countries. Germany had already completely opened its market for issues by non-resident companies. But even Italy, which operated the tightest exchange regime within the Community, had allowed issues of international institutions. Also the Netherlands, which had voiced such misgivings about seeing its hard earned savings withering away to less frugal countries, in practice took a pragmatic viewpoint and had allowed foreign issues on its capital market.[19] An important consideration was that, like Germany, the Netherlands was confronted with speculative inflows. It slowly began to realize that the difficult post-war years of reconstruction had ended and that it was necessary to change gear and retake its prewar position of a structural capital exporter.

The committee also briefly discussed a Commission paper on *taxation* of capital transactions, which showed that the absolute level of taxation in some countries was a hindrance to truly free capital flows. The committee generally favoured the harmonization and possibly the abolition of such taxes, but acknowledged that this was within the competence of other bodies (a special working party of taxation experts having been established).

All in all, the Commission proposals received a *cool reception* in the committee. The cooperative spirit which had prevailed during the negotiations on the 1960 Directive seemed to have evaporated and the committee members entrenched themselves in their national positions, apparently each waiting for the other to move. Although all countries adhered to the liberalization obligations under the 1960 Directive, apart from a minor deviation in Italy, they apparently did not wish to accept further common obligations, but wished to retain the right to set their own pace. The committee's report to the Commission thus did not contain any proposal for concrete steps forward, but confined itself to good intentions and further examinations. In its annual report on 1961 the committee would repeat that further coordination of policies would be needed in order to make progress. The time elapsed since the 1960 Directive had been too short to initiate further measures.

5.6 THE SECOND DIRECTIVE OF 1962

Late 1962 the Monetary Committee resumed its discussion of capital liberalization on the basis of a new Commission paper which dealt with the unresolved issues of the discussion of the previous year. Yet, again not much progress was made. Considerable pressure was brought to bear on ***Belgium*** to merge its two exchange markets, or at least to transfer direct investment flows to the regulated market, but to no avail. The Belgians pointed out that the exchange rate differential since the settlement of the Belgian Congo affair had been very small and that therefore no action was needed. Belgium was willing to reconsider the matter if a large differential were to re-appear. The argument exasperated chairman van Lennep: when the differential had been large the Belgian members had advocated that the discussion be resumed in more quiet times. Now that the situation had been normalized it was asked to postpone the discussion until problems would re-emerge. In this way the matter would never be thoroughly discussed. But it did not help. The Belgians would not budge.[20]

As to foreign *issues* on domestic capital markets there were some concessions: France and Italy would allow issues on a limited scale by international organizations (such as the European Investment Bank) and thus followed the example set by the Netherlands. However, the French stuck to their opposition to liberalization of transactions in shares of undertakings for collective investment in securities (unit trusts).

There was a new proposal of the Commission to liberalize non-trade related *medium-term and long-term credit by banks.* The Netherlands, France and Italy, however, did not move, although their considerations differed. The Dutch authorities continued to be fearful of large-scale demand for capital on their domestic market because of the relatively low Dutch interest level. As long as guilder issues of non-residents were authorized only in individual cases, they considered it undesirable that this regime could be circumvented by the taking up of bank credit by non-residents. In the French case the argument was phrased differently: France wished to shield its domestic capital market and be able to follow its own interest and credit policy, as long as there was no monetary unification in Europe. For Italy similar considerations prevailed.

There was not much of substance left to be included in a new directive. Yet, the Commission wished to maintain the momentum. In its final proposal for a new directive all small steps to which countries had agreed were inserted. These included some new relatively unimportant categories of capital transactions which more or less had been forgotten in the 1960 Directive and now were placed in the nomenclature attached to the directive. Thus the Second Directive, adopted by the Council on 18 December 1962, merely served as a *supplement* to the 1960 Directive. Short-term and medium-term credits, which had been liberalized only for trade-related transactions, now were unconditionally liberalized for services as well. This curious inclusion was an answer to the specific problems posed by the Belgian dual market. Various cross-border payments for services had to be executed in the free financial market, because Belgium considered them to be of a capital character. In discussions on a directive on trade in services other member states did not want to accept this and thus implicitly sanction Belgium's dual market. As a pragmatic solution it was decided to include these payments for services in the capital directive.[21]

All in all, these changes were not impressive and they did not fundamentally change the state of liberalization obligations achieved in the 1960 Directive. Apparently the political and economic limits to unconditional liberalization had been reached. Whereas the 1960 Directive to a great extent had consolidated liberalization measures which the authorities had already autonomously decided to effect, the pain threshold had now been reached for further steps which would impose obligations on member states. The level of economic integration still was relatively low, as was the degree of policy coordination. Despite their favourable balance-of-payments situation, France and Italy did not wish to take further common steps as long as monetary policy coordination was not strengthened. At the same time they were gradually dismantling their controls on an individual basis. France had abolished its devises-titres market in April 1962 and thus had considerably eased transactions in shares.[22] The Netherlands had progressively opened up its well-organized capital market by allowing issues of non-residents. But it wished to keep its authorization procedures in place. The Belgian-Luxembourg dual market formed the rallying point where all other member states could unite in their objections. Indeed, in the discussions in the Monetary Committee a disproportionate amount of time was devoted to the dual market system.

The focus on the *dual market* was not so much inspired by economic as by political motives. The Belgians combined a de facto restrictive system with the claim to be liberal. Because of this position they did not support the restrictive member states in their opposition to certain liberalization proposals of the Commission. This provoked the latter to denounce the restrictive character of the dual market, just as the truly liberal countries would do. In an atmosphere where the original cooperative spirit had been lost and quid pro quos were asked in exchange for liberalization, for them it was not acceptable to undertake further obligations if the Belgian-Luxembourg Economic Union (BLEU) could back out because of its supposed liberal system. Quid pro quos implied equal pain for everybody. Under this pressure the Belgians nevertheless held on to their position.[23] The underlying cause must be found in the demands of the BLEU. The position of the Belgian franc could just as much fall victim to speculative pressures as other potentially weak currencies, particularly because of the unbalanced fiscal position in Belgium. However, for Luxembourg direct capital restrictions were not acceptable because this would frustrate the development of a specialized financial centre. As the system implied the segregation of stocks (foreign currencies held by residents and Belgian francs held by non-residents) and not only flows, the dual market could not possibly be reinstated under a safeguard clause once it was dismantled. The maintenance of the dual market therefore must be regarded as a compromise between the two BLEU partners for which there was no viable alternative.

The drive towards common liberalization ground to a halt. Political considerations, such as in the case of Belgium, domestic regulations, for France and the Netherlands, and tax considerations, particularly for Italy which suffered from lax fiscal ethics, all were put forward as obstacles to further liberalization. Member states more and more were inclined to demand *quid pro quos* from others. In short, the political will to arrive to a common accord dissipated. All in all countries wished to determine the pace of liberalization of their own accord and were not willing to be forced by further common obligations. The members of the Monetary Committee, who had so enthusiastically started their deliberations as advocates of European integration, had entrenched themselves in their national positions. In these circumstances the good atmosphere of cooperation between the Commission and the Monetary Committee deteriorated. The 1962 Directive generally was perceived by the public at large as a modest achievement in which the ambitions of the Commission were not fulfilled.

5.7 THE THIRD DIRECTIVE: A FAILED ATTEMPT

The 1962 Directive having been a modest exercise, partly designed to deal with the Belgian problem, the Commission wanted to press ahead. Before the adoption of the Second Directive, the Commission had already prepared a memorandum on the still existing capital restrictions, which, so it hoped, would form the basis for a Third Directive. The Commission wished to liberalize three categories of capital transactions: a) issues of foreign securities on domestic capital markets; b) the introduction and quotation of foreign securities on domestic stock exchanges; and c) investments in foreign shares by domestic institutional investors.

Moreover, the Commission wished to tackle 'hidden' restrictions by abolishing *administrative and legal domestic* regulations which formed a hindrance to the free movement of capital. To this end the Commission developed some general principles which should apply in the EEC, such as non-discrimination of domestic regulations vis-à-vis non-residents, openness in criteria used for issuance calendriers and for the introduction of foreign securities on domestic stock exchanges. It also suggested improvements and possibly harmonization of the presentation of financial company data, e.g. in annual reports. Although domestic regulations in a formal sense often did not discriminate, they restricted de facto capital movements. They were, in varying forms and with varying intensity, applied in all EEC countries on varied grounds. Some of them, such as the investment regulations for pension funds and insurance companies had been designed to protect the interests of small savers and policyholders. Others were part and parcel of a country's industrial policy. It was clear that the Commission had trodden on delicate ground. This immediately became clear when it consulted the Monetary Committee.

The *Monetary Committee's advice,* prepared by the Alternates, gave a hint of the problems to come. It was acknowledged that discriminatory regulations concerning the domestic capital market indeed were against the spirit of the Treaty of Rome. However, it was stressed that these were difficult and delicate matters as long as the harmonization in other sectors, in particular with respect to taxation, had not progressed. The committee therefore called for a gradual and cautious approach. Although there was some sympathy for the proposal to abolish restrictive regulations with respect to the issuance of foreign securities in EEC member countries – this would give meaning to the unconditional liberalization of the trade in securities –, there were great hesitations with respect to changing regulations for investment in foreign shares by institutional investors. The rationale of these regulations was the protection of the small savers who had entrusted their savings to the institutional investors from transfer and exchange risks. As long as there was no economic and monetary unification such risks were deemed to be real. However, a step in the right direction might be the liberalization of issues of securities in domestic currency by – or guaranteed by – foreign governments. In such cases both the transfer and exchange risks would be negligible. Even here, however, the Dutch member Posthuma referred to the right under Article 68.3, included on a Dutch initiative, to exclude foreign government loans from the liberalization obligation. With these discouraging reactions the committee had set the pace for further liberalization measures. But the Commission did not resign itself to such a cautious wait-and-see policy.

In August 1963 the Commission presented a *draft proposal* for a Third Directive which went considerably further than the committee's advice.[24] In particular, the draft proposal provided for the abolition of regulations which would limit investment in foreign securities by instutional investors, as long as they were provided with an exchange-guarantee clause. The Commission felt that thus the exchange risk had been taken care of. The intra-European transfer risk could not in its eyes be considered very large. Sound as the economic reasoning of the Commission might have been, it seriously underestimated the judicial and competence problems in member states. Several supervisory authorities – with respect to the stock exchange, insurance companies, commercial banks, etc – were involved, all with their own philosophy of supervision.

The proposals did not go down well with the committee. The resistance must be ascribed in the first place to the fact that the Commission had gone further than the committee's advice.[25] The committee did not want to be kicked around and this was an opportunity to show the Commission who would call the tune. Apparently, irritations had grown over time. It was the first time that the committee had expressed itself in such no uncertain terms. Opposition came from all sides. But first and foremost from France and the Netherlands.

In the *French* eyes the Commission ran ahead of a situation which as yet did not exist and perhaps never would arise, that is a unified capital market in a full economic union. As long as the member states conducted their economic policies in an autonomous manner, harmonization of policies in these delicate areas could only come about in a cautious and gradual manner. In France a wide variety of investment regulations was applied with respect to different financial institutions, because some, such as pension funds, had to be placed under a stricter regime than others. If the Commission wished to proceed further it should perhaps come up with a differentiated scheme. The *Dutch* found it a wrong course on principle to create at the level of the EEC the conditions for the free movement of capital before a certain degree of uniformity was reached with respect to those aspects of economic policy which influenced domestic savings and their channelling.

It was noteworthy that even the *German* members, up till then staunch supporters of the Commission initiatives, also reacted with pique. The Commission was reminded that Germany had no exchange restrictions in place and that it could not be expected to dismantle domestic administrative regulations before the other EEC countries had fulfilled their Treaty obligations of – in the German view – abolishing all exchange restrictions. With this reasoning Germany, which up till then had defended capital liberalization as a case of enlightened self-interest, now also brought the quid pro quo argument into the discussion. Politically logical, this attitude impeded further common progress and brought the subject of capital liberalization more than ever before in the arena of negotiations. Up till then the Commission had prodded member states in bilateral talks to make progress. Now countries watched each other to see who would move first. Negotiations could only be concluded in a package deal.

The reception in the Monetary Committee had been disastrous. The committee concluded that a gradual liberalization of domestic regulations which hindered the free movement of capital, in parallel with further liberalization of exchange restrictions on the one hand and further progress in economic policy coordination on the other hand, was logical and useful. At the same time these complex matters, which threatened to impinge on their autonomy as regards economic and monetary policies, deserved a more thorough and balanced preparation than they had been given up till now. In short, the committee seemed to have buried the Commission's proposals in an elegant manner. The committee having given its disapproval, there was no chance that the Council would go along with the Commission's proposals. But was the burial elegant? In the annual reports of the Monetary Committee the subject of capital liberalization had always figured prominently. But in the committee's Annual Report on 1963 not a single word was devoted to capital liberalization. This silence was unelegant towards the Commission, if not ominous.

What caused this disappointing attitude of the committee? Institutional clashes apart, a real problem figured in the background. The *economic climate* was deteriorating. The first five years of the EEC had been exceptionally favourable: the annual average rate of increase of gdp in the period 1958–62 had been a little over 6%, whereas the annual rate of increase of consumer prices remained relatively well contained at a level under 4%. This situation changed towards the end of 1962. As shown in Figure 9 inflationary pressures rose and, especially in France and Italy, increasing signs of overheating were attended by a deterioration of the balance of payments. For the first time economic developments within the Community began to diverge significantly.

On the international front as well the sky became clouded. The *United States* and the *United Kingdom* experienced substantial capital outflows which in continental Europe threatened to undermine domestic monetary stability. After Germany had already taken measures in 1960 to ward off short-term inflows, in 1963 for the same reason France also had to ban the payment of interest on non-resident accounts.[26] Moreover, in order to prevent evasion of the direct credit restrictions, the taking-up of loans abroad by residents was restricted. For the first time France applied the same motive – control of domestic monetary expansion – to capital restrictions as the Dutch had done, who operated a similar monetary control system of domestic credit ceilings. The Commission wisely had not proposed to liberalize short-term capital transactions. But in the increasingly unstable international climate the member states did not wish to tinker with other capital regulations in Europe either.

5.8 FURTHER EFFORTS OF THE COMMISSION

In subsequent years the Commission made several attempts to get the Third Directive accepted in amended forms. In January 1964 a *new draft* was sent to the committee, which to a considerable extent met the earlier objections of some countries. The committee advised that this proposal went in the

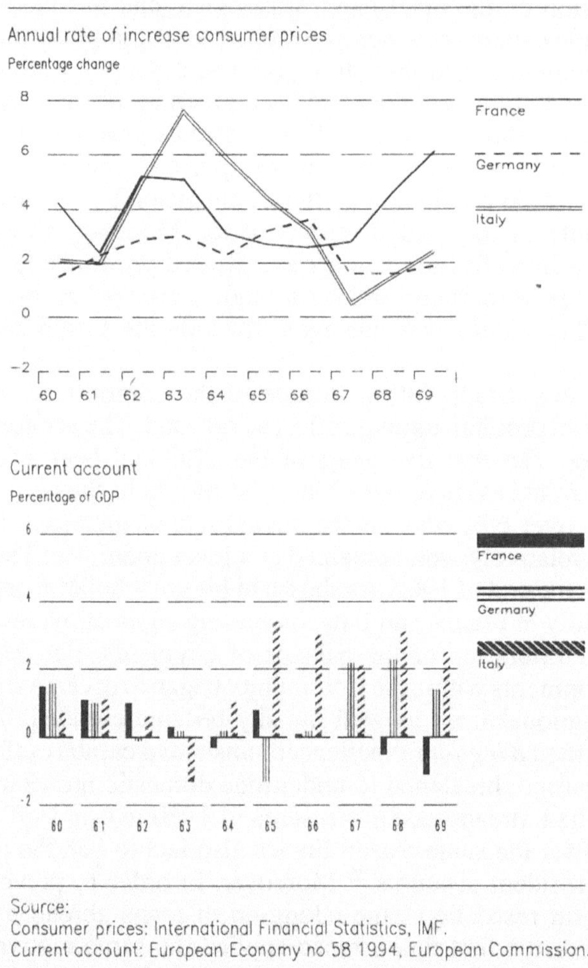

Fig. 9. Diverging economic developments in the 1960s.

desired direction; some modifications were proposed.[27] The Commission went back to the drawing board and then submitted on 9 April 1964 a new draft directive directly to the Council.[28] This proposal, however, was shelved by the ministers. There could be no other conclusion than that in those circumstances there was no way to reach agreement on further liberalization obligations. Germany, Belgium and Luxembourg did not want to move in the sphere of domestic regulations as long as the other countries kept exchange restrictions in place. France wished to consider changing its domestic regulations only in the framework of a wider development towards economic integration. Italy was dragging its feet as well. So was the Netherlands, which, however, possibly under the influence of chairman van Lennep, was willing to accept the directive. In practice it was already moving towards a much more liberal regime.

An underlying consideration was that further liberalization would not be opportune in the prevailing *cyclical phase* characterized by overheating.[29] Germany was trying to curtail demand by raising interest rates and this might be frustrated if German industry could finance itself freely on other markets. France and the Netherlands were operating a system of credit restrictions, which they did not wish to see circumvented by their industry taking up credit in third countries. It was thus felt by the Monetary Committee, in its third annual examination of capital restrictions since the adoption of the 1960 Directive, that further capital liberalization would be *counterproductive* to efforts underway to rebalance the overheated European economies.[30]

In an attempt to bring the discussion to life again the Commission entrusted a group of experts, headed by Claudio Segré, to study the complex issues of integration of national capital markets. The *Segré report*,[31] published in 1966, underlined the linkages between freedom of capital movements and progress in other domains, such as monetary and economic policies. It forcefully advocated the removal of obstacles which different domestic regulations and fiscal regimes posed to capital movements.

Mid–1965 the Commission tried to speed up the treatment of the Third Directive by adding some *new obligations* for the countries which still operated exchange restrictions: France, Italy and the Netherlands. It thus hoped to have a more balanced proposal, acceptable to the 'liberal' countries Germany, Belgium and Luxembourg which had made it clear that they were only willing to soften their domestic regulations after the other countries had taken steps to dismantle part of their existing exchange restrictions. Inter alia the Commission proposed that foreign issues and financial credits, up till then falling under the conditional regime, should be liberalized unconditionally up to certain amounts. The Commission also proposed to abolish the possibility of reintroducing restrictions on transactions under the conditional regime which had been liberalized.

These proposals met with objections from the Italian and Dutch members.[32] However, on the initiative of chairman van Lennep who wished to make progress, a Dutch *alternative plan* was developed which provided for the parallel placement of foreign bonds on all European capital markets in order to prevent these bonds from being issued only on the capital market with the lowest interest rate (the Dutch capital market). This showed that the Dutch were willing to take liberalizing measures as long as they could rest assured that this would not in practice mean that the Dutch capital market would become overburdened.

In the subsequent meetings of the Monetary Committee the discussions dragged on without much progress.[33] A situation was finally reached where the Netherlands and Italy were willing to open up their markets up to certain limits (foreign issues up to 1.5% of their gross domestic savings), but France

TABLE 13

Public finances in the EEC 1960–1969 as percentage of GDP.

	Average 1960/1963	1964	1965	1966	1967	1968	1969
Belgium	−1.9	−0.8	−1.6	−1.0	−1.3	−2.6	−1.8
France	0.4	0.7	0.7	0.6	0.0	−0.8	0.9
Germany	1.9	0.7	−0.6	−0.2	−1.4	−0.8	1.1
Italy	−1.0	−0.8	−3.8	−3.8	−2.2	−2.8	−3.1
The Netherlands	−0.3	−1.5	−0.8	−0.9	−1.3	−0.9	−0.5
EEC	0.5	0.2	−0.9	−0.8	−1.1	−1.3	−0.1

Note: Net lending (+) or net borrowing (–); general government. EEC-weighted average of 5 countries.
Source: European Economy no 58, 1994, European Commission.

was not even willing to go this far. On the other hand, Belgium and Germany were firm in their opinion that these concessions were not enough to make the Third Directive acceptable to them. The negotiations had become completely bogged down in haggling over details. A desperate attempt by the Commission in 1967 to get the Third Directive in an amended form accepted in the Council failed.[34]

It was generally felt that the lack of a sound and well-coordinated *policy mix* in the EEC was one of the fundamental reasons why time and again the proposals of the Commission failed and the capital liberalization process in Europe was getting nowhere. The divergences between the economic performances of the European countries had increased and public finances in many countries started to deteriorate (see Table 13). The burden of adjustment and the fight against inflationary pressures thus increasingly came to rest on monetary policy. In particular France and the Netherlands were concerned that further liberalization would add to this burden by increasing the demand for capital, causing upward pressure on the interest rate. In its Annual Report on 1965 the Monetary Committee suggested that other countries, too, should consider the introduction of a system of direct credit controls, as was operated in France and the Netherlands. Capital liberalization had reached a deadlock also because of the increasing concern over international monetary developments. The Bretton Woods system started to show cracks. The United States had taken steps in the mid–1960s to curb its continuous capital outflows, which had met only with limited success.[35]

In the meantime, on the initiative of chairman van Lennep, a discussion was started on the opening-up of the European capital markets to the *less developed countries*. Capital outflows which would finance investment in less developed countries would form a useful counterpart to the surplus on current account registered by the EEC as a whole. The practical outcome of this discussion was that the regional development banks gained access to the domestic capital markets on the same conditions as the World Bank. However, this was more of a gesture, which did not have much practical impact.

While the discussions in the framework of the EEC were deadlocked, on an *individual* basis countries did take steps to gradually liberalize capital movements. After France had abolished its devises-titres market as early as 1963, the Netherlands followed suit in 1966 with the abolition of the comparable closed-circuit market for cross-border transactions by residents in securities. End 1966 Michel Debré, the French Finance minister, took the radical step of liberalizing most capital movements and switching to a *positive system,* implying that all capital transactions were permitted unless they were explicitly prohibited.[36] Most remaining restrictions on short-term capital movements were abolished. The switch to a positive system was accompanied with the introduction of a system of minimum reserve requirements. Actually the whole range of monetary policy instruments was under active consideration with a view to moving to a more *indirect* system, which would operate through movements of short-term interest rates.[37] This resulted in a period of relative liberty for capital movements in France which was to last only 16 months, until May 1968.

The French transition to a positive system was an important, daring step. The law's declaration of intent was simple: 'Les relations financières entre la France et l'étranger sont libres.' In parliament Debré argued that the French franc having become a strong currency, the relaxations of exchange control which had already taken place could now be codified. An important further argument was the development of Paris as a financial centre. For this freedom of capital movements was rightly considered a precondition.[38] But the introduction of a positive system was heavily contested by the technical apparatus.[39] The Banque de France initially was hesitant as well, arguing that as long as monetary cooperation in Europe was inadequate capital movements should be regulated in one way or another. Moreover, the French central bank needed time to undertake the monetary reform which would have to accompany capital liberalization.[40]

The switch to a positive system implied a considerable easing if not abolition of administrative permissions. Now the French domestic capital market – no longer governed by exchange controls – could be gradually opened up to foreign issues through an easing of domestic regulations. The waiting-list on the French calendrier was a long one – 12 months! – and there was thus a certain scepticism as to the practical openness, the more so because the calendrier was determined by the Minister of Finance on the basis of priorities of the national economic plan. The system of administrative controls for direct investment flows, both incoming and outgoing, remained in place as well. A situation now had developed where France had abolished nearly all

TABLE 14

French balance of payments 1968–1969 in billions of francs.

	1968	1969
Trade balance	–0.4	–4.8
Current account	–5.3	–8.7
Long-term capital	–5.9	–1.6
Short-term capital	–1.0	4.4
Net errors and omissions	–5.7	0.5
Official reserves	–17.9	–5.4

Source: International Financial Statistics, IMF

exchange controls with respect to short-term capital movements, while maintaining some domestic regulations which in practice could curtail long-term capital flows. The main purpose of these regulations was, as it always had been, the furtherance of domestic economic priorities and the avoidance of the taking over of French companies by foreign, in particular US interests. Nevertheless, the French intentions constituted a sensational departure from the previous system and must be regarded as part and parcel of the Fifth Plan which envisaged opening-up the French economy to foreign competition. The traditional fear of speculative capital movements had been set aside.

5.9 'LES ÉVÉNEMENTS' OF MAY 1968 IN FRANCE

The ultimate blow to any move forward in Europe was given when France was forced to reintroduce capital restrictions in the aftermath of what the French authorities preferably called 'les événements' of May 1968. Social unrest, which started at the universities but quickly spread to labour, led to widespread strikes causing serious disruptions of economic activity. The troubles were accompanied by an enormous *flight of capital* which the authorities tried to stem through the temporary closing of the exchange and gold markets and the reintroduction of severe restrictions on short and long-term capital flows (see for balance-of-payments figures Table 14). The provisions of the January 1967 decree introducing a positive system of exchange control were suspended. For the first time since the signing of the Treaty of Rome the safeguard clauses had to be invoked by a member state. France availed itself of the possibility of Article 109, the 'urgency clause', which provided that in case of a sudden crisis in the balance of payments a member state may take the necessary protective measures. France took, in agreement with the

Commission, temporary emergency measures in the trade sphere as well. Rumours of an impending devaluation of the French franc increased, but the authorities continued to resist this despite the loss of competitiveness as a consequence of the generous wage settlements agreed upon in order to end the strikes. Thus, in an attempt to regain confidence, the government tempted fortune by lifting all exchange controls early September 1968, while at the same time tightening monetary policy.

The resistance to adjusting exchange rates was formidable despite fresh waves of vast amounts of speculative flows. The exchange market again had to be closed. In an emergency meeting of the Group of Ten on 20–22 November 1968 in Bonn pressure was exerted upon Germany, which was confronted with large current account surpluses, to revalue the Deutsche mark. But Germany, too, preferred taking regulatory measures, like raising border taxes and imposing direct restrictions on speculative flows, to contemplating revaluation. Capital inflows into Germany were further discouraged by the imposition of a 100% reserve requirement on the growth of Deutsche mark deposits held by non-residents. After the Bonn meeting General de Gaulle declared that the French franc would not be devalued. Instead, exchange controls were reintroduced. The brief experiment with free capital movements in France had definitely come to a close. The restoration of the French external situation took more time than initially foreseen and when a new wave of speculation occurred in the spring of 1969, Germany intensified its controls on speculative short-term inflows, while France tightened monetary policy further. It was to no avail. France devalued in August by 11%, the first adjustment of the exchange rate of the French franc since 1958, and Germany revalued the Deutsche mark one month later by a little over 9%.

The Monetary Committee, for the first time since the establishment of the European Community, was consulted on the parity changes. A large part of the deliberations was devoted to the consequences for the common agricultural policy. France, which after the frustrating events did not wish to risk again a crisis of confidence in the exchange rate, kept the capital controls in place after the devaluation. This was not challenged in the committee. Germany, on the other hand, abolished all restrictions after the revaluation of the Deutsche mark. However, the restoration of full freedom of capital movements in Germany, as it had existed in the early part of the 1960s, was not to last long either. The intra-European speculative capital flows in 1968 and 1969 were small compared to the tide which would flood Europe from across the Atlantic early in the next decade.

5.10 CONCLUSION

The start of the EEC had been promising. Rather soon secondary legislation had been enacted which gave a meaningful content to the Treaty obligation to liberalize capital movements to the extent necessary to ensure the proper functioning of the Common Market. Those types of capital transactions were affected which had a clear link with trade or direct investment. The *two directives* which were agreed upon constituted largely a consolidation of the status quo in the member states. Nevertheless, they could be regarded as a step forward, because the provisions in principle saw to it that restrictions would not be reintroduced unless by way of a common procedure. This exerted some restraining influence on member states. The fact that countries liberalized further on a unilateral basis but were not yet prepared to codify this in obligations underlines the importance of the common obligations to which they had agreed in the first decade of the EEC.

After this promising start it became increasingly difficult to make further progress. *Short-term capital movements* were not brought under the liberalization directives, even though some countries on an individual basis began to abolish restrictions at the short end as well. The wish to remain in control of domestic monetary policy as well as the fear of speculative capital flows forged a powerful alliance. Countries for the time being wished to retain the powers to maintain or impose restrictions on short-term flows without having to go through cumbersome Community procedures, although a majority of member states acknowledged that in due course also short-term capital movements would have to fall under Community obligations. Even Germany, the strongest advocate of the freedom of capital movement, had imposed restrictions on short-term capital inflows for the larger part of the decade. There was no attempt on the part of the Commission to include them in the liberalization obligations.

The Commission trod on difficult terrain when it tried to bring other types of capital transactions under the liberalization directives. It struck upon objections closely related to the three motives for maintaining exchange control, which had come up during the negotiations on the Treaty of Rome and discussed in Chapter 3: (a) *Member states were not yet prepared to open up domestic capital markets.* Foreign demand on domestic capital markets was a politically sensitive issue, being regarded as a drain on national savings and leading to potentially upward pressure on domestic capital market rates. Further unconditional liberalization in the medium and long-term sphere impinged on national regulations concerning domestic capital markets, where countries wished to determine their own marching pace. (b) *Member states followed a different monetary philosophy*, with some, notably France and the Netherlands, needing capital restrictions as a complement to domestic monetary policy instruments. (c) *The fear for disturbing speculative capital movements was still present.* Although the fear for speculative outflows had diminished as European economies flourished, there remained a latent fear. Later in the decade it was rather speculative inflows which were perceived as a problem.

The attempts of the Commission to broaden the liberalization obligations were mainly directed towards the opening-up of domestic capital markets. In the view of the Commission this could lead towards the development of a truly integrated *European capital market* which, so it was felt, would strengthen the functioning of the Common Market. The Commission targeted areas such as the admission of foreign issues on domestic markets, the quotation of foreign securities on domestic stock exchanges and the liberalization of unit trusts. In doing so the Commission became increasingly attentive to domestic regulations, such as investment rules for institutional investors which discriminated between domestic and EEC assets.

These Commission attempts towards a common approach failed because of institutional and structural obstacles, notwithstanding the substantial progress towards deregulation and liberalization in *individual* member states. Particularly in France, before the 1968 events, there was a courageous effort to liberalize capital movements far beyond the agreed obligations and modernize monetary policy instruments. For a short while French and German exchange control systems approached each other closely and plans were developed in France to move towards an indirect monetary control system as well. This alignment, however, proved to be short-lived when the *French 'événements'* caused a major set-back. When the economic and international climate worsened towards the end of the decade and tensions in the exchange markets increased the authorities became disinclined to further liberalization. So, ten years after the start of the EEC, at the very time when the customs union between the six EEC members was completed, restrictions on the free movement of capital had to be reimposed. At the time these measures were taken, it was thought that they would be of a temporary nature. It could not be foreseen that it would take another 15 years before attempts toward capital liberalization could be resumed.

NOTES

1. La libération des mouvements de capitaux en application de l'Article 67.1 du Traité de Rome (1959), European Commission.
2. Banca d'Italia, Annual Report 1961, p. 77.
3. Banca d'Italia, Annual Report 1960, p. 87–92.
4. Memorandum of 9 April 1959, Ministry of Finance.
5. See discussion in Chapter 2, p. 15.
6. In an earlier internal draft of the memorandum it was argued that for transactions in securities a separate, free exchange market should be established which could absorb the shocks which were likely to occur in this sector. However, the idea of a dual exchange market (trade and investment-related capital transactions through the fixed exchange market, finance-related capital transactions through a free market) met with opposition from Governor Holtrop and eventually was abandoned.
7. Note concernant la proposition de directive sur la libération des mouvements de capitaux, dated 17 December 1959.

8. The Commission had split the unconditional liberalization regime into two parts (lists A and B) in order to accommodate a different treatment of certain categories of capital transactions in multiple exchange rate systems. Transactions on list A – mainly direct investment and trade credits – should be executed at an exchange rate which was not allowed to diverge appreciably and lastingly from the official rate for current transactions. As regards the transactions on list B – mainly listed shares – the authorities merely should 'endeavour' to avoid appreciable and lasting divergences. The motive for this different formulation was that the list A transactions were deemed most essential for the functioning of the Common Market and therefore should not be hampered by the exchange rate fluctuations on the free market. For list B transactions this was felt to be less urgent. The régime conditionnel was put in list C and the third category, where there was no obligation to liberalize, in list D.
9. Directive on the liberalization of transactions in shares of undertakings for collective investment in securities (85/583), dated 20 December 1985. See chapter 7, p. 167.
10. There was one exception: long-term trade credits were not unconditionally liberalized as opposed to short and medium-term credits. The Commission had wished to liberalize all trade credits, whereas the committee initially wished to limit the liberalization obligation to trade credits shorter than one year. Eventually a compromise was struck and medium-term trade credits were included in the liberalization obligation (see also Chapter 7, Note 39).
11. Monetary Committee, Annual Report 1960.
12. Since the beginning of 1959 France had gradually liberalized its extensive exchange controls. On 1 January 1960 the Office des Changes, established in October 1940, had been closed because of its diminished activities. The remaining tasks had been partitioned between the Banque de France and the Ministries of Finance and Economic Affairs. When the directive was published on 20 July 1960 in effect no French exchange regulations had to be amended (Banque de France, Annual Report 1960, p. 25). As regards the Italian exchange regime, there was, however, a difference of opinion between Italy and the Commission whether the treatment of shares was in conformity with the directive.
13. Articles 1.2 and 2.2 of the First Directive. Italy, too, was confronted with multiple exchange rates because exported bank notes, a notable source of illegal or tax-inspired capital outflows, could not, after being re-imported, be credited to non-resident accounts. Therefore, there was an unofficial lira exchange rate quotation which differed from the official exchange rate. In January 1962 this restriction was lifted. France and the Netherlands both operated closed-circuit free markets in shares. Because these fell under the less strict regime of Article 2.2, these markets were not affected.
14. Addendum to the proposal of the Commission to the Council for the First Directive, 1960.
15. Banque de France, Annual Report 1960, p. 24.
16. Banca d'Italia, Annual Report 1960, p. 88.
17. Emminger (1986), p. 98.
18. Conclusions du premier examen annuel des restrictions applicables aux mouvements de capitaux entre les Etats membres, report of the Monetary Committee to the Commission, dated 7 July 1961.
19. The Netherlands proceeded cautiously. The issues were allowed 'provisorily' on the basis of an 'exceptional' authorization and for limited amounts.
20. The Belgian authorities were to propose that in case of large differentials special permits could be given to conduct direct investment transactions in the regulated market. They wished to define this as 'on average 2% over the last 90 days or 3% over the last 30 days', but this was not acceptable to the Commission which did not want to go further than 2% over the last 15 days.
21. The inclusion of payments for services in the EEC directive implied a deviation from the OECD code which treated all services payments as current payments, in line with established practice. However, so it was argued in the Monetary Committee, the OECD

had not taken a strict line against the dual market system: transactions were considered liberalized if they were channelled through the free market. The EEC was taking a stricter line.

22. The devises-titres market, started in April 1955, implied that proceeds from sales of foreign securities expressed in foreign currencies and owned by French residents (so-called devises-titres) might be sold in a free market to other residents, who in turn could use them only to purchase securities quoted in foreign markets. This system was comparable with the Dutch system of special investment accounts ('herbeleggingsrekeningen'). The Banque de France intervened in the devises-titres market in order to exercise a moderating influence on exchange rate fluctuations. Actually the exchange rate differentials since end–1958 had been relatively small. In an internal memorandum of the Banque de France (1 February 1962) its abolition was advocated: 'le régime de la devise-titre est un héritage d'une période où la balance française des paiements se soldait avec persistance par de lourds déficits, où les réserves officielles de change étaient manifestement insuffisantes, où le franc était attaqué sur tous les fronts'. All these were bygones and its abolition would satisfy the IMF, its European partners, the US and the French citizens, who would now no longer be incited 'to export their capital illegally or buy gold on the Paris market'. The latter was regarded as undesirable. The abolition of the devises-titres market implied that transactions in shares by residents could now be channelled through the official market.
23. In the 1960s preparations had been made to abolish the dual exchange market, but they were cancelled at the last minute when a crisis showed it could still play a useful role.
24. Projet de troisième directive pour la mise en oeuvre de l'article 67 du Traité, dated 23 August 1963.
25. In a report by the Dutch members of the meeting of the Monetary Committee in November 1963 there is an undeniable sense of irritation: the committee had carefully considered its advice, but the Commission had felt that it could brush away these considerations. The Commission's proposals moreover showed signs of poor preparation.
26. Decision of 21 April 1963 by the Conseil National du Crédit. The payment of interest on accounts held by central banks and international institutions was exempted. The prohibition was lifted on 9 November 1966, only to be reintroduced during the crisis in the Bretton Woods system.
27. Avis du Comité Monétaire, dated 16 March 1964.
28. Proposition de Troisième Directive pour la mise en oeuvre de l'article 67 du Traité, COM(64)128, dated 9 April 1964.
29. There was a serious concern that inflationary impulses might be transferred from one member state to the other. In its meeting on 15 April 1964 the Council had adopted a recommendation which called upon member states to adopt measures in order to restore internal and external equilibrium. A concrete measure proposed was that all countries should limit the expansion of government outlays to 5% in order to curtail inflationary pressures. Countries indeed took deflationary measures which met with some success.
30. Meeting of the Monetary Committee in May 1964.
31. Le développement d'un marché européen des capitaux (1966), European Communities, Luxembourg.
32. The French members were not present because of the empty-chair policy France conducted from July 1965 until January 1966. However, had they been present, doubtless they would have voiced objections as well.
33. Meetings of the Monetary Committee in December 1965, and February and April 1966.
34. See Ruding (1969), p. 212 et seq., for an elaborate discussion of this modified directive. He attaches much importance to the distrust felt by Germany, Luxembourg and the Netherlands, that in practice the required liberalization would take place at an equal scale in France, and to a lesser extent in Belgium and Italy. The latter countries made much more use of domestic regulations for admission to the domestic capital market, e.g. prior authorization of issues by the Minister of Finance in France. The lack of transparency of

these regulations fueled the fear that the capital markets of those countries which hitherto relied primarily on exchange controls would after the liberalization become overexposed to foreign demand for capital.

35. See Chapter 2, Note 2.
36. Law of 28 December 1966, which entered into force on 31 January 1967.
37. Icard (1994) reports that these considerations resulted in the publication in June 1969 of the Report on the money market and credit conditions, written by Marjolin, Sadrin and Wormser (Rapport sur le marché monétaire et les conditions de crédit). They criticized the selective credit policy at subsidized rates and recommended an active monetary policy with interventions on the money market to influence short-term interest rates. Icard judges these proposals as 'very far-reaching and also quite modern for an economy that was still largely regulated.' Some of the recommendations were implemented, but they had to be suspended in the economic turmoil which followed the oil shock in 1973.
38. Debré quoted in Teyssier (1973), p. 270.
39. In his memoirs Teyssier (1973, p. 265), one of its administrators, decries the transition to a positive system in vivid terms: 'Un pays doit être maître de son destin. A quoi bon une armée, une marine, une aviation, et même des bombes atomiques, si l'anéantissement peut venir d'ailleurs!', meaning speculative capital outflows.
40. Banque de France, memorandum dated 5 May 1966.

CHAPTER 6

The 1970s: Lost Control

All diese Fortschritte in Richtung auf größere Freiheit in der Weltwirtschaft, die uns heute so selbstverständlich erscheinen, erforderten jahrelang eine unendliche Kleinarbeit.

Otmar Emminger, 1986

6.1 INTRODUCTION

At the turn of the decade the strains in the international monetary system had become very pronounced. The large balance-of-payments deficits of the United States had cast doubts on the sustainability of the fixed exchange rates and engendered vast speculative capital outflows out of the US dollar. But the European economic and political situation, too, was full of uncertainties. The political troubles in France in 1968 – 'les événements de mai' – had been followed by repeated speculative attacks on the intra-European exchange rate relationships. Following a defeat in the referendum held in April 1969 General de Gaulle had resigned. The new administration under president Pompidou was defining a new, less intransigent course for French external policies, including the possible lifting of the French veto on EEC membership of the United Kingdom. The continued upward pressure on the Deutsche mark, both vis-à-vis the US dollar and most other European currencies, had provoked a crisis atmosphere in Germany. There was widespread reluctance to let the currency appreciate out of fear of a deterioration of the competitive position of German industry. When in the face of continuous capital inflows such appreciation could not be avoided in the end – the Deutsche mark was revalued by 9% in October 1969 – the 'great coalition' (christian-democrats and socialists) headed by chancellor Kiesinger had already been forced to step down, reflecting the serious differences of opinion within the administration as to how to handle the crisis situation. But when the speculative inflows from across the Atlantic contined to swamp the German money market, the new socialist-liberal government under Willy Brandt also struggled with the question whether the Deutsche mark should be allowed to float or whether controls on capital inflows should be imposed. Opinions on this issue were sharply divided within the Zentralbankrat of the Bundesbank as well. The crisis in the international monetary system prompted the European Community into action. Numerous meetings of the Monetary Committee were devoted to discussing possible measures to cope with the voluminous cross-Atlantic speculative capital movements. The exchange control measures taken by the US administration to stem the continuous outflows had little effect. When it increasingly became clear that no international agreement on more fundamental measures could be reached, the European countries were driven into each other's arms. Gradually consensus emerged on a twofold European reaction to the turbulences in the exchange markets: (1) *closer intra-European cooperation* in the economic and monetary field would be pursued, in order to reduce uncertainty and restore confidence among market operators, and (2) *capital controls would be re-established* in order to ward off remaining speculative capital movements. Faced with the new situation the Commission completely reversed its earlier position in favour of capital liberalization. Anything was preferable to floating which was considered to undermine the foundations of the Common Market and to complicate the common agricultural policy.

The wish to cooperate more closely in the economic and monetary field had been a constant theme in the deliberations of the Monetary Committee. In its Annual Report on 1966 the committee had evaluated the functioning of the EEC in the first ten years since the signing of the Treaty.[1] One of the main findings was that the gravest threat to the accomplishment of the goals of the Common Market had not been the restoration of trade or capital restrictions – as had been the main fear of the drafters of the Treaty –, but rather the *internal imbalances* within the member countries themselves. Thereby the maintenance of price stability had been jeopardized. The problems caused by inflation differentials had been compounded by major cyclical divergences among member states. These had prompted policy reactions which in turn had repercussions on the policies of other countries. The main lesson to be drawn from this was that the conditions for internal macro-economic and financial equilibrium of the individual member states deserved much more policy attention of the Monetary Committee. Economic and monetary *policy coordination* should be strengthened with a view to minimizing these negative repercussions. These considerations and the emergence of exchange rate tensions prompted a major political initiative at the end of the 1960s to deepen the institutional and procedural commitments of the member states. It was felt that this should be done before new member states would be admitted to the Community. In an enlarged Community the risk of negative repercussions of uncoordinated economic policies would be even larger.

6.2 THE WERNER REPORT, A DOOMED ATTEMPT

In the breakthrough *Hague European Summit* meeting in December 1969 an attempt was made to breathe new life in the European integration ideal. Under its new president Pompidou, France took a more outward-looking attitude. Its negative demeanour within the EEC, evinced by the empty-chair policy, was now left behind and the French veto on EEC membership of the United Kingdom was lifted. From now on the Community would open itself to new members. However, before initiating negotiations with prospective new members the Community's goals and institutions should be strengthened. In their communique, the Heads of State or Government expressed the wish 'to see the Community develop into an economic and monetary union through the implementation of a phased plan'. To this end an Ad Hoc Group, under the chairmanship of Pierre Werner, Premier and Minister of Finance of Luxembourg, was established to elaborate such a plan. On 8 October 1970 the group finalized its report.[2]

The *Werner report* took as its starting point the anomaly that due to the increasing linkages between the European economies autonomy over national policies had weakened, while no compensation for this loss of national autonomy had been created at the Community level. The lack of effective coordination of economic policies in the Community, prescribed in the Treaty, and a continued bias towards particularism among member states were seen as lying at the heart of the insufficient progress towards further liberalization of capital flows and financial integration. Therefore all attention should be directed towards strengthening policy cooperation between member states, with a view to reaching the final objective of *economic and monetary union.* Such a union, to be achieved in three stages, would 'realize an area in which goods and services, people and capital will circulate freely and without competitive distortions, without thereby giving rise to structural or regional disequilibrium', as well as 'the total and irreversible convertibility of currencies, the elimination of margins of fluctuation in exchange rates, the irrevocable fixing of parity rates and the complete liberation of movements of capital'.

The main elements of economic and monetary policy-making would have to be centralized.[3] This would require the creation of new institutions to which national powers would have to be transferred:

- a *Centre of decision for economic policy,* which would formulate economic policy of the Community and would monitor national budgetary policies; this institution would be responsible for the external exchange rate policy of the Community and would be politically accountable to a European Parliament;
- a *Community system for the central banks,* which could be based on the structure for the Federal Reserve and which would execute the internal monetary policy in the Community, as well as the commonly agreed exchange rate policy through interventions on the foreign exchange markets.[4]

The aim of the *first two stages,* the second stage being essentially a reinforced first stage, was to progressively strengthen the coordination of economic policies with a view to both *stabilizing the exchange rates* and to enabling the *gradual liberalization of capital movements* as necessary steps towards the final stage of economic and monetary union. National decisions on budgetary policy were gradually to be taken in the light of Community guidelines. To this end there would be prior consultations among Community member states and their performance would be closely monitored with the help of a system of indicators. In these preparatory stages the coordination of general economic policy-making was to be principally the responsibility of the Council of Ministers. The Committee of Governors of the EC central banks would play an important role in both internal and external monetary policy-making, but the general guidelines of monetary and credit policy were to be determined in the Council as well. The central banks were requested to work towards a progressive *narrowing of the fluctuation bands*.

The Werner report noted with concern that both exchange restrictions as well as domestic regulations hampered the free *movement of capital*. The resulting differences in the costs and conditions of credit among countries were contrary to fair competition and the eventual establishment of an economic and monetary union. In the envisaged first stage the Werner report took up the earlier proposals of the Commission to abolish restrictions in a somewhat amended form. It advocated the liberalization of issues of securities by EEC residents on all EEC capital markets (subject to ceilings which could be gradually raised), of short and medium-term non-trade related credits, and of the quotation of shares originating from member states on all EEC stock exchanges. The report furthermore called for the abolition of domestic regulations for institutional investors which limited investment within the Community. Finally, the Werner report advocated the coordination and harmonization of domestic regulations concerning the capital market.

A number of observations can be made with respect to these proposals. In the first place the proposals again fell short of full liberalization of capital movements. It was envisaged that efforts in the second phase primarily should be directed towards the establishment of an integrated *European capital market*. Apparently the freeing of short-term capital movements was to be left to the final stage of economic and monetary union. Secondly, the proposals considerably diverged from the *erga omnes principle*. They were explicitly directed towards the establishment of an exchange and regulatory regime which discriminated between EEC and non-EEC capital movements. Finally, there was no reference to the desirability of abolishing the *Belgian dual market*. In the face of the international exchange turmoil the spreads between the financial franc and the official Belgian franc rate had increased to as much as 10%. This omission was all the more remarkable because at the same time the Werner report called for the progressive narrowing of the fluctuation bands for the official intra-EEC exchange rates.

The report stopped short at a rather general description of the institutional set-up of the final stage of the economic and monetary union and did not deal in detail with the institutional structure and the division of responsibilities between the system of central banks and the political executive. It was left unclear whether the system of central banks could operate independently of government or Community instructions, an institutional feature which gained a prominent place in the Delors report and subsequently in the Maastricht Treaty twenty years later.

The institutional vagueness of the Werner report, especially in the monetary field, and the non-committal character of the economic policy coordination in the transitional stages formed inherent weaknesses of the report. The Werner report was rich on the need for cooperation, but was short on the targets to be achieved through this cooperation. It did not prescribe the objective of price stability for the national central banks, nor did it provide for indications of the acceptable size of national budget deficits. Its grandiose concept of economic and monetary union was not yet supported by a common economic philosophy among the member states. The compromise formulations used could barely hide the fact that there were underlying fundamental differences. The disagreements would become manifest rather soon. When on 22 March 1971 the Council adopted a *Resolution on the attainment of economic and monetary union in stages*, the definition of the Werner report's final objective was accepted, but the relinquishment of national sovereignty in the non-monetary field was described in much vaguer terms. The proposal for a Centre of decision for economic policy was not taken up by the Council, without any provision being made for alternative constraints on national budgetary policies. The institutional set-up of the economic part of the union thus was weakened considerably.

At the same time the Council adopted a *Decision on the strengthening of the cooperation between the national central banks*. But also here there were underlying divergent views on the objectives of monetary policy. The initiative towards economic and monetary union therefore soon would fail when, despite all good intentions and strengthened cooperation procedures, economic and monetary developments within Europe increasingly started to diverge. Thereby the opportunity for liberalization of capital movements slipped away as well.

6.3 THE ESTABLISHMENT OF THE SNAKE

In the Council Resolution of 22 March 1971 it was provided that in the framework of the ultimate goal of the introduction of one European currency the mutual *exchange rate margins* would, by way of trial, be *narrowed,* as suggested in the Werner report.[5] This plan had barely been conceived, when in May 1971 the speculative capital movements again swelled after the publication of a study by the five German economic institutes, in which either floating or a revaluation of the Deutsche mark was advocated. The Deutsche mark had become the safe haven for funds moving out of the US dollar and the continued capital inflows threatened to blow up the money supply. Monetary policy, which had been tightened following the 1969 revaluation in order to curb inflationary pressures, had become completely overstretched. At

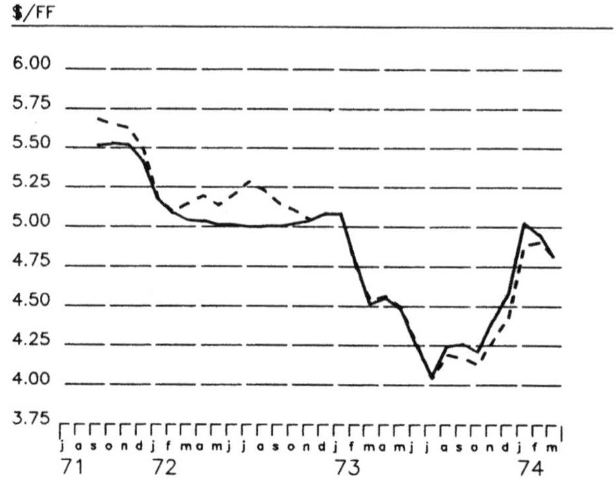

Official franc exchange rate — Financial franc exchange rate

Source: Quarterly bulletin, DNB.

Fig. 10. The French dual market 1971–1974.

times measures had been taken to discourage short-term capital inflows. These measures had affected capital movements only in an indirect manner and were not in contravention of the EEC directives, nor of the OECD Liberalization Code.[6] They were, however, not successful.

There were serious differences of opinion among the monetary authorities as to how to react to the continuing inflows. At stake was the issue whether the *Deutsche mark* should be allowed to float or whether direct controls on capital inflows should be imposed. The Bundesbank favoured the imposition of direct capital controls on inward flows, although it was unlikely that at short notice adequate exchange controls could be introduced which would effectively discourage further capital inflows. For the German government the step towards a generalized system of direct controls was not yet acceptable for reasons of economic philosophy. The government, loath to abandon its market-oriented approach, decided to float the Deutsche mark unilaterally on 10 May 1971.[7] Nevertheless, the reintroduction of the prohibition against the sale of German money market paper to non-residents, only lifted in 1969, as well as a ban on interest payments on bank deposits held by non-residents, constituted a prelude to an increasing willingness towards interventionism.[8] The Dutch monetary authorities, which likewise found it impossible to draw up strict exchange controls in time, let the guilder float in tandem with the Deutsche mark.

The speculative capital movements out of the US dollar implied a shift in the fortunes of the *French franc*, which up till then primarily had been prone to speculative capital outflows, but now was attracting inflows. In the course of the year several measures were taken to curtail these inflows. After the suspension of the convertibility of the US dollar on 15 August 1971 the upward pressure on the European currencies was such that direct restrictions on inflows were considered to be unavoidable. France tried to avert the risk of an appreciation of its currency vis-à-vis the US dollar by introducing a *dual exchange market* with similar characteristics as the Belgian dual market, while at the same time further strengthening its restrictions on capital inflows. Current transactions could be settled in the official market, where the Banque de France intervened, whereas all other transactions, including those for tourism and travel, had to be led through the free market, where the 'franc financier' floated (see Figure 10). At the same time the authorities were reluctant to abolish the heritage of the 1968 crisis – controls designed to curtail capital outflows – although there were some relaxations. The security currency market ('devises titres') initially was maintained,[9] as were maximum foreign exchange allowances for French travellers. This anomalous situation was characteristic of the activist, fine-tuning attitude of the French authorities in using exchange controls. Whereas the Belgian two-tier market was vindicated by the lack of direct capital controls, France utilized both. In the Monetary Committee the French members indicated that France intended to leave long-term and intra-EEC capital movements as much as possible unaffected. A brave face was put on it, but in practice it proved to be impossible to separate intra-EEC and extra-EEC flows. Moreover, there was a pull on the French franc from two sides: against the tendency to appreciate vis-à-vis the US dollar, there was the tendency to depreciate vis-à-vis the Deutsche mark.

France was the only European country to maintain an effective dollar parity. Belgium and Italy no longer kept their exchange rates within the agreed margins. *Belgium* had provided that capital inflows could only be executed on the free market where the Belgian franc carried a premium. Previously market operators had had a choice to settle a number of capital receipts from abroad either in the free or in the official market and thus could select the most advantageous exchange rate. *Italy,* which was not confronted with large-scale inflows and thus did not have to fear an appreciation, decided to let the lira float freely. In *the Netherlands* the so-called O-circuit was established, a closed bond circuit which was intended to curtail foreign demand for Dutch guilder paper. In March 1972, as a complement to the reserve requirements for banks, Germany introduced the Bardepot, which called for a non-interest-bearing deposit of part of the proceeds of credits taken up by residents abroad.[10] In many countries there were accompanying measures to limit the growth of domestic liquidity as well, mainly in the form of reserve requirements.

In the currency turmoil of the beginning of the 1970s the *Benelux* countries actively tried to maintain a measure of exchange rate fixity within Europe. In August 1971 they had agreed on narrow fluctuation margins against each other's currencies in the hope that this would set an example which might be followed by other European countries.[11] These attempts to persuade the other member states to proceed to a joint floating of the EEC currencies failed because of diverging economic developments and policy goals, France wishing to maintain its parity.[12] Only in the framework of the *Smithsonian agreement*, where on 18 December 1971 new parities were fixed, implying a devaluation of the US dollar vis-à-vis the Deutsche mark of 13%, could the European countries reach agreement to establish an exchange arrangement, which would become known as the *snake*. Starting on 10 April 1972 the arrangement functioned as 'the snake in the tunnel', intra-European exchange rate fluctuations being limited to narrower margins than the fixed margins (the tunnel) vis-à-vis the US dollar. The establishment of the snake was the most concrete left-over of the recommendations of the Werner group. It was, however, to operate under conditions diametrically opposed to monetary integration, capital controls having been tightened considerably. Technically it was not possible to differentiate between intra and extra-EEC capital flows, despite weak attempts to this effect by France. The snake therefore was not so much a first step on the road to economic and monetary union as well as a defensive move to preserve a measure of internal exchange rate stability within Europe.

European countries had stumbled over one another to close the lock-gates. However, the plethora of measures did not end the exchange crisis. The imposition of capital controls was merely a *symptom* of the shaken confidence in the international monetary system, the seriousness of capital flight out of the United States and the resistance of European countries to a revaluation of their currencies. Actually, the dramatic events brought about an evolution in the thinking of European authorities concerning capital restrictions. Before this time, in some countries capital controls were regarded mainly as a complement to domestic financial and monetary policies, the Dutch monetary authorities providing a striking example of this attitude. In other countries the monetary authorities had been mainly concerned with the risk of speculative capital outflows and the consequent undue downward pressure on the exchange rate. Now, after the suspension of dollar convertibility, there was a new motive: to avoid *upward* pressure on the exchange rate. Appreciation of the European currencies vis-à-vis the US dollar would cause an unwarranted deterioration of their competitive positions, so it was felt. Capital controls were imposed out of fear of a loss of European jobs.

6.4 CAPITAL CONTROLS CODIFIED IN THE 1972 DIRECTIVE

The blow which the 1968 events in France had dealt to the process of capital liberalization in Europe had been magnified by the problems surrounding the collapse of the Bretton Woods system. The suspension of official interventions and the subsequent floating of the Deutsche mark and the guilder in May 1971 had raised serious problems for the Community. The temporary abolition of fixed exchange rates and the consequent disturbance of the common agricultural policy were undermining the foundations of the Common Market. The speculative capital movements were driving the member states apart. France, which already had an elaborate machinery for exchange control at its disposal, had tried to maintain the par system in combination with stringent exchange controls. Germany, which in the 1960s had been the staunchest supporter of capital liberalization, was not yet ready to revert this position, both in an ideological and a practical sense, but it was showing signs of weakening resolve.

In this changed atmosphere the *Commission*, in a complete *reverse* of its earlier drive for liberalization, had presented in June 1971 proposals which would require member states to have at their disposal the necessary instruments to ward off undesirable capital inflows.[13] These proposals followed inconclusive discussions in the Monetary Committee on measures to deal with the speculative flows, which disturbed the monetary situation in some member states, especially in Germany, and were hindering the pursuit of the steps provided for the first stage of economic and monetary union. An important motive for the Commission, which was decidedly against any move towards floating, was that capital controls might contain speculative movements and thus preserve the system of fixed exchange rates. Although most member states had the instruments alluded to in the Commission proposal at their disposal, it was indicative of the disarray within the Community that no quick agreement could be reached. All member states had taken different countermeasures in the face of speculative capital inflows. Another factor was that the German authorities among themselves were not yet clear as to what the appropriate response should be. Later in the year, after the suspension of dollar convertibility and the subsequent Smithsonian agreement, thoughts had developed. Consensus among the member states had grown that indeed measures were called for to curtail the speculative capital flows which continued to disrupt the exchange markets. It was acknowledged that the restrictive measures which individual member states had already taken detracted from the obligations under Article 67. The Monetary Committee, which held numerous debates on the monetary problems, concluded that the serious international disturbances and their repercussions on internal liquidity justified such a departure from the liberalization obligations of the Treaty.[14]

In a final discussion of the draft in the Monetary Committee it was decided to have regular discussions in the committee with a view to *coordinating* the exchange controls of member states. This was a far cry from the obligation, both under the First Capital Directive as well as under the committee's own statutes, to examine yearly whether existing exchange regulations could be abolished. The last such examination had taken place in December 1965. Afterwards it was relegated to oblivion. It suited the committee members quite well, so it seemed. The mood had changed dramatically.

In the directive, which ultimately was adopted by the Council on 21 March 1972,[15] the member states were obliged to have instruments available which could curtail undesirable capital flows and neutralize their effects on the domestic monetary situation. These instruments should include regulations governing *money market transactions by non-residents*. In order to neutralize the monetary effects of capital inflows, countries were obliged to have rules in place for the *net external position of credit institutions* as well as *minimum reserve ratios for holdings by non-residents*. Furthermore, a *general derogation* from the First Capital Directive was extended with respect to financial loans and credits by non-residents to residents.

Restrictions under the directive would have general application; there was no differentiation between capital movements within the EEC or with third countries. The *erga omnes principle* thus was upheld. Opinions had differed as to whether capital controls should discriminate between EEC member states and third countries. In the eyes of the Commission Europe should manifest itself as a bloc. In meetings of the Monetary Committee, the Commission representatives had taken the position that member states should harmonize their capital controls vis-à-vis third countries, while simultaneously liberalizing intra-EEC capital flows. Most other members opposed this, on the grounds of the erga omnes principle as well as for *technical reasons*. It was technically nearly impossible to distinguish between intra-EEC and extra-EEC capital flows. If at all possible, such discriminatory regulations could be easily circumvented. Moreover, the lack of consensus on policies within Europe triggered intra-EEC speculative capital movements with equal force.[16]

6.5 THE COLLAPSE OF THE BRETTON WOODS SYSTEM AND THE OIL CRISIS

In the beginning of 1973 yet another wave of speculative capital movements foreboded the final demise of the Bretton Woods system. On 22 January 1973 Italy, following the example of France, established a dual exchange market in order to stem considerable outflows of capital. Germany took further administrative measures to stop capital inflows, but they proved to be largely ineffective. Finally, it was decided to close the exchange markets. After a devaluation of the US dollar of 10% the exchange markets were reopened on 14 February. Within a fortnight the exchange markets had to be closed again after another tide of speculation. The failure of massive interventions by the Bundesbank to change the sentiment had convinced the German monetary authorities that continuation of the fixed parity would undermine monetary policy beyond repair and thus would threaten domestic price stability. The European countries decided to maintain the snake, but to abolish the fluctuation margins vis-à-vis the dollar (the 'tunnel'), thus marking the end of the Smithsonian agreement. On 19 March 1973 the exchange

TABLE 15

The snake arrangement.

% change vis-à-vis European central rate (UCME)		Germany	Belgium	Denmark	The Netherlands
1973	19 March	+3			
	29 June	+5.5			
	17 September				
					+5
1976	18 October	+2			
				–4	
1977	4 April				
				–3	
	29 August				
				–5	
1978	16 October	+4	+2		
					+2

Note: The United Kingdom withdrew from the arrangement on 23 June 1972. Italy withdrew on 13 February 1973. France withdrew on 21 June 1974, re-entered on 10 July 1975 and withdrew again on 15 March 1976. Norway and Sweden were temporarily associated with the snake arrangement.

markets reopened, marking the start of the era of *floating exchange rates*. At the same time controls on capital inflows in several Community countries were tightened further in order to prevent or mitigate upward movements of the exchange rate.

Later in the year the *oil crisis* erupted, causing a dramatic change in the fortunes of major currencies. Oil-importing industrial countries experienced a sharp deterioration in their terms of trade and consequently were faced with large ex ante deficits on the current account of their balances of payments. The oil crisis gave the final blow to the project of European economic and monetary union. The snake had been the only substantive, visible left-over of the attempts of the Werner Report towards monetary integration. Already at an early stage, in June 1972, the United Kingdom had been forced to leave the snake, as the first European country switching over to a full-fledged float (see Table 15). When in early 1974 France and Italy had to withdraw as well from the arrangement in the wake of the oil crisis, the aim of achieving a monetary union had to be regarded as completely illusory. Herewith, also the issue of capital liberalization was pushed into the background. In fact, there was widespread agreement that 'the regulation of capital flows by direct (restrictive) means is of great importance in the current situation in preventing, as far as possible, disequilibria occurring as a result of the differences in preference that funds from the oil producing countries seeking investment show for the currencies participating in the scheme (i.e. the snake agreement)'.[17]

Many countries quickly dismantled the controls on *inward* capital flows, which they had installed during the previous years, in order to facilitate the financing of the expected current account deficits. Furthermore, in countries with serious balance-of-payments problems capital controls on *outward* capital flows were intensified. An even more serious threat to the Common Market ensued when Italy, which was suffering from high inflation and rising balance-of-payments deficits, took restrictive measures in the trade field. Developments in Europe thus had taken a serious turn. Not only had capital movements been curtailed substantially, but with the Italian measures even the raison d'être of the Community – the free trade of goods – was jeopardized. European member states drifted apart and the *coordination* of economic and monetary policies remained *a dead letter* until the establishment of the European Monetary System in 1979.

Since the anchor that the fixed exchange rate system had provided was lost, a *new policy orientation* had to be chosen. In some countries the conviction had grown, partly stimulated by the vivid academic debate on the pros and cons of fixed and floating exchange regimes, that monetary policy under a floating regime, possibly supported by exchange restrictions, could be conducted in a more autonomous manner. But views differed about the primary aim of monetary policy and thus about the way this increased autonomy should be put to work. In Germany, monetary policy was set by a strong independent central bank which regarded the maintenance of price stability as the main target for monetary policy. This primary objective was written into law. But in countries like France and Italy monetary policy, being a shared responsibility of the Treasury and the central bank, was one of many instruments to support the general economic objectives of the government. These objectives typically concerned economic growth, the provision of employment as well as price stability. It was precisely the trade-off which was seen to exist between these objectives which detracted from the pursuit of price stability. The 1973 oil crisis had sparked off an exceptional severe cost push inflation and cyclical downturn which revealed inexorably the diverging policy priorities of European member states. For a time the ways of member states would part.

6.6 THE GERMAN EXPERIMENT WITH CAPITAL CONTROLS

Since the mid–1960s Germany had increasingly felt the impact of *capital inflows*. It had only reluctantly allowed the Deutsche mark to appreciate in 1969. When afterwards the tight monetary policies, aimed at curbing inflationary pressures, attracted speculative inflows, in turn blowing up the money

TABLE 16

The German capital account 1969–1974 in billions of Deutsche Marks.

	1969	1970	1971	1972	1973	1974
Current account	7.5	3.1	3.3	3.7	13.9	27.5
Long-term capital	−19.3	0.9	4.5	14.5	14.0	−6.0
- Securities	*−6.7*	*1.2*	*5.1*	*14.6*	*6.3*	*−2.4*
- Other	*−12.6*	*−0.3*	*−0.6*	*−0.1*	*7.7*	*−3.6*
Short-term capital	4.3	16.2	3.3	−6.2	−3.6	−22.2
Net errors and omissions	−3.1	1.8	5.7	2.6	1.0	−1.2
Official reserves	−10.6	22.0	16.8	14.6	25.3	−1.9

Source: International Financial Statistics, IMF.

supply which the Bundesbank precisely tried to control, it was clear that something had to give. Initially the choice was being seen as between letting the exchange rate appreciate, either through a revaluation or by a float, and the establishment of exchange controls. When in 1971 it was decided to rely primarily on an appreciation of the exchange rate and to take only indirect control measures, this still could be regarded as a victory of those officials who believed in the free functioning of markets. The market orientation of the post-war German administrations and the abstinence from direct controls had contributed to the *Wirtschaftswunder*. There was great reluctance, especially in the Ministry of Economic Affairs, to throw this successful legacy overboard.

When in mid–1972 there was a *replay of events* with domestic monetary stability being undermined by another wave of capital inflows, prompted by the withdrawal of sterling from the snake, the free-marketeers were outnumbered by the proponents of taking measures to curb the inflows. Now the German cabinet after a heated debate decided to support Bundesbank president Klasen in his demand for the imposition of further direct capital controls. Minister Schiller, who was in favour of introducing a common float of the European currencies vis-à-vis the US dollar, was outvoted. This clash caused the downfall of 'super' minister Schiller who was to be succeeded by Helmut Schmidt, also combining the economics and finance portfolios. The German cabinet seemed to be convinced by the reasoning of the Bundesbank that these controls would be able to stem the inflows and thus stabilize the exchange rate. This was all the more welcome because the cabinet feared the fall-out of a possible loss of competitiveness on the parliamentary elections which were to be held at the end of 1972.

If the measures taken up till then to curb inflows could with some indulgence be regarded as still being of a *market-oriented nature* – inflows not

TABLE 17

German capital control measures 1970–1974.

April 1970	Reactivation of a minimum reserve requirement of 30 per cent on the growth of external liabilities of banks.
May 1971	Prohibition of payment of interest on bank deposits of non-residents and requirement of prior authorization for all purchases by non-residents of German money market paper.
March 1972	Imposition of a cash reserve requirement ('Bardepot') of 40 per cent for liabilities incurred vis-à-vis non-residents. Raising of the reserve requirement on the growth of external bank liabilities to 40 per cent.
July 1972	Requirement of prior authorization for all purchases by non-residents of domestic fixed-interest securities. Raising of the Bardepot to 50 per cent and of the minimum reserve requirement to 60 per cent.
February 1973	Extension of the prior authorization requirements to all types of credit instruments, such as securities and mutual fund shares, and borrowing above DM 50,000.
June 1973	Further tightening of the Bardepot and minimum reserve requirements.
January 1974	Abolition of the marginal reserve requirement.
February 1974	Reduction of the Bardepot to 20 per cent and abolition of authorization requirements for credit instruments other than domestic fixed-interest securities with a maturity of less than 4 years.
September 1974	Abolition of the Bardepot provisions.

being forbidden, but merely being made more expensive –, now a threshold was passed (see Table 17). Further measures would by necessity have a *dirigistic character* and would imply an outright ban on certain categories of capital inflows. The effectiveness of the Bardepot, introduced in March 1972, was eroding through the diversion to other instruments without Bardepot provisions. In order to close the loopholes, the sale of fixed-interest bonds denominated in Deutsche marks to non-residents was restricted. A similar ban had already been imposed by Switzerland and it was feared that speculators now would concentrate on Germany. Later on the restrictions needed further tightening because new loopholes were continuously found and actively exploited. After the transition to the floating rate regime Germany maintained its capital restrictions. In a short period Germany had moved from a situation in which there were almost no controls (in the late 1960s) to a situation by the middle of 1973 where as regards capital inflows one of the most extensive sets of restrictions was operated.

Initially, the main German motive had been to avoid an undue appreciation of the exchange rate. At a later stage, the wish to insulate domestic monetary developments from the outside world became the preponderant objective. Domestic interest rates were raised to unprecedented levels in order to wring out inflationary tendencies (see Figure 11). Capital controls were aimed at

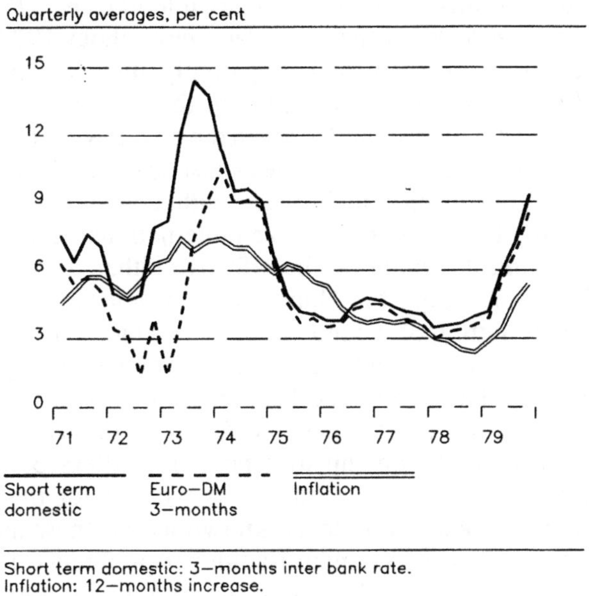

Fig. 11. German interest rates 1971–1979.

preventing short-term inflows from undermining these stabilization efforts. All these measures, however, were not capable of resisting speculation at times of currency unrest. The restrictions were evaded on a large scale. The so-called *'Koffergeschäfte'* (illegal physical cross-border transactions) for the year 1973 were estimated at DM 4 billion and the illegal taking-up of credit abroad at DM 7 billion.[18] Although measures were taken to curtail shifts in leads and lags, their effect was limited because of the large impact of only minor shifts in payment patterns, which could not be controlled. The authorities were particularly discouraged that ever more measures were needed to close unrestricted channels and other loopholes. The Bundesbank initially relied on cooperative behaviour of the commercial banks.[19] In this respect it was to be disappointed. German industry and the commercial banks did not cooperate in accordance with the spirit of the capital control measures, but were actively engaged in the search for loopholes.

Within a short period the *Bundesbank* reversed its attitude with respect to capital controls. Whereas in 1971 the central bank had actively encouraged the government to impose capital controls, in the course of 1973 the Bundesbank had come to the conclusion that these controls did not significantly influence the size of capital inflows in the face of the high level of German interest rates relative to US interest rates. Against purely speculative capital movements restrictive measures were ineffective. In a system of floating exchange rates, where the Bundesbank was freed from the obligation to intervene in support of the US dollar, they could be only of secondary importance.[20] The government nevertheless decided to keep them in place throughout 1973, proving the stickiness of controls once imposed. Apparently, there was a fear that their release would precipitate the appreciation of the Deutsche mark. However, they were to a large extent dismantled when the oil crisis changed the fortunes of the European currencies, including the Deutsche mark. Only minor controls on short-term inflows were kept in place with a view to discouraging the development of the Deutsche mark into an international reserve currency. In this respect the controls would not be effective either, as will be discussed further in Chapter 7. Soon, the Bundesbank developed its own range of instruments for the setting of monetary policy in a medium-term framework. In 1974 it announced a *target* for the growth of the monetary aggregate (central bank money) which had shown the best correlation in the transmission to inflation and had shown a stable demand function. Interest rates were used to influence monetary growth, up to a point regardless of the short-term consequences for the domestic economy as well as for the neighbouring countries. This new focus came to be known as the 'new assignment'. In the course of the 1970s the German traditional preference for freedom of capital movements again would come to the fore. Its brief experimentation with direct capital controls had been a dramatic failure.[21]

6.7 THE FRENCH RESPONSE TO THE CURRENCY TURMOIL

France had supplemented its extensive exchange control system with restrictions on *inflows* in the wake of the dollar crisis. During 1972, when the exchange markets were relatively calm, some control measures were suspended, only to be reintroduced with greater force in 1973, when a new bout of speculative inflows occurred. The exchange controls were complemented inter alia through the introduction of a marginal cash reserve of 100% on incremental French franc deposits of non-residents.[22] As in Germany, the controls were largely ineffective in warding off speculators as inflows continued to pour in and to swell the official reserves of the Banque de France.[23] However, it was considered that in their absence the situation might have even been worse, and the controls were tightened further after the collapse of the Bretton Woods system in order to prevent an excessive appreciation of the French franc. With the oil shock later in the year there was yet another change in the fortunes of the French franc. The prospect of sizeable balance-of-payments deficits exerted downward pressure on the exchange rate and immediately led to a plethora of further controls on capital *outflows*. The authorities believed that these controls were more effective than those on inflows. This discrepancy was partly explained by the fact that in outflow crises it was mainly residents who should be kept under control – the French franc not being a widely held international reserve asset – whereas in inflow

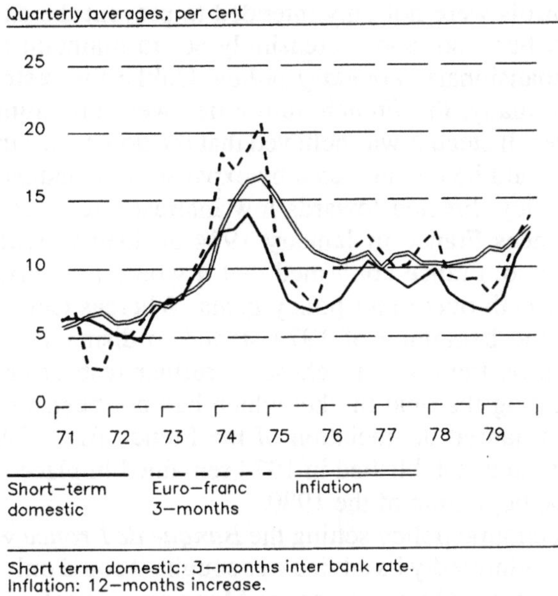

Fig. 12. **French interest rates 1971–1979.**

TABLE 18

The French capital account 1969–1974 in billions of French francs.

	1969	1970	1971	1972	1973	1974
Current account	-8.7	-1.1	0.9	-0.5	6.4	-18.6
Long-term capital	-1.6	0.6	0.1	-3.3	-11.0	-1.3
- Securities	*0.4*	*1.5*	*1.3*	*0.8*	*-3.0*	*-1.0*
- Other	*-2.1*	*-1.0*	*-1.2*	*-4.0*	*-8.0*	*-0.2*
Short-term capital	4.4	8.6	14.4	6.7	-3.0	12.6
Net errors and omissions	0.5	2.0	2.8	5.2	-0.8	5.5
Official reserves	-5.4	10.1	18.2	8.1	-8.4	-1.7

Source: International Financial Statistics, IMF.

crises the whole outside world jumped on the French franc. A contributing factor was that French banks were responsible for proper execution of the exchange control measures and that a large control apparatus was available. Unlike the private German commercial banks, which were prepared to help clients circumvent controls, the French banks stood under firm government control and were more compliant with the rules.

The capital controls were not only intended to prevent the exchange rate from depreciating, but also, and increasingly so, to maintain a margin of manoeuvre for expansionary *monetary policy.* Unlike the restrictive monetary stance in Germany, the French authorities were unwilling to follow deflationary policies. Instead it was believed that the downward impact of the rise of oil prices should be counteracted by expansionary budgetary policies and a monetary policy directed towards low interest rates (see Figure 12). In these circumstances France in January 1974 decided to withdraw from the snake. In doing so, France confirmed that it would give priority to fostering economic growth over other policy goals. Whereas Germany and the Netherlands from the beginning of 1974 started to dismantle their capital restrictions, France on the contrary chose to further restrict capital movements while abolishing the dual market which had not been very effective. Nevertheless, a substantial depreciation of the French franc followed. The extensive control system established in 1974 remained in place more or less unchanged until the beginning of the 1980s.

In the French economic policy setting the *Banque de France* was subordinated and, although admittedly its advice was sought, it could only execute the monetary policy as decided by the Treasury. Monetary control was not directed towards restriction of the growth of the monetary aggregates, but rather continued to be directed to the provision of cheap credit to targeted sectors of the economy. The crisis situation at home, with substantial inflationary pressure, resulted in the mothballing of the earlier monetary reform plans of Marjolin, Sadrin and Wormser.[24] Although some elements were implemented in the beginning of the 1970s, giving greater room for market influences on interest rates, the oil shock provoked a reorientation of monetary policy. In fact a step backwards was taken by reverting to the use of direct instruments, such as the *encadrement du crédit*, combining credit controls with different credit windows for chosen industrial sectors. There was reluctance to use increases in interest rates as an instrument to curb monetary growth, also since the subsidized, selective credits were not very sensitive to changes in interest rates. As a substitute, capital controls were used to insulate domestic interest rates from those prevailing in Germany or the United States. France re-entered the snake arrangement in 1975 but the general reluctance to follow restrictive monetary policies in case of need forced France again out of the snake. French policies generated a relatively high inflation rate and consequently downward pressure on the exchange rate. The use of differentiated credit ceilings made the monetary control system prone to political pressure from influence groups, which were all the more difficult to resist because institutional opposition was lacking in the absence of an independent central bank.[25]

For the whole period of the 1973 oil crisis until the end of the 1970s French real interest rates were negative (see Figure 12). In an attempt to boost confidence – both internally as well as externally – the Banque de

TABLE 19

Monetary targets in France and Germany.

In %	France Target	France Outcome	Germany Target	Germany Outcome
1975	·	·	±8	10
1976	·	·	8	9
1977	12.5	13.8	8	9
1978	12	12.2	8	11
1979	11	14.4	6–9	6
1980	11	9.8	5–8	5
1981	10	11.4	4–7	4
1982	9	11.5	4–7	6
1983	12.5–13.5	11.0	4–7	7

Target: France – M2; Germany: Zentralbankgeldmenge.

TABLE 20

French and German economic performance compared.

	1972–1975		1976–1979		1980–1983	
	France	Germany	France	Germany	France	Germany
Average in %						
Inflation rate	10.9	6.4	10.9	3.7	13.5	5.1
GDP growth rate	2.7	1.3	3.5	3.8	1.5	0.5
Average in % GDP						
Current account	0.0	1.5	0.3	0.6	–1.1	–0.2
Fiscal deficit	–0.2	–1.6	–1.1	–2.7	–2.0	-3.1

Fiscal deficit: Net lending general government.

France followed the example of the Bundesbank in publishing *monetary targets*, beginning in 1977. However, without any change in the conduct of monetary policy these targets were set much higher than in Germany and generally were overshot (see Table 19).

From 1976 until 1979 French annual money growth on average was 13.5%, domestic credit expansion nearly 12%, inflation 11% and the depreciation of the French franc vis-à-vis the Deutsche mark ran at an annual rate of 7% (see Table 20).

TABLE 21

Spreads between official and financial exchange rates (May 1971-March 1974).

%	Maximum	Mean spread	Standard deviation
Belgium	2.5	0.04	0.67
France	5.5	–0.46	2.35
Italy	7.5	3.9	2.08

Source: Marion (1994), p. 220.
Note: France operated a dual market from August 1971 to March 1974, Italy from January 1973 to March 1974.

6.8 ITALY: AN ECONOMY UNDER SIEGE

Initially Italy was less afflicted by the international monetary turbulence in the beginning of the 1970s. Speculative capital inflows seeking refuge from the US dollar bypassed the Italian economy, which unlike most other continental European countries was not considered to be a safe haven. In the face of increasing domestic political instability, which had negative repercussions on the economy, the lira itself came under severe downward pressure, outflows taking the form of illegal export of lira bank notes. Already in 1970 measures had been taken to counter such outflows, which ran in the order of $ 2 billion per year, and these measures were continually tightened. In January 1973 the authorities introduced a *dual market,* following the earlier example of France, in an attempt to preserve the nearly depleted official reserves, while maintaining direct controls. As in France, there were additional considerations, in particular the wish to shield the domestic economy as much as possible from the turmoil on the exchange markets. When in February also the commercial lira was allowed to float an important reason was 'to avoid jeopardising the recovery of the economy which was just getting under way.'[26]

In the highly indexed economy the subsequent depreciation of the lira led to mounting inflation and further downward pressure. The Italian economy was tumbling down in an inflation-depreciation spiral. Mid–1973 an *emergency EEC loan* was taken-up, after extensive discussions in the Monetary Committee, which was accompanied by a further tightening of exchange controls and monetary policy. At the same time a third parallel market developed for lira bank notes – in addition to the commercial and financial lira – where the lira was traded at a discount of on average 4% below the financial rate. Capital outflows in the form of bank notes, partly disguised as fictitious tourism expenses, had increased tremendously. The dual market was soon abolished because cross operations occurred as soon as the gap between the commercial and financial rates widened. The exchange rate differentials were

TABLE 22

Italy: economic indicators 1973–1979.

In per cent	1973	1974	1975	1976	1977	1978	1979
Inflation rate	10.9	18.5	17.1	17.1	18.1	12.0	14.8
GDP growth rate	7.0	5.5	–2.7	6.3	3.7	3.7	6.1
% of GDP							
Current account	–1.5	–4.3	–0.2	–1.5	1.0	2.1	1.6
Government deficit	–8.3	–7.3	–11.9	–8.5	–10.5	–13.5	–9.8

Source: International Financial Statistics, IMF.

much larger than those in Belgium or France (see Table 21) and attracted another category of offenders, namely bounty hunters who were not so much interested in exporting capital as in collecting the premium. Whereas in 1971 the Banca d'Italia still had professed great confidence in the effectiveness of exchange controls, it now had to acknowledge that 'the experience of 1973 emphasized the difficulty of controlling capital movements with administrative regulations (...) when, given the country's general economic situation, larger depreciations are expected.'[27] Together with France, Italy was forced to leave the snake arrangement in the beginning of 1974. The authorities had put their trust in vain in the protective powers of capital controls.

Later in 1974 in the light of a serious *deterioration of the trade balance* (see Table 22) even more drastic steps were taken. A temporary non-interest-bearing deposit of 50% was required on certain imports. Nearly half of imports being affected, this had a price raising effect of 3 to 4% – still marginal as compared to the price and exchange rate fluctuations –, but more importantly it decreased bank liquidity. The measure went against the essence of the EEC, but Italy's claim that it was taken on the grounds of the clause d'urgence of Article 109 was accepted by the Commission. The Commission felt it had no choice in doing so in the rather dramatic circumstances, where 'the international and domestic press were alike convinced that bankruptcy was the inevitable outcome and only speculated as to when it would happen', and where there was no possibility of access to the international capital markets because of the already high external indebtedness.[28]

Despite financial assistance provided by the EEC and by the IMF, as well as the continued application of tight exchange controls, the economic environment deteriorated further until in the beginning of 1976 an even more serious *lira crisis* erupted. Control of domestic liquidity creation was lacking, partly due to budget deficits running in the order of 10% of gdp, providing ample liquidity for speculative movements against the currency, despite tight controls. The situation worsened so dramatically that the foreign exchange market had to be closed for forty days. In the meantime restrictions were tightened, but when the market reopened on 1 March 1976 there was a sharp drop in the exchange rate. In these circumstances emergency measures were taken, some of them strongly condemned by the international community, which merely provided short breathing spaces.[29] The Banca d'Italia and the Foreign Exchange Office were 'faced with the unpleasant task of presiding over a process which, as far as the management of monetary and foreign exchange flows is concerned, is coming to resemble an economy under siege'.[30] When finally decisive fundamental measures were taken, supported by an IMF program, the external situation started to improve quickly. In the course of 1977 the exchange restrictions gradually were relaxed. The central bank had become exasperated by the continuous operation of exchange controls. Despite the multitude of exchange restrictions, residents apparently could rather easily, albeit at some cost, bring capital out of the country through illegal means. These outflows were motivated both by the distrust in the economic and political situation and by fiscal considerations. The restrictions were *ineffective* remedies which temporarily may have softened the problems, but in doing so did not contribute to real solutions, particularly as some restrictions were maintained for a prolonged period of time. They most likely postponed such solutions. As in France, monetary policy was traditionally directed towards the ample provision of liquidity, given the underdeveloped domestic capital market, and was characterized by reluctance to raise interest rates in view of the wish to foster economic growth and the need to finance burgeoning fiscal deficits. Continued easy monetary policies and a selective credit policy for an increasing number of so-called prioritary sectors, could only lead to inflation, monetary financing of budget deficits and capital flight. In the end, of course, the wish to maintain low interest rates could not be realized either. Its unorthodox loose budgetary and monetary policies, covered up by exchange controls, had brought Italy to the brink of bankruptcy.

6.9 THE NETHERLANDS: LIBERALIZATION GAINING PACE

When in May 1971 the guilder, together with the Deutsche mark, had been allowed to float, an important consideration had been that it was impossible to introduce at short notice sufficiently adequate exchange controls to discourage further capital inflows. Preparations for such controls in case of need were completed when on 15 August 1971 the dollar convertibility was suspended. The so-called *O-circuit* was established, a closed bond circuit with similar characteristics as the French devises-titres market and the British investment currency market, but unlike these markets not aiming at controling capital outflows but rather intended to curtail foreign demand for Dutch guilder paper (see Figure 13). Subsequently further restrictions were enacted, culminating in the imposition in March 1973 of a negative interest rate on non-resident accounts.[31]

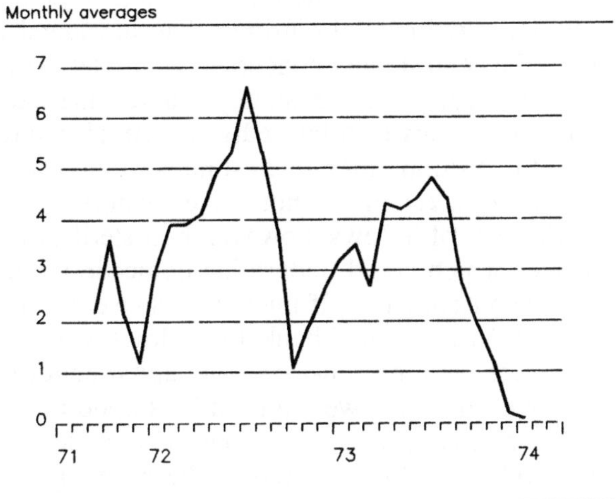

Fig. 13. The Netherlands 0-guilder premium 1971–1974.

Just as these events had influenced the attitudes towards capital restrictions in all European countries, they constituted an *evolution* in the thinking of the Dutch authorities. Before this time, exchange controls had been regarded mainly as a complement to domestic financial and monetary policies. Now there was a new additional motive: as other countries the Dutch wished to avoid an undue appreciation of the exchange rate of the guilder and thus an unwarranted deterioration of the competitive position.

The evolution in thinking was reflected in the subsequent drafts of *the law on external financial relations,* which every time seemed to be overtaken by events. A first draft of this law, which was to replace the Exchange Control Decree (Deviezenbesluit) of 1945, had been presented in 1967, envisaging a single law which gave only limited powers to impose capital controls. Then, 'after each wave of exchange unrest the draft, which had not yet been sent to parliament, was reviewed with an eye to whether the authorities would have been able to handle the situation. Each time this led to additions'.[32] Finally a draft law was submitted to parliament on 4 July 1972. The timing, however, was rather unfortunate because this submission followed the recent adoption of the 1972 Directive. When in 1973 the system of fixed exchange rates disintegrated beyond repair, it was considered questionable whether it would be wise policy to limit the powers of the authorities to impose restrictions. The draft law was withdrawn. For a resumption of the liberalization drive the Dutch authorities assumed that two conditions had to be fulfilled: the restoration of a well-functioning international monetary system and a reasonable degree of consistency between the economic and monetary policies of the major countries.

The Netherlands was of the opinion that *monetary policy* was better equipped to check undesired capital outflows than unwanted inflows. If in the case of outflows the central bank concerned would let the resulting contraction work its way through to the money market, the capital outflows inevitably would be slowed down. Admittedly, this could lead to a disorderly money market or, if the resulting high interest rates would last long, undesirable cyclical consequences. Yet, in the short run exchange rate considerations should prevail. In the case of inflows, however, non-sterilization would lead to lower interest rates which could undermine domestic monetary stability and have inflationary consequences. If interventions were sterilized through mopping-up operations by the central bank, the inflows would only continue, so it was felt. Yet, there were no illusions that capital controls were useful instruments in the long run. They were a third-best option in circumstances of extreme international divergences in economic and monetary policies. But their imposition would not help to overcome these divergences and might even perpetuate them.

Exchange controls were increasingly seen as having important *drawbacks* both for the Dutch economy and for the effective functioning of the monetary authorities. Among these drawbacks the tendency of restrictions to spread to other transactions figured prominently. In the Dutch case the ban on borrowing abroad by residents soon had to be extended to other categories, up to the point that this was hindering genuine direct investment flows.[33] Another drawback was that the commercial banks, which initially were compliant, as in Germany were developing loopholes for their clients.[34] This involved the risk of overburdening the good relationship between the banks and the monetary authorities. Finally, there was great reluctance on the part of the Nederlandsche Bank, which was entrusted with the execution of the capital controls, to expand the needed technical apparatus.

After the turmoil had somewhat subsided the Dutch authorities were quick to ease restrictions. The closed bond circuit was abolished on 1 February 1974, when the premiums, which in earlier years had risen as high as 6.5 percent, had returned to virtually nil. Further relaxations came about in the following years and on 26 January 1977 then Minister of Finance Duisenberg presented a somewhat amended bill on external financial relations to parliament, resuming the proposal to change to a positive system. The negative system had become so complex that the number of Bank staff who knew their way in the maze of regulations gradually were depleted. Pending parliamentary approval of the bill, it was decided to move to a de facto *positive system* in September 1977. At the same time, issues of securities and loans on the domestic capital market by non-residents were permitted, provided they would take their place in the queue, like domestic issuers. However, restrictions on capital inflows were maintained in order to prevent the prevailing domestic credit restrictions, introduced at the beginning of 1977, from being frustrated. In the following years these restrictions were gradually relaxed when the current account of the balance of payments began to show a deficit. The policy of the Nederlandsche Bank, rightly termed 'moderately monetarist' – the money supply being a vital but not the only policy variable – actually was characterized by considerable fine-tuning: in view of the current account deficit domestic credit restrictions were applied, complemented by restrictions on short-term capital inflows; at the same time medium and long-term capital inflows were liberalized in order to facilitate the financing of the same current account deficit. The bill on external financial relations eventually was adopted on 28 May 1980, more than twenty years after the first legal work had been initiated, and took effect on 1 May 1981.[35] All these years the authorizations were based on the Exchange Control Decree of 1945, as a living monument to prove the stickiness of capital restrictions.

6.10 COMPARISON OF THE DUTCH AND FRENCH ATTITUDES

In the course of the 1970s the Dutch attitude towards capital controls gradually evolved in a pragmatic manner. As we have discussed earlier, there were certain *similarities* between the French and the Dutch control system and range of monetary instruments. In the first decade of the EEC France and the Netherlands were allies in their defence of capital controls. Both countries applied controls to inflows as well to outflows. Both countries relied on direct credit controls as a primary monetary instrument. But on closer scrutiny there were important *differences,* which became more evident in the course of the 1970s as the countries drifted apart as regards policy formulation. Of course, there was first a difference of *gradation:* the French controls on capital outflows were far more extensive than the Dutch controls. So was the technical apparatus. The foreign exchange regulations department in the Nederlandsche Bank numbered in the mid–1970s a staff of only a dozen persons, whereas in the case of France hundreds of civil servants were involved. There was also an important difference in *vision.* The French authorities considered restrictions on outflows more effective than those on inflows, whereas in the Netherlands it was rather the reverse. The Dutch authorities were convinced that monetary policy was better capable of checking capital outflows than inflows. This implied that the Netherlands primarily utilized capital controls if monetary policy could not be effective in warding off capital movements, viz. in support of restrictive monetary policies. In France, on the other hand, capital controls precisely were intended to avoid the deployment of monetary instruments, i.e. the raising of interest rates to ward off outflows.

In essence, the difference between the Dutch and the French attitude regarding capital controls boiled down to a differing degree of willingness to utilize the *interest rate* in order to defend the exchange rate. In the course of the 1970s the Netherlands visibly became more liberalized as opposed to the French financial and monetary system. The Netherlands and France had been close allies in various policy areas especially in the international monetary arena, e.g. in their defence of the fixed rate system and their orthodox position vis-à-vis gold, as well as their rather interventionist attitude in economic and financial matters. But in the inflationary climate of the 1970s the Netherlands aligned itself increasingly with Germany, which was fighting inflation by orthodox macro-economic means.

6.11 THE BELGIAN-LUXEMBOURG DUAL MARKET

The rather satisfactory operation of the Belgian dual market had prompted other member states to experiment with such a system as well. The dual market was considered by the authorities as a *useful instrument* because it safeguarded the official exchange rate and the official reserves against speculative capital flows, while at the same time upholding the notion of freedom of capital movements. The IMF staff consistently supported the practice in its Article IV consultations with Belgium, albeit each time for a period of a year. Although the dual market in theory did not obstruct the free movement of capital, the latter in practice was hampered by rather far-reaching *domestic regulations*. The domestic financial markets were characterized by mutual partitioning (the so-called 'cloisonnement'), partially inspired by the wish to secure the provision of credit to the government. The parastatal Commission Bancaire regulated the issues on the domestic capital market; in practice the amount of foreign issues, which also needed the permission of the Ministry of Finance, had been negligible. In his decision the Minister could take into consideration the vital national interests. Like France, the Belgian authorities furthermore discouraged the take-over of domestic firms by non-residents. Approval procedures had been established in 1967 when Petrofina was threatened by a US take-over, in contravention of the liberalization obligations. Finally the local securities market was lacking in depth and therefore was not attractive to foreign investors. In sum, there were practical and administrative obstacles which prevented large cross-border capital flows.

The National Bank of Belgium was strongly supportive of the dual market system. From time to time it intervened in the free market, as the Banque de France did when it operated a dual market system. After the 1960 Congo crisis, the system had only briefly come under strains in 1969 when the devaluation of the French franc had triggered market expectations of a devaluation of the Belgian franc as well. Although the dual market system may have played a role in repulsing both attacks, more probably it was the fundamentally strong current account position of Belgium, consistently in surplus, which convinced the markets that a change in the official rate would be unwarranted.[36] The dual system had the advantage that in principle it could deal not only with speculative outflows but also with inflows, without changing administrative regulations. But in the exchange turmoil in the beginning of the 1970s inflows

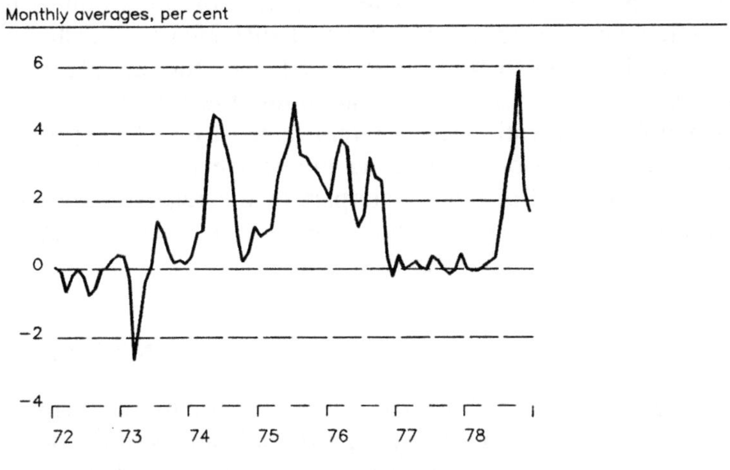

Difference between free and official exchange rate of the Belgian franc.
Source: BIS.

Fig. 14. The Belgian dual market 1972–1978.

strained the system, the financial Belgian franc being for a time stronger than the commercial one. It was eventually impossible to operate the system without the introduction of quite far-reaching *further controls*.[37] Also the dual market system itself was tinkered with. Before May 1971 several capital transactions could be executed both on the free and the official market, to the effect that the system provided exclusively a weapon against capital flight but offered no protection against speculative inflows. After a change in the exchange regulations all links between the two markets were severed through the prohibition of all transfers between the markets. The Belgian and Luxembourg authorities all along maintained that the abolition of the dual market would necessitate recourse to other control techniques which not necessarily would imply an improvement. Nevertheless, there was a certain measure of *surprise* among other member states that Belgium in the era of floating exchange rates maintained the dual market. All other EEC countries, which had experimented with multiple exchange rates, abolished them rather soon. The advantages for the Belgian and Luxembourg authorities apparently outweighed the disadvantages. Among the latter: a control apparatus was needed, just as for direct exchange control; changes in the financial franc rate could provide undesirable signals which could amplify pressures on the official exchange rate; the effectiveness of monetary policy could be reduced, in so far as an increase in official interest rates in order to support the exchange rate could lead to a reflow on the free market rather than to support of the official rate.

In sum, the dual market system, like other types of capital control measures, was not effective in warding off large and sustained capital flows in crisis situations. It then had to be supplemented with further measures, which, however, were likewise incapable of stemming the speculative tide. In quiet times, when the differential was not very large, it may have provided some protective shield, possibly preventing minor speculative movements from running out of hand. But the counterpart of the relative *external freedom* of the double market system in quiet times was a rather heavy *domestic regulation* of the financial system in Belgium.

6.12 EUROPEAN INTEGRATION AT A STANDSTILL

The European countries had drifted apart. Each country had tried to find its own way in the disarray caused by the external shocks of the demise of the Bretton Woods system and the oil crisis. Capital controls were utilized in varying intensity to insulate the domestic economy from those shocks, with very little success. The *new members* of the EEC, Denmark, Ireland and the United Kingdom which had joined on 1 January 1973, did not provide any additional stimulus towards coordination or liberalization. On the contrary, they had adhered to the EEC more because of its Common Market aspect than because of further integration ideals. Moreover, they all had a history of extensive exchange control, which in practice was condoned by the Commission.[38] Therefore, the balance between liberal and restrictive countries initially swayed in favour of the latter.

Attempts were made to give body to the need to coordinate economic policies. In 1974 a *Council Decision on the attainment of a high degree of convergence of economic policies* was adopted, but its procedures were rather weak. There was no pressure on member states to follow the guidelines with respect to budgetary policies. As regards capital controls there was no serious discussion in the Monetary Committee on a common European approach.[39] Some countries on an individual basis gradually relaxed controls, but in other countries the controls increasingly were considered to be a fact of life.

From the mid–1970s onwards the lack of policy consensus within the Community stood in the way of progress towards economic and monetary integration. The Werner Report was written against the comfortable background of a relatively long period of economic growth and price stability. Budgets in the Community were in approximate balance and *government debt* at the end of the 1960s averaged less than 30% of gdp. By contrast, the 1970s saw the average *inflation rate* in the Community rise to double digit figures and government debt to well over 40% of gdp (see Figure 15 and Table 23). In the face of such serious divergences from inflation-free sustainable growth the European mechanisms of coordination were powerless.

A new initiative was needed. Diverging economic policies resulted in exchange rate instability, which formed an obstacle to further European inte-

TABLE 23

Fiscal imbalances in the EEC as a percentage of GDP.

	1971	1972	1973	1974	1975	1976	1977	1978	1979
Fiscal deficit									
weighted average	−1.2	−1.7	−0.9	−2.0	−5.2	−3.7	- 3.0	−3.7	−3.5
Government debt									
weighted average	30	31	35	34	38	40	41	42	42
average	36	36	37	37	39	41	42	43	45

Note: Fiscal deficit – net lending (+) or net borrowing (–) of general government; average of actual EEC member states; European Economy no 58, European Commission. Government debt – gross public debt; OECD Economic Outlook 55.

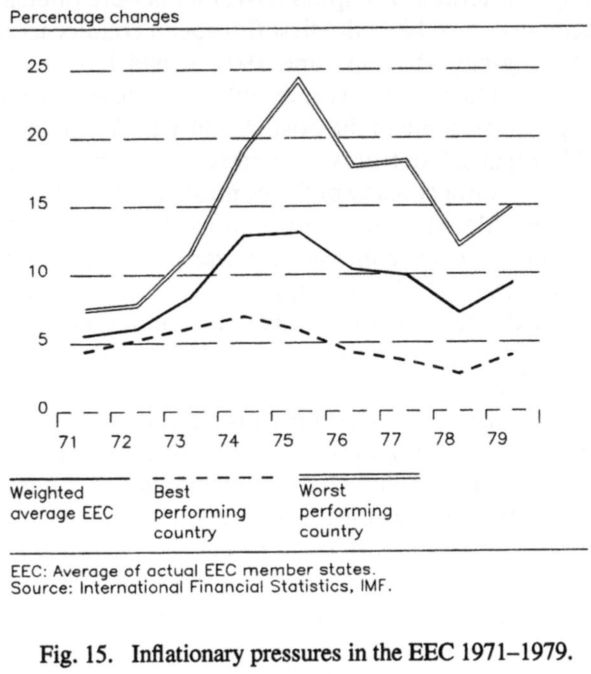

Fig. 15. Inflationary pressures in the EEC 1971–1979.

gration. The masterplan of the French president Valéry Giscard d'Estaing and the German chancellor Helmut Schmidt to establish a *European Monetary System,* proposed in 1978, was precisely intended to redirect Europe on the path of cooperation. It envisaged the establishment of a zone of monetary stability. In view of the major macro-economic derailments of the 1970s this was an ambitious goal, which provided an important signal that European countries again wished to grow towards one another. In the resolution, establishing the EMS, there was no reference to capital liberalization. This absence was telling for the priority of member states. Restoration of stable exchange rates ranked first and foremost. The liberalization of capital movements was pushed in the background. In the meantime, however, an important development took place in the United Kingdom, which while not taking part in the EMS embarked on a new economic approach which would impart a new impetus to the goal of capital liberalization.

6.13 THE LIBERALIZATION IN THE UNITED KINGDOM

The dismal events of the 1970s reached a major *turning point* when the newly elected Thatcher government in the United Kingdom came into power. After having tested the water with some relaxations of exchange control, in October 1979 all remaining restrictions on capital movements were lifted at one stroke.

The United Kingdom had been the first European country to adopt a floating exchange rate regime when in June 1972 it had left the snake after a membership which had lasted only two months. Although with the transition to floating the original rationale of the post-World War II capital controls, codified in the 1947 Exchange Control Act, namely to preserve foreign exchange reserves, was lost, the authorities kept the controls in place.[40] In his memoirs Nigel Lawson notes: 'People had lived with exchange control for so long that it was not in any real sense an issue: it was a fact of life.'[41] There was always the fear that their abolition might cause a run on the pound, with serious political backlashes, and there was thus a preference for maintaining the status quo.

When the United Kingdom had become a member of the EEC on 1 January 1973 a number of *transitional provisions* were agreed which provided time to adjust domestic policies and regulations. With respect to capital movements the Treaty of Accession provided that the liberalization under the Capital Directives could be postponed until 1 January 1975 in the case of direct investment, and until 1 July 1975 for other categories of capital movements in the personal sphere. However, in 1975 the United Kingdom experienced large balance-of-payments deficits and asked for an exemption from the entry terms. Also with respect to other aspects of the Community the United Kingdom asked for delays and in March 1975 Prime Minister Harold Wilson, when reporting to the House of Commons on these 'renegotiations' with the EEC, said that the United Kingdom would avail itself of the Treaty safeguard clauses to protect the balance of payments from capital outflows. The Commission granted a delay for one year on the basis of the provisions of Article 108.3.[42] These delays had to be repeated several times, since the United Kingdom after the sterling crisis of November 1976 had if anything further tightened its exchange controls. In the discussions in the Monetary Committee these measures routinely were approved, although recommendations were given for a tightening of monetary and fiscal policy. Afterwards some relaxations were carried through.

The UK economic performance in the 1970s continued to be mediocre as the economy under the hoped-for autonomy for domestic monetary and fiscal policy under the system of floating rates had run aground. Stimulative policies had conjured up inflationary forces and led to repeated attacks on the exchange rate. The net result had been *stop-go policies* which had frightened off both domestic and foreign investors. The Conservative government was elected in 1979 after a 'winter of discontent' when major strikes in the public sector, lasting over six weeks, had paralysed the country. The ideological platform of the incoming government assigned a high priority to deregulation and the unhampered free functioning of the markets. Capital liberalization fitted in well with this platform. The abolition of exchange controls was a sign of belief in economic potential and a reflection of increased self-confidence and economic strength. However, the decisive factor was *oil.* The prospect of a substantial improvement in the current account because of oil proceeds had triggered fears of a disproportionate appreciation of the pound sterling exchange rate. This would further hurt the weak non-oil industrial base in the United Kingdom. A relaxation of exchange controls was expected to cause capital outflows because of the pent-up demand for foreign assets by residents.[43] This would help to dampen the upward pressure on the exchange rate.[44] The United Kingdom with its newly found treasure of North Sea oil was positively affected by the rise of oil prices resulting from the second oil shock. Actually 1979 was the first year in which the United Kingdom moved from being an oil importing to an oil exporting country and the pound reached petro-currency status. Another factor, very much felt within the Bank of England, was the wish to maintain the position of London as one of the main financial centres of the world.

When Chancellor Geoffrey Howe announced the abolition in the House of Commons on 23 October 1979 it was a leap in the dark, but circumstances on the currency markets could not have been more propitious. Nevertheless he later remembered: 'I count this one of the most important achievements of my Chancellorship – and certainly the most fraught with worry ... It still stands as the only economic decision of my life that caused me to lose a night's sleep.'[45] The extremely complicated structure of exchange rules and regulations, the hundreds of civil servants who had to judge the applications for capital movements and control possible breaches in the rules, this huge edifice was demolished overnight.

It was an important decision both in political and in economic terms. Capital liberalization marked the start of further *deregulation*, giving free rein to market forces. It was followed by the removal of direct controls as an instrument of monetary policy, because leakage – the tapping of banking facilities abroad – was no longer frustrated by exchange controls. There was a request from the Bank of England to the banks not to encourage borrowing abroad, but it was to no avail. The marginal reserve requirements on increments of interest-bearing deposits, intended to curtail funding for credit, popularly known as the 'corset', had to be withdrawn in June 1980. This was followed by an overhaul of monetary policy in 1981, in which indirect means of monetary control were introduced.

As far as the consequences for the exchange rate of the *pound sterling* were concerned, it is difficult to set apart the effects of liberalization from the strong upward pressure on the exchange rate emanating from the orthodox Thatcher government policies and the oil factor. Artis and Taylor (1989) conclude that the most important effects have been on the size of portfolio investment flows and on a greater degree of financial integration through the removal of differentials between Euro rates and domestic interest rates. All in all the increase in overseas demand for sterling assets probably was smaller than that in the demand by UK residents for overseas assets in response to the lifting of exchange controls.[46] Considered on its own, there must have been some downward, though unquantifiable, pressure on the exchange rate.

It was rather paradoxical that the 1972 EEC Directive, requiring member states to maintain powers to impose exchange controls, stood in the way of repealing the 1947 Exchange Control Act in the United Kingdom. Although the directive thus did not directly hinder the actual liberalization of capital movements, it implied that the relevant legislation had to be kept intact. It was only in the context of discussions on the 1988 Directive, in which full liberalization of capital movements was to be codified at the Community level, that the Act finally could be repealed.

6.14 CONCLUSION

At the turn of the decade a *new motive* for the imposition of capital restrictions had emerged. The continuous capital outflows from the United States put upward pressure on the European exchange rates. For a long time appreciation vis-à-vis the US dollar was resisted by the authorities out of fear for a loss of competitiveness. Capital controls on inflows were called in, even in traditionally liberally-oriented countries as Germany. In an about-turn the Commission, which in the 1960s had been the most vocal advocate of capital liberalization, now called upon the member states to impose controls in order to contain speculative capital movements. The Commission's main motive was the wish to preserve the fixed exchange rate system.

The Werner Report had concluded that economic and monetary union could be achieved within a decade, provided that the political will existed to realize that objective. But the underlying differences of opinion as to the road to economic and monetary union were not fully discussed. By the mid–1970s the momentum had been completely lost. This can be attributed to the change in the international environment, such as the collapse of the Bretton Woods system, together with the first oil price shock, whereupon the large member states in the Community each formulated a *different policy response*. This lack of consensus on the way Europe should adjust to the changed international environment and the insufficient political willingness to pursue the integration ideals resulted in a stalemate.

The establishment of the *snake* could be seen as an attempt to counter the adverse international climate and preserve stability within Europe. But this attempt was doomed because there were serious underlying disagreements among European countries about a common policy response to the oil shock. Expectations that more flexible exchange rates would enlarge the scope for autonomous domestic economic management were shattered when exchange rate movements quickly translated themselves into domestic inflation-devaluation spirals. Capital controls were not able to enhance substantially the freedom of the authorities to choose their own growth and inflation paths.

Although in a number of countries the tightening of capital controls in the beginning of the 1970s was primarily intended to counteract speculative *extra-European* capital flows, controls were to remain a more permanent feature to curtail *intra-European* capital flows as well when attempts to seek closer cooperation faltered. Exchange restictions spread in Europe in an uncoordinated manner. The EEC was enlarged with countries which had a tradition of even more extensive systems of capital controls: the United Kingdom, Ireland and Denmark, countries which had not yet associated themselves with the goal of economic and monetary unification. Countries in the 'economist' camp, such as Germany and the Netherlands, condoned the use of exchange controls by other countries in so far as they were believed to hinder capital movements into the Deutsche mark and the guilder. Countries in the 'monetarist' camp, such as France and Italy, regarded capital controls as a useful safety valve as long as economic convergence was lacking. Financial markets in Europe at the end of the 1970s were less integrated than they had been in the mid–1960s.

The decade clearly showed the *limited effectiveness* of capital controls. Faced with strong disturbances or diverging fundamentals they were powerless. Disillusionment as to the effectiveness of exchange controls was great, especially among the central banks which were involved in the execution and tried to close the loopholes in vain by ever tighter measures. Among them the Bundesbank, which had briefly advocated capital controls, figured prominently, but also the Nederlandsche Bank, which had been among the proponents of control, and the Banca d'Italia were growing sceptical. One of the central bankers had said that as central banks 'we try to make the best of a bad situation trying to render controls as effective as possible; on the other hand, few people are in a better position than we are to judge the limitations of restrictions and the endless red tape and arbitrariness which they inevitably imply'.[47] Although the limited effectiveness was generally recognized, member states did not draw the same conclusions. Only Germany, where the experiment with controlling capital inflows hardly fell short of a disaster, was quick in dismantling its restrictions. France played it safe and kept its post-Bretton Woods crisis control system more or less in place, in line with its interventionist economic philosophy.

To a certain extent capital controls may have shielded *domestic monetary policy* in quiet times with stable exchange rate expectations. This was probably the case in Belgium, France and the Netherlands, explaining in part the stickiness of controls. However, they were largely ineffective as regards their main objective, preserving the official reserves and the exchange rate. In Italy the repeated tightening of exchange controls gained the character of near-panic measures in the face of very serious macro-economic disturbances. Consequently, the capital controls did not succeed in restoring confidence, but rather impressed upon the markets the image of drifting policies. More and more the view gained ground that capital controls in so far as they were effective gave the wrong signals, stifling economic development and conditioning unsound macro-economic policies. Capital controls created the illusion that policies could diverge within Europe.

Germany began to frame its monetary policy in terms of domestic monetary targets. In fact, internal stability was put first and foremost. Late in the decade, the *United Kingdom* completely liberalized capital movements in a radical break with its stalemated economic past. It is interesting that both countries came to these steps on purely *domestic grounds*. They had not been preceded by European deliberations. Yet, they had great consequences for Europe. The German quest for domestic price stability, accompanied by strict budgetary and monetary policies, would set a standard for other European countries. With the United Kingdom, switching over to a liberal-oriented policy, Germany gained a powerful ally in breathing new life into fostering the development of a truly common market, also as regards capital movements. The British action lay at the basis of the evolution of dynamic and competitive financial markets in Europe. In the end other countries could not afford to remain on the sidelines.

NOTES

1. Monetary Committee (1967), 9th Report on the activities of the committee, p. 5–15.
2. Report to the Council and the Commission on the realization in stages of the economic and monetary union in the Community ('Werner' Report), Official Journal of the European Communities, 11 November 1970.
3. As regards economic policy-making the Werner report stipulated that 'the essential features of the whole of the public budgets, and in particular variations in their volume, the size of balances and the methods of financing or utilizing them, will be decided at the Community level'. In the monetary sphere 'the creation of liquidity throughout the area and monetary and credit policy will be centralized'.

4. The immediate establishment of a European fund for monetary cooperation was envisaged, which would take over the short and medium-term support mechanisms of the EEC and would eventually manage the exchange reserves of the central banks of the Community. In the final stage this fund would be integrated into the system of Community central banks.
5. Official Journal of the European Communities, 27 March 1971.
6. In March 1964 a withholding tax (Kuponsteuer) of 25% on proceeds of Deutsche mark bonds held by non-residents was announced, originally motivated by the wish to curb capital inflows which threatened to undermine domestic monetary stability. The tax, however, was maintained for budgetary reasons when the original motive had long disappeared, only to be repealed in 1984. From 1 December 1968 to 31 October 1969, a cash reserve of 100% had been set against increases of non-resident deposits with a view to limiting inflows. On 1 April 1970 an additional minimum reserve requirement of 30% was imposed on increases in deposits of non-residents over and above the customary reserve requirements.
7. There were differences of opinion within the Zentralbankrat of the Bundesbank as well. Emminger (1986, p. 177 et seq.) reports that a majority of 11 members, including Bundesbank president Klasen, was in favour of a 'Devisenbannwirtschaft' against a minority of 7 members who favoured a temporary floating of the Deutsche mark. Emminger reports that the introduction of a dual market according to the Belgian model was considered as well. The German government supported the position of minister Karl Schiller and thus sidestepped the opinion of the Bundesbank. It could do so because activation of capital controls under the Aussenwirtschaftsgesetz could only be decided upon by the government.
8. With the switch-over to a positive system of capital controls, codified in the Aussenwirtschaftsgesetz of 1961 (Article 23), a measure of restrictiveness was maintained by the introduction of a ban on the payment of interest on bank deposits of non-residents. The ban was lifted in December 1969, only to be reintroduced in May 1971. Later, in 1973, the imposition of a negative interest rate was considered, but the idea was rejected partly because of disagreement as to which institution should be the beneficiary of the proceeds: the Bundesbank, the Bund or the Länder.
9. After two months the devises-titres market was merged with the financial franc market on 20 October 1971.
10. The legal basis for the Bardepot instrument had been provided by an amendment of the Aussenwirtschaftsgesetz at the end of 1971. With the introduction of the Bardepot the Bundesbank had to rebuild the technical apparatus which after the transition to a positive system in 1961 had shrunk to nil. It seemed logical to entrust the execution to the department dealing with the minimum reserve requirements (Hauptabteilung Bankwesen und Mindestreserven). However, its director, Rolf Gocht, who as a member of the Monetary Committee had been one of the most outspoken proponents of capital liberalization, had so little sympathy for the control measures that the operation of the system was delegated to another department (Hauptabteilung Ausland).
11. The Netherlands and Belgium observed mutual fluctuation margins of 1.5% on either side of the parity.
12. See A. Szász (1988), p. 141–45, for a vivid description of the various attempts to arrive at a common European policy response.
13. Draft directive on regulating international capital flows and neutralizing their undesirable effects on domestic liquidity, dated 23 June 1971.
14. Monetary Committee (1972), 13th Report on the activities of the committee, p. 21.
15. The text is reproduced in Annex 5.
16. After the adoption of the 1972 directive, an ad hoc Working Group on 'Short-term capital movements' was mandated by the Monetary Committee to make an inventory of all available instruments to curb undesirable capital inflows and to examine their execution. In its report, dated 9 October 1973, it could only conclude that it was impossible to

harmonize exchange regulations and to introduce a preferential regime for intra-EEC capital transactions as long as political impulses for closer integration were lacking.
17. De Nederlandsche Bank, Annual Report 1973, p. 17.
18. Other evidence of the 'Koffergeschäfte' was provided by the fact that German securities were traded in Switzerland at a premium of 3 to 5% above the German quotation (Handelsblatt, 5 August 1974). At the same time the existence of interest differentials showed that the controls were effective up to a certain point in deflecting capital flows.
19. In July 1972 the Bundesbank concluded a gentlemen's agreement with the commercial banks in which the banks were requested not to assist in transactions which could lead to undesired capital inflows. In fact cooperation was poor. Notably, the foreign branch activities of German banks, particularly in Luxembourg, expanded considerably. One commercial bank reportedly sent out students to borrow in Luxembourg the basic amount for which no cash reserve was required, which subsequently was deposited on a resident account. Enforcement was hampered by the minor penalties in case of infringement of the regulations. With respect to the Bardepot provisions the Bundesbank sued approximately 40 offenders, winning most of the cases. However, no proceedings were instituted with respect to non-authorized transactions in securities.
20. Bundesbank, Annual Report 1973, p. 20 and 21.
21. For some years to come a number of indirect capital controls would continue to feature in the German system for monetary policy reasons. Among these discriminatory reserve requirements and restrictions on short term issues figured prominently.
22. Reserve requirements were introduced in France in 1967 and were mainly applied as an instrument to counteract capital inflows. When direct quantitative credit controls eventually were abolished in the 1980s (after a brief experimentation with indirect monetary control from 1 October 1970 until the First Oil Crisis), reserve requirements were targeted towards controlling the growth of the money supply.
23. Governor Wormser of the Banque de France once jokingly said that in the face of impending parliamentary elections (in 1973) socialist leader Mitterrand and communist leader Marchais provided for two guardians at the gate, who would discourage investors from converting US dollars into French francs. However, this did not hold true as the wish to unload dollar assets was overwhelming (see Emminger (1986), p. 241 et seq.).
24. Compare Chapter 5, note 37.
25. Goodman (1992), p. 123 et seq.
26. Banca d'Italia, Annual Report 1973, p. 65.
27. Banca d'Italia, ibid., p. 66.
28. Banca d'Italia, Annual Report 1974, p. 204. The Commission authorized the derogation from the EEC obligations ex post on 8 May 1974. The Monetary Committee established a working group under the chairmanship of De Strycker, vice-governor of the Belgian National Bank, in order to monitor developments under the financing arrangement provided by the EEC.
29. The compulsory import deposit scheme was restored for a period of 3 months, affecting nearly 90% of imports. Prior authorization, requested from the Commission under Article 108.3, was readily given. In September 1976 foreign exchange restrictions were tightened further and an emergency 10% tax was imposed on purchases of foreign currency and payments abroad. However, as soon as the tax expired tensions reappeared with a vengeance. The special tax was reintroduced, now for a period of 4 months. When a law was adopted condoning past foreign currency offences, some flight capital repatriated.
30. Banca d'Italia, Annual Report 1975, p. 197. Looking back on the unfortunate episode it was concluded: 'The intensification of controls has afforded some relief from the effects of expectations; however, it has not only narrowed the range of alternatives open to business for legitimate commercial purposes, but has brought a burdensome increase in the formalities to be performed at three levels: that of businessmen themselves, that of the foreign exchange departments of the banks and that of the authorization and control

functions entrusted to the Italian Foreign Exchange Office. The array of instruments available for such interventions now appear to have been exhausted; the reinstatement of those that have fallen into disuse is forbidden by the international community and the continued application of those that are still valid is onerous.'

31. On 9 March 1972 the payment of interest on non-resident accounts was prohibited. On 17 July 1972 measures were taken to contain capital movements through shifts in leads and lags and through foreign credits to residents. Moreover, the taking-up of intercompany loans by Dutch multinationals in third countries, a notorious loophole, was prohibited.
32. See Szász (1974), p. 308.
33. The Netherlands did not go so far as Germany which banned all direct investment inflows unless financed in Germany itself. See Szász in Swoboda (1976), p. 173.
34. Szász (in Swoboda (1976), p. 175) mentions the following example: '... when we forbade the payment of interest to non-residents on guilder deposits, we soon discovered that an important part of these deposits were swapped by the banks: though these deposits were officially dollar deposits, the holder was to receive guilders in the end so that, for practical purposes, these were guilder deposits which escaped the prohibition of interest payments. Such a practice could not have developed without the cooperation of the banks.'
35. The adoption of the bill was delayed because parliament insisted that first legislation with respect to the imposition of (financial) sanctions and the supervision of the credit system was to be enacted. Although the bill was a step forward, the authority to impose restrictions was far-reaching and was still motivated by the same considerations as held earlier by Governor Holtrop. The main purpose of exchange restrictions continued to be the support of domestic financial and monetary policy. To this end the Nederlandsche Bank was authorized to restrict certain categories of capital inflows in case domestic credit ceilings were applied, and the Bank, in agreement with the Minister of Finance, could restrict capital outflows if the Dutch domestic capital market would become overburdened. Furthermore, the Minister of Finance, after having heard the advice of the Bank, could impose restrictions in case of large-scale speculative capital movements.
36. See Lamfalussy in Swoboda (1976), p. 177 et seq.
37. Lamfalussy (ibid.) mentions as a striking example that in February 1973 the Belgian commercial banks were prohibited from accepting Belgian franc deposits from non-residents on so-called 'convertible' accounts beyond a given maximum amount.
38. Upon accession to the EEC the new member states were granted transitional periods. *Denmark* had transitional periods ranging from 1 January 1975 for non-residents' purchases of Danish securities to 1 January 1978 for purchases by residents of foreign securities. When high domestic interest rates in combination with the prospect of EMS membership attracted massive foreign interest in Danish government bonds, Denmark reimposed in February 1979 restrictions on capital inflows under the safeguard clause of Article 73. *Ireland* received special treatment up to 1 July 1977. The Irish pound being linked to the British pound, exchange regulations roughly corresponded to the exchange control applied in the United Kingdom, although the regulations generally were more lenient with respect to direct investment, both inward and outward. There was close cooperation between the British and Irish authorities in order to prevent 'back door' evasion of the controls of one country by the residents of the other country. The *United Kingdom* could avail itself of transitional arrangements until 1975 (see for discussion par. 6.13).
39. In April 1974 the Monetary Committee had formulated a new mandate for the group on short-term capital movements (compare Note 16). In the first instance the group should exchange information on capital controls applied in the member states. At a later stage it should try to reach consensus on elements of a common minimum set of instruments as well as on the coordination of the use of such instruments. Ultimately it should examine how a distinction could be made in the use of instruments with respect to intra-EEC and extra-EEC capital movements. Also in the beginning of 1974 the Monetary Committee in conjunction with the Committee of Central Bank Governors established a working

group on the 'Harmonization of instruments of monetary policy'. A tremendous amount of effort was put into cataloguing instruments and analysing their respective merits, but in the absence of any drive towards integration dust was piled on the conclusions of these groups.

40. The various restrictions were set out in A guide to United Kingdom exchange control, Bank of England, February 1977. Major restrictions included: the requirement of prior permission for investment abroad; certain types of capital transactions had to be led through the investment currency market; restrictions on the holding of other foreign currency assets, such as bank deposits (except for trade); and restrictions on lending of sterling to non-residents, including trade credit.
41. Nigel Lawson (1992), p. 39.
42. Commission Resolution 75/487/EEC, dated 23 July 1975. The German government raised objections to the procedure followed by the Commission. In particular it was deplored that the Monetary Committee had not been consulted on the matter and that no formal decision by the Council had been taken. Against this the Commission argued that no consultations or decisions were needed because the United Kingdom had not requested mutual assistance. However, the Commission mended its ways on later occasions when the Monetary Committee was consulted for approval of further delays in the liberalization of capital movements by the United Kingdom.
43. One factor was the abolition of the investment currency market, where the premium stood at over 40% at the end of 1978. The value of premium-worthy securities was estimated at £5.3 bln, implying a premium of £1.6 bln. It was expected that attempts by investors to restore the pre-abolition share of overseas assets in portfolios could give rise to capital outflows. The lifting of barriers and the resultant psychological impact were expected to lead to an increase beyond this pre-abolition share. The possibility to finance overseas direct investment in sterling might also give rise to capital outflows; see Bank of England (1981, p. 369 et seq.).
44. Nigel Lawson (1992) recalls having urged for a substantial relaxation of exchange control as early as 1977. Exchange rate considerations were a major factor, as was the consideration that in the longer run capital invested abroad would yield a useful stream of foreign exchange as North Sea oil gradually ran out. Abolition of exchange control, however, was not mentioned in the Conservative manifesto.
45. Geoffrey Howe in a lecture in 1991, quoted in Lawson (1992), p. 40.
46. See Bank of England (1981).
47. Szász in Swoboda (1976), p. 172.

CHAPTER 7

The 1980s: Liberalization and Deregulation

While some countries have almost completely liberalized capital movements, others fall far short of their obligations. The European Commission's zeal in proposing new commitments has in the past not always been matched by the same attention to have old obligations respected. It can grant dispensation by empowering member countries in difficulties to take temporarily so-called safeguard measures. In one case this dispensation has been in force without interruption since 1968, when De Gaulle's France got into trouble because of the students' revolt. One should assume that the specific circumstances justifying it at the time have changed since then (and I do not only mean that those students have hopefully graduated by now).

W.F. Duisenberg, 1985

7.1 INTRODUCTION

The decade of the 1970s in many respects had been a lost decade for Europe. Ill-conceived plans and unrealistic time schedules had left European countries floundering about for newborn faith in the integration ideals. However, the decade had ended on an optimistic note with the establishment of the *European Monetary System*. Admittedly, the EMS was not without its ritualistic jargon: the ECU being at the centre of the system, whereas of course in practice the Deutsche mark was to form the focal point for the participating currencies; and the divergence indicator signalling the need for policy action, whose frequent ringing, however, was left unanswered.[1] But if all the frills were cut out, a pragmatic system it was, resembling closely the snake in its essential operational elements. Unlike the snake, the EMS was not placed in the framework of the Werner Report's goal of Economic and Monetary Union. This implied that there was no institutional pressure for capital liberalization. Such liberalization was not needed because the arrangement lacked the goal of monetary unification.[2] It was not wished for either because capital movements were still seen as potentially threatening for exchange rate stability. The founding fathers of the EMS were convinced that without exchange rate stability, there would be no resumption of European integration. The system was a realistic attempt to precisely reach this goal of 'a zone of monetary stability in Europe'.[3] Later, it could be seen if the foundation had gained sufficient strength to build the European house further.

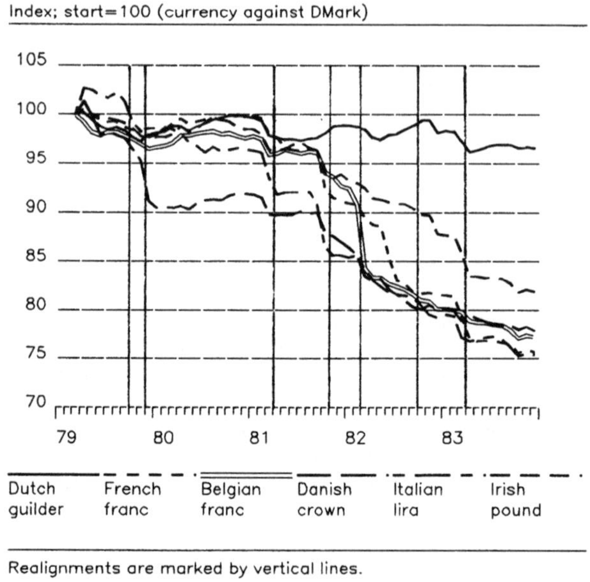

Fig. 16. The EMS 1979–1983: a shaky start.

The Exchange Rate Mechanism of the EMS had a shaky start. As shown in figure 16, in the first years there were frequent and sometimes sizeable *realignments,* partly because of different policy responses to the Second Oil Crisis of 1979, and there were relapses into a tightening of exchange controls on the part of some of the participants. Since the inception of the system, there had been a continuous debate, reminiscent of the debate preceding the Werner report, between those participants who aimed to transform the EMS as quickly as possible into a final system (the 'monetarists') and those participants who wanted to make this dependent on progress in economic convergence and in the liberalization of capital movements (the 'economists').[4] In particular there had been repeated French-inspired proposals for the strengthening of the EMS mechanisms for which the Commission let itself happily be used as an intermediary. These proposals aimed at enhancing symmetrical responses to tensions within the system, therewith sharing-out the burden of adjustment among the currencies under downward pressure and those under upward pressure, the latter for all practical purposes being the Deutsche mark. Although these initiatives were always framed in technical terms, the policy issues involved were scarcely hidden.[5]

In fact, the customary issue in any exchange rate mechanism, i.e. the distribution of the *burden of adjustment,* was at stake all along, as well as the decision-making process with respect to monetary policy in Europe. As long as countries whose currencies were under downward pressure had not put their house in order, Germany was not willing to jeopardize its own stability by coming to the rescue of weaker currencies. The Dutch monetary authorities supported this position, arguing that the pursuit of a European zone of monetary stability could only be successful if the anchor currency was not hindered in its anti-inflation policies. The continuous stream of proposals to intensify monetary cooperation, carrying along in their slipstream suggestions to amplify credit mechanisms, antagonized Germany and the Netherlands. These countries grew tired of being put on the defensive and having to say 'no' against these proposals to finance the deficits of the weaker currencies in the system without visible adjustments on their part. They went on the *counteroffensive*. In search for a mechanism which would enhance discipline among the weaker members of the system, they chose one of the long-forgotten objectives of the Community: the liberalization of capital movements. And their forum was the Monetary Committee.

7.2 CAPITAL LIBERALIZATION REINTRODUCED ON STAGE

In contrast to the leading role the European Commission had played in the liberalization directives in the early 1960s, it now was the *Monetary Committee* which, after some hesitations, took the lead in 1982. In the intervening years since the inception of the EMS the Monetary Committee had been absorbed in discussions on the institutional set-up of the EMS and on proposals for the strengthening of the system's mechanisms. Among the latter, plans to increase the liquidity and acceptability of the ECU figured prominently. As far as the institutional set-up of the EMS was concerned, discussions focused on the provision in the EMS Agreement that not later than two years after its start the European Monetary Fund would be created. In this Fund the existing arrangements and institutions would be consolidated. The European Monetary Fund figured no less than ten times on the agenda of the Monetary Committee in the period 1979–81. But it all came to nothing. In the wake of the Second Oil Crisis attention in the Monetary Committee shifted to the financing of balance-of-payments deficits, and in particular to an enlargement of the Community loan mechanisms.

The constant push for a shift of part of the adjustment burden to the creditor countries, implied by the proposals to strengthen the EMS and the enlargement of credit facilities, fuelled the fear among the strong-currency countries that the wish to maintain exchange rate stability would come at the expense of domestic monetary stability in their own countries. In particular Commission proposals for *non-institutional changes in the EMS*, put forward early 1982, had divided the member states. The proposals comprised intra alia increased acceptance obligations of ECUs, facilitation of intramarginal interventions, stabilization of the ECU exchange rate vis-à-vis third currencies, and promotion of the private use of the ECU. This was supported by France, Italy and Belgium and strongly opposed by Germany and the Netherlands. The latter resented being presented continually with steps, which by themselves might be rather limited, but taken together always went in one direction of shifting the burden of adjustment to the hard-currency countries. Discussions on the final objectives of these steps were evaded and the hard-currency countries thus found themselves in the uncomfortable position of being constantly on the defensive. Presumably the Commission and France wished to develop the ECU gradually as a global reserve currency, possibly alongside national currencies, whereas Germany and the Netherlands saw the ultimate goal as an economic and monetary union, with clearly defined institutional responsibilities in the Treaty. They sought means of bringing the differences of opinion in the open and see which steps could be taken which would not prejudice any of these ultimate objectives. A logical step would be capital liberalization, which was anyway one of the Treaty obligations, and which would be required for both objectives. It had the advantage over the other divisive EMS proposals that in principle all member states could agree that this was a sine qua non for further monetary integration.[6]

Capital liberalization was not an extraordinary desire. It was in the air. The United Kingdom had liberalized in 1979, and so had Japan in 1981. The Reagan administration had adopted a deregulatory attitude. In the framework of the EEC the Netherlands authorities, which had grown irritated over the yearly packages of EMS amendments while others did not live up to their Treaty obligations, viz. capital liberalization, decided to make an issue of it. In the Ecofin Council meeting on 15 March 1982, when the Commission proposals were discussed for hours, the Dutch finance minister van der Stee proposed to reconsider the liberalization of capital movements in Europe and not to confine this to ECU-denominated capital. One of the initiators, André Szász, put the issue of capital liberalization on the agenda of the Monetary Committee in July 1982. This marked the beginning of a new era since the adoption ten years earlier of the 1972 Directive which had institutionalized capital restrictions in Europe. It also marked the beginning of a constructive attitude of the hard-currency countries towards monetary integration, after their initial hesitant stance towards the EMS.

Szász called for the development of a common philosophy among member states with respect to capital liberalization. A first step could be to reinstate the regular annual examination of the use of capital restrictions, as provided for in the First Capital Directive of 1960 and in the statute of the Monetary Committee. Against the rules, the practice had developed that derogations from the liberalization obligations had been granted for an unlimited duration (see Table 24). He advocated that the committee should resume its normal task of examining whether the circumstances still justified recourse to such derogations.

In the committee there was sympathy from the side of Germany and the United Kingdom, the only two member states which had liberalized all capital movements themselves. *Germany* was attracted by the idea that liberalization

TABLE 24

Application of safeguard measures.

Country	since	ended	Treaty basis
France	1968	1986	109.1
Italy	1974	1977	109.1
	1981	1987	109.1
United Kingdom	1975	1977	109.1
	1977	1979	108.3
Denmark	1977	1979	108.3
	1979	1984	73
Ireland	1977	1988	108.3
Greece	1985	1990	108.3

Note:
Article 73: disturbances in the functioning of the capital market;
Article 108.3: (threat of) difficulties in the balance of payments;
Article 109.1: sudden crisis in the balance of payments.
At the end of the transitional arrangements, which are not presented in this table, the Commission applied Article 108.3 directly for Denmark, Ireland and the United Kingdom.

would strengthen market forces and thus would put pressure on governments to follow stability-oriented policies, with more emphasis on the maintenance of price stability. For the *United Kingdom* the integration ideal implicit in the Dutch and German argument played a less important role. Liberalization of capital movements fitted well in the more modest British concept of Europe as one market without barriers where economic development was fostered by the free play of market forces. The issue, however, was extremely sensitive for *France*. For the Trésor capital liberalization was a difficult exercise, both in political as well as in psychological terms. In the French view there was no urgency at all. Instead, all attention should be directed towards the strengthening of the EMS. If liberalization was to be discussed at all, then only in the framework of discussions on improving the mechanisms of the EMS. By explicitly formulating this link, capital liberalization again was to be made part of wide-ranging European negotiations.

There were attempts within the Monetary Committee to persuade France. The issue, so it was pointed out, was not the total abolition of restrictions in the short run. From a European viewpoint the real issue was that a certain degree of liberalization would be needed for any meaningful form of monetary and

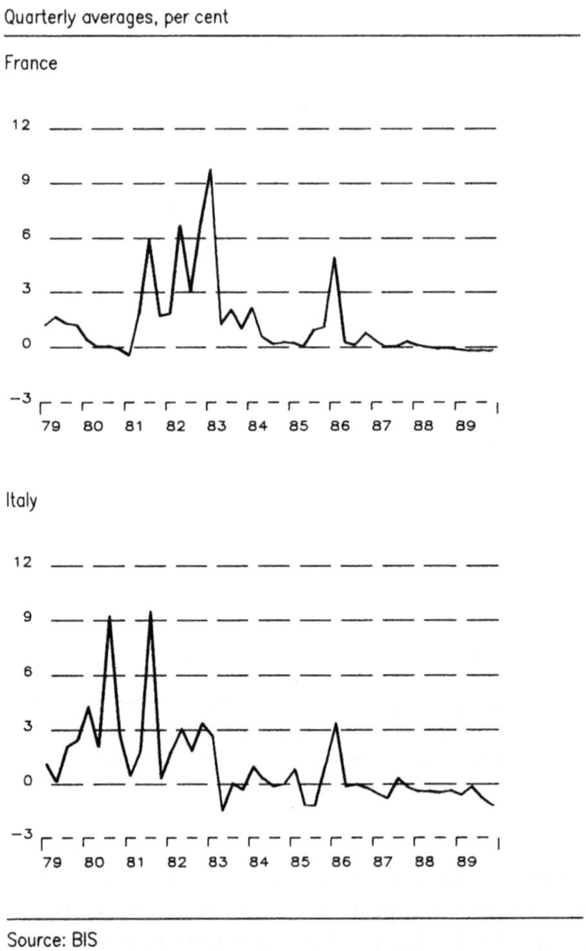

Fig. 17. French and Italian Euro interest rate differentials 1979–1989.

economic integration. But the French committee members saw major risks in capital liberalization and wanted only to postpone the whole exercise. The position of France was clear. In the 'monetarist' tradition France ranked monetary cooperative arrangements higher than market-driven convergence. In the absence of symmetric arrangements it felt vulnerable to speculative attacks. Abolition of capital controls would expose the French franc even more. Therefore it held the existing exchange restrictions close to its chest, as if they were its principal bargaining chip in the further development of the EMS.

7.3 A STRATEGIC REORIENTATION IN FRANCE

The uncomprising, dogmatic attitude of France can best be understood in the context of the *political and economic situation in France* in the beginning of the 1980s. Shortly after the election of François Mitterrand as the first socialist president under the Vth Republic, a socialist government had taken office in the summer of 1981. Soon the government embarked on expansionary policies in order to lift France out of the recession. Capital restrictions were regarded as a cornerstone in this policy in that they separated domestic financial markets from the outside world. At the same time the nationalization of financial institutions was initiated with a view to making them instrumental in the government's reflationary strategy. Both developments antagonized the international financial community and sparked off speculative capital movements against the French franc. Speculation initially was countered by a further tightening of exchange controls, which sharply increased differentials between domestic and Euro interest rates (see figure 17). Eventually a devaluation of the French franc could not be avoided (8.5% in October 1981). Neither could another one (by 10% in June 1982), when the French go-it-alone reflationary policies proved unsustainable in the face of a world-wide recession. Not much later additional capital controls were imposed to stem the continuing outflows. But it was a waste of effort. The capital controls were porous. Outflows continued and they were accommodated by double-digit growth rates of domestic credit, as long as the central bank was forced to play its part in giving an impulse to the French economy.

The major confidence crises, which hit the French currency, eventually led to a *volte-face* in French economic policies in March 1983 when France for the third time within 18 months had to devalue (this time by 8%). From now on France would turn towards stability-oriented policies. It had realized that with its open economy it was not possible to go against the international tide. It had run against external constraints, among which the dwindling of its official foreign reserves was an important one. France had to make a strategic choice. Either it could break apart from the EMS and follow an isolationist course. This, however, would bring European integration to a halt. Moreover, there was the genuine fear that such a course would lead to a free fall of the French franc. Or it could align itself with Germany in its quest for domestic price stability, keeping open the perspective of further European monetary integration. It chose, with grandeur, for the latter direction, combining it with a major reformulation of its financial and industrial strategy. The latter implied the *opening-up of markets* with the aim of enforcing rationalization upon the French industry through the forces of competition. Accompanying measures to deregulate and liberalize the financial markets were taken in the coming years. One of the chief architects of this new economic policy was the then Minister of Finance Jacques Delors, who later was to become the President of the European Commission. The new stability-oriented policies of the French government strengthened greatly the Franco-German axis in Europe, which traditionally had been the driving force behind European integration. This was fertile soil permitting the issue of financial integration again to be put high on the European agenda. But the Commission needed considerable prodding.

7.4 THE CHANGE OF ATTITUDE OF THE COMMISSION

The Dutch initiative, supported by Germany and the United Kingdom, to bring capital liberalization back on the European agenda had been given a frosty reception on the part of the Commission. As we have seen the attitude of the Commission had been transformed from that of an enthusiastic supporter of liberalization in the beginning of the 1960s to an outright sceptic. But in the wake of the French reorientation, there gradually was a change of heart in the Commission's thinking.

A contributing factor was that the Commission had come under increased *external criticism* for its permissive attitude. The Commission had tolerated the intensifications of the existing exchange restrictions in France in the course of the years 1981–83.[7] All these restrictions had been effected unilaterally, without prior consultation and without examination whether the conditions for the use of safeguard clauses were fulfilled. When the *European Parliament* questioned these developments, the Commission had answered that the new restrictions fell within the limits of the safeguard granted to France more than a decade ago, in December 1968, in accordance with Art 108.3. Rulings of the *Court of Justice* indirectly condemned this attitude and called on the Commission to observe the procedures of the Treaty strictly, i.e. to examine regularly whether the circumstances justified the application of the safeguard clause and to see to it that derogations would only be temporary.[8] A similarly permissive attitude of the Commission vis-à-vis the restrictions on trade and capital flows imposed by Italy had provoked another indignant reaction of the European Parliament. In a resolution the parliamentarians sharply criticized the failure of the Commission to act in accordance with the spirit of the Treaty.[9] The Parliament was concerned about the increasing number of unilateral actions taken by member states, which clearly ran counter to the spirit of the Treaty. The Commission was called upon to act more vigorously as guardian of the Treaty.[10]

In April 1983, not long after the third French devaluation, the Commission issued a communication to the Council on *financial integration* in the Community,[11] in which an attempt was made to give new impetus to the process of capital liberalization. The Commission acknowledged that the continued recourse to the safeguard clauses was inappropriate: 'Otherwise, direct exchange controls become a permanent economic policy instrument, which is incompatible with the intentions of the Treaty'. In its paper the Commission sided with the French position that any progress would have to depend on the simultaneous strengthening of the EMS mechanisms, as well as on improved EEC procedures to bring about economic convergence. The Commission argued that progress in these three areas was interrelated and would be mutually supportive. Greater exchange rate stability and closer economic convergence would facilitate the gradual removal of capital controls. Conversely, the liberalization of capital movements would contribute to greater discipline in economic policy by making the external consequences of domestic policy mistakes visible at an earlier stage. However, the road chosen by the Commission was not one of general capital liberalization as promoted by the majority of the Monetary Committee, but rather one of liberalization of *EEC-related* or *ECU-denominated capital transactions*. The Commission's leitmotiv was not yet capital liberalization per se, but rather the promotion of its pet child the ECU. As Vice-President Ortoli formulated: 'A useful means of progressively establishing a Community financial market would be to facilitate ECU financial transactions, particularly in those countries which operate exchange controls.'[12]

Apparently, the Commission wished to *shield the EEC internal financial market* from the outside world. In its paper the Commission reproachfully stated that European savings dissipated through the Euromarket into US dollars 'for ill-defined economic purposes and subject to somewhat uncertain arrangements, as recent events have shown', the latter being an obvious reference to the vicissitudes of the American currency and the international debt crisis. The Commission wanted to replace the role of the US dollar by the ECU, thus hoping that international financial flows would shift to Europe and in particular to EEC deficit countries. It would then be a matter of striking the appropriate balance between the 'constraint of internal adjustment and the advantages of external financing'.[13]

There was French support for the Commission's *favouritism vis-à-vis the ECU* on political grounds: the EMS in practice functioned too much as a Deutsche mark zone, implying that French policies had to adjust to German policies. But there was opposition from other sides to such positive discrimination of the ECU. The German viewpoint was that it would be of little use to deploy the financial instrument of the ECU as long as there was no common monetary policy in the EEC and no European central bank with appropriate powers to control and maintain the value of the ECU. Besides, Germany, supported by other countries with a liberal exchange regime and well-developed financial centres such as the United Kingdom and the Netherlands, was vehemently opposed to any shielding of EEC financial markets from outside influences. Yet, despite all opposition, the Commission's memorandum was indicative of a gradual shift from its detached attitude vis-à-vis exchange restrictions to a more favourable stance towards capital liberalization. After the experiences both in the snake and, again, in the Exchange Rate Mechanism of the EMS, the Commission had come to the conclusion that capital controls had only a passing effect on exchange rate stabilization and did not contribute to adjustment of economic policies: 'Fluctuations in capital movements are sometimes due as much to speculation as to the trend of basic economic variables'. Moreover, experience had shown that short-term capital flows were difficult to regulate, because 'operators are very clever at finding ways through the tangled web of national rules'.

The change of attitude in the Commission's thinking, encouraged by the outside criticism of its permissive application of the safeguard clauses, reflected a greater awareness of the advantages of the establishment of a *European capital market.* Although it phrased its proposals initially in the framework of the promotion of the ECU and the shielding from external disturbances, the Commission was convinced that European industry needed free access to capital in the member states. When at a later stage the framework of a shielded European capital market on the basis of positive discrimination of the ECU did not prove to be a realistic proposition the Commission, mindful of the interest of European industry, retained the concept of capital liberalization and accepted this being brought about in an open, non-discriminatory manner. Thus these first Commission proposals on financial integration can be considered as a run-up to the far-reaching implications for capital liberalization of the White Book which was to appear two years later.

7.5 ACTIVE GRADUALISM

In the course of 1983 and 1984 numerous meetings of the Monetary Committee were devoted to the financial integration dossier. The Ecofin Council was regularly informed of the state of the discussions in the Monetary Committee. Ministers, however, did not discuss themselves the issues in a substantive manner until a very late stage. The de facto negotiations were delegated to the Monetary Committee.

7.5.1 Promotion of the ECU

In a meeting in Venice in the autumn of 1983 the committee discussed the matter at length. The Commission stressed that its proposals were intended to strike a 'political balance' between mutual intra-European capital liberalization, with the possibility to introduce common restrictions vis-à-vis third countries, on the one hand and the promotion of the ECU on the other hand. There was fierce opposition from Germany, the Netherlands, Denmark and the United Kingdom to the implicit discrimination vis-à-vis third countries. For Germany in particular the rejection of the *erga ommes principle* was unacceptable, as it had been ever since the subject had been brought up. But now there was an additional reason. After the policy of active discouragement of the build-up of external Deutsche mark holdings had been given up by the authorities in 1981 in view of its apparent failure, the Deutsche mark had evolved into an internationally traded reserve currency. The monetary authorities now tried to make the best of it. Its *reserve currency status* would be irreparably damaged if transactions were to be curtailed by EEC-wide capital restrictions vis-à-vis third countries. France, on the other hand, stood ready to liberalize ECU transactions but did not wish to go beyond that, seeing no room for further generalized liberalization.

The discussion in the Venice meeting was overshadowed by a fundamental debate on the why's and how's of a *promotion of the ECU,* the quid pro quo demanded by the restrictive countries. From the Dutch side the question was put quite bluntly and repeated in the central bank's annual report: 'A number of countries, including the Netherlands, are loath to make agreements about further technical refinements as long as existing agreements, which are often of a more fundamental importance, are not fully complied with and as long as it remains unclear what such refinements are meant to achieve.' The Bundesbank was not less outspoken: 'Convergence (...) and freedom of money and capital movements are the areas in which progress is necessary in order to secure the EMS in the long run. On the contrary, questions concerning the role of the ECU bear the risk that they detract from the real needs for a durable holding together of the EMS. In any case the attention given to the ECU in the public discussion bears no relationship to its importance for the monetary integration process.'[14] Germany and the Netherlands apparently took the position that the liberalization of capital movements was a goal in itself, to be aimed at both on its own merits as well as in accordance with the Treaty provisions. They felt that it was not acceptable to demand concessions in the form of ECU promotion schemes or enlarged financing mechanisms in exchange for measures by other member states which were called for in the Treaty anyway.

The question *why* the role of the ECU should be strengthened had been evaded, so it was felt. Some countries probably aimed at an economic and monetary union, but were disinclined to discuss the fundamental premises of such union, reasoning 'let's begin by 'perfecting' the ECU'. Other countries probably wished to see the ECU develop into an international reserve asset. Apart from these possible *long-term goals* of developing the ECU, it was questioned how the ECU in the near future could serve a useful role in countering speculative capital flows or be instrumental in bringing about economic convergence. In short, there was considerable scepticism with respect to the added value which the promotion of the ECU would bring in relation to the liberalization of capital movements. And there was a genuine fear that in the end technical measures would be taken with respect to the ECU in the central bank sphere, whereas with respect to capital liberalization it would remain merely a matter of good intentions in the political sphere.

Nevertheless, the fact that there was a political link between capital liberalization and the *strengthening of the EMS* was eventually accepted by the major participants. France and Italy, as the major restrictive countries, indicated a willingness to dismantle capital controls in exchange for improvements in the EMS mechanisms. However, they wished to do so in a gradual manner because they saw great risks in a quick dismantling in a situation of high inflation and external imbalances. Only recently France had still been forced to draw on one of the Community loan mechanisms.[15] When these large countries moved, Denmark and Ireland did not resist gradual liberalization any longer, as long as they could determine the pace on their own. Belgium did not actively engage in the discussion, because it maintained, as it had done all along, that under its dual market system for all practical purposes freedom of capital flows was established. All along, it sided with France in its demands for a strenghtening of EMS mechanisms. Germany, the United Kingdom and the Netherlands reluctantly had to go along with the idea of a package deal. But they insisted that the promise of relaxation of controls should not prove to be an empty gesture. Therefore, to start with, the Commission and the Monetary Committee should take up their statutory obligation to examine existing restrictions and safeguards regularly, as had already been demanded in mid–1982.

In the meantime the liberalization movement gained force. On 1 January 1984 *Denmark* decided to abolish at one stroke the major remaining exchange restrictions. As the United Kingdom had experienced earlier in 1979, no significant disturbances on the domestic capital market followed and the Danish members in the committee professed great satisfaction with the results achieved. In the spring of 1984 the European Commission finally heeded the exhortations of the Monetary Committee and initiated a series of official bilateral talks on the justification of the continued use of the safeguards of France, Italy and Ireland under Article 108.3.[16]

7.5.2 Formulation of a Package Deal

The contours of a possible package deal began to take shape when a shopping list of desiderata was formulated by the ministers of finance in the informal *Ecofin meeting in Rambouillet* on 12 May 1984. This list had three headings: economic convergence, financial integration and the strengthening of the exchange arrangement of the EMS. Apart from capital liberalization, the last two headings combined a variety of topics, ranging from preferential treatment of ECU-denominated transactions, extension of the official and private use of the ECU, to a narrowing of the margins for the Italian lira and the entry of the pound sterling in the exchange arrangement. It was clear that the most extravagant wishes, among which the latter, sooner or later would have to be dropped from the list. But the shopping list made one thing clear: from the viewpoint of the restrictive countries there had to be a quid pro quo for capital liberalization in their countries. And this quid pro quo was to be the ECU.

At the request of the Monetary Committee, the Alternates headed by Jean-Jacques Rey from the Belgian National Bank, were asked to report on concrete steps with respect to the liberalization of capital movements. On a German initiative the liberalization process was nick-named '*active gradualism*'. This implied that Germany accepted that the restrictive countries embarked on a process of gradual liberalization – as distinct from the British and Danish examples – but that concrete visible steps would be set which would transcend the already existing obligations. Therefore it was suggested that certain capital items should move up the lists to the unconditional regime.[17] As a back-up exercise to the Commission's examination of the justification of safeguard measures, the Monetary Committee should resume its annual examinations of the whole range of capital restrictions. Both the European Commission and the Monetary Committee thus implicitly, in a rare show of self-accusation, were chastised for their absent-mindedness over the past years to see to it that the Treaty obligations were fulfilled.

The report of the Alternates was discussed in the Monetary Committee in September 1984. As could be expected, there was firm support from the German, British and Dutch sides for further steps towards capital liberalization which in their view would reinforce the *disciplinary effects* of the EMS on economic policies. But also France could now accept the active gradualism with respect to capital liberalization, promoted by Germany, as long as this would be accompanied by symmetrical efforts by others, in particular with respect to the promotion of the position of the official and the private ECU, on which separate discussions were underway both in the Monetary Committee and the Committee of Governors. The Italians and Irish, by subscribing to the temporary character of the safeguard clauses, accepted that in time they would have to abolish the controls on capital transactions which fell under the 1960 and 1962 Directives. The French chairman of the Monetary Committee, Michel Camdessus, in summing up the debate in the committee, elaborated on four elements which would distinguish active gradualism both from 'gradualisme prudent' and 'gradualisme hardi': (1) the temporary nature of safeguard clauses, (2) enlargement of liberalization obligations, (3) de facto liberalization of certain EEC-related capital transactions, and (4) the drawing-up of a negative list of measures in the grey zone of informal restrictions. This was encouraging.

The breakthrough on the principle of capital liberalization was confirmed at the political level in the *informal Ecofin meeting in Dromoland Castle* (Ireland) in October 1984. The ministerial discussions focused on the technical improvements in the EMS mechanism on the understanding that capital restrictions would be abolished in due course. In the meeting further evidence was furnished that France, which had been the driving force behind the call for promotion of the ECU, gradually was taking a more pragmatic standpoint. When demands for Community-wide positive discrimination of the ECU were dropped, the contours emerged up of a package which would be acceptable for all. Obviously, the political tide had changed at last.

The *Committee of Governors* was invited to work out a package which eventually would comprise: the raising of the interest rate on ECUs held by central banks to market-related level; the setting-up of a mobilization mechanism under which ECUs would be exchangeable for dollars; extension of the obligations to accept ECUs in the settlement of intervention debts; and the extension of the circle of holders of official ECUs to third countries or international institutions.[18] These were minor changes, which did not in any way affect the main characteristics of the ECU or the functioning of the EMS. But they served a useful political purpose in demonstrating that a step-by-step approach was followed with respect to both the development of the ECU and capital liberalization.

Apparently, there had been an evolution in French thinking since the reorientation of *France's economic strategy* in 1983. This reorientation encompassed a major deregulation of the financial sector in stages, which needed to be supplemented eventually by the liberalization of exchange control. At the same time the change of direction in monetary policy influenced the functioning of the French financial markets. The beginning of the disinflation process, accompanied by a rise of real interest rates, enabled the Treasury to finance its budget deficit in a non-monetary way, and enabled the commercial banks to issue bonds. This in turn paved the way for the Banque de France to prepare a wide-ranging change in the quantitative credit control mechanism, which came into effect in 1985, as well as a reform of the money market.[19] The French authorities thus followed a well thought-out *sequencing* order, in which first deregulation of the financial sector, restoration of real interest rates and more market-oriented ways of monetary control were implemented, while still making use of the shield of capital controls. When the French macro-economic situation would have been strengthened – the current account returning into a surplus in 1984 – and the financial sector would be strong enough to withstand foreign competition, the capital controls could be withdrawn. Its declaration of intention to this effect was an important political signal.

7.5.3 Examination of Derogations

In December 1984 the Monetary Committee held its first annual examination of capital restrictions since 1965. Twenty years had passed. Yet, there still were collisions between the committee and the Commission. The Commission felt that the Monetary Committee was only authorized to examine whether there were possibilities to expand the liberalization obligations. In its view, it was precisely because of the fact that such extensions were not feasible that the yearly examinations had fallen into abeyance. The examination of the existing safeguard clauses was a matter for the Commission.

The Commission's viewpoint was in flat contradiction with the provisions of the Treaty and the First Capital Directive.[20] Accordingly this position was strongly contested by members of the committee, who still had a vivid memory of the lethargic attitude of the Commission vis-à-vis the application of the safeguard clauses. The outcome was that the derogations would be monitored more strictly, both by the Commission and by the Monetary Committee, and that their *duration* would be limited in time. The restrictions would be continually reviewed and were to be gradually abolished as the difficulties which originally justified them diminished. As a first step expiry dates were set for the remaining recourse to safeguard clauses by France (two years) and by Italy and Ireland (three years).[21] In a show of good will France and Italy relaxed their restrictions somewhat, although the French easing had no bearing on the transactions for which the safeguard clause had been invoked.

7.6 PRESENTATION OF THE WHITE BOOK

A further contribution to the changed sentiment in Europe was made when on 1 January 1985 Jacques Delors, who as a minister of finance had steered France through turbulent times to a new economic orientation, was appointed the President of the European Commission. He gave an invigorating impulse to the European integration process. Soon after his appointment he came forward with an ambitious plan to breathe new life into European integration by focusing on the completion of the *Internal Market.*[22] In the meeting of the European Council on 29 and 30 March 1985 in Brussels this goal was further specified: a single large market should be achieved by the end of 1992. The Commission was called upon to draw up a detailed programma with a specific timetable. These plans were elaborated by Commissioner Lord Cockfield and culminated in the publication of the White Book in June 1985, in which the Commission presented its proposals to complete the Internal Market by 1 January 1993.

In the White Book the *complete liberalization* of capital movements was taken up as an essential ingredient of the Internal Market. No longer was there any reference to Community-wide positive discrimination of the ECU, the idea having been clearly rejected by the Monetary Committee. European industry and private individuals would need an efficient capital market for the free movement of goods, services and persons not to be a dead letter, so it was argued. The integration of national financial markets would foster the economic development in the Community through an optimal allocation of savings. Beyond these traditional arguments in favour of free capital flows, there was a new argument, reminiscent of the Werner Report of the early 1970s, which had come up in the discussion on the financial integration paper. Capital liberalization would exert a disciplinary effect on domestic economic policies needed for exchange rate stability, which in turn was seen as an essential condition for the proper functioning of the Internal Market.[23] Therefore capital liberalization should move in parallel with a strengthening of the European Monetary System.

As far as the concrete plans with respect to capital liberalization were concerned the Commission gathered up the threads. Plans were reconfirmed to phase out in time recourse to the safeguard clauses. Plans were reconfirmed as well to enlarge the unconditional liberalization obligations for transactions in shares issued by collective investment undertakings (unit trusts) as well as in the mortgage lending field. Certain transactions would be added to the list of unconditional liberalization obligations.[24] All these plans were not new. But the time framework in which they were put added a sense of urgency. And there was the clear aim that all operations of Community interest should be gradually liberalized.

All in all the White Book contained daring steps on the road to integration. It appealed to governments and the public at large, where the mood was ripe for liberalization and deregulation after the disappointing results of interventionist policies in the 1970s. But it also presaged the later proposals for the more final and definitive step of economic and monetary union. In taking the logical step towards the fulfilment of the original goal of the founding fathers of the EC – the establishment of a common (now called internal) market – the White Book at the same time called attention to the further-reaching step of ultimate unification. This process would eventually call for the surrender of national sovereignty.

7.7 DISCUSSIONS ON THE SINGLE EUROPEAN ACT

In order to implement these ambitious plans it was felt necessary to insert into the Treaty of Rome provisions which would facilitate the decision-making with respect to the establishment of the Internal Market and broaden the latter's range. In the Milan summit on 28 and 29 June 1985 an Intergovernmental Conference was convened to work out amendments to the EEC Treaty with a view to achieving concrete progress on European Union.

7.7.1 Freedom of Capital Movement

The Commission proposed that in the new so-called Single Act the definition of the Internal Market would also encompass the free movement of capital. In doing so, the Commission set a further step beyond the targets specified in the White Book, because its proposal implied that capital liberalization no longer was confined to transactions of Community interest. The Commission wished to seize the occasion of the Treaty amendment to get rid of the *escape clause in Article 67* which provided that capital liberalization would be abolished only 'to the extent necessary to ensure the proper functioning of the Common

Market.' In order to achieve this, the Commission used the device of defining the Internal Market as comprising an area without internal frontiers in which the free movement of goods, persons, services and capital would be ensured under the same conditions as in a member state.[25] This formulation would lead to a situation in which on 1 January 1993, the date foreseen for the completion of the Internal Market, residents of the EEC could rightfully claim that cross-border capital movements should be completely freed as long as they were not curtailed at home. This would apply, even if secondary legislation to implement the capital directives would not be forthcoming in the meantime.

The central banks and ministries of finance were somewhat taken aback, because this proposal as well as an accompanying one to strengthen Community procedures in the monetary field had important implications in their fields of competence but initially were not dealt with in the relevant bodies, i.e. the Ecofin Council and the Monetary Committee. The *Intergovernmental Conference* which was called upon to prepare the Treaty modifications could not be founded on prescribed procedures and they got alarmed only at a rather late stage of the negotiations. The member states were not yet ready for direct applicability of Community law in the field of capital movements. Eventually the following text for a new article 8a was adopted: 'The internal market shall comprise an area without internal frontiers in which the freedom of goods, persons, services and capital is ensured in accordance with the provisions of this Treaty.' The latter ensured that the relevant existing provision, i.e. the escape clause of Article 67, was left intact. Apparently the member states did not wish at this stage to tie their hands with respect to capital liberalization.

7.7.2 A Monetary Dimension

Accompanying attempts by the Commission to introduce a monetary dimension in the Treaty, as it were through the backdoor, got an even more frosty reception. The idea that Europe should be given a *monetary identity* had been forcefully pushed by France after the adoption of the EMS package.[26] But the vagueness of the concept had turned off others and prompted initiatives first to discuss the long-term goals of the EMS. In the European Council meeting in Milan in June 1985 it had been stressed by the Chairman of the Ecofin Council that given the fact that in the area of monetary integration technical measures could have far-reaching political effects, and in view of the balanced functioning of the EMS, it would be appropriate that the further development of the EMS would remain a matter for the finance ministers and the two competent committees, i.e. the Monetary Committee and the Committee of Governors. The Commission proposals negated this political declaration by proposing to include the European Monetary System as well as the objective of economic and monetary union in the Treaty.[27] The progressive bringing about of such union should be endeavoured by increased cooperation within the EMS, under the aegis of the European Monetary Cooperation Fund which would be the organ responsible for running the EMS. The EFMC would be replaced eventually by a European Monetary Fund, with institutional autonomy.[28] The inclusion of economic and monetary union as one of the objectives of the Treaty would imply that institutional measures in the field of monetary policy could be taken by the Council pursuant to Article 235, even if no monetary powers were conferred upon the Community.[29]

In a hastily convened meeting of some Monetary Committee members, on the occasion of the IMF and World Bank annual meetings in Seoul, it became clear that Belgium, France and Italy were positively inclined towards the inclusion of a monetary dimension in the Treaty. However, Germany categorically refused such a clause. The granting of monetary competences at the Community level without further specifications would imply by definition that the decision-making procedures of the Treaty would apply, i.e. the Council decides on a proposal of the Commission. This would contradict the independence of the Bundesbank, written into German law, and might trigger a constitutional crisis at home. The British were also opposed, albeit on different political grounds: the objective of EMU in their view showed little sense of reality and was deemed to be totally out of character with the other changes which were more of a modernizing and updating character.

With the encouragement of the Commission, the Belgian government at a rather late stage came forward with similar proposals for the inclusion of economic and monetary union in the EC's mission statement in Article 2.[30] However, these proposals, as those of the Commission, did not contain any provisions with respect to the decision-making in such union nor to the task and the position of the national central banks. To the disappointment of France – Minister Bérégovoy: 'Peut-on évoquer l'Europe sans dimension monétaire?' – the proposals fell down. The awkward handling by the Commission of this matter had antagonized the monetary authorities in a number of countries.[31] It was clear that too little time had been allowed to have a thorough discussion with respect to future European monetary integration. The concept of economic and monetary union had too many important implications for it to be forced through.

Eventually, at the request of Germany, a clause was inserted in the Single Act which explicitly decreed that 'in sofar as further development in the field of economic and monetary policy (would) necessitate institutional changes, the provisions of Article 236 shall be applicable' *(Article 102a)*. This referred to the article which provided the procedures for amendment of the Treaty, requiring ratification by all Member States in accordance with their respective constitutional requirements. If there had been any lingering doubt as to the monetary powers of the EEC, from now on it was clear that any institutional step in the monetary field would require a change of the Treaty of Rome. Moreover, it was explicitly stipulated that the Monetary Committee and the Committee of Governors should be consulted regarding institutional changes in the monetary area. The only concession made was that the title of the new Chapter for Article 102a – Cooperation in economic and monetary policy – was supplemented with the addition 'Economic and monetary union', significantly within brackets.[32]

7.7.3 Assessment

The Single European Act was adopted by the European Council in Luxembourg in December 1985 and signed by the member countries in February 1986. How should one judge the outcome of the Single European Act? As far as the *monetary dimension* was concerned the outcome was not impressive. The Commission had tried to force through monetary arrangements, without having granted member states sufficient time to think them over. Opinions as to the ultimate goal of integration still diverged and in the end countries hardened their positions, rather than making compromises. It would be some years before the subject of monetary integration would come up again when, after thorough preparation in the Delors Committee, another Intergovernmental Conference could be convened, which eventually agreed on the Treaty of Maastricht on European Union. By this time ministers of finance had already secured that they were to be the ones who would draft the Treaty texts on economic and monetary union and not their colleagues from the foreign affairs departments. They would not let themselves be taken by surprise for a second time.

As far as *capital liberalization* was concerned the accomplishments on paper were not impressive either. Eventually, some declaration of intent was wrangled out of the discussions and inserted into the Treaty: the highest possible degree of liberalization should be attained and unanimity would be required for measures which would constitute a step back as regards the liberalization of capital movements (Article 70). But this reference was more in the nature of a political declaration than that it implied any commitment on the part of member states. But the *dynamic ingredients* of the Single Act were very powerful indeed. They consisted of two major ingredients concerning the decision-making process: *qualified majority voting* and the principle of *mutual recognition,* as already spelled out in the White Paper. The first meant that powerful alliances could be forged which could overcome a veto of individual states. This would facilitate the adoption of secondary legislation with respect to the liberalization of capital movements. The second ingredient implied that the cumbersome process of trying to reach harmonized rules within the EC, for instance with respect to financial services, was abandoned. From now on, member states would only have to agree on a minimum degree of harmonization. This had to be mutually recognized, but could be expanded upon by individual member states if they wished to do so.

7.8 COMMISSION PROPOSALS FOR A NEW DIRECTIVE

Despite the political agreement that capital liberalization and strengthening of the EMS should go hand-in-hand, it took some time before the March 1985 agreement on a package of technical measures to strengthen the EMS was followed-up by concrete measures in the field of capital liberalization. In the Monetary Committee Szász, who as chairman of the Alternates of the Committee of Governors had presided over the completion of the package, stated that, the central banks having done their fair share, it was now up to the treasuries to take their part in the Rambouillet understandings, i.e. to fulfil the liberalization obligations of the Treaty.[33] In the wake of the publication of the White Book the Commission had finally started work on a *new directive* after having received political backing from the Ministers in the Ecofin Council meeting in June. Preliminary Commission proposals were eventually discussed in the Monetary Committee in December 1985 on the basis of a report of the Alternates.[34]

In general, the proposals to broaden the liberalization obligations were positively received in the committee. Some members, however, warned the Commission not to be overambitious in reforming the existing directives. There was a *diminishing need for detailed classification* of capital transactions in the eyes of those countries which had already freed all capital transactions. An outspoken position in this respect was taken by the British members. London had been the scene of an extremely rapid development of new financial instruments. It was clear that in this process of innovation the distinctions between different sorts of capital transactions were getting blurred more and more. Instead of the subtle fine-tuning of the Commission, it might in their view be preferable to leave the directives as they were, so that each country could decide for itself when it wished to follow the British example of radical liberalization at one stroke. There was the fear among some that the directive might actually *discriminate* with respect to countries which had liberalized their capital transactions. If those categories which now also had to be liberalized were easily brought under the existing safeguards, the end result would be that liberal countries which did not avail themselves of derogations would be confronted with expanded obligations, whereas the restrictive countries would continue to be protected under the safeguard clauses.[35]

On balance the modest proposals of the Commission for merely partial liberalization of capital movements were in line with the agreed 'active gradualism' approach. But they constituted a disappointment for those who would have expected a more ambitious approach in the slip-stream of the White Book. In fact the Commission had done no more than resume its attempts to expand on the 1960 and 1962 Directives. It had proposed similar transactions to be unconditionally liberalized in its failed attempt for a Third Directive in the 1960s. Now that it had picked up the thread some countries resumed their ritual of raising technical objections. There was a genuine risk that the time-consuming negotiations on a new directive actually might slow down rather than accelerate the process of liberalization and that the political momentum would get lost. What was lacking was a longer-term vision. However, for this the member states would not have to wait long.

In the meantime some concrete progress was made by the adoption by the Council of a directive on the liberalization of transactions in shares of undertakings for collective investment in securities (unit trusts). A draft directive to this effect had been on the table since 1979 but the discussions had dragged on. As was discussed in Chapter 5, France had objected to its inclusion in the First Capital Directive. After adoption of another directive which harmonized the protection of investors and coordinated the supervision of these unit trusts, the road had been freed for the first concrete progress in capital liberalization in Europe since 1962.[36] More was to follow soon.

7.9 A NEW AMBITIOUS INITIATIVE OF THE EUROPEAN COMMISSION

In the discussions on the Single European Act the Commission had already tried to insert freedom of capital movements as an integral part of the Internal Market. That proposal had been one bridge too far for member states. But the Commission's thoughts had evolved considerably since then. Eventually the *strategic decision* was taken to give top priority to the liberalization of capital movements and to aim ultimately for the complete freeing of all capital transactions, regardless of their duration or their purpose. It is significant that the President of the European Commission, Jacques Delors, first outlined the Commission's initiative before the Committee of Governors. It seemed to be an attempt to improve the relationships which had become strained during the negotiations on a Single European Act.

In the Basle meeting on 13 May 1986 Delors mentioned two fundamental reasons for the choice to give high priority to *full capital liberalization*. The first reason was the link with the White Book and the objectives of the Single European Act, where the unification of the financial area should be considered as a constituent part of the establishment of the large internal market by 1992. The second reason advanced by Delors derived from the fact that greater freedom for the movement of capital would be a necessary condition for making monetary cooperation more effective. He concluded from this that both the development of the EMS as well as of the ECU must be based on a wide measure of freedom for capital movements within the Community. Allowance should be made for gradual adaptation by lagging countries, but liberalization should not be postponed unduly because greater freedom for capital movements would bring pressure for achieving convergence of economic policies.

The strategy outlined by Delors had a highly *political dimension*. The Commission's claim that all capital transactions, i.e. including short-term movements, were an integral part of the Internal Market implied an outright negation of the escape clause of Article 67, which it had tried in vain to remove from the Treaty in the Single Act. By referring to more effective monetary cooperation being dependent on capital liberalization the Commission heeded German insistence that it was not prepared to consider further EMS packages unless concrete liberalization steps had been taken in other countries.[37] But Delors took things one step further: by embracing the goal of full capital liberalization, he gambled on setting in motion a dynamic process which would eventually bring German monetary policy into the European orbit.

In the liberalization programme which the Commission presented two phases were distinguished.[38] The *first phase* consisted of three fields of action: (1) general liberalization for the transactions covered by the 1960 and 1962 Directives should be achieved through the termination of the safeguard measures which several countries had applied for so many years; (2) the transitional arrangements for the new members should be ended as soon as possible; (3) enlargement of the liberalization obligations through the adoption of a new directive. The first two fields of action provided reassurance for the liberal countries which had feared that further liberalization obligations would only apply to them and not to the derogation countries. As regards the enlargement of liberalization obligations, the Commission proposed to include all transactions in financial securities, including non-listed securities not dealt with on a stock exchange, and long-term commercial credits.[39] Moreover domestic regulations should allow companies to issue securities on any market within the Community on the same conditions as those applying to resident issuers. By ending discriminatory treatment the linkages between the European national financial markets would be improved.

The *second phase* would lead to the full liberalization of capital movements and thus would imply the effective lifting of all remaining exchange controls. In practice this would mean that the liberalization obligations would extend to short-term flows such as financial loans, money-market operations and the opening of sight and other deposit accounts. The Commission wished to follow a tight *time schedule*,[40] while recognizing that not all member countries would be able to take the necessary steps at the same time. Therefore, safeguard clauses would be applied, but they were to be closely monitored. Expressis verbis it was admitted that capital liberalization would be a two-speed process.

The Commission had come up with an ambitious, far-reaching programme which went considerably beyond what most member states seemed prepared to contemplate. It was most likely that the operation of the EMS would be complicated through complete freedom of capital flows. The proposals drew heavily on the hoped-for economic convergence. Here the Commission took a *calculated risk*. If greater freedom of capital flows would have to be bought at the price of more frequent realignments or larger fluctuation margins within the EMS, the end result would be worse than the existing situation. These risks were very much realized at the time.[41] On the other hand, if there was a time when economic conditions were favourable to try an attempt to leap forward, it was now. The German objections to contemplating further institutional steps with respect to the EMS and the ECU as long as capital restrictions remained intact in other countries would continue the stalemate the Commission was fearful of. The argument that any further strengthening of the EMS was not on the cards had propelled the Commission to direct its attention to capital restrictions. It seemed right to embark on a dynamic process which, if successful, would bring high rewards. Financial liberalization would force the central banks to coordinate ever more closely, opening up the perspective of changing the EMS from a Deutsche mark zone into a truly commonly managed system with the perspective of monetary union.

7.10 THE RECEPTION OF THE COMMISSION'S PROGRAMME

At the time of introduction of the Commission proposals in May 1986 only 3 EEC countries, Germany, the United Kingdom and the Netherlands, had virtually abolished restrictions on capital flows for all practical purposes. But the announcement of the Commission more or less coincided with a major relaxation of restrictions in France, including the abolition of the devises-titres market and an easing of direct investment abroad, which made it possible to end the use of the safeguard clause, in force since 1968. The *breakthrough in France* provided an important political signal for other countries. Other member states still had more far-reaching restrictions in place, sometimes necessitating quite an extensive bureaucratic apparatus for control. Ireland and Italy continued to have safeguard measures in place, whereas Greece and the new members Spain and Portugal were under various transitional arrangements, agreed at or, as in the Greek case, extended since their entry into the EEC.[42] In Belgium and Luxembourg the dual exchange market still had its place, although the differential between the financial franc rate and the official franc rate normally was small. Denmark continued to avail itself of certain short-term capital controls. Many of these restrictions affected not only the commercial and the banking sector. The general public at large was equally confronted with limits on the amount of travel money, restrictions on the purchase of foreign equity or of foreign assets, such as second homes. The restrictions therefore had a negative psychological impact on the sense of European citizenship. But the position of some of the major restrictive countries was rapidly changing. Among those, the French attitude was of paramount importance. If France were to liberalize in a decisive manner, the regimes of other countries would become more exposed. Their being out of step with the core of Europe carried political costs, as well as risks in the financial markets.

7.10.1 The French Position

Since its entry into the European Monetary System in 1979, France had tightened further its exchange controls, in order to ward off speculative capital outflows. These found their logical counterpart in a system of direct monetary control, with special credit ceilings and interest subsidies for specific industries targeted by the government, which, as discussed earlier, had been a constant characteristic of French monetary policy, apart from a brief experimentation with indirect instruments in the beginning of the 1970s. The tightening of exchange controls had peaked in May 1983 with the introduction of the *'carnet de change'*, a drastic measure which controlled the allowance for foreign nonbusiness travel up to a maximum of merely FF 2000 ($ 270) per year per person. Also the use of personal credit cards abroad was forbidden. Galy (1986) estimates that both measures reduced French tourist expeditures abroad in 1983 by 13%. As regards the primary goal of exchange control – maintenance of the external value of the currency and the preservation of official exchange reserves – it was clear that exchange restrictions were powerless in the face of unsound policies, the French franc having been forced to devalue by more than 25% in just 18 months between 1981 and 1983. The tightening of restrictions provided only short-term relief, but this effect quickly dissipated. It provided a dangerous sense of comfort that short-term solutions could prevent a haemorrhage of offical reserves. The policies pursued and their attendant restrictions had completely undermined the confidence of the public at large, depleted the official reserves of the Banque de France and had failed to contribute to spurring economic growth. The disastrous developments and the disillusionment as regards the effectiveness of the regulation of economic life led to a turnround in French policies, aimed at a transformation of the way the economy functioned. Already at the end of 1983 the unpopular carnet de change was withdrawn.

Apart from the ineffectiveness of exchange control there were three other *inconveniences* which underlined the need for a reorientation of policy. (1) The bureaucratic procedures implied by the tightening of exchange control became a heavy burden. Especially the workload for the banks in keeping files for the 'domiciliation' of imports and exports, enabling the matching of trade and financial data, became cumbersome. (2) The system invited evasion. The big French enterprises used their political weight to obtain derogations from the burdensome controls, with considerable success. This in turn caused serious competitive distortions for the small and medium-sized enterprises which had less political clout. (3) Commercial and financial activities of French industry and banks were diverted to other centres. Especially the establishment of the financing divisions of Renault and Peugeot in Geneva, as well as the development of activities of French banks in London and Luxembourg caused grave concern among the authorities.

There were thus real *economic drawbacks* of the exchange control system in the French economy. These came on top of the ineffectiveness of the controls, following a general move towards lower costs of financial transactions through technological developments, which enhanced the possibilities to evade the restrictions. France, as a modern state, could no longer afford to stay on the sidelines of the international move towards deregulation of financial markets. But first the domestic economy needed strengthening. To this end there were basic reforms in industrial policy under then Minister of Industry Laurent Fabius. Subsidies to inefficient firms were discontinued. Frontier sectors were targeted in order to bring about industrial modernization. Quantitative credit controls were abolished and financial markets were deregulated. Thus it was sought to restore a climate of confidence, encouraging saving and investment by the private sector. Minister of Finance Bérégovoy – in 1983 still one of those who favoured dropping out of the EMS – was later to say that he wished to liberalize not only in order to observe the obligations under the EC Treaty, but also to make life easier for the French population at large.[43] The deregulation and liberalization process was supported throughout the political spectrum. When the socialist-led governments under Prime Minister Mauroy (1981–84) and Fabius (1984–86) were succeeded by the centre-right Chirac government (1986–88) the gradual dismantling of restrictions was continued. The economic climate was propitious for such liberalization: after the change of policies in 1983 France made good progress in the fight against inflation and the restoration of balance-of-payments equilibrium. From end–1983 until end–1985 the restrictions were gradually eased by removing their most annoying aspects. At the Luxembourg summit on 2 and 3 December 1985 President Mitterrand announced that capital liberalization would continue at such pace that all restrictions for which France had obtained derogations would be lifted before the end of 1986.

For France the proposals of the Commission were introduced at the appropriate time, synchronized as they were with the substantial relaxation of foreign exchange controls in May 1986. It had embarked on an irreversible process of gradual unwinding of restrictions. But France tried to gain political advantages by linking it to the European integration dossiers. Further progress should take place in the sphere of what could be called *'institutional' sequencing*, i.e. further liberalization was to be made conditional upon firm agreement on stronger monetary cooperation between the EEC countries. This form of institutional sequencing, in which quid pro quos were asked from partner countries to compensate for liberalization, was presented under the heading of the umbrella term 'strengthening of the EMS.'

7.10.2 The German Position

There were three mainstays in the German position with respect to capital liberalization: (1) liberalization was good in itself because it improved the allocation of resources; (2) it would contribute to disciplining economic policies; and (3) it should be applied erga omnes, i.e. in a non-discriminatory fashion for EEC and non-EEC countries alike. The German attitude was inspired by free market ideology, but it was also influenced by the experience of prolonged surpluses on current account. Capital exports by nonbanks were considered to facilitate the task of the monetary authorities in two important ways. By helping to prevent current account surpluses from feeding into monetary aggregates inflationary pressures were allayed. And by helping finance the current account surpluses, undue upward pressures on the exchange rate were diminished as well.[44]

As a traditional surplus country Germany frequently had to cope with inflows of funds which disrupted the formulation and implementation of monetary policy. The dilemma between the external constraints and the requirements of the domestic economy had been the leitmotiv of German monetary policy. The brief attempt to alleviate this dilemma by the imposition of restrictions on capital inflows in the beginning of the 1970s had not been a success and the last regulations were lifted in 1981.[45] The restrictions partly had been aimed at limiting the *reserve role of the Deutsche mark* in the post-Bretton Woods years through a policy of determent. In fact, there had been an important change in the attitude of the authorities vis-à-vis the Deutsche mark's international role. The acceptance of the role of the Deutsche mark as an international reserve currency prompted a turnround in domestic regulation as well. The requirements with respect to the form of domestic paper were eased gradually in line with developments elsewhere. Liberalization in third countries provoked a certain competition between monetary authorities in deregulation: the easing of form requirements was now explicitly motivated by the wish to sustain the Deutsche mark's international reserve role.[46]

The progress achieved in the convergence of economic developments and monetary stability in Europe had created much scope for liberalization in other European countries as well, so it was felt. This would enhance discipline in economic policies of the countries concerned and thus strengthen convergence within the EMS.[47] In the German position there was a distinct ideological undertone – freedom of capital movements was good per se –, but Germany was realistic enough to acknowledge that countries should not prematurely liberalize short-term capital flows, i.e. not before a certain degree of convergence had been established. Therefore it had sympathy for a degree of gradualism. The complete freeing of capital flows would place high demands on stability-oriented policies, in particular with respect to price stability. If countries were not able to fulfil these demands, there would be a risk of serious backlashes which could prompt demands for a further strengthening of the EMS and could lead to disturbing inflows. Germany was opposed to institutional back-ups in the EMS because this would merely weaken discipline and postpone adjustment. Liberalization, so it was argued by Bundesbank director Gleske (1986), would rather boost the confidence in the currency.

The experience in the United Kingdom and Denmark seemed to vindicate this standpoint. Such confidence was hampered if conflict situations were resolved with 'dirigistic' capital controls. The message was clear: Germany's vision of an integrated Europe was a market-oriented one with economic agents being as free as possible in making their decisions. Only on that basis was it willing to discuss institutional changes in the economic and monetary setting of Europe.

7.10.3 The Dutch Position

The Dutch authorities were satisfied with the active stance of the Commission: 'Thus a better climate (would be) created for policy discussions on the advancement of European monetary cooperation and the role which the ECU could play here.'[48] However, they initially held that *existing* obligations with respect to capital liberalization should be fulfilled first, before *new* ones could be accepted. They feared that new obligations would simply be brought under the existing safeguards for the restrictive countries, implying that it would only be the liberal countries which would take additional obligations on board. The Netherlands, which unlike Germany used direct methods of monetary control, wished to retain the possibility to impose restrictions on inward capital flows to close the external gap when imposing domestic credit ceilings. If it were prevented from applying controls on borrowing in third countries in case of a domestic credit ceiling, direct monetary control measures could be easily circumvented.[49] It was felt that it would be hurtful to Dutch pride ever to invoke the safeguard clauses for this purpose.

When at the end of 1981 the domestic credit ceilings were completely lifted, the legal basis for controls on capital inflows disappeared as well.[50] Domestically it was felt increasingly difficult to keep the controls in place. Industry had grown used to taking up credit with commercial banks abroad. All in all, the Dutch no longer held an ideological position with respect to capital restrictions as they had done in the Holtrop era, but were rather pragmatic. They had changed from a negative system to a *positive system* in 1977, largely because of doubts as regards the effectiveness and fairness of exchange restrictions. This doubt was also enhanced when it became evident that prosecution for non-compliance was rare and that in no single instance had offenders been sentenced. The token reference in the annual reports of the Nederlandsche Bank that 'investigations were held to check compliance with the exchange control regulations' only scared off jellyfish. The move towards a more market-oriented approach gained force among the monetary authorities.

As a first step, important *deregulations* of the Dutch capital market were carried through. Regulations had been in place with the aim of ensuring orderly market conditions as well as maintaining a strict separation of liquidity and capital in order to attain monetary objectives. However, the rapid development of financial markets, spurred by innovations and technical progress, as well as their internationalization made it increasingly difficult to enforce national rules. A major consideration was the wish to maintain Amsterdam's position as a financial centre and to ensure that transactions in guilder-denominated paper would continue to take place as much as possible in the Netherlands. The deregulation, effective as from 1 January 1986, involved the virtual abolition of all requirements as to form, thus ending the strict separation of liquid and capital assets, as well as a considerable easing of the calendar requirements. As a logical sequence the second step was taken shortly afterwards. The remaining restrictions on capital outflows were lifted and the Exchange Control Regulations Department, which had already shrunk to only 3 professional staff members, was dismantled. On 1 October 1986 the Netherlands became the fourth OECD member country which had liberalized all capital movements.

7.10.4 The Belgian Position

Belgium kept a low profile in the discussions on capital liberalization, in order to avoid drawing too much attention to the dual market. Although the ultimate goal of full freedom of capital movements was supported, the dual market, where differentials between the two markets had decreased to 0.5%, was functioning satisfactorily and was not questioned at home. When it was questioned by other member states the Belgian authorities reacted irritated.[51] They formulated conditions which other member states would have to fulfil before abolition of the dual market could be contemplated. In particular, actual liberalization of exchange controls should take place in France and Italy. But also further-reaching measures should be taken, such as participation of the pound sterling in the EMS and reduction of the fluctuation margin of the Italian lira.[52] From this it was clear that Belgium and Luxembourg would sell their dual market dearly.

7.10.5 The Danish Position

Denmark had not experienced an easy entry into the EEC. Although it had managed to stay in the snake – together with Germany and the Benelux countries –, the 1970s were a decade of persistent current account deficits, run-away inflation, extensive controls on capital exports and repeated devaluations. Interest rates were kept high to attract capital inflows and domestic monetary policy was conducted through direct controls on credit expansion. Monetary policy and exchange controls were arranged with a view to allowing private capital imports to finance part of the current account deficits and preventing capital outflows from becoming too bulky. There was a growing conviction that these policies merely prolonged the stagnation of the real economy. It was felt that the restrictions were ineffective and outdated in

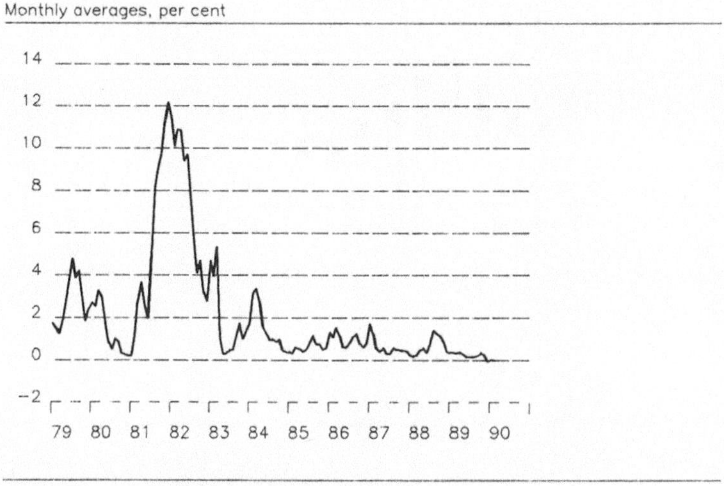

Fig. 18. The Belgian dual market 1979–1990.

an integrated world, and that they had produced distortions in the national financial system. Some transactions, such as the purchase of foreign shares, had been banned for over half a century.[53]

In the beginning of the 1980s a radical change was carried through and Denmark switched over to a *hard-currency policy* in the EMS (see Figure 19). Interest rate policy from now on was to be the main policy instrument to peg the Danish krone to the other hard currencies in the EMS. In line with this change of policy direct domestic monetary controls were abolished and exchange controls were dismantled at a rather quick pace. Denmark's experiences with vigorous capital liberalization were positive. The hard-currency policy gained considerable credibility, when it was shown that the central bank indeed was prepared to let market forces work their way through into interest rates. Denmark thus became, like the United Kingdom, a convert to the gospel of capital liberalization and joined forces with other liberal-minded countries like Germany and the Benelux countries.

7.10.6 The Italian Position

Since the beginning of the 1980s proposals for a *reform* of the extensive exchange control system had already circulated in Italy. Parliament had been offered draft laws in 1981 and 1983, which aimed at reforming the regulations which since 1976 had considered violations to be criminal offences, as well as at changing from a negative to a postitive system of exchange control. The impulse to proceed towards such liberalization came from the perception

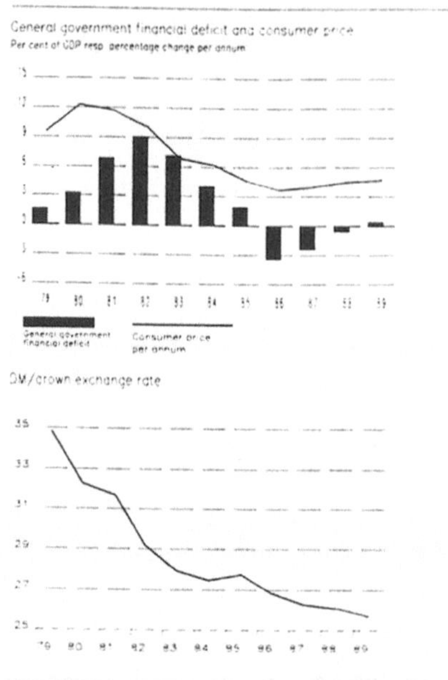

Fig. 19. Denmark's switch-over to a hard-currency policy.

among the authorities of the contradiction of the strong presence of Italy in the international trade and financial system, Italy belonging to the Group of Seven, and the persistence of restrictive domestic regulations. In the Banca d'Italia it was increasingly felt that an easing of restrictions and a streamlining of administrative procedures would improve the allocation of resources and, by increasing the efficiency of the domestic capital market, would eventually make capital cheaper.[54] In fact the perceived contradiction between Italy's position in the world economy and its domestic regulatory and institutional framework gave rise to a vivacious political and cultural debate.

The adoption of the relevant legislation, switching-over to a positive system, nevertheless was continually delayed because of the precarious economic situation. The balance of payments continued to be fragile in the early 1980s, inflation was too high and there were repeated devaluations of the Italian lira. A process was started to gradually remove barriers and restrictions with respect to capital movements. Total liberalization was not the starting-point in the process but might eventually be its conclusion. Full liberalization was viewed as being not without risk and Italy would in practice ask for long transition periods.

7.11 THE 1986 DIRECTIVE

In line with the outcome of the Monetary Committee's discussions towards the end of 1985 and as a follow-up to the programme presented by President Delors the Commission came forward with a new draft directive for the first phase.[55] In this proposal the Commission had dealt with some of the concerns which had been voiced with respect to the earlier draft, notably by excluding short-term securities from the liberalization obligation. Although the directive now received a warm welcome in the Monetary Committee,[56] again there was a battle of words over *parallelism.* Although all countries in principle could subscribe to the notion that capital liberalization should move hand-in-hand with increased convergence, there were considerable differences of opinion as to the operational implications of parallelism. Implicitly, the sequencing of liberalization measures was at stake.

The 'restrictive' weak-currency countries still had drawn a demarcation line for further liberalization measures between long-term and short-term capital transactions in order to avoid the risk that speculative short-term capital flows would jeopardize exchange rate stability. The sequencing of capital liberalization had been partly determined by the relative strength of the national currency. In the realignment discussions in the *informal Ecofin meeting in Ootmarssum* in April 1986 this link was explicitly established by Minister of Finance Balladur. After an initial request for a devaluation of the French franc by 8 to 9%, which was deemed excessive by most other countries, the parties settled for a range of 6% to 7%. Balladur declared that, in the case of an adjustment of 7%, all restrictions which fell under the safeguard clause would be lifted. If, however, other countries insisted on an adjustment of only 6%, France would liberalize less. The EMS partners did not allow themselves to be blackmailed, and an adjustment of 6% was eventually agreed upon. Shortly afterwards, France liberalized nevertheless up to the point that the safeguard measures could be withdrawn.

For further liberalization France wished to have assurances that hard-currency countries would stand ready if the French franc would get under speculative attack, either by giving financial support to shore up official reserves or by taking measures, preferably interest rate decreases, which would enhance the relative attractiveness of the weak currencies. The view that a proper sequencing of liberalization measures required ample financing possibilities for weak-currency countries was most forcefully espoused by the European Parliament. President Delors was reminded of his proposals that the *financing mechanisms* of the EC would be used not only in case of balance-of-payments difficulties, but also as a form of support on the road to capital liberalization.[57] The Parliament proposed that instead of the application of safeguard clauses recourse should be had to financial support and EC loans.[58] In its meeting on 17 November 1986 the Council finally adopted the directive which was to enter into force on 28 February 1987.[59]

TABLE 25

Third amendment of the 1960 Directive.

July 1982	The Monetary Committee exhorts the Commission to come forward with proposals for capital liberalization.
20 April 1983	The Commission outlines new initiatives in its paper to the Council on Financial Integration.
4 May 1983	First discussion of the Commission proposals in the Monetary Committee.
17–18 October 1983	A package deal comprising capital liberalization, promoting the ECU and strengthening of the EMS is discussed in the Monetary Committee.
26 March 1984	Preparation in the Monetary Committee of the informal Ecofin meeting.
12 May 1984	Informal Ecofin meeting in Rambouillet in which the contours of a package deal began to take shape.
24 May 1984	Further discussions in the Monetary Committee on a package.
September 1984	Discussion in the Monetary Committee on a report of the Alternates.
4 December 1984	Resumption in the Monetary Committee of yearly examinations of capital restrictions.
19 December 1984	The Commission sets expiry dates on the safeguard clauses for France, Italy and Ireland.
March 1985	Agreement among central banks with respect to a package of measures designed to promote the ECU.
June 1985	The Commission presents a White Book on the completion of the Internal Market.
17 December 1985	The Commission proposal of a new Directive on capital liberalization is discussed in the Monetary Committee.
23 May 1986	Presentation of a programme by the Commission to fully liberalize capital movements in two phases.
18 July 1986	Discussion in the Monetary Committee.
10 September 1986	Presentation of the final proposal for a directive by the Commission.
17 November 1986	Adoption by the Council of the third amendment of the 1960 Directive.
28 February 1987	Entry into force of the Directive.

It was approved unanimously after the Italian, Greek and Danish ministers had withdrawn their *reservations*. They could not have blocked the directive anyway, because a qualified majority had been secured. However, Minister Goria of Italy, supported by his Greek colleague, made a unilateral declaration for the Council minutes in which he advocated the simultaneous development of financial instruments to cope with destabilizing capital movements. As far as he was concerned there would be a price tag on the next liberalization round.[60]

7.12 CONCLUSION

The first years of the European Monetary System were characterized by repeated exchange rate tensions under the influence of continuing large inflation differentials. A tightening of exchange controls in France and Italy did not succeed in stemming speculative flows, which time and again forced the authorities to devalue their currency. In an attempt to secure support form their hard-currency partners in the Exchange Rate Mechanism yearly packages to strengthen the EMS were tabled, which in practice entailed additional financing obligations for the latter with potentially inflationary consequences. Irritations mounted in Germany and the Netherlands when they were forced on to the defence and risked, by declining the packages, as being perceived as obstructing the monetary construction of Europe. In search of developing a constructive attitude, the Dutch authorities proposed to take up again the nearly-forgotten issue of capital liberalization. This fitted in well with the global drive towards liberalization and deregulation.

The initiative was immediately seized by Germany which was attracted by the disciplinary effect of freedom of capital movements on macro-economic policies. Another side to the sequencing argument thus emerged, with countries in the 'economist' camp, as Germany, reasoning that monetary cooperation would only be possible if other countries, such as France, would follow more strict, stability-oriented policies. The United Kingdom, too, supported the initiative because it would strengthen the market orientation of the Community.

The *Commission* needed considerable prodding before it came into action. First, in line with French preferences, the road of discriminatory liberalization in favour of the ECU and EEC countries was tried out. This, however, ran into fierce opposition from those countries which had already fully liberalized capital flows and strongly advocated adherence to the erga ommes principle. When France, after its reorientation of policies in 1983, had successfully modernized its domestic financial system, while restoring external equilibrium and regaining a measure of domestic price stability, a significant liberalization of capital movements could be carried through. The Commission, under the visionary leadership of Delors, seized the opportunity to come forward with a programme for full capital liberalization. Delors invariably and successfully sensed the lay of the land and adjusted his policies accordingly. From now on the Commission would play the leading part. Capital liberalization could prove to be the dynamic element, lacking in the post-Werner era, which could create internal momentum by introducing elements of external discipline. In the improved economic climate the liberalization process could gather momentum and in its slipstream bring monetary integration closer. By aligning himself with a proposal of the hard-currency countries, and therewith discontinuing the perpetual opposition of these countries towards the

EMS packages, Delors had made a political and strategic choice, which if successful could bring great rewards.

The *position of France* in this respect was crucial. Initially, France was hesitant. But growing self-confidence was evident in successive French governments. Whereas previously the risks of free capital flows had been stressed, there was a growing feeling that because of its balanced economic policies France now finally could afford to capture the gains of free capital flows without having to be overly concerned about their potentially destabilizing effects. Capital liberalization increasingly was seen as a sign of strength and as a reward for good policies. A multi-speed Europe was more and more visible. There was a leading group, composed of Germany, the Benelux countries and Denmark, which had a low inflation rate, virtually no exchange restrictions and exchange rate stability. Apart from the last aspect, the United Kingdom formed part of this leading group as well. There was a lagging group, composed of Spain, Portugal, Greece and Ireland, which as far as economic development was concerned still had a long way to go. And there was an intermediate group, consisting of France and Italy, which could seek its allies on either side. France was ready to break away from the 'Southern' pack and to join this first group.

The outcome of the 1986 Directive fell short of the modest conception of the first phase by the Commission. In particular the transitional periods had been lengthened instead of shortened; short-term capital transactions still were excluded from the liberalization obligation. Thus there was not yet a breakthrough towards full capital liberalization. The discussions nonetheless had shown that the arguments in favour of capital restrictions had become weaker; in particular their effectiveness seemed to be limited and, if anything, decreasing. On the other hand, the arguments in favour of liberalization were gaining force, especially the advantages of efficiency. But apart from these underlying economic motives, there were important international considerations. When, following Germany, which, apart from a temporary experimentation, had been a steady supporter of liberalization, the United Kingdom in 1979 and now also France were clearly moving in a liberal direction, this had important consequences for other European countries as well. With a third large European country having become inclined towards liberalization, the European pursuit of the free movement of capital could no longer be stopped. It was clear that the adoption of the second phase of Delors' programme would not come about easily. Italy had accepted the directive with visible reluctance. Other restrictive countries were not bursting with impatience and would come up with costly proposals for compensation. The Commission would now have to show whether it wished to go all-out for forcing capital liberalization on its member countries.

Among the *central banks* there was support for the liberalization because of growing scepticism as to their effectiveness. But there also were fears. There were especially doubts as long as convergence of budgetary policies was lacking. It was feared that with progressive liberalization the burden of adjustment would fall lopsidedly on monetary policy. On the other hand partial liberalization contained a dynamic element because it became increasingly easier to circumvent restrictions through the construction of special financial instruments which fell under the liberalized regime. Thus the liberalization drive could not be stopped easily, once it had gathered speed. Partly for this reason some countries, particularly the United Kingdom and to a lesser extent Denmark, had opted for a shock treatment by liberalizing all capital movements at one stroke. But the United Kingdom did not yet participate in the Exchange Rate Mechanism of the EMS. The crucial question was whether France and Italy, which did follow a policy of exchange rate stability, would be prepared to follow suit.

NOTES

1. Resolution on the Establishment of the European Monetary System and related matters, Brussels, 5 December 1978. Although article 2.1 provided that 'a European Currency Unit (ECU) will be at the centre of the EMS', in operational terms the system functioned on the basis of a grid of bilateral exchange rates. Article 3.5 provided that 'a threshold of divergence will be fixed at 75% of the maximum spread of divergence for each currency'. However, the presumption that the authorities of a currency crossing this threshold would correct the situation by adequate measures, in practice was not carried into effect.
2. It may be argued that the European Commission considered the EMS as a step towards monetary unification. At the time of the inception of the ECU – 'at the centre of the system' – the Commission may already have had in mind its development as a parallel currency which eventually was to supersede the national currencies. In later communications this intention was explicitly stated (e.g. in its note on 'Financial integration', April 1983). This was a different concept from Werner's proposals for the progressive narrowing of fluctuation bands and the eventual irrevocable fixing of parities. Neither of these approaches was yet intended by the participating countries. If anything, the French authorities wished to develop the ECU into an international reserve currency. The Council Resolution of 5 December 1978 merely provided that the EMS within two years would be consolidated into a final system, entailing the creation of a European Monetary Fund, whose functions still had to be defined. See also Szász (1988), p. 164–166.
3. Resolution of the European Council (ibid.), article 1.1.
4. See Ludlow (1982), p. 4–7 for a discussion of the debate between 'economists' and 'monetarists' in the run-up to the Werner report.
5. France had two motives to propose changes in the EMS: the wish to present the EMS not as the Deutsche mark bloc into which it had developed, but as a truly European system, implying an enlargement of the role of the ECU; and the wish to reach a more symmetric distribution of the adjustment burden, by putting additional obligations on the creditor countries. The French proposals took the form of packages of technical improvements in the EMS. These packages gave rise to lengthy discussions where the underlying policy disagreements were fought out 'in code'(e.g. Szász (1988), p. 169 et seq.). In its Annual Report on 1981 the Nederlandsche Bank disapprovingly writes: 'With progress towards convergence of policies proving more arduous, tendencies are gaining ground within the EMS to focus on technical aspects. (...) Monetary techniques ought not to be an excuse for failure in other areas.'
6. Later, in the Annual Report of the Nederlandsche Bank on 1984, p. 18, the point would be made clearly that diverging objectives of the member states did not necessarily entail a

standstill: 'After all, those travelling from The Hague to Groningen and Leeuwarden take the same train as far as Zwolle. Thus, by the same token, if the ECU is to be promoted either as an international reserve asset or as a common currency, the intermediate station of completely free capital movements is a sine qua non. This would also mean that the undertakings to liberalise capital flows previously entered into would actually be honoured. Let us work towards this goal first of all.'

7. France had modified its exchange controls in the wake of speculative pressures on 21 May 1981, 25 March 1982 and in April 1983 with a view to encouraging capital inflows and discouraging outflows.
8. In case 36/83 (ECSC re deviations from Treaty provisions) the Court of Justice had ruled that the requirement for the maintenance of restrictive measures is that the conditions under which the original authorization is given still apply. If those conditions were to disappear, the authorization should be withdrawn. This contradicted the opinion of the European Commission that the restrictive measures taken by the French administration in the beginning of the 1980s could still fall under the authorization given in 1968.
9. On 18 June 1982 the European Parliament adopted a very critical resolution on the lax attitude of the Commission vis-à-vis Italy, which in September 1981 had reintroduced compulsory deposit measures. The Commission, which had authorized similar measures in 1974, again authorized them unquestioningly under the safeguard clause of Article 108.3.
10. Although in theory the Commission's position could be challenged before the Court of Justice by a member state, in political terms this was neither a viable nor a desirable route. Likewise, the Council of Ministers in theory could amend or revoke the authorization given by the Commission with a qualified majority in accordance with Articles 108 and 109. However, such majority could not be reached as long as France, Italy, Ireland and Denmark maintained exchange controls under the safeguard clauses of the Treaty and could form a blocking minority. Therefore, in practice all depended on the good will of the Commission.
11. Communication of the European Commission to the Council of Ministers on 'Financial integration', 20 April 1983, COM(83)207.
12. Vice-President Ortoli quoted in ECU Newsletter, May 1983.
13. Communication of the Commission, COM(83)207, p. 17, Note 6.
14. De Nederlandsche Bank, Annual Report 1984, p. 17. Deutsche Bundesbank, Annual Report 1984, p. 70.
15. In May 1983 France was granted ECU 4 billion under the oil facility (Community loan mechanism), which had been established in 1975, in the face of rather outspoken protests of some member states which considered the use of this facility improper. Later this facility was merged with the medium-term financial assistance mechanism into the so-called single facility for medium-term financial assistance.
16. Bilateral talks with Denmark were no longer needed because its use of the safeguard clause under Article 73 (disturbances on the domestic capital market) had been lifted after a major liberalization exercise on 1 January 1984. The European Commission did initiate talks with Greece, which still could benefit from transitional safeguard arrangements, in order to see whether there was room for some relaxation of capital controls.
17. The unconditional regime applied for lists A and B (compare Chapter 5, Note 8).
18. These proposals had been contained in a report of the Committee of Governors on the possibilities for strengthening the EMS which was presented in Dromoland Castle. The package in its final form was accepted in March 1985.
19. See Icard (1994).
20. See Chapter 4, p. 62 and 71, and Chapter 5, p. 88.
21. Decisions 85/14, 15 and 16/EEC, dated 19 December 1984.
22. The European Council, in its meeting on 3 and 4 December 1984 in Dublin, had agreed that steps should be taken to complete the internal market, albeit without further specification.

The completion of the internal market should be accompanied by a strengthening of the EMS. In his inaugural speech for the European Parliament on 14 January 1985 Delors had advanced that 'a strengthened EMS (...) could re-open the path to economic and monetary union mapped out by the Werner report almost 15 years ago'.

23. The White Book provides in paragraph 126 that: '... Action to achieve greater freedom of capital movements would need to move in parallel with the steps taken to reinforce and develop the European Monetary System. Exchange rate stability and convergence of economic policies help the gradual removal of barriers to the free movement of capital; conversely, greater financial freedom leads to greater discipline in the conduct of economic policies'. See also discussion in Chapter 7.4, p. 155.
24. These operations concerned the issue of securities representing risk capital, transactions in securities issued by Community institutions and long-term commercial credits. They were largely the same categories of transactions as had been proposed at the time of the discussion on the Third Directive in the beginning of the 1960s.
25. Proposal by the European Commission to amend the Treaty of Rome, dated 7 October 1985.
26. Under the heading of the strengthening of the 'monetary identity' of Europe France advocated that the Monetary Committee should come up every year with a balanced package which should contain steps in four related areas: convergence, capital liberalization, development of the ECU and enlargement of the participation in the ERM. Others considered such a yearly package to be a strait-jacket which could obstruct progress in separate areas.
27. President Delors had mentioned the possibility of a clause on monetary cooperation to be inserted into the Treaty during the informal Ecofin meeting on 20 and 21 September 1985 in Luxembourg. The Monetary Committee and the Committee of Governors both formulated an opinion concerning the Commission proposals on Monetary Provisions, which were discussed in the meeting of the Ecofin Council on 18 November 1985. See for a detailed discussion Louis (1988).
28. New Commission proposal for Monetary Provisions in the Treaty of Rome, dated 16 November 1985, in which Article 2 of the Treaty was to be supplemented as follows: 'The objective shall be to achieve economic and monetary union of the Member States in accordance with Articles 103 to 107 of this Treaty, thus bringing about parallelism between alignment of economic and monetary cooperation.' Article 107 was to be supplemented by clauses concerning the European Monetary System, the ECU, the EMCF and the European Monetary Fund ('with institutional autonomy').
29. Article 235 provides for supplementary powers for the EC, not provided for in the Treaty, to act in order to attain one of the objectives of the Community.
30. Belgium had been approached by the Commission to come forward with a proposal of its own in the Intergovernmental Conference. The purpose of the request was to lend additional political weight to the proposal on a monetary dimension in the Treaty. Minister of Foreign Affairs Tindemans complied with the request against the advice of the National Bank.
31. It has been suggested in talks with officials that the Commission approach had been particularly counterproductive with respect to a possible entry of the pound sterling into the EMS. The fear that the EMS would prove to be the hell's gate of economic and monetary union through the inclusion of a monetary dimension in the Treaty stiffened British opposition.
32. Interpretations of Article 102a vary. For an elaborate discussion see Louis (1988). The inclusion in Article 102a of the EMS and the ECU was heralded by some as a strengthening of the monetary competences of the Treaty, while others stressed that the article at the same time acknowledged that cooperation shall respect existing powers in this field. The Commission added a Declaration to the Single Act, supported by the Presidency, in which it considered 'that the provisions inserted in the EEC Treaty with reference to the Community's monetary capacity are without prejudice to the possibility of further

development within the framework of the existing powers.' Margaret Thatcher in her memoirs (1993, p. 555) describes that she hoped that by adding to the phrase 'Economic and Monetary Union' the gloss 'cooperation in economic and monetary policy' the limits the Single European Act placed on it would be signaled. Lawson in his memoirs (1992, p.894) disapprovingly writes of this that she mistakingly had heeded Foreign Office advice that what remained of the reference to EMU was 'little more than hot air'. In Lawson's view Thatcher had instead allowed the genie out of the bottle (p. 902), as became clear in the Hanover summit in June 1988.

33. Szász indicated that the Committee of Governors on a Dutch initiative would start a discussion on the long-term perspective of the EMS. In this way more clarity could be reached regarding the future role of the ECU. The Monetary Committee would conduct a discussion in parallel.
34. In the draft directive the Commission proposed to place three categories of capital restrictions on the list for which there was an unconditional obligation to liberalize: the issue of securities, transactions in non-tradable securities and long-term commercial credits (5 years and more). This went somewhat further than the earlier proposal in the White Book (compare Note 24). Furthermore, the Commission proposed to merge the unconditional lists (A and B) and the conditional lists (C and D).
35. Liberal countries, as Germany and the Netherlands, were particularly irritated that the Commission in its draft directive tried to curtail the powers of the Monetary Committee by restricting the committee's examination to the transactions which figured on the conditional list only. This meant that the committee would no longer be involved in the examination of the safeguard clauses and would have to leave this completely to the Commission. Given the Commission's track record, this was unacceptable for the liberal countries.
36. Directive (85/583/EEC), dated 20 December 1985, brought transactions in shares of unit trusts on the list of transactions to be unconditionally liberalized. It was supplemented by Directive (85/611/EEC), also dated 20 December 1985, which coordinated the legal and administrative regulations with respect to unit trusts. Both directives were effective from 1 October 1989.
37. Minister Stoltenberg: '.. a further strengthening of the EMS is absurd as long as there is no further liberalization of capital movements ..' (Die Zeit, 15 March, 1985). Bundesbank director Gleske: '.. the dismantling of the still numerous restrictions on capital movements that stand in the way of real monetary integration are the areas in which progress is required in order to consolidate and further develop the EMS ..' (Handelsblatt, 25 April 1985).
38. Programme for the liberalization of capital movements in the Community, Communication from the Commission to the Council (COM(86)292), 23 May 1986.
39. It would seem an anomaly that precisely long-term commercial credits had not been placed under the unconditional regime in the 1960 and 1962 Directives. The reason for this was of a practical nature: long-term commercial credits being not very common, they had been subject to special authorization procedures in several countries with the aim of verifying that there was a genuine link between the credit and the underlying commercial transaction. In this manner it could be ensured that the restrictions on financial credits were not circumvented. The authority to control such a link with commercial transactions was recognized in the draft directive.
40. Prompt revision of the safeguard clauses for France and Italy, so as to incorporate the easing of restrictions which had been carried out in the meantime; the presentation to the Council, early in the summer of 1986, of a proposal for a directive with respect to phase one; the submission to the Council towards the end of 1987 of a new directive incorporating the full liberalization of capital movements in phase two.
41. For instance, at the symposium 'L'Europe des services financiers', organized by the European League for Economic Cooperation in Brussels on 11 and 12 December 1986, EC Director-General Russo admitted that the full liberalization of capital flows would

not facilitate the operation of the EMS. In particular it would be necessary for monetary authorities to subordinate domestic interest rate policy to exchange rate stability.

42. Italy had kept in place the system of interest-free bank deposits for transactions in foreign securities, although it had lowered in steps the required percentage. Ireland still kept in place restrictions on transactions in foreign securities. There was a special regime for the new members of the EEC: in November 1985 the transition period for Greece had been extended until end–1988. Under the Accession Treaty Spain and Portugal had bargained for transition periods until end–1988 and end–1990 respectively.
43. In Favier and Martin-Roland (1990), p. 489, Pierre Bérégovoy stated, as quoted by the authors: 'The franc would have floated, it would have fallen, then it would have recovered and opinion would have supported its regained strength. Then it would have been possible to reintegrate the EMS. I remain persuaded that, sooner than having to accept a discipline imposed from the outside, we would have been able to find the strength to discipline ourselves.'
44. See also Koenig and Ledig (1989) for an elaborate survey of the interrelationship between capital movements and German monetary policy.
45. Germany had up till 1981 kept in place restrictions on the sale of short-term Deutsche mark paper to nonresidents. The authorities wanted to control the holdings of such paper in foreign hands in order to suppress the development of the Deutsche mark as an international reserve currency. These attempts, however, were in vain and the German authorities gradually gave up their resistance. On 17 March 1980 the maturity of interest-bearing paper which was allowed to be sold to nonresidents was lowered from four to two years. On 4 November the maturity was lowered to one year and on 19 February 1981 the restriction was abolished altogether. On 12 March the last remaining obstacles to inward capital movements were de facto lifted. It should be noted that also in the case of Germany exchange rate considerations played a role. The abolition of these last controls on inflows helped to underpin the Deutsche mark against continued upward pressure on the US dollar. The coupon tax on nonresidents' interest income, which did not constitute a capital restriction per se but was likewise intended to fend off capital imports when it was introduced in 1964, was not lifted until 1984.
46. On 1 May 1985 issues with variable interest and zero-coupon certificates were allowed, albeit in the longer end of the market (above 3 years). Also foreign banks in Germany were allowed to participate in issuing syndicates. This deregulation was propelled by the expansion these instruments had shown in the dollar segment of the market. A brief spell of weakness of the Deutsche Mark vis-à-vis the US dollar had precipitated decision-making in this area, which explicitly was meant to boost the Deutsche mark's international role.
47. Deutsche Bundesbank, Annual Report 1986, p. 75–76.
48. De Nederlandsche Bank, Annual Report 1985, p. 19.
49. In a written comment from the Dutch members of the Monetary Committee on the directive proposed by the Commission, dated 4 July 1986, a symmetrical application of the safeguard clause was demanded, whereby under certain circumstances balance-of-payments reasons (to check outflows) as well as monetary policy reasons (to check inflows) could justify measures, both being a consequence of the combination of liberalized capital flows and still imperfect convergence. Although the Commission considered the risks for monetary policy to be small, it argued that the 1972 Directive was still valid and could be applied in such circumstances, as could Article 73. Under the latter article control measures in Denmark, taken for domestic monetary reasons, had been authorized in the past as well. It was, however, questionable whether the Commission was right that the 1972 Directive could be invoked, because this directive was based on Article 70 which only applied to the coordination of exchange rate policies vis-à-vis third countries, i.e. non-EEC countries. Obviously this would not help the Dutch.
50. The law concerning financial relations with foreign countries (1980) contained ample possibilities to impose controls on capital inflows (see Chapter 6, Note 35). There was,

however, a certain fear that such restrictions, which needed to be approved in parliament, would not be comprehended well and would give rise to counterclaims for checking capital inflows by relaxing monetary policy and decreasing domestic interest rates.

51. In an interview with L'Echo de la Bourse on 8 May 1985 Jean Godeaux, Governor of the National Bank of Belgium said that he 'found it paradoxical and even irritating at times that some of Belgium's foreign partners pointed to the two-tier foreign exchange system as an example of an obstacle to complete financial integration within the Community.'
52. Interview with Jean Godeaux (ibid.).
53. Freiberg-Jensen and Hald (1986), p. 13.
54. Banca d'Italia, Annual Report 1985, p. 161.
55. Proposal for a Council Directive amending for the third time the first Council Directive for the implementation of Article 67 of the EEC Treaty, COM(86) 326 final, published in Official Journal of the European Communities, No. C 229/3, 10 September 1986.
56. Meeting of the Monetary Committee on 18 July 1986.
57. Press conference of Jacques Delors, President of the European Commission, on 22 May 1986.
58. Resolution of the European Parliament, dated 10 October 1986.
59. Directive of the Council of 17 November 1986 amending for the third time the first Council Directive for the implementation of Article 67 of the EEC Treaty, Offical Journal of the European Communities, No. L 332/22, 26 November 1986.
60. Spain and Portugal had lifted reservations on an earlier occasion when they were granted additional terms after the end of the transitional period provided for in the Accession Treaties. Furthermore, a transitional period for the application with regard to a number of transactions under the present 1986 Directive was granted until 31 December 1990 for Spain and 31 December 1992 for Portugal. This was one of the first instances where the Commission had applied the two-speed principle by differentiating transitional periods according to the economic development of the member state. It was at least curious that these extensions were already granted at this juncture, regardless of the economic situation at the end of the agreed transition period.

CHAPTER 8

Towards the Full Liberalization of Capital Movements

L'ouverture des frontières financières est une chance qu'il ne faut pas laisser passer, mais la construction du grand marché européen ne doit pas aboutir à mettre en panne l'Europe monétaire.

Edouard Balladur

8.1 INTRODUCTION

It had taken a long time to reach agreement on the 1986 directive. From the initial call in the Monetary Committee in mid–1982 for a resumption of the liberalization process to the entry into force of the directive in February 1987, nearly five years had been needed for reaching agreement on an enlargement of the liberalization obligations. Yet, these were not wasted years. The lengthy discussions were needed to bring about a *change in official thinking*, both among the officials as well as among the politicians. Countries had been able to try out cautiously the effects of a gradual relaxation of domestic regulations and exchange controls. Helped by macro-economic policies directed towards price stability and budgetary discipline, these steps generally had been received well in the financial markets. Nonetheless, at times there was a flare-up of tensions in the markets, usually sparked by political interference with interest rates.

A rather painful experience was the *realignment* within the EMS on 12 January 1987, in which the French franc and some other currencies had to be devalued by 3%. It was generally felt that this realignment 'à chaud' was not justified on fundamental grounds, but was forced by pressures in the markets after uncoordinated interest and intervention policies and a noticeable lack of verbal discipline on the part of some of the authorities involved.[1] At the same time, it was acknowledged that the changing environment in which financial markets operated made the maintenance of the remaining restrictions ever more ineffective. The increasing capital mobility was caused not only by the liberalization of exchange controls which had already taken place, but also by financial innovations, technical developments and domestic deregulation. The advantages of increased efficiency in the allocation of capital, which had played a role in the change of attitude of the Commission, as discussed in Chapter 7.4, could only be fully exploited if all capital movements were liberalized. The translation into agreed common obligations would be the subject matter of political negotiations. After a brief discussion of the changed financial environment this chapter deals with the political process leading up to the acceptance by all member states of full and unconditional freedom of capital movements as a Community obligation.

8.2 THE CHANGING FINANCIAL ENVIRONMENT

The increasing integration of national markets and the growth of international financial markets had made it ever more difficult to isolate domestic financial markets from external influences, especially the more developed ones. Four main influences were at work:

8.2.1 The Role of Innovations

The traditional distinction between short-term and long-term financial transactions had become increasingly blurred through financial innovations such as the introduction of interest rate options, financial instruments with variable interest rates and the like. This decompartmentalization of market segments had important implications for the transmission mechanism of monetary policy. Monetary instruments typically affect the short end of the market and many restrictions with respect to short-term capital flows were precisely intended to strengthen the effectiveness of domestic monetary policy actions. Because of innovations the traditional concepts of monetary aggregates became less reliable as indicators of the monetary policy stance, while at the same time the lags of their working-through in the domestic price level were affected.

8.2.2 The Administration of Controls

The increased size, number and sophistication of international financial operations, partly on account of technological advances, made it increasingly difficult to control capital transactions. Control being dependent on compliance by the commercial banks, considerations pertaining to cost and competitiveness came into play. The reporting requirements and strict surveillance of the banking system involved considerable costs for the banks as well as for the controlling authorities. Especially in France the requirement of so-called *domiciliation* dossiers, enabling the matching of financial and trade data, had become extremely burdensome. The banks came under increased competitive pressure from banks in third countries which sometimes had less strict control systems in place. At times, there was evidence of complicity of the banks in circumventing such controls.[2]

8.2.3 The Effectiveness of Controls

The effectiveness of controls varies inversely with the state of development of domestic financial markets. The more developed these markets are, the greater the possibilities for legitimate substitution. The markets for goods and services having become more and more integrated, industrial and investment companies had developed ingenious ways of circumventing controls by intercompany transactions or by using non-bank channels, thus leading to disintermediation. Countries experienced that over time controls, once imposed, had to be constantly reinforced and extended in scope in order to maintain their effectiveness.[3] Given the fungibility of capital, the prolonged closing of certain channels for capital transactions had the effect of deflecting flows to alternative, less controlled or regulated channels. Controls gave rise to disintermediation and to the migration of short-term operations to the international (Euro)markets or their spill-over into longer-term operations. In some instances capital restrictions thus had the unintended effect of developing the international markets for the currency in question, just as the controls in the United States had given rise to the development of the Euromarket in the 1960s.

8.2.4 Financial Integration

In nearly all European countries financial markets had developed rapidly because of deregulation and capital liberalization. Institutional investors had been given more leeway in the management of their assets and had become active cross-border players in the financial markets. The deregulation of institutional investors necessitated the freedom to protect assets against exchange rate changes. This protection could mainly be provided at the short end of the market (forward exchange transactions, interest rate options and futures, short-term financial transactions). Therefore, the corollary of financial integration was that there were increasing market pressures to abandon the remaining capital controls on the short end of the market.

To many observers the final step to full liberalization seemed inevitable and highly desirable. The question no longer was: why liberalize, but rather how soon. For full freedom of capital movements short-term transactions, still restricted in many countries, had to be liberalized, in particular financial loans to non-residents in domestic currency, cross-border transactions in money market paper and the opening of deposit accounts by residents in foreign currencies. *Economic conditions* were propitious for capital liberalization: the inflation differential, as measured by the gdp deflator, of France vis-à-vis Germany had declined from a high of 8.2% in 1982 to a mere 1.2% in 1986. As shown in Figure 20 in other countries inflation differentials had decreased as well.

8.3 COMMISSION INITIATIVES FOR FULL LIBERALIZATION

After the conclusion of the discussions on the first phase of its liberalization programme, culminating in the acceptance of the 1986 Directive, the Commis-

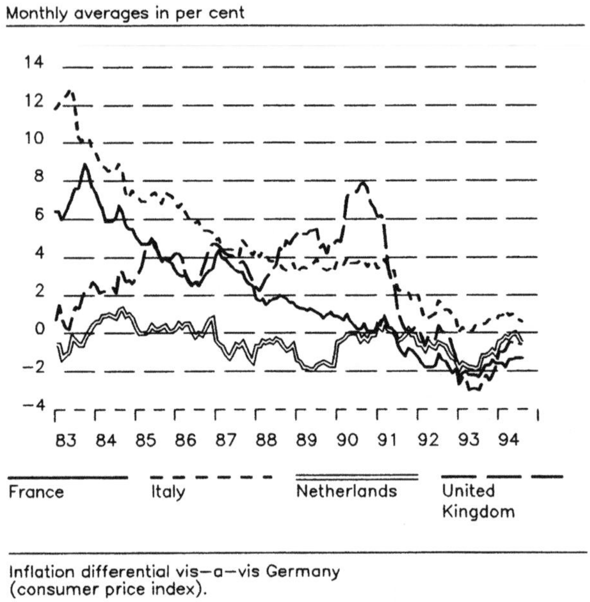

Fig. 20. Convergence of inflation in Europe.

sion was quick to start discussions on the second phase. Late 1986 thoughts were ventilated for the steps to be taken towards the complete liberalization of capital movements in due course.[4] In the Commission's words: 'The logic of (European) financial integration inevitably leads to the ending of all restrictions on capital movements and to the lifting of all types of discriminatory treatment.' In the document the Commission dealt with the implications for the conduct of *monetary policy* as well as with a number of related issues, which will be discussed in section 8.4. Full liberalization would imply, within the context of the EMS, a relative loss of national autonomy with respect to monetary policy. It would become impossible to isolate Euromarket interest rates from those prevailing on the domestic money market. Therefore short-term interest rates could hardly be used any longer to pursue purely domestic objectives. Increased capital mobility following full liberalization did not need to be destabilizing, however, as long as nominal divergences were reduced and strengthened coordination procedures would assure stable exchange rate expectations. Monetary policies in particular would have to be coordinated more closely. To this end the Commission proposed a greater role for symmetrical, non-sterilized *intramarginal interventions*. It also wished to develop an *EC-wide monetary aggregate*. This would help create a situation in which the basic monetary choices would have to be as collective as possible. A set of 'rules of the game' would have to be put in place to give content to the coordination procedures.

At this stage the Commission did not elaborate further, but the implications were clear: in an environment of full freedom of capital movements the Commission would like to make the use of domestic monetary policy instruments, presumably interest rates, the subject of Community coordination. *Common decision-making procedures* with respect to monetary policy would in practice imply more symmetrical interest rate adjustments in case of exchange rate pressures. Symmetrical sterilization of intramarginal interventions would imply that Germany would be confronted with increased intervention obligations as well. The Commission thus supported the long-standing French claim that German monetary policy called the tune too loudly and that the EMS should be operated in a more symmetrical way. Jacques Delors, the President of the Commission, had lamented publicly that 'the West German government lacks the same interest in the construction of Europe now that it had in former years'.[5] But the Commission did a fine *balancing act*. Traditionally inclined to follow French convictions it had to allow for German considerations as well. With its strategic choice for full capital liberalization it had heeded Germany's vision of European integration. It now remained to be seen whether the Commission would stick to its choice with no strings attached or whether it would postulate conditions to be fulfilled simultaneously.

8.3.1 Reactions of Member States

A wide-ranging discussion was held in the Monetary Committee in February 1987. The fundamental issue was whether full capital liberalization would contribute to convergence and thus to exchange rate stability, or whether accompanying measures in the field of monetary policy would be needed. *Germany,* so it became clear, was unwilling to consider any transfer of monetary policies to the EC level, as was implied in the Commission document. While Germany acknowledged that exchange rate tensions were more likely to arise when capital movements were fully liberalized, monetary policy remained the responsibility of the member states. Strengthened coordination thus could not be interpreted in such a way that the goal of domestic monetary stability in Germany would be subordinated to the maintenance of the EMS parities. As long as convergence was not complete the EMS should therefore leave room for exchange rate adjustments.[6]

Some smaller countries, such as the *Netherlands* and to a certain extent *Denmark,* took a rather relaxed attitude with respect to the de facto loss of monetary autonomy, which in any case had already been eroded considerably. But in their view, strings were attached: countries should be prepared to use market-oriented monetary instruments and accept the interest rate consequences of external constraints. Policies should be directed to domestic price stability in order to combine free capital flows with exchange rate stability. This was in line with their traditional fear of realignments of other currencies which always could undermine confidence in the national currency as well.

Price convergence at higher levels was considered to be not good enough, because of the intrinsic merits of price stability and the inherent unsteadiness of higher inflation rates. The Dutch particularly disliked the *inflationary consequences* of the Commission's proposals. The call for increased intra-marginal interventions and symmetrical interest rate adjustments in their eyes were aimed at hedging in German monetary policy. They involved the risk of postponing adjustment in the weaker-currency countries. Thus the potential conflict between internal and external stability eventually would increase, endangering the stability of the Exchange Rate Mechanism.

The *French* professed sympathy for the Commission's ideas. For them the strengthening of the EMS remained an important theme, which should accompany the move to freedom of capital movements. The French concern was that capital liberalization in itself did not further the European cause because it was mainly a reflection of the world-wide deregulation and globalization of international financial markets.[7] As a follow-up to the mandate given after the January 1987 realignment the French members of the Monetary Committee had presented a *memorandum* in which proposals were made for a *new package deal* to strengthen the functioning of the EMS.[8] In this memorandum the French members mounted their hobby-horses once again with respect to the functioning of the EMS, in line with their 'monetarist' approach towards monetary integration. France demanded symmetric macroeconomic adjustment measures in hard-currency and weak-currency countries alike as well as symmetric intervention obligations, backed by greater resources. One way of achieving the latter would be that EC central banks would hold each other's currencies in their official foreign reserves. These proposals were based on the fear that the EMS could break apart in the face of increased capital mobility. All progress made with respect to convergence would then dissipate. Therefore, the French held that capital liberalization should not proceed too quickly. In any case, it would be a great step backwards if France were to be compelled to once again have recourse to the use of safeguard clauses.

Italy, which considered its regained external equilibrium to be precarious, went a step further by calling for *institutional changes*. In the Italian view full liberalization, by creating a new environment, called for new rules with respect to monetary policy coordination, such as the collective fixing of domestic monetary targets. The latter would require the transfer of powers to a centralized European institution which would then oversee the development of these monetary objectives.[9] In this respect the Italian attitude came closest to that of the Commission. The implication was clear: the Bundesbank might have provided a useful anchor for disciplining weak-currency countries, now that convergence was progressing this dominant position was no longer acceptable. German monetary leadership was challenged.

The discussion made clear that there was no agreement on the fundamental question whether full capital liberalization necessitated accompanying measures in the monetary field. Although it was accepted by all that capital

TABLE 26

A political tally of attitudes towards capital liberalization.

		pro	contra	intermediate
1.	Full liberalization	Germany Netherlands UK	Greece Denmark* France** Italy Ireland	Belgium
2.	Erga omnes	Belgium Denmark Germany Italy (?) The Netherlands	–	France** UK**
3.	Extension of safeguard clauses	Belgium France Greece Ireland Italy Netherlands	Denmark Germany Luxembourg UK	–
4.	Stricter coordination of monetary policies	Ireland Italy Netherlands	Denmark Germany UK	Belgium France
5.	EC credit mechanism to support capital liberalization	Greece Ireland Italy	Denmark Germany Netherlands UK	–

Note:
* Liberalization first to be applied only to industrial sector.
* France favoured preferential EC system for financial services, the UK reciprocity.

liberalization would promote discipline on economic policies, France and Italy, supported by a number of restrictive countries, asked for quid pro quos in the operation of the EMS. Despite this continuing divergence of views, the Commission could feel strengthened by the discussion in the Monetary Committee. No fundamental objections to full capital liberalization had been raised. And it was taken for granted that the pace of progress should not be dictated by the countries with the lowest degree of liberalization, but by those countries which had made real progress. For countries which could not keep the pace, transitional arrangements would be made. The Commission reported to the Council that the implications of full liberalization would be multiple and major, but that none of them would represent an insurmountable obstacle.[10] It would be an irreversible process, providing a challenge to the EMS, but also an opportunity to strengthen it. As far as the Commission was concerned, it declared that it would set *no preconditions* for full capital liberalization. This was an important declaration, removing the sting from the Commission's call for increased symmetry. As discussed in Chapter 7 the Commission put its hope on a dynamic process, in which capital liberalization would stimulate the adoption of the accompanying measures which it favoured. The Commission had set out a strategic course and now it would stick to it.

8.3.2 Two Rival Schools of Thought

The Commission had derived from the discussion in the Monetary Committee that there were two rival schools of thought as to how to resolve in the long run the '*triangle of incompatibilities*' between the coexistence of exchange rate stability, free movement of capital and autonomy over monetary policy (at least in certain countries). One school relied on the common adherence to the objective of *monetary stability*, i.e. domestic price stability. This would spontaneously generate coordination of monetary policies, subject to a certain degree of flexibility in the EMS. This school of thought was based on the view that capital flows were basically induced by macroeconomic policies and their credibility. The other school favoured an *institutional solution* with collective monetary decision-making, accompanied by increased financial solidarity to defend exchange rates. According to the latter view destabilizing capital flows might also develop as a result of exogenous factors that were neither linked to the stance of domestic policies nor to the fundamentals. Such exogenous factors could be sharp swings in the exchange rate of the US dollar or expectations of a realignment involving the main EMS currencies.

At the request of the Commission a *group of experts*, chaired by professor Tommaso Padoa-Schioppa, vice director-general of the Banca d'Italia, was invited to study the implications of capital liberalization.[11] The group gave unequivocal support to the school favouring an institutional solution. Its main conclusion was that '... the elimination of capital controls, coupled to the requirement of exchange rate stability, (...) will require moving closer to unification of monetary policy. In a quite fundamental way, capital mobility and exchange rate fixity leave no room for independent monetary policies. In these conditions, it is pertinent to consider afresh the case for a strengthened organisation of monetary coordination or institutional advances in this field'. It suggested to move to a 'European central banking system with considerably enhanced policy coordination and executive responsibilities'. In such a system the targets of monetary policy would be jointly agreed or set through a common procedure and the attainment of these targets closely coordinated.The report also called for the simultaneous strengthening of EMS mechanisms to counter speculative capital movements along the lines of the French memorandum. However, the report was remarkably silent on the need to coordinate budgetary policies. Although it noted that the system for coordination of budgetary policies under the 1974 Convergence Decision had been ineffective, it favoured relying on the restraint the capital market would exert on state borrowing. In this respect the report was considered to be rather lopsided by many members of the Monetary Committee, some of whom moreover preferred the common pursuit of domestic price stability above symmetrical monetary policy cooperation.[12] Its findings did not play an immediate role in the further decision-making with respect to the capital liberalization directive. But its call for monetary unification had touched a string.

The *informal Ecofin meeting in Knokke* on 4 April 1987 provided a first opportunity for Ministers to discuss the further strengthening of the EMS and the full liberalization of capital movements after the January realignment. Some Ministers, among which Gerhard Stoltenberg of Germany and Onno Ruding of the Netherlands, in the 'economist' tradition, argued that capital liberalization could and should precede further measures with respect to the EMS. In their view the dynamic interaction of free capital flows and domestic policies would contribute to a strengthening of the EMS, especially by bringing to bear substantial pressure for a higher degree of convergence. Others held the opinion that the EMS should be strengthened further before capital flows could be fully liberalized. Minister Edouard Balladur was a vocal spokesman: 'Il faut avancer avec pragmatisme sur les deux fronts à la fois', echoed by Jaques Delors: 'Liberalization of capital movements and reinforcement of the EMS must go hand in hand'.[13] Chairman Eyskens could not yet firmly conclude that both dossiers, on capital liberalization and strengthening of the EMS, were linked. But he made clear that a common position to be aimed at could not contain a fundamental revision of the EMS, but rather would have to be limited to technical improvements. It was decided that both dossiers would continue to be discussed in the Monetary Committee and the Committee of Governors with the aim of reaching such a common position. The Commission was invited to come forward in the autumn of 1987 with concrete proposals for the second phase, leading up to full capital liberalization.

8.4 THE MONETARY SAFEGUARD CLAUSE AND THE ERGA OMNES PRINCIPLE

Several *related issues* were discussed in the intervening months. One of these concerned the implications for the financing of public deficits, if protected home markets were to be opened up. It turned out that the privileged access to domestic funds by public authorities was not yet seen as a problem. However, the issue would be taken up later in the context of the EMU negotiations. Three important questions remained: the need for safeguard clauses in the new directive; the future status of the 1972 Directive, with the related question whether intra-EC capital liberalization would equally apply to third countries; and, finally, the need for enlarging the existing financing mechanisms in the Community.

8.4.1 The Monetary Safeguard Clause

The Commission favoured the incorporation of a specific, so-called monetary safeguard clause, which would allow controls on short-term inflows or outflows to be imposed in case of serious *disturbances* either in the conduct of *monetary policy* or in the stability of the *exchange rate*.[14] The Commission argued that the existing safeguard provisions of Articles 108 and 109 could not be invoked in all circumstances because they expressis verbis were limited to crisis situations. Given the uncertain international monetary environment, there could be instances where national monetary policies were disturbed because of cyclical divergences, even when fundamental economic factors would appear to be basically sound. The Commission took the view that such special circumstances could warrant controls as well. Article 73 could not be invoked either, because the legal services of the Commission considered that the term 'capital market' could not be interpreted widely to include money-market and other short-term financial operations. Because it was acknowledged that such controls lost effectiveness over time, the validity of the monetary safeguard clause should be limited to 3 or at most 6 months.

Germany, the United Kingdom, Denmark and Luxembourg were not in favour of a monetary safeguard clause. They considered such a clause to be an unfortunate signal to the financial markets which could weaken confidence in the Exchange Rate Mechanism, particularly with respect to the weak currencies. But there was a majority, consisting mainly of precisely these weak-currency countries, which was in favour of such a safeguard clause: France, Italy, Belgium, Spain, Portugal, Ireland and Greece. There was the example of *Italy* which had taken restrictive measures late in the summer of 1987 when the lira had come under temporary pressure. These measures had met with a certain degree of success. It was felt that this case provided a good example of the kind of instances when temporary restrictions, to be covered by the monetary safeguard clause proposed by the Commission, would be useful.

TABLE 27

Dutch non-bank capital flows in billions of guilders.

	1963	1973	1983	1988	1993
Direct investments	2.8	10.8	27.5	111.6	246.8
Dutch securities	2.7	9.6	63.6	260.7	717.6
Foreign securities	3.1	14.4	62.4	162.2	579.9
Total long-term	9.8	39.8	168.6	551.9	1,565.6
Total short-term	0.5	0.2	21.0	128.8	458.3
Total	10.3	40.0	189.6	680.7	2,023.9

Note: Gross total of inflows and outflows.

The *Dutch* authorities initially took a completely different approach in an attempt to maintain a measure of limited monetary autonomy. They pleaded for an *asymmetrical safeguard clause* which would only apply to capital *inflows*. Such restrictions would largely be of a technical character, since they would be designed to supplement domestic credit restrictions if internal monetary stability was threatened. The Dutch argued that safeguard measures on outflows were of a different nature. They could even be counterproductive by undermining the credibility of the currency, since foreign capital would be mousetrapped in a country with restrictions on outflows.

The Dutch found themselves in an awkward position. By not aligning themselves with the traditional liberal countries, they had played in the hands of the more restrictive countries and thus *swayed the balance* in favour of a safeguard clause. Internally, however, the discussion served a useful purpose, because it triggered a fundamental debate on the methods of monetary control. Historical data suggested that restrictions on credit-taking with banks abroad as a supplement to domestic credit ceilings would affect at most 10 per cent of total capital imports. The restrictions could be easily circumvented by specially created short-term paper, by swaps, or by intra-group credits. The apparatus to control these loopholes was simply not available.[15] The monetary effect of such controls therefore was highly questionable; they had merely symbolic significance in the light of the sharply increased capital movements (see Table 27). In these circumstances the Dutch abandoned their request for an asymmetrical safeguard clause and decided to ally with those liberal countries which resisted any safeguard clause. At the same time, it was conceded that in an open economy as the Netherlands it would no longer be possible to control domestic liquidity creation. Instead, the focus of monetary policy was shifted towards supporting the long-standing exchange rate policy, i.e. the link of the Netherlands guilder to the Deutsche mark. A complete *overhaul of monetary instruments* followed. The instrument of direct credit restrictions was discarded and in future the Nederlandsche Bank would rely solely on market-oriented indirect means of controlling monetary developments. It was the final demise of the monetary tradition of Holtrop which had governed for so long a time – and with considerable success – the monetary policy actions of the Nederlandsche Bank.

In the meantime Germany and the United Kingdom had taken the position that if a monetary safeguard clause was to be the price for full liberalization, it was worth paying as long as the *duration* of controls was limited and the application would remain under *Community control.* In any case, such restrictions should not be taken on the initiative of the Commission, but should be decided by the member states concerned. In the end a position emerged where the dividing line between countries pro and countries contra a safeguard clause approximately coincided with the dividing line between more and less liberal countries.

8.4.2 The 1972 Directive and the Erga Omnes Principle

The Commission proposed to incorporate the monetary safeguard clause into an amended version of the *1972 Directive,* which in its view should be retained alongside the new liberalization directive. The 1972 Directive was considered to remain important, because the Community should not deprive itself of the means for a coordinated regulation of capital movements to and from third countries, in particular in the event of violent external shocks. The *erga omnes principle*, adhered to by most countries, was considered by the Commission as merely a political declaration. It had no plans to write this principle into Community legislation. On the contrary, it might be useful to leave third countries in doubt as to whether the Community might actually impose capital controls vis-à-vis them. In the background the concern lingered that the upheavals of the US dollar might again bring unrest to the European Monetary System. Periods of dollar weakness had typically pushed the Deutsche mark up and exerted pressure on the other EMS currencies. In extreme cases the Community should be able to shield itself from such external disturbances.

Apart from some token support of France and Italy, the Commission proposal to retain the 1972 Directive and enlarge its scope did not receive much sympathy. Italy had not applied the liberalization obligations which followed from the 1986 Directive on an erga omnes scale, arguing that the liberalization of portfolio transactions for non-EC countries would be too large a burden for its weak domestic capital market. The Commission's concept of a shielded European capital market was fundamentally different from the concept of a *Europe open to the outside world*, favoured in particular by Germany and some other countries. Germany wished to abrogate the directive altogether, whereas other countries equally felt that it could be dispensed with as long as the monetary safeguard clause was incorporated into the new directive.

Nonetheless, some countries wished to reserve their own attitude as to a strict application of the erga omnes principle on purely domestic grounds. For this they did not need an EC directive but they favoured an interpretation of the erga omnes principle which would allow them to take measures in the grey zone of domestic regulations, especially with respect to the financial services sector. France for example favoured the *positive discrimination* of EC institutions in some areas, and wished to protect its own financial services sector.[16] And the United Kingdom, although embracing the erga omnes principle, favoured *reciprocity* vis-à-vis third countries. The British in particular were fearful that a wide interpretation of the erga omnes principle would weaken the negotiating position of the Community with respect to Japan. Japanese financial institutions were aggressively entering European markets and it was felt that this would be only permissible if the Japanese domestic financial market would be opened up to foreign financial institutions as well.

8.4.3 The European Credit Mechanisms

The Commission favoured extending *financial support* to those member states which would liberalize in spite of a precarious external position. It proposed to combine the existing Community credit mechanisms and change their application. It was envisaged that the combined credit mechanism could be used not only in the traditional manner, i.e. in support of adjustment programs of member countries in balance-of-payments difficulties, but also in support of capital liberalization. These proposals met with mixed feelings in the Monetary Committee. Of course potential users of the credit facilities such as Italy, Spain, Greece and Ireland, were in favour, and saw a political trade-off between the extension of the credit mechanisms and the transitional period which would be allowed to them. Other countries did not consider such extension urgent. In any case the usual conditionality tied to Community loans should be maintained, if not strengthened. The previous experiences with respect to the contribution EC loans had made to adjustment was not encouraging. All in all the positions ran along the dividing line between potential creditors and potential debtors, as had also been the case on the monetary safeguard clause.

8.5 TRANSITIONAL ARRANGEMENTS

Some member states had got cold feet with respect to the timing of the full liberalization of capital movements. France suggested that as a first step liberalization could be limited to transactions by *commercial enterprises* only.[17] A similar idea to subdivide the second phase had been voiced by Denmark. However, the Commission did not see any possibility for differentiation, arguing that the remaining short-term operations were all highly substitutable. The limitation of liberalization to such operations carried out by commercial enterprises, as had been effected in France, would be too complicated to codify at the Community level. On the other hand, a differentiation in timing as between the liberalization in individual member states was advisable, since the starting positions were very different. The deadline of end–1992 set for the completion of the internal market should, however, represent the absolute limit for the transitional arrangements in the view of the Commission.[18]

By accepting *transitional arrangements,* the Commission embraced the argument that sequencing was justified to a certain degree. The Commission based its judgment on three evaluation criteria: (a) *The degree of development of the national financial system*

The commercial banks and other financial institutions should be sufficiently robust in order to hold their own against a very competitive international environment and not be swamped by foreign institutions. In the eyes of the Commission this presupposed a diversified body of institutions and instruments, operating under predominantly market-oriented conditions. Furthermore, money supply and credit control should be based chiefly on indirect methods, i.e. through movements in interest rates. Finally, the public sector deficit should be of such a size that it could be financed at market conditions, without excessive costs. If these conditions were fulfilled capital liberalization would have no harmful side-effects.

(b) The level of external debt

A very high external debt ratio might discourage spontaneous new capital inflows. In such circumstances a serious consolidation programme would have to be carried through, aimed at strengthening the balance of payments. Such a programme might be jeopardized by a premature, radical liberalization of capital flows.

(c) The degree of integration in the Community

Countries like Greece and Ireland, and the newly acceding countries Spain and Portugal, were not yet fully integrated into the Community. Moreover, they did not yet participate in the Exchange Rate Mechanism of the EMS, with the exception of Ireland. The latter's membership, however, was complicated by the non-participation of the United Kingdom. This criterion was considered to be so important as to make it impossible to finalize the full liberalization of capital movements within five years, i.e. before the end of 1992, without accompanying measures, such as an extension of financing facilities. Indeed under the umbrella term of 'cohesion' the Commission proposed to develop special funds in support of the process of catching-up with the more developed countries of the European Community. This was the price tag attached to Community-wide capital liberalization.

In their initial reaction to the Commission proposals for transitional periods, the member states concerned showed a clear reluctance to move fast. For Spain and Ireland the Commission had proposed a final date of 1990, whereas for Portugal and Greece the deadline was set at 1992. All these countries opted for later dates: Portugal even mentioned 1995. Their main argument was that sequencing was required and that *entry into the Exchange Rate Mechanism* of the EMS had priority over capital liberalization. To have both at the same time was not possible, it was felt. In order to placate the lagging countries the Commission pushed hard to reach agreement on its proposals for special funds for those countries which wished to liberalize.

8.6 QUESTIONS OF COMPETENCE

In its proposals the Commission had taken a wide definition of the obligation to liberalize: *domestic regulations* which would discriminate against non-residents were not allowed. The liberalization obligation would not only imply the abolition of exchange controls which restricted transfers, but would ultimately also apply to any regulation which would limit the possibility to conclude or perform the underlying transaction. Although this attitude was widely accepted, it could give rise to questions regarding the division of responsibilities between national monetary authorities and the Commission. It was acknowledged that, for reasons of monetary control, the commercial banks would have to comply with rules which in practice could have the effect of restricting capital flows. In particular this was the case for limits on the net external position of financial institutions or for compulsory reserve ratios on their external assets or liabilities. Such measures would be needed in the future as well for monetary or supervisory reasons and therefore the Commission proposals provided for the exclusion of such measures from the general obligation to liberalize. However, for this grey area a notification and monitoring procedure was proposed in which not only the Monetary Committee and the Committee of Governors played a role, but also the Commission itself. In this manner the Commission could monitor that monetary instruments were not used improperly with the ulterior motive of limiting capital movements.

Especially from the German side it was feared that this could impinge on the *national responsibilities* in the monetary field as they had been reconfirmed in the Single Act. They argued that only the two competent committees, in which the Commission was represented anyway, should monitor this. The Commission always could turn to the Court of Justice if it felt that Community legislation had been infringed.[19] Obviously the Commission could only take this step after having heard the advice of the two competent bodies. Eventually a compromise was reached and Article 2 of the 1988 Directive, which is reproduced in Annex 6, would state that the Commission would be notified of those measures to regulate the liquidity of the banks which would influence capital transactions with non-residents; the two competent bodies would advise the Commission whether such measures were indeed confined to what was necessary for the purpose of domestic monetary regulation.[20]

Another question of competence came up, reminiscent of the earlier discussion in 1984. Again, it concerned the respective roles of the Commission and the Monetary Committee. The Commission in its draft had not envisaged a role for the committee as regards the examination of remaining restrictions. It had assumed that such a task would automatically lapse with the establishment of full freedom of capital movements. Besides it felt that the surveillance of compliance with the directive was the task of the Commission. The members of the Monetary Committee again did not agree: safeguards and transitional arrangements could have important policy implications and should thus remain a matter for discussion by the committee.

The jury is still out on the question which approach would be the most effective one to enforce compliance. On the one hand, the Monetary Committee might be expected to provide the right environment for exercising peer pressure on countries to comply, not only with the letter, but also with the spirit of the liberalization directive. On the other hand the Commission feared that in the grey area of indirect controls a united front of member states might emerge within the committee, which would seek to preserve the status quo. That this fear was not completely unfounded became evident in later examinations when the peer pressure did not materialize when the Commission raised possible infringements of the liberalization directive in the four large member states (see also discussion in Chapter 9.2.4).

8.7 THE BASLE/NYBORG AGREEMENT

In the run-up to the Nyborg informal Ecofin meeting in September 1987 both the Committee of Governors and the Monetary Committee focused on the package to strengthen the EMS, which had begun to take shape since the Knokke meeting. As to the management of the EMS understandings were reached on the proper use of *interest rates* to defend the exchange rate and the more flexible use of the *fluctuation margins*. If *realignments* were needed, they should be small and infrequent. The most important aspect of the so-called Basle/Nyborg agreement among central banks (Basle) and ministers (Nyborg) was that a common strategy was developed to withstand speculative pressures. Large-scale interventions should no longer be the chief line of defence, because experience had convinced the Monetary Committee members that such interventions by themselves could be counterproductive and were a cause of instability.[21] The new set of instruments was designed both to deter speculation as well as to punish speculators by showing that speculation was costly (high interest rates), and unrewarding (the full use of the fluctuation band in combination with small realignments implying only limited changes in market rates).

There was also some expansion of the *financing facilities* of the EMS. This was reluctantly accepted by the Bundesbank. It had agreed to this because the EMS had proved to be a stabilizing element and partner countries had strengthened visibly their stability-oriented policies. And it had taken into account the Governors' view that all central banks should give priority to price stability in their monetary policy.[22] This fundamental orientation was worth a price. Germany again had made concessions. Some observers in Germany feared that by giving other countries an inch, they would take a mile. The Commission and France had always been quite open in their strategy of reaching the ultimate goal by means of small steps. This meant in practice that every concession by Germany would be followed by fresh French demands.

This was not a hypothetical risk. President Delors had already sent a memorandum to the informal Ecofin in Nyborg in which he presented some new proposals which had far-reaching *institutional* implications. In particular he proposed to transfer the monetary coordination from the Committee of Governors to the dormant European Monetary Cooperation Fund and to open the possibility to create ECUs against Community currencies.[23] The German reaction was predictably negative. Such steps could only be taken in the perspective of the ultimate target of Economic and Monetary Union. This obviously was a risky course as long as there was no political consensus on EMU and governments were not prepared to surrender necessary powers in the non-monetary area.

The Basle/Nyborg agreement, underneath the sobering resolutions on the management of the EMS, constituted one of the distinct turning points in the history of capital liberalization. It would be the beginning of a long period of quasi-exchange rate stability, thus providing a background which was conducive to both capital liberalization and the resumption of the debate on economic and monetary union. To a certain extent in the Basle/Nyborg agreement for the first time economic policy considerations, and in particular the need to achieve convergence as a precondition for exchange rate stability, took precedence over technical refinements of the system. The Commission's attitude was an interesting one as well. On the one hand the forward thrust was clearly discernible, on the other hand the traditional regulative position is still there, as the ambiguous memorandum of Delors showed. This potentially defensive line would remain sotto terre in the coming years but would re-emerge in 1993 when Delors, shaken by the EMS crises would call for the reimposition of capital restrictions. The Commission, while still maintaining the line of full liberalization as set out in its plans, remained fearful that the risk was increased that markets would amplify the exchange rate repercussions of external disturbances or perceived policy divergences of a temporary nature. Some others shared this fear as well. The operational consequence which the Commission drew was to insist on safeguard clauses, transitional periods and support mechanisms to avoid the EMS being shaken by too brutal shocks. In Nyborg, however, these Commission fears were brushed aside.

8.8 A EUROPEAN FINANCIAL AREA

After the Basle/Nyborg agreement, aimed at strengthening the EMS, attention again could be focused on the capital liberalization dossier. The Commission presented in October 1987 a new document on the creation of a European financial area in which its views were further elaborated in the light of the first round of discussions in the Monetary Committee.[24] The new directive would seek to reach full capital liberalization by the end of 1988, apart from transitional periods for lagging countries. The timing of the Commission document was somewhat awkward because on *Black Monday* – 19 October 1987 – share prices had plummeted world-wide, giving rise to concern over financial fragilities in the international system. These concerns were raised by the rapidity with which stock exchanges in different financial centres nosedived. This covariance was partly ascribed to the deregulations which had taken place.

8.8.1 Discussion in the Monetary Committee

In the discussion in the Monetary Committee, which took place only a few days later, the stock exchange collapse was very much on the minds of participants, but it detracted in no way from their willingness to positively appraise the main thrust of the Commission proposals. The full liberalization of capital movements at one stroke was now accepted by all, on the understanding that transitional periods would be granted to the lagging countries. And it was agreed by a large majority that there would be *no preconditions* for full capital liberalization as long as there was parallel progress in related areas. This was an important political signal. For the first time, the quid-pro-quo approach, still demonstrated by France in the 1986 Ootmarssum realignment discussions (see page 177), was abandoned. Apparently, France on domestic grounds had already decided for itself that it would abolish exchange control altogether.

The most hesitant attitude vis-à-vis full capital liberalization was adopted by *Italy.* Had the problems which were associated with increased capital mobility been discussed sufficiently in the Monetary Committee? In the Italian view, there were actual dangers that both exchange rate and monetary stability would be jeopardized. If monetary coordination could not be brought a step further – and this became increasingly apparent in the German attitude – other ways to strengthen the cohesion among EMS members should be explored. This brought back a familiar theme in the Italian demands: expansion of the EC credit mechanisms and enlargement of the financing possibilities in surplus countries. With respect to the latter the Italians proposed to establish a new Community *recycling mechanism* which would enable deficit countries to attract funds on the capital markets of the surplus countries.[25] These were the kind of demands which scared off countries like Germany: cohesion in their view was to be brought about by adjustment in the deficit countries, not by the financing of the balance-of-payments deficits which would imply their continuation.

The Commission insisted on maintaining the *1972 Directive,* albeit in a modified form, despite the outspoken resistance in the Monetary Committee. Part of this modified directive would be a declaration of intent which would state that the member states would endeavour to attain the same degree of capital liberalization vis-à-vis third countries as within the Community. This implied that member states were not bound by the erga omnes principle. The Commission also proposed that it could issue a recommendation to activate monetary instruments in order to regulate capital movements to or from third countries causing serious disturbances to the exchange rate stability in the EMS. Only the Italians and to a lesser extent the French seemed interested. For France the main issue of importance was that the erga omnes principle would not be a legally binding obligation, but rather a political declaration of intent. In no way should this prevent the Community from taking steps vis-à-vis third countries if their policies were a hindrance for the good functioning of the EMS. For Germany such common measures would be unthinkable. They would constitute a step backwards in the liberalization process.

8.8.2 The Belgian Dual Market

The Commission had left no doubt that full capital liberalization would not be compatible with any multiple exchange rate practices. However, Belgium, supported by its Luxembourg partners in the monetary union, held its *dual exchange market* close to the chest. It was again argued, as on previous occasions, that this did not constitute a capital restriction, but rather should be regarded as an imperfection in their exchange regime – a 'flaw' – of a nature similar to the use of the wide band in the ERM in the case of Italy or the floating of the British pound outside the ERM. The implication obviously was that the dual regime only had to be abandoned if the latter 'imperfections' had been removed as well.[26] This argument was contested by others on procedural as well as substantive grounds. As regards *procedure,* it had been agreed that there would be no preconditions and the Belgian double exchange market could not form an exception. There was considerable peer pressure. Belgium and Luxembourg were put through the wringer by their two big neighbours: France and Germany. As regards *substance,* it was pointed out that for the operation of a dual market administrative regulations and a control apparatus were necessary as well, just as in case of exchange restrictions. The uncertainty with respect to the exchange rate in the dual market brought along additional costs and therefore did hamper capital movements, as it was intended to do. The staff at the Nationale Bank of Belgium who were controlling the dual market were not acting in a very different manner from those in other bureaucracies dealing with exchange restrictions. For them it was just as difficult when, with the eventual abolition of the dual market, they had to be converted into statisticians. From now on they could only register capital flows but no longer had the power to delegate applicants to the free market by the stroke of their pen.

The *reluctance* of Belgium and Luxembourg to drop the system when it increasingly seemed obsolete, can be traced back to several factors: – for long, the entrenched domestic acceptability of the system weighed heavily against the shade it was conceivably casting on the international status of the Belgian franc;

– twice in the past, and as early as in the 1960s, preparations had been made to abolish the system, but were cancelled at the last minute when a crisis showed it could still play a useful role;

– once dismantled the system could not easily be reinstated under a safeguard clause;

– the *Luxembourg* authorities were very supportive of the dual exchange market. The system provided Luxembourg with an institutional guarantee that capital flows would not be regulated by direct administrative controls. This was of the utmost importance to the position of Luxembourg as a financial centre. The Luxembourg authorities feared that if the dual market was to be banned, the Belgian monetary authorities could have recourse to other means of interfering with capital flows under Community regulations, which would harm the position of Luxembourg.

8.8.3 Draft Directives

After this discussion in the Monetary Committee the Commission presented its *draft directive* on the full liberalization of capital movements in November 1987.[27] This directive was accompanied by two other draft directives, one to amend the 1972 Directive and another one to revise the medium-term financial instruments of the Community. President Delors presented the proposals both in the Ecofin Council and in the meeting of the Governors.[28] In the circle of the *central bankers* President Delors raised the issue of the wide band of the Italian lira and the dual exchange market for the Belgian franc. The position of the Commission was that the lira should move to the narrow band and that the dual market should be abolished, but that it was open-minded as regards the precise timing, as long as the transitional period would be short. However, as far as the Commission was concerned, the entry of the pound sterling into the ERM was nearly a precondition for the proper functioning of a European financial area. Despite the events on Black Monday, the Commission would proceed with the necessary steps to bring about one integrated financial area in Europa. This should be regarded as an act of faith in the functioning of market mechanisms and in the capability of the Community to respond to these events. Although on the whole the reception among Governors was positive, there was a brief Italian-inspired discussion whether it was really necessary to bring about full freedom of capital flows soon. Could countries not decide for themselves on the timing as long as they promised to fulfil their obligations in this respect before the end of 1992? But President Delors did not flinch. Four countries had already fully liberalized, four other countries, including Italy, were perfectly capable of doing so in 1988 in the eyes of the Commission. For the remaining four countries the Commission had already proposed transitional periods up until the end of 1992 at the latest.[29]

In the *Ecofin meeting* in the following week President Delors reiterated that the degree of organization and the quality of the supervision of the financial markets, one of the evaluation criteria, could be regarded as equal in 8 out of the 12 Community countries. Therefore these countries did not need any transitional periods. Chairmen Ciampi (Committee of Governors) and Littler (Monetary Committee) reported on the state of the discussions in their respective committees. It was typical of the European decision-making process that ministers refrained from commenting on substance, but confined themselves to discussing the procedure to be followed. Ministers agreed that the technical working groups of the Council were not allowed to start their work until the final advice of both committees had been received by the Ecofin Council.

In the Alternates of the Monetary Committee, which prepared the committee's advice, the general support for full capital liberalization was reaffirmed, apart from another last-ditch Italian attempt to *subdivide* the liberalization process into two steps: first the non-bank transactions and then the bank transactions. It was argued that such gradual implementation would permit the harmonization of supervisory rules and the coordination of monetary policies to catch up with the capital liberalization process. There was, however, no support for this approach. In practice such a distinction could not be made easily and soon market operators would have found loopholes. Moreover, it ran against the accepted policy line that no preconditions should be attached to full capital liberalization.

8.9 FISCAL QUESTIONS

All along in the negotiations on the liberalization of capital movements the implications for the collection of taxes in member states were an important issue. There was a genuine fear among governments that with increased capital mobility funds would flow to countries with lower tax rates. The Commission on the other hand was concerned that if a certain degree of *tax harmonization* were to be a precondition for full capital liberalization, the whole process would be bogged down in interminable negotiations. On this it was probably right. Taxation notoriously was the most difficult area to agree upon, not least because of the ultimate authority to tax of national parliaments. Although it was accepted by member states that other dossiers should not form a precondition, pressures mounted on the Commission to undertake some action and come forward with proposals for measures aimed at harmonization or prevention of tax evasion. The Commission obliged and announced to aim at establishing a framework of harmonized rules in the tax field by 1992. Member states thus could be satisfied that an environment would be created in which possibly negative side-effects of full capital liberalization would be minimized. Commissioner Lord Cockfield toyed with three ideas: a general *withholding tax* on interest payments, an obligation for all banks to *disclose information* on interest income to tax authorities or a more *intensive cooperation* between the European tax authorities. He seemed to have a preference for the first, most far-reaching solution.[30]

The Monetary Committee invited the Alternates, strengthened with some seconded tax experts, to study the tax problem. Fiscal issues were very much in the minds of the members of the countries which still maintained capital restrictions. These countries feared in particular that in a liberalized environment the small savers would find easier access to financial outlets in third countries. Italy shared a long border with Switzerland and feared *tax evasion*. France was equally afraid that its citizens would transfer their savings to countries with a mild tax regime. For some countries, such as Denmark and Ireland, the taxation of interest income or of wealth was a politically sensitive issue, not least because it constituted a significant part of fiscal revenues. This could not easily be replaced by other sources. Ireland for instance maintained a withholding tax of 25 per cent; when introduced this had already given rise to considerable capital flight. It was felt that this could only become worse if capital transactions were to be fully liberalized. If the directive were to be adopted soon, there should be a sufficiently long transitional period before its entry into force. This period could be utilized to solve the fiscal problems, either by taking measures at home or by harmonizing tax rules at the Community level. It was noteworthy that the countries which had already liberalized did not consider the taxation issue to be important. They pointed to their own favourable experiences, where the magnitude of tax evasion was of such a relative small size that it did not give cause for changes in taxation legislation.[31] The British explicitly warned against Commission initiatives in this sphere. They were afraid that proposals such as the establishment of a withholding tax on interest income would hamper the competitive position of the European capital markets and would involve the risk of capital flight to the United States and Switzerland.

The discussion in the Alternates showed that there were no ready-made solutions for the fiscal problems.[32] Taxation was a mine field. It was clear that there was *no consensus* in sight. Hope could be drawn from the experience of liberal countries, which indicated that tax evasion by small investors remained limited because of the high costs involved in foreign transactions. Nevertheless, the French proposed to incorporate into the directive a clause which would call on the Commission to make parallel progress in the field of tax harmonization. Eventually, this was agreed, together, as mentioned before, with a later date of implementation of the directive (1 July 1990). In the final text of the directive Article 6.5 required the Commission to submit proposals before 31 December 1988, aimed at eliminating or reducing risks of distortions or tax evasion, and the Council would take a position on this issue before 30 June 1989. However, it was noted that all common tax regulations would require unanimous approval.

8.10 ENHANCED SUPERVISION

Some members in the Monetary Committee from countries which still maintained restrictions considered that different *regimes of national supervision* of financial institutions in practice might lead to distortions in or barriers to the free flow of capital. They were of the opinion that further regulation in this area would be required as a precondition for full liberalization. Interestingly enough, the supervisors themselves did not share this view.[33] The supervisors were already engaged in the drafting of directives with a view to establishing a unified internal banking market in 1992. This was predicated upon the assumption that monetary cross-border flows would be fully liberalized. Their work was directed towards achieving sufficient 'minimum' harmonization in order to secure mutual recognition of supervisory regimes. This would enable them to apply the principle of home country control and the recognition throughout the Community of licences granted in a single country. The supervisors pointed out that full liberalization existed already in a number of countries, without this ever having been made dependent on supervisory legislation.

Liberalization and deregulation did not imply complete laissez-faire. Instead, it was necessary to provide a dependable and trustworthy legal framework in order to prevent imprudent or fraudulent behaviour. In fact many countries introduced *new legislation* to counter unworthy behaviour, such as insider trading or the offering of financial services in a misleading manner. The tightening of supervision and prudential control of financial institutions was already underway. The innovations resulting from financial engineering had made it more difficult to assess the risks involved for the commercial banks. Therefore solvency requirements for the banks had to be strengthened. Because of the international financial integration this strengthening of prudential control had to be internationally coordinated, in order to avoid regulatory arbitrage, with institutions seeking locations with the mildest supervisory regime. This coordination took place mostly in the Basle Committee. The EC was to adopt secondary legislation giving effect to the Basle agreements in the course of the next few years.

8.11 COMPLETION UNDER GERMAN CHAIRMANSHIP

In the first half of 1988 Germany had taken over the chairmanship of the Community. The German authorities, who had become more *assertive* in the course of the years with respect to full capital liberalization, considered the finalization of the capital directive one of their prime targets among the desiderata of the Internal Market. For them it was extremely important that the completion of dossiers which had been linked to full capital liberalization, i.e. tax harmonization and enhancement of supervision, were not regarded as a precondition for the adoption of the directive. The other dossier which had been linked all along to capital liberalization, i.e. the strengthening of the EMS, had been temporarily closed by the adoption of the Basle/Nyborg Agreement. However, there were increasing signals that there was more to come as regards monetary integration. Indicative in this respect was the embracement by the German Minister of Foreign Affairs Hans-Dietrich Genscher of the initiative of the French Finance Minister Balladur for the further strengthening of monetary cooperation through concrete moves towards the creation of a Monetary Union and a European Central Bank.[34] Balladur, who had presided over the deregulation and modernization of the French financial system, had tried to revive the idea of a European central bank with increasing force in the latter half of 1987. Now, with full capital liberalization within sight, a favourable cyclical situation and much improved convergence, the most important preconditions had been fulfilled. France closed a pact with Germany that end-June 1988, when the capital directive would be approved, a study would be undertaken of the stages leading towards such a European central bank.

The deadline for the finalization of the directive implied a tight schedule and the Monetary Committee devoted a number of meetings to the subject in the first six months of 1988. The *erga omnes principle* was accepted by all, but Germany stood alone in wishing to have this included as an obligation in the directive. Other countries continued to fear that such an obligation would weaken the negotiating position of the Community, especially if it would prejudice the EC position in the field of financial services. The requirement of reciprocity should be maintained as a powerful tool to gain access for European financial institutions to third markets, particularly in Japan. There was, as had become increasingly clear in the course of the discussions, no support for maintaining the 1972 Directive, as requested by the Commission.

The Commission proposal to make the directive *effective* within 3 months after its adoption was deemed to be too strict and Chairman Littler in February proposed a compromise of 6 to 12 months. However, Italy in particular asked for a longer period because of the possible consequences of the differences in tax regimes. The Monetary Committee could not reach agreement and left the issue to Ministers, which eventually decided that the directive would become effective on 1 July 1990, i.e. in a period of two years. Belgium and

Luxembourg, however, were allowed to maintain the dual market until the end of 1992. The Ministers also decided on the transitional periods for the four countries which were granted respite. As to the need for a *monetary safeguard clause* opinions still differed. However, if there were to be such a clause, the Monetary Committee agreed that it should apply (a) only for short periods of time; (b) exclusively to transactions not yet liberalized; (c) only in exceptional circumstances; and (d) by a Community procedure.[35] Eventually a compromise was reached, under which the Council would decide before 31 December 1992 whether a monetary safeguard clause was still needed.[36]

As to the Community *credit mechanisms,* consensus was reached that the two existing mechanism should be merged into a single facility.[37] This facility would be financed primarily by the contracting of loans by the Commission on the capital markets. There was, as could be expected, considerable haggling over amounts, but eventually a compromise was reached within the Monetary Committee on a maximum of ECU 16 billion. Access quotas for individual member states were to be decided on a case-by-case basis. The suggestion of the Commission that there should be a separate window to provide stand-by credit arrangements to countries in the process of capital liberalization met with considerable resistance. A majority was of the view that balance-of-payments problems should remain the main trigger for the use of Community credit mechanisms. It was, however, conceded that the threat of such problems would also qualify countries for the mechanism, and at a proposal of Spain it was recorded in the minutes of the Council meeting that the possible consequences of capital liberalization could constitute such a threat. Although this was not legally binding, it gave sufficient comfort that the Commission and the Council would take capital liberalization efforts into account, when deciding on requests for EC financing.

Shortly before the final Ecofin meeting in June 1988 a new problem emerged. Denmark considered it to be of vital importance that the Danish law which prohibited the sale of *second homes* to non-residents could not be circumvented by the capital liberalization directive. The term 'vital importance' of course was ominous, because this could block acceptance of the directive. This would obviously be a very bad signal for the financial markets, so it was felt. Denmark succeeded in incorporating a clause into the directive which stated that national regulations with respect to the sale of second homes in border areas would not be affected by the directive.[38]

In the meeting of the Ecofin Council on 24 June 1988 the directive was adopted.[39] Finally, after more than thirty years member states had agreed that the escape clause – 'to the extent necessary to ensure the proper functioning of the Common Market' – implied the full liberalization of capital movements. At the same time the directive on the establishment of a single credit facility was approved. An important hurdle on the road to monetary integration had been taken. Now the biggest hurdle, economic and monetary union, could be given a new try. In the following weekend, on 27 and 28 June, the *European*

Council in Hanover gave a mandate to a committee of central bank governors and independent experts under the chairmanship of Jacques Delors to study and propose concrete steps which should lead to economic and monetary union.

8.12 CONCLUSION

The negotiations on full capital liberalization were completed with success in a relatively short period, thanks to the agreement that there would be no preconditions. The demands for quid pro quos, which at times had slowed down the liberalization process, now lacked force. The *Commission* showed great determination and did not let itself get side-tracked in the parallel issues which were put on the table. It had made the strategic choice for the full liberalization of capital movements in Europe and grasped the window of opportunity provided for by the favourable cyclical situation and the relative calm within the European Monetary System. The Commission rightly refused to put its weight behind the calls for parallel progress in other areas. Its motives were threefold: European industry needed a well-functioning integrated European capital market (*efficiency* argument), capital liberalization was a precondition for further steps towards economic and monetary union (*integration* argument), and the disciplinary effect on policies would align the member states (*convergence* argument). The adoption of the 1988 Directive was a landmark in the history of the Community.

The Commission was prepared to do *concessions* which were needed to bring about agreement. It had to accept longer transitional periods from the struggling member states, postponement of the date of entry and the incorporation of a monetary safeguard clause. But these were minor concessions in view of the end goal. It was more dissatisfied with the abolition of the 1972 Directive, as the last vestige of a shielded European capital market, but it gave up the fight against consistent German opposition.

France had become more and more in favour of capital liberalization – the formation of one European financial area – as a condition for strengthening the competitive position of Europe. And France, which had lost faith in the effectiveness of capital controls, now was conviced that it was in its own interest to abolish capital restrictions. It had put much efforts in the restructuring of its financial system in order to establish Paris as one of the leading financial centres in Continental Europe. Its support of the liberalization process was decisive. At the same time France advocated progress with the '*construction monétaire européenne*'. In the French view capital liberalization was linked with the development of a common long-term vision on the economic and monetary shape of Europe. In this respect the *Dutch initiative* in 1982 to put capital liberalization on the European agenda had served its purpose. It had in the intermediate years brought out the differences of opinion into the open.

It had once again galvanized the debate between the 'economists' and the 'monetarists', but the debate had not ended up in dividing the member states, as it had done in the 1970s, but it had succeeded in assembling countries in a constructive way. The gamble of the Commission, which had regained the initiative and pushed member states further than they initially were prepared to go, had paid off. Edouard Balladur tentatively concluded that the historical quarrel between the monetarists and the economists might have been overcome at last.[40]

The *Basle/Nyborg agreement,* important as it was with respect to the understandings among central banks on how to beat off speculative attacks, had been meagre in its institutional improvements. It fell far short of the demands France had spelled out in its memorandum of February 1987. In fact, this memorandum must be regarded as the last convulsions of the yearly EMS and ECU packages. France having made the decision on domestic grounds to abolish exchange control, its demands for monetary concessions from the Germans lacked strength. There were increasing signs that what up till then had been a coherent bloc of restrictive countries, the ECU block, coinciding more or less with the 'monetarist' school, was falling apart. France changed coalition. Many Southern member states and Belgium had put high stakes on the maintenance of capital restrictions, and were only prepared to dismantle them in exchange for increased financing mechanisms and symmetric intervention obligations in the EMS. The French change of heart drove a wedge in this bloc.

Italy in particular was left in the cold. It had taken over the leadership of the camp which cautioned against full capital liberalization. Italy had insisted on the incorporation of a monetary safeguard clause and it had continued to come forward with proposals for enlarging the EMS financing mechanisms, including the strengthening of the role of the dormant European Monetary Cooperation Fund. It had come to resent what it perceived as the deflationary bias of the European Monetary System, the system lacking a 'growth motor'.[41] But with the French-German rapprochement on monetary matters Italy stood alone in its rather fargoing claims.

Germany could be satisfied. It had consistently advocated full capital liberalization and it had not been forced to make concessions which could have weakened autonomy over domestic monetary policies. Its increased assertiveness in advocating stability-oriented policies in Europe had got a hearing. In the course of the years it had been joined by other partisans, in particular the United Kingdom and the Netherlands, and now France had come along as well. Germany's constant insistence on the principle that the freedom of capital movements was a precondition for further steps towards monetary integration had paid off. Now that this hurdle had been taken, the time had come to give serious consideration to the long-term vision of European monetary cooperation. The positive German response to the French initiatives in this field, especially from Minister Genscher, led to the establishment of the Delors Committee with a mandate to study concrete steps towards the creation of a European economic and monetary union. It was a resounding reward for the Commission's persistence in advocating the full freedom of capital movements.

NOTES

1. In the preceding months in discussions in the Monetary Committee it had been concluded that realignments in the EMS should be carried out '*à froid*', i.e. in a timely manner and at a time chosen by the authorities, rather than '*à chaud*', i.e. forced upon the authorities by market pressures. Nevertheless the January 1987 realignment was forced by speculation on a German interest rate decrease – which did not materialize – in the wake of downward pressure on the US dollar. The events had left President Delors with doubts whether the existing system of 'dialogue and concertation' would be adequate to cope with such tensions (Financial Times, 13 January, 1987). The realignment elicited a request from the Ecofin Council to the Monetary Committee and the Committee of Governors to examine ways of strengthening the operating mechanisms of the EMS. This would lead to the *Basle/Nyborg agreement.* Moreover, efforts were intensified to dampen the downward trend of the exchange rate of the US dollar, which France saw as being at the root of the problems within the EMS. These efforts were crowned with the conclusion of the *Louvre Accord* on 22 February 1987.
2. OECD (1982), p. 6. See also Chapter 6, note 19.
3. There were two aspects here: (1) restrictions sharpened the minds of market participants in finding loopholes, which subsequently had to be closed as well, (2) some restrictions, such as those with respect to leads and lags, had only a short-lived net effect on the capital account: the shortening of the period in which exporters had to surrender foreign exchange to the banks in France had only a once-for-all effect and prompted the authorities to decree a further shortening when the exchange rate came under downward pressure.
4. Note of the Commission on Implications of the full liberalization of capital movements within the Community, dated 5 December 1986.
5. Financial Times, 23 March 1987.
6. Note by Bundesbank Director Leonhard Gleske, presented to the meeting of the Monetary Committee on 12 February 1987.
7. Cf. the influential commentator Paul Fabra on the Internal Market: 'En réalité, la liberté de circulation pour les capitaux est à la fois l'un de volets les plus importants et les moins 'européens', car le mouvement actuellement en cours concerne la globalisation des marchés financiers du monde entier'. Le Monde, 24 March 1987.
8. The memorandum was announced in February 1987 in the Ecofin Council, which asked the Monetary Committee to examine the proposals.
9. Note by Banca d'Italia Director-General Lamberto Dini, presented to the meeting of the Monetary Committee on 12 February 1987.
10. Note of the Commission to the President of the Council on Implications of the full liberalization of capital movements in the Community, dated 19 March 1987.
11. Padoa-Schioppa (1987), Efficiency, stability and equity: a strategy for the evolution of the economic system of the European Community, Brussels. The report was presented to the Commission on 10 April 1987.
12. The Monetary Committee and the Alternates held a relatively brief debate on the report. Scepticism as to the most radical elements of the report prevailed and it was generally felt that the report exaggerated the problems which could arise from the full freedom of capital movements. There was, however, French support for some of the proposals to be

implemented in the short run, such as the enlargement of financing mechanisms, which came close to those put forward in their own memorandum.

13. Minister Balladur quoted in Agence Economique et Financière, 3 March 1987; President Delors quoted in Financial Times, 23 March 1987.
14. Note of the Commission on The regulation of short-term international financial flows in a situation in which capital movements are fully liberalized, dated 26 May 1987.
15. The Dutch exchange restrictions up till mid–1983 prescribed an authorization procedure for guarantees given by the parent company for credits taken up abroad by foreign subsidiaries, a notorious loophole. Such authorization was routinely granted if normal intra-company payment terms would not be altered. In practice, however, the latter was not checked.
16. The French Minister of Finance Edouard Balladur had made his position clear in an interview with Agence Economique et Financière on 3 March 1987: 'Si la Communauté doit s'affirmer vis-à-vis des tiers comme un espace largement ouvert sur l'extérieur, elle doit en même temps mieux protéger ses intérêts face aux prestataires non communautaires de services financiers. A défaut, certains grands pays tiers pourraient bénéficier grandement du marché intérieur des services financiers, tout en conservant eux-mêmes des réglementations protectionnistes.'
17. The French proposal for subdividing the second phase may not have been without self-interest. France was already preparing a substantial easing of exchange control with respect to commercial enterprises, which came into effect on 21 May 1987.
18. Note of the Commission on Preparation of a new directive for the implementation of Article 67 of the Treaty, Scope of the obligation to liberalize capital movements and periods within which the obligation could take effect, dated 23 July 1987.
19. The Court of Justice had ruled in the Brugnoni and Ruffinengo case that all administrative restrictions hampering liberalized capital movements should be removed (see Chapter 3.8).
20. There were no official notifications of measures to regulate liquidity, which might affect capital flows. The Commission, which was aware of such measures, in practice took a rather pragmatic viewpoint, as long as the measures (1) were taken exceptionally, (2) did not discriminate and (3) were confined to commercial banks. When the Commission in 1991 inventoried the measures, which in some countries were in place, they were regarded as not problematic.
21. Monetary Committee (1988), Twenty-ninth activity report, p. 6. The report by the Chairman of the Monetary Committee to the informal Ecofin Council is annexed to the report, p. 15–23.
22. Deutsche Bundesbank, Annual Report on 1987, p. 71. In the report which the Committee of Governors presented at the Nyborg meeting it was underlined that the gradual dismantling of capital controls implied 'that all partners should pursue in a closely coordinated manner policies that foster stability of domestic prices and costs and external balance as a basis for lasting exchange rate stability: in particular, countries should agree that central banks would be committed to giving priority to the objective of price stability in the conduct of monetary policy.'
23. The proposals of President Delors, dated 30 July 1987, could be considered as an alternative to the earlier proposal for cross-currency holdings in the reserves of the EC central banks, which was contained in the French memorandum of February 1987. The latter proposal, supported by the United Kingdom, envisaged that EC central banks would build up not only Deutsche marks in their official reserves, but also the currencies of the other EC countries, if these could be considered to be sufficiently liquid. Not unexpectedly, there was considerable opposition from surplus countries like Germany and the Benelux countries, which feared to be overfed with currencies which in case of need could not be used. The more or less automatic financing of interventions in support of weak currencies would imply that the disciplinary effect of the EMS would diminish. The proposals eventually were dropped when it became clear that they received insufficient support.

24. Note of the Commission on The creation of a European financial area, dated 19 October 1987.
25. In its Annual Report on 1987 the Banca d'Italia elaborated on this proposal for a Community recycling mechanism. Its purpose should be to alleviate pressures which would result from capital liberalization, but which would not be justified by changes in economic fundamentals. To this end financial funds should be extracted from the domestic capital markets of the traditional capital exporting countries. On 24 February 1988 Treasury Minister Giuliano Amato presented a memorandum in which it was provided that the European Monetary Cooperation Fund should be entrusted with the recycling of funds. In the same memorandum strong support was expressed for the monetary safeguard clause. Finally Italy signalled that it was willing to renounce its six per cent fluctuation margin if the pound sterling would also be brought in the EMS, and the normal fluctuation margin of 2.25 per cent would be widened for all countries.
26. Belgium and Luxembourg took a cautious attitude in the debate due to the political delicacy of the subject. Their preoccupation was to keep the dual market in place temporarily so as to secure a smooth transition to complete liberalization. This attitude should, however, not detract from the fact that both countries did support the Commission's initiatives for full liberalization.
27. Proposal for a Council Directive for the implementation of Article 67 of the EEC Treaty, SEC(86)1660, presented by the Commission to the Council.
28. Meeting of the Committee of Governors on 10 November and meeting of the Ecofin Council on 16 November 1987.
29. The four countries which had fully liberalized were Germany, the United Kingdom, the Netherlands and Denmark; the four countries which in the eyes of the Commission did not need a transitional period to fully liberalize as well were France, Italy, Belgium and Luxemburg, whereas transitional periods were proposed for Spain, Portugal, Greece and Ireland.
30. Lord Cockfield in the Ecofin Council meeting of 16 November 1987.
31. A notable exception was provided by the introduction of a withholding tax on interest income in Germany in 1989, which was replaced after six months when it had given rise to sizeable capital outflows. Nonetheless, the withholding tax was reintroduced in a modified form in 1993 after a ruling of the Constitutional Court.
32. Meeting of the Alternates of the Monetary Committee, jointly with taxation experts, on 28 March 1988. Four possibilities were considered:
    - a general *withholding tax* throughout Europe; drawback: difficult to decide on the appropriate level: if the tax rate would be too low, it would not be effective; if it would be too high, it would prompt investors to move their capital outside the EC.
    - a general obligation for the banks to *declare interest income* to the tax authorities; drawback: work load for the banks and the tax authorities.
    - a strengthening of the *mutual assistance* of tax authorities; drawback: only effective in case of presumption of fiscal fraud.
    - the channeling of investments abroad through *agreed intermediaries*; drawback: hampering of the free movement of capital through administrative controls.
33. Reply of Mr O'Grady Walshe, chairman of the EC Banking Advisory Committee, to an enquiry by Mr Tietmeyer in his capacity as chairman of the Monetary Committee, 26 August 1987.
34. In a speech for the European Parliament in Strasbourg on 20 January 1988 Minister Genscher said: 'Wir müssen das Europäische Währungssystem weiter entwickeln. Nach den wichtigen Beschlüssen der Zentralbankgouverneure und Finanzminister von Basel und Nyborg ist zu fragen, wie groß heute noch der Spielraum für weitere Fortschritte bei der Stärkung des EWS ohne neue institutionelle Vorkehrungen ist. Möglicherweise ist er nur noch gering, so daß darüber hinausgehende Zielsetzungen auch die Frage nach der institutionellen Schwelle aufwerfen. (...) Die Krise der internationalen Finanzmärkte hat in

dramatischer Weise die Notwendigkeit verstärkter Zusammenarbeit im Währungsbereich unterstrichen. (...) Hätten wir aber schon eine Europäische Währungsunion und eine Europäische Zentralbank, so wären wir weit besser gewappnet gewesen. Wir müssen deshalb konkret auf die Schaffung der Währungsunion und einer Europäischen Zentralbank hinarbeiten, die auch in der Logik eines Europäischen Binnenmarktes liegen. Entscheidend ist, daß dies Währungsunion zu einer Stabilitätsgemeinschaft wird'.

35. Monetary Committee (1988), Twenty ninth Activity Report, p. 21.
36. When in 1992 the monetary safeguard clause was reviewed in the Monetary Committee and the Committee of Governors it was decided to maintain the clause for another year. The clause, which had not been invoked, would lapse anyway at the start of the second stage of EMU on 1 January 1994 for which no such clause was provided in the Treaty on European Union.
37. The weaker member states had been placated earlier by the decision of the European Council in February 1988 to double the size of the structural funds over the period up to 1993.
38. Article 6.4 states that 'existing national legislation regulating purchases of secondary residences may be upheld until the Council adopts further provisions'.
39. Council Directive of 24 June 1988, published in Official Journal of the European Communities, No. L178/5, 8 July 1988; see Annex 6.
40. Edouard Balladur in an article in the Financial Times, The EMS: advance or face retreat, dated 17 June 1987.
41. Giuliano Amato in an interview with Reuters, dated 24 February 1988.

CHAPTER 9

Towards Economic and Monetary Union

It is the somewhat tragic fate of the central bank to stand more or less alone in the fight for the value of the money. The main interest groups in society without any doubt in the abstract are proponents of stable money. However, they are always just that bit more interested in other, more pressing matters.

M. W. Holtrop, 1956

9.1 INTRODUCTION

The adoption of the *1988 Directive* was greeted with relief by the Commission. It had been a major accomplishment to agree on the obligation for all member states to completely liberalize capital movements. In the course of the following two years the remaining restrictions on short-term capital flows in Denmark, France and Italy were removed and the dual exchange market, operated in the Belgium-Luxembourg monetary union, was abolished. These steps were often taken at an *earlier date* than was called for under the directive. But also the countries which had been granted longer transitional periods generally moved forward in a decisive manner. In the negotiations the latter had been dragging their feet. But the momentum created by the adoption and implementation of the directive set spurs to the authorities. In doing so, they could profit from the generally favourable economic climate in Europe and the absence of expectations of major exchange rate adjustments. But there was also an important political consideration: they did not wish to miss the connection with the other EC members. There was a clearcut move towards full liberalization within the Community and all countries wanted to be part of this.

The coming years would be dominated by the discussion which all along had accompanied the proposals for capital liberalization: *European monetary integration.* The French had consistently advocated the closer coordination of monetary policies, ever since the Community had been created. In the 'monetarist' tradition France had advocated monetary arrangements even if economic convergence and domestic stabilization had not yet been fully accomplished. But it had fallen short of demanding monetary unification. In fact, what France was after up till then, was not the rendering of monetary sovereignty to a supranational level, but the sharing of policy decisions on monetary policy with other countries, in practice with the Bundesbank. The latter consistently had been refused by Germany, which had considered all French ideas – be it with respect to the ECU or with respect to reserve pooling or a common dollar policy – inspired by one single goal, impinging on the autonomy of the Deutsche Bundesbank. The French authorities had come to the conclusion that the road of monetary coordination, as well as that of financial integration through the promotion of the ECU, would come to a *dead-end,* because it would always clash with the independence of the Bundesbank and the confidence the financial markets gave to the Deutsche mark above other currencies, including the ECU. Therefore, France *changed* its *strategy.* As mentioned in Chapter 8, in the course of 1987 the first indications were given that France no longer would insist on further institutional advances of the EMS or on official promotion of the ECU, but that it would be interested in the establishment of an economic and monetary union and in the creation of a European Central Bank.

After a discussion of the *implementation* of the 1988 Directive, this chapter deals with the provisions on capital movements in the *Treaty on European Union.* In this Treaty the transition to and the final stage of economic and monetary union are outlined, with rules to prevent excessive budget deficits and provisions for the establishment of an independent European Central Bank. In EMU a number of the traditional tasks of the Monetary Committee will become redundant. Therefore, the Treaty provides for the set-up of a relabeled committee, with newly defined tasks and, possibly, a modified composition. The chapter ends with a review of the events in the aftermath of the adoption of the Maastricht Treaty, when large-scale capital flows seriously undermined the cohesion of the European Monetary System, leading up to a substantial widening of the fluctuation margins. This did raise some doubts as to the wisdom of the full liberalization of capital movements, but some muted calls for throwing sand in the wheels of free capital flows were firmly resisted by the member countries.

9.2 THE FOLLOW-UP TO THE 1988 DIRECTIVE

Following the adoption in June 1988 of the directive providing for the full freedom of capital movements most countries moved swiftly. The liberal club in Europe, Germany, the Netherlands and the United Kingdom, was already in compliance with the directive and thus did not have to undertake any action.

9.2.1 Full Liberalization in the Leading Group

Denmark was the first of the other 9 member states still maintaining restrictions to fully comply with the liberalization directive. On 1 October 1988 the few remaining regulations were abolished. *France* in another major overhaul of its control system lifted most restrictions in March 1989.[1] When the last

TABLE 28

The abolition of exchange controls in the EEC.

United Kingdom	1979	Italy	1990
Germany	1981	Spain	1992
The Netherlands	1986	Portugal	1992
Denmark	1988	Ireland	1992
France	1989	Greece	1994
Belgium/Luxembourg	1990		

obstacles finally were removed effectively on 1 January 1990, well ahead of the deadline, France had become the fifth EC member state to have fully liberalized capital movements. More than twenty years after its first attempt in the late 1960s to liberalize capital flows and modernize monetary policy, its second attempt had been completed successfully, without setbacks on the financial markets.

Although *Belgium* had earlier insisted on an extension of the deadline for the abolition of the dual exchange market until end–1992, it proceeded much earlier when it was clear that other countries would live up to their commitments. Especially the de facto liberalization of all capital movements in France triggered the move to abolish the dual exchange market in Belgium and Luxembourg on 5 March 1990. *Italy* soon was to follow suit. After the adoption of the liberalization directive Italy had introduced a new exchange law in October 1988, switching to a positive control system under which all cross-border transactions were permitted unless explicitely prohibited. This change had been under debate since the beginning of the 1980s, but its adoption had been delayed for some time because of the fragile economic and political situation. Under the new law specific restrictions were retained for the time being for certain short-term transactions. The switch was positively received in the markets. Upward pressure on the exchange rate, also caused by the large interest rate differential of 6.5% vis-à-vis the Deutsche mark, even necessitated temporary measures to dampen a surge in capital inflows.[2] The ground for full liberalization was prepared by the adoption of the narrow fluctuation margins in the ERM for the lira in January 1990 and a few weeks before the deadline in an atmosphere of much improved confidence all remaining restrictions were removed. With Italy, the 8 member states, which President Delors had singled out as capable of fully liberalizing capital movements, had indeed fulfilled their obligations on time. On 1 July 1990 the *first phase of EMU* started with the full freedom of capital movements firmly implanted in the heartland of the European Community. When on 8 October 1990 the *United Kingdom* finally considered the time ripe to take the pound

TABLE 29

Stabilization in Ireland.

in per cent	1979–83	1984–88	1989–93
annual rate of increase			
consumer prices	15.9	4.6	3.0
% of gdp			
budget deficit (–)	–12.1	–8.7	–2.1
currrent account	–11.0	–2.6	1.5

Source: International Financial Statistics, IMF; European Economy 58, European Commission.

sterling in the ERM success seemed complete. All member states which practiced full freedom of capital movements maintained their exchange rates in the narrow fluctuation band.

9.2.2 Gradual Progress in Derogation Countries

The other countries which had been granted extensions gradually dismantled capital controls as well. *Ireland* removed those restrictions which still fell under the safeguard clause of the earlier liberalization directives before the end of 1988, as foreseen. Therefore, from that time it only maintained exchange controls relating to short-term capital movements.[3] Its liberalization measures were as much influenced by the push factor of the EC obligations as by the perceived pull factor of the beneficial effects of improved confidence on investment in Ireland. The authorities had noted that investors responded positively to an economic climate with as little as possible restrictions on capital movements.[4] At the same time Ireland was an example of a country in which policy adjustments, especially in the fiscal policy area, and capital liberalization went hand-in-hand successfully (see Table 29). Its current account balance had improved from a deficit of 6.8% of gdp in 1983 to a sizeable surplus from 1988 onwards. But it proceeded cautiously with respect to short-term flows: Ireland did not want to see its fiscal adjustment programme jeopardized by sudden speculative outflows. It would further relax controls in the course of the years but would wait until the latest permitted date, 1 January 1993, to fully abolish exchange control.[5]

Spain, which operated a fairly restrictive exchange control system, notably with respect to capital outflows, took a series of liberalizing measures in the course of the years. Under one of those relaxations the French example to favour the ECU was followed: Spanish residents were free to open current account or savings deposits denominated in ECU in September 1989. Generally, liberalization was carried through at an earlier stage than was called for in the Treaty on Accession. Under the influence of relatively high nominal interest rates and rapid economic growth, spurred by heavy investment, Spain was confronted with sizeable inflows which, with limited success, were counteracted by reintroducing certain restrictions on capital inflows.[6] The tendency of the peseta to appreciate was dampened after the entering into the ERM in June 1989, although the peseta continued to be strong. This permitted an acceleration of the liberalization process. In September 1991 Minister of Finance Solchaga in a surprise move announced that all remaining exchange restrictions would be abolished as from 1 February 1992, almost a year ahead of schedule.[7]

The announcement was accompanied by plans to grant the Banco de Espana greater autonomy. Both moves were intended to increase credibility in the markets.

Portugal had operated a restrictive control system characterized by detailed, bureaucratic regulations. It had negotiated long transitional periods up to 7 years for the commitments under the previous directives, including the 1986 directive, in the Treaty on Accession. Its membership of the EC implied a fundamental reform of its regulatory practices, which were mainly inspired by the fragility of the external position and the relatively small size of the Portuguese financial markets. An important motive had been as well to keep domestic savings for its own economic development and support domestic credit control. After the adoption of the 1988 Directive Portugal took some measures to soften the impact of restrictions on basic capital movements. But it first gave priority to modernizing its domestic financial system and undertaking a market-oriented reform of monetary policy. To this end the system of credit rationing and privileged treatment of government debt was abolished, and in April 1991 the authorities introduced a new system of indirect monetary policy instruments. The domestic banking sector was restructured and recapitalized as well in order to be able to withstand the foreign competition which would follow liberalization. These domestic reforms, which virtually revolutionized the domestic financial market, were regarded by the authorities as a necessary precondition for a sustainable liberalization of capital movements.

Like Spain, Portugal was confronted with substantial capital inflows which caused problems for monetary policy. In July 1991 restrictions on inflows were temporarily reintroduced, particularly on purchases of short-term paper by non-residents. The persistence of high interest differentials and the absence of expectations of a devaluation acted as a powerful stimulus for capital inflows in 1991, estimated at a net inflow of autonomous capital of 11.6% of gdp, of which a substantial part was considered to be of a volatile nature.[8] The substantial interventions of the central bank in order to take the upward pressure off the escudo blew up domestic liquidity and undermined the efforts to contain inflation. Portugal did not ask for an extension of the transitional period but instead it announced in August 1992 the complete liberalization of all capital movements by the end of the year. From now on, so it was announced, the conduct of monetary policy would be primarily determined by the exchange rate target of the escudo, which had entered the ERM in the spring of 1992.

The *progress* in Ireland, Spain and Portugal had been *impressive*. Especially the Iberian countries came from a situation of a very regulated economy, with heavy government involvement. In a few years time, in a catching-up process which inspired confidence, they had transformed their financial sector and liberalized capital movements. The currencies were dragged along in the currency turmoil in the ERM in 1992 and temporarily reintroduced restrictions after the September crisis, which will be discussed in paragraph 7. Nonetheless, all countries had fully liberalized capital movements on 1 January 1993. Only *Greece* asked for an extension of the transitional period with two years, until 1 January 1995 for short-term capital operations. The Commission was of the opinion that a shorter period would be appropriate, and the Council eventually granted an extension until 30 June 1994.

Outside the European Community the liberalization drive gained momentum as well. In particular the *EFTA countries* which sought rapprochement to the EC aligned their regulations to the standard set by EC legislation. When on 22 October 1991 agreement was reached on the European Economic Area the directive on the liberalization of capital movements was accepted as well together with 12.000 more pages of EC secondary legislation. Some minor exceptions were formulated, mainly with respect to existing property and direct investment regulations.

9.2.3 Effects on Capital Flows

Countries experienced a large increase of capital flows, both inward and outward, after they had liberalized capital movements. In most cases on a net basis a surplus of *inflows* was registered in the period just following liberalization. Therefore, periods after capital liberalization typically were associated with a virtuous circle of net capital inflows, upward pressure on the exchange rate, permitting a decrease in domestic interest rates. But not in all cases this was associated with improved macroeconomic performance, measured by the size of budget deficits and the rate of inflation. This suggests that other factors are at work as well. One major factor may be that indeed the removal of capital controls contributed to the *credibility* of the exchange rate commitment of the authorities, because the exposure to market forces was perceived to exert a disciplinary effect on policies. This had been argued all along by liberal countries, like Germany, but still the proof of the pudding was in the eating. Bartolini and Bodnar (1992) on the basis of the experiences in Italy have advanced that 'by raising the potential costs of exchange rate stability, the removal of capital controls increased the credibility of the commitment to the EMS and therefore contributed to calming devaluation expectations'. The

TABLE 30

Disequilibrium in Italy.

in per cent	1979–83	1984–88	1989–93
annual rate of increase			
consumer prices	17.3	7.1	5.7
% of gdp			
budget deficit (–)	–10.0	–11.5	–10.0
current account	–0.8	–0.4	–1.1

Source: International Financial Statistics, IMF; European Economy 58, European Commission.

actual stability in the EMS, the publication of the Delors report in May 1989 and the joining of the British pound sterling and the transition of the Italian lira to the narrow band in January 1990 were instrumental in this stabilizing of exchange rate expectations. In this sense, capital liberalization in Europe was instrumental in increasing the trust of financial market operators and investors in the future course of economic policies in EC member states. The commitment to domestic price stability played a crucial role.

What was less well understood, however, was that inflows following capital liberalization were of a fleeting nature. The fact that net capital inflows occurred was related to *portfolio adjustments* of non-residents, which were willing to hold a relatively larger share of the currencies in a liberated exchange environment. These flows were based on the perception of an increased commitment to exchange rate stability. When the portfolio adjustments had run their course, financial markets took a fresh look at the macroeconomic fundamentals. The net inflows had, however, given the authorities the perception of financial ease. In some cases they may have contributed to continued laxity in fiscal policies. *Italy* is a case in point. Since the transition to a positive exchange regime in 1988 the government and the private sector had increased external borrowing. Thus domestic demand was kept strong and the current account deficit was easily financed. Interest rates decreased and thus gave no warning signals. Despite repeated calls by the Banca d'Italia on the government to decrease the huge public deficit the apparent financial ease undermined the resolve of the authorities.[9] Paradoxically, the disciplinary effect of free capital movements thus was lacking (see Table 30).

Portugal and Spain, too, which maintained relatively high interest rates in order to control inflation, encountered problems for domestic monetary policy because of increased capital imports. The strong potential for economic catch-up since the entry in the EC and the opening-up of the domestic markets, supported by credible policies, attracted massive inflows and permitted the liberalization of outflows. It proved, however, difficult in these circumstances to bring the rate of inflation under control, which remained substantially above the EC average. Also here, tighter fiscal policies might have been warranted to lower price expectations, which were lagging, and moderate wage demands.

9.2.4 Indirect Barriers

In a discussion in the Monetary Committee in July 1990 satisfaction was expressed with the progress achieved with respect to capital liberalization. The committee requested that the Commission now shift its attention to the identification and reduction of indirect controls, viz. domestic regulations which still hampered capital flows. In a checkup the Commission identified a number of country-specific, mainly *minor controls* which were considered to be in contravention of the Community obligations. Examples were the prohibition in Germany of purchases of certain categories of government bonds by non-residents and the limitations imposed in Italy on physical cross border movements of bank notes. France and the United Kingdom continued to maintain certain restrictions regarding direct investment.[10] It brought these infringements to the attention of the Monetary Committee at the end of 1990, which urged the member states to take action. Some obliged but in a number of instances the authorities maintained that the identified restrictions did not constitute an obstacle for the free flow of capital but were maintained for other reasons.[11]

A number of *domestic regulations* which hampered the free movement of capital were identified by the Commission as well.[12] These included measures in the sphere of (1) *tax discrimination*, (2) *prudential rules* for institutional investors, such as pension funds, and (3) regulations regarding the *admission on domestic markets* of securities denominated in a foreign currency. The latter were governed by 'gentlemen's agreements' where admission was dependent on authorization of the home country authority. Member states in a number of cases objected to the inclusion of certain regulations as indirect controls, disputing the interpretation of the Commission. Obviously indirect controls formed a *grey area* which left much more room for different interpretation than direct controls.

The discussion up to a point vindicated the Commission's reluctance to cede its enforcement powers to the scrutiny of the committee, as discussed in Chapter 8.6. The Commission's acts, unlike its complacent attitude in the 1970s, now proved its ardour for reaching as complete possible liberalization of capital movements. After the discussion it was felt within the Commission's services that the committee was not the best location for debating country specific problems, since the peer pressure, which was so evident in earlier years, no longer materialized in the grey areas of indirect controls, once more so now that the four large member states were put on the rack.

9.3 THE FOLLOW-UP IN TAXATION AND SUPERVISION LEGISLATION

During the negotiations on the liberalization directive a strong link had been laid by the French and the Italians with progress in the harmonization of taxation and supervision legislation. The Commission maintained that the last major barrier to the creation of a truly integrated European capital market was the existence of differential *taxation* systems. The opportunities for tax evasion being a source of economic distortion, the Commission favoured a Community-wide approach to fight tax evasion. Actually, in the 1988 Directive a provision was included that the Commission would come forward with proposals with respect to taxation before 31 December 1988. However, when this date approached President Delors had to inform Ministers that the Commission would miss the deadline.[13] The Commission was studying the harmonization of taxation of returns on capital, in particular on income and interest earnings, where different regimes were disrupting capital flows. Ministers prodded the Commission to come forward soon with proposals. But their motives differed. The German Minister Stoltenberg did so because he wished to speed up the pace of capital liberalization and was fearful that member states would use the delay as an excuse to postpone moves towards liberalization. The French Minister Bérégovoy was particularly interested in the harmonization of taxation of returns on capital. In his eyes there was a link with capital liberalization, if not of a legal nature than at least a moral one.

The political link *France* had laid between capital liberalization and fiscal harmonization was a strong one. At the same time it was clear that there would be no back-tracking if fiscal harmonization would not come about. Minister Bérégovoy in a forum organized by the French weekly l'Expansion on 5 January 1989 made this perfectly clear: 'En ce qui concerne l'harmonisation de la fiscalité sur l'epargne, remettrions-nous en cause la libération des capitaux? Je vous ai repondu non (...) Sur la libération des capitaux la décision est prise, je croix qu'il est bon de respecter les décisions prises. (...) La décision de libération des capitaux je la considère comme irrévocable.' In the preparation of the 1988 Directive France had laid an equally strong link with monetary issues. However, also in that instance, as discussed in Chapter 8, France did not insist. This behaviour shows that freedom of capital movements for France indeed constituted an *aim in itself*.

On 8 February 1989 the Commission presented a draft directive with respect to a *withholding tax* on interest income and on *mutal assistance* between the tax authorities. The proposed measures were intended to tackle tax fraud and tax evasion. At the same time it was clear that this could not be solely dealt with on a European scale. Fraud and evasion constituted problems of global dimensions, which should be dealt with in international negotiations as well. The proposals to harmonize taxation proved to be controversial, as expected. Countries had implemented different regimes, which they considered to be superior compared to the regimes in other countries. There was a fundamentally different approach between those countries operating a withholding tax and those countries which relied on information by the banks on interest paid. Some were vehemently opposed to a withholding tax. Among them *Luxembourg* figured prominently. Its forgiving tax regime attracted capital evading taxation at a large scale. This had given rise to a booming financial services industry, which it did not wish to see wither away, possibly to the benefit of other tax havens outside the territorium of the European Community. In the coming years it did not prove possible to reach agreement, except for cooperation among tax authorities in exchanging information, and at the time of writing the draft directive is still in limbo.

When it became apparent that it would prove to be very difficult to make progress with respect to fiscal harmonization, France, Spain and other countries prepared administrative measures providing for the reporting of transfers to third countries in order to keep open the possibility of fiscal control. There was a genuine fear of 'délocalisation' of French savings abroad. But in the course of 1990 it became apparent that these fears had not materialized on any grand scale, just as the countries which had liberalized before, had predicted.[14]

As regards *supervision,* the other parallel dossier, much more progress was made. In the framework of the collaboration between the supervisory authorities in Basle, at the premises of the BIS, agreements were reached on the harmonization of supervisory arrangements and on the division of responsibility between the various supervisors, which was partly based on preparatory work in the EC. The Community in the course of the years adopted secondary legislation giving effect to the Basle agreements and providing for transparent rules. In 1989 the Council adopted a directive, which took up the Basle Agreement's risk weightings for the assets of credit institutions as well as the requirement for credit institutions to have capital equal to 8% of their risk-weighted assets.[15] In the same year the Second Banking Directive was adopted which made it possible that a single licence was recognized throughout the Community. In this directive the principle of home control with respect to supervision was established. There was thus important parallel progress in the supervisory area, which accompanied the drive for liberalization of capital movements.

9.4 THE DELORS REPORT

It had been agreed that there would be no preconditions for capital liberalization. But the adoption of the 1988 Directive had removed an important obstacle for a resumption of the discussion on monetary integration. In speeches held by president Mitterrand and Minister Balladur in the latter of half of 1987 France had argued for a progressive approach towards monetary union and the establishment of a European Central Bank.[16] Apparently such moves were seen as providing an answer to the discontent France at times had professed with respect to the deflationary bias implied in the functioning of the ERM as a Deutsche mark based exchange arrangement. The *French initiatives* were soon supported by the German Minister of Foreign Affairs Genscher, who grasped their political significance. His motives were not mainly of an economic nature. Foreseeing openings to the East, which would expose Germany, he saw the binding force of monetary unification which would determine Germany's position as a Western European nation.[17] The liberalization of capital movements, the relative stability within the Exchange Rate Mechanism of the EMS and the healthy cyclical position of the European economies proved to be fertile soil for the warm reception of these ideas.

The *European Council* on 27 and 28 June 1988 *in Hanover* stated that, 'in adopting the Single Act, the Member States of the Community confirmed the objective of progressive realization of economic and monetary union'. This was a benign form of rewriting history as our discussion on the Single European Act in chapter 7 has shown.[18] The statement was dictated by political opportunism and gave an important signal. The political leaders of Europe wished to take Europe a significant step further. They established a committee composed of the central bank governors and some independent experts, chaired by Jaques Delors, President of the European Commission, with the task of 'studying and proposing concrete stages leading towards this union'.

The committee presented its report one year later to the *European Council* meeting *in Madrid* in June 1989.[19] The committee could take as its starting point that one of the necessary conditions for monetary union, namely complete liberalization of capital transactions and full integration of banking and other financial markets, would be met with the completion of the Internal Market programme. Incompatible national policies now would quickly translate into exchange rate tensions and put an undue burden on monetary policy. More intensive and effective policy coordination thus was needed. The Delors committee particularly called attention to the fact that in the economic field policy coordination remained insufficient.

The *Delors report* provided a blueprint for an economic and monetary union to be implemented in three distinct phases. The report pleaded for the establishment of an *independent system of central banks* that would have as its primary task to ensure the price stability of the new European currency in the final phase of EMU. The central bank's institutional position was better secured than in the Werner report. On the other hand the Werner report had gone further in its plea for a supranational European budgetary authority. The Delors report confined itself to the formulation of binding rules aimed at *preventing excessive government deficits*. The parallel currency strategy for the ECU was rejected. The committee could merely agree that there should be no discrimination against the private use of the ECU. The report was unanimous. But a controversial issue remained on the table: a group of 'monetarist' countries headed by France favoured the early establishment of a *European Reserve Fund* in the first phase. This Fund would pool part of the national central banks' reserves and would as appropriate intervene on the exchange markets. Others, particularly Germany, rejected this approach and pointed out that such a proposal would involve an institutional change which would require a new Treaty in accordance with Article 102a, inserted by the Single European Act. In the 'economist' vision common interventions could thwart domestic monetary policy objectives and thus would only be acceptable in the final phase of EMU, in which they would fit naturally.

Although the European Council in Madrid did not accept the Delors report in its totality, no more than the European Council earlier had done with the Werner report, the beginning of the *first* stage of EMU was declared on 1 July 1990. After extensive preparations in the Monetary Committee and the Committee of Governors two Intergovernmental Conferences were called on respectively EMU and the closely linked European Political Union. The IGC on EMU had at its disposal a blueprint of the statutes of the European System of Central Banks, prepared in the Committee of Governors, which would become responsible for the common monetary policy in the final phase of EMU. The IGC started under Luxembourg presidency in the first half of 1991 and finished its proceedings under Dutch presidency in the second half of the year.

9.5 PREPARATIONS UNDER THE LUXEMBOURG PRESIDENCY

The drafting of the Treaty on European Union provided a good opportunity to write the principle of the unconditional and full freedom of capital movements formally into European law.[20] Because of the achievement reached in the 1988 Directive the matter was not a controversial one and relatively little time was spent on the drafting of the new texts. The ministerial IGC meetings were prepared at the deputy level in meetings of the so-called personal representatives. With respect to capital liberalization the Monetary Committee, too, was involved and prepared an advice for the IGC.[21] Commission proposals for a draft Treaty suggested that in a new Article 67 the freedom of capital movements would be established as a *direct Treaty obligation* and not one depending on secondary legislation, i.e. through the adoption of directives. The Commission considered that the logic of the Internal Market, which would make it practically impossible to enforce controls, would render intra-European capital controls an anachronism.[22] The new article would replace all existing directives, including the 1988 Directive, and would simply provide that all restrictions on capital movements would be prohibited. The Articles 68 through 73 were considered outdated or redundant in the final phase of EMU because they either dealt with the gradual liberalization of capital movements or with exemptions.[23]

Equally uncontested was the Commission proposal that member states would be allowed to take measures to prevent infringements of their laws and regulations in the field of *taxation* and *prudential supervision,* or to be able to collect *statistical information.* Although the principle of full freedom of capital movements thus would be firmly implanted in the Treaty, some issues were still left open for discussion which could constitute exceptions to the principle of freedom of capital movements: (a) should the *erga omnes principle* be written in the Treaty; (b) should the Community avail itself of the possibility to impose restrictions vis-à-vis third countries for political reasons, such as *financial sanctions*; and (c) how long should the *transitional* arrangements be and would there remain a need for *safeguard clauses* in the third stage?

9.5.1 The Erga Omnes Principle

As to the regime vis-à-vis third countries a majority was of the opinion that the EC should apply the principle of full freedom of capital movements even to those countries which themselves had a less liberal regime. An important reason was that a number of member states did practice such freedom already. If other member states were to continue restrictions vis-à-vis third countries, these could be easily circumvented via the liberal countries. It was noteworthy, however, that in the French proposals for a new Treaty text reference was made only to full freedom of capital movements between EC residents. The most fervent proponents of the erga omnes principle on the other hand were the Germans and the Dutch who feared that the threat of exchange restrictions vis-à-vis third countries would increase the uncertainties in the financial markets. The British, while taking a liberal line, were concerned about the link between full capital liberalization and the freedom to establish in the Community. They wished to maintain the right to demand *reciprocity,* especially in the sphere of financial services. A simple suspension of the procedure to grant an authorization would still remain possible, it was agreed by the Commission. But it was a question whether this should be written expressis verbis into the Treaty. In particular the term reciprocity could form a dangerous precedent which could weaken the erga omnes principle for capital movements.

But there were more fargoing proposals to take exception to the erga omnes principle. Spain and Italy were of the opinion that also in cases of seriously *disturbing short-term capital movements* or in cases of grave *political crises* it should be possible for the Union to curtail capital movements to or from third countries. The Commission agreed to such temporary measures which in essence would constitute a continuation of the monetary safeguard clause at the Community level. The Germans, British and Dutch resisted such dilution of the erga omnes principle. In their view such disturbances could best be dealt with by means of interest rate adjustments or by allowing the common exchange rate to move. In any case the capital and money markets of the

European Union in the final phase would be of such a large size that external shocks could be absorbed easily.

9.5.2 Sanctions

At the time of the beginning of the discussions in 1991 the Gulf War had just ended and the issue of financial sanctions vis-à-vis Iraq therefore was a topical one. The Commission regretted that the provisions of the 1988 Directive did not equip the Commission with the right to initiate concerted action in such a case to an individual third country. The only exemption which therefore should be made on the principle of free capital flows would concern the situation of a major political, military or economic conflict with third countries. This should be dealt with on a Community-wide basis, analogous to the EC competences in the sphere of trade. To this effect a text for a Community regulation dealing with the imposition of sanctions to third countries was proposed, which was generally accepted.[24]

9.5.3 Transitional Arrangements and Safeguard Provisions

As to the coming into effect of the Treaty obligations it was proposed that *Portugal* and *Greece* would be allowed to maintain the temporary derogations which were granted to them under the 1988 Directive at the latest until 31 December 1995. For all other countries 1 January 1994, ie the starting date of the Second Phase of EMU, would be the date on which all capital movements would have to be completely freed. There were no objections voiced against this Commission proposal.

On the basis of the discussions the Luxembourg presidency produced a text which was discussed by the Ministers in the framework of the IGC.[25] Most notably the wishes of some member states to take restrictive measures vis-à-vis third countries for non-political economic reasons in exceptional circumstances were retained. A wide definition was proposed for circumstances which *in the third phase* could justify the taking of such temporary *safeguard measures* by the Union: if capital movements caused or threatened to cause serious difficulties for the operation of the Economic and Monetary Union the Council at a proposal of the Commission could take restrictive measures with a qualified majority. At this early stage there was only a brief discussion among Ministers, mainly to underline specific national interests. Most noticeably the Danish minister wished to retain the right to take preventive measures with the aim of avoiding infringement of national tax legislation. Another theme, reminiscent of the discussion on the 1988 Directive, was that Denmark did not wish the freedom of capital movements to impair in any way the existing domestic legislation which prohibited the sale of second homes to non-residents.

The discussions on capital movements showed that *caution* prevailed. While the principle of full freedom was confirmed, member states wished to hedge against unforeseen circumstances, both in the run-up to EMU as well as in its final phase. It was generally accepted that the existing *safeguard clauses*, contained in Articles 108 and 109, were to be maintained in their essential meaning for the duration of the second stage, i.e. until intra-EC exchange rates would have been irrevocably locked, unlike the monetary safeguard clause which would automatically lapse at the start of the second stage.[26] These provisions gave member states with (threatening) balance-of-payments difficulties the possibility to take safeguard measures for a limited period of time, with the consent of the Commission. Also the clause d'urgence was retained, giving a member state the right in case of a sudden crisis to take safeguard measures on its own accord. The Council was to retain the power to modify or establish the measures with qualified majority. Of course, in the third phase of monetary unification these articles would have to lapse, because national balances-of-payments would have lost their meaning and a common exchange rate policy would be followed by the ESCB. Countries which would not participate in the monetary union by way of derogation or would opt-out, and would thus follow their own exchange rate policy, would retain the right to invoke Articles 108 and 109.

9.6 FINALIZATION UNDER THE DUTCH PRESIDENCY

When on 1 July 1991 the Netherlands took over the presidency of the EC, the draft text of the Treaty, as forwarded by the Luxembourg presidency, was still a fairly straightforward one.[27] It contained four articles, stating respectively the freedom of capital movements; the right to take measures for statistical, taxation or supervision purposes as long as they did not constitute a disguised restriction; the right for Greece and Portugal to retain safeguard measures until end 1995; and, finally, the clause to take safeguard measures when capital movements to or from third countries (threatened to) cause serious difficulties for the operation of EMU.

In preparing a new draft, it was decided to deal explicitly with *financial sanctions*; in the Luxembourg version this was covered by general provisions. In the comprehensive draft Treaty text, which would form the basis for political negotiations, presented on 29 October 1991, the exceptions on the principle of free capital movements, now including sanctions, were upheld. It was, however, left open for political negotiation if the *general safeguard clause* in the third phase, in which the Union could impose restrictions vis-à-vis third countries, should be decided upon by qualified majority, as proposed in the Luxembourg text, or unanimously.

Although the third phase might be way off, in fact this was an important fight on the principle whether the future European Union would present itself as an *outward-looking open area* or, in line with the Commission's proposals for a European financial area in the mid–1980s, as primarily an *internal market* which should be able to *shield* itself against external shocks. Although a tally in the ministerial IGC on 11 and 12 November 1991 showed that actually only a minority of countries favoured such decisions to be taken with a qualified majority, by way of a compromise this was accepted by the majority with the proviso that such measures could not exceed a period of six months. As if to underline the case of the liberal countries, it was added that such safeguard measures could only be taken 'in exceptional circumstances' and then only 'if such measures are strictly necessary'. This formulation of course would not stand in the way of any lenient interpretation. Moreover, it was added that the Council could act only after having consulted the European Central Bank.

In the final weeks before the Maastricht summit there were further attempts to impinge on the general liberalization principle, which met with a certain measure of success. It did not prove easy to uphold the *erga omnes principle*. Eventually in Article 73c it was agreed that the Community endeavoured to achieve the objective of free movement of capital between member states and third countries to the greatest extent possible (see Annex 7 for all relevant Treaty provisions). But in addition to the Dutch presidency text, countries would be allowed to continue to apply those restrictions vis-à-vis third countries which existed on 31 December 1993, i.e. at the eve of the second phase, with respect to direct investment, establishment, the provision of financial services and the admission of securities on domestic capital markets.[28] By means of this provision countries could keep in place the few protective domestic regulations with respect to underlying transactions they had and could thus negotiate with third countries deregulatory measures, while demanding reciprocity.[29] The Union could also adopt common regimes in these areas with respect to third countries, but unanimity would be required if this were to represent a step backwards in Community legislation.

With these remaining departures from the erga omnes principle a latent *micro-economic motive* for capital restrictions had again surfaced, as was earlier the case in the discussions on the 1988 Directive. At earlier stages macro-economic motives had been advanced for the maintenance of restrictions. In Chapter 3 some of these motives have been discussed, and in Chapter 6 a new motive, still of a macro-economic character, had come into play, namely the wish to avoid an appreciation vis-à-vis the US dollar and for Germany to temper the development of the Deutsche mark into an international reserve currency. But now micro-economic motives were advanced which carried in essence a protectionist character. The British wished to use the reciprocity argument in order to extract concessions from third countries. And the French wished to retain the possibility for positive discrimination of the establishment in France of European industry.

Member states would retain the right to apply a different *fiscal regime* with respect to capital depending on the place where it was invested or the residence of the owner (Article 73d(1)a). This provision was additional to the clause in the original Luxembourg text for Article 73d which allowed measures to prevent infringements of national law in the field of taxation and prudential supervision. It was added that measures could also be taken which were justified on grounds of public policy or public security, despite hesitations from the German side as to the precise meaning of such provision. This was not entirely cleared up, but a provision was added that such measures should not constitute a means of arbitrary discrimination or a disguised capital restriction (Article 73d(3)).[30]

Finally Article 73g was agreed upon, which would allow restrictions to be taken in case of *financial sanctions*. Such restrictions could be either taken by the Community as a whole, but on grounds of urgency a member state could also do so on its own initiative 'for serious political reasons'. However, the Commission and other member states should be informed immediately of such measures. The Council could by a qualified majority decide that the member state should amend or abolish such restrictive measures.

All in all, the Treaty text on capital movements does not unequivocally embrace the erga omnes principle. The sheer length of the exceptions and their sometimes vague wording bears testimony of the wish of member states to *retain a margin of manoeuvre* vis-à-vis third countries. The importance of the Treaty is primarily that the freedom of capital movements now is *directly applicable*. Thus the scope of freedom of capital movements is extended beyond what is 'necessary to ensure the proper functioning of the Common Market', the escape clause contained in the Treaty of Rome. Now capital freedom was put on the same footing as the other freedoms foreseen by the founding fathers. This implied that freedom of capital had direct effect and conferred legal rights on individuals.

An important element for the effective freedom of capital movements is that the Treaty on European Union contains stringent provisions to bar the privileged access of governments to financial markets from 1 January 1994. This is done via two routes. First, Article 104 forbids *central bank financing of governments*. This serves at the same time to underline the independence of central banks vis-à-vis governments. Second, according to Article 104a any regulation which *favours government financial instruments* or forces financial institutions to buy government debt instruments is forbidden. On the basis of these articles decisions were adopted which spelled out in detail the prohibitions. By putting governments on the same footing as private credit-takers, governments have a much greater interest in good-functioning financial markets. It constitutes a powerful argument for the irreversibility of the liberalization of capital markets.

9.7 THE FUTURE OF THE MONETARY COMMITTEE

In the third and final stage of EMU monetary policy will have been centralized in the European System of Central Banks. Also there will be a single exchange rate policy of the Union, under a shared responsibility of the Ecofin Council and the European Central Bank. This changed institutional environment implies that the tasks of the Monetary Committee will undergo important changes. So as to underline this switch the Treaty on European Union provides that the committee will be renamed *Economic and Financial Committee* at the start of the third stage. In Article 109c important advisory functions are foreseen, in particular concerning the policy mix between the common monetary policy and the national economic policies of member states, the avoidance of excessive budget deficits, the external exchange rate policy and the situation regarding the movement of capital. Because of the increased competences of the Ecofin Council in the Union, it is likely that the position of the new Economic and Financial Committee in the preparation of the Council meetings will further increase. In a formal sense, though, elements of the old advisory function of the Monetary Committee will be maintained.

As to the composition of the Economic and Financial Committee it is only provided that each member state will appoint at most two persons, as well as the Commission and the European Central Bank. It is a matter of debate whether national *central bank representatives* will be member in the new committee. In the Committee of Governors, when discussing these matters, some doubts were expressed as to the wisdom of the participation of the ECB in the committee, because of its explicit mandate to prepare the work of the Council with respect to the EMU. The independent position of the European System of Central Banks, so it was felt, might be endangered. These fears, however, were brushed aside in the Intergovernmental Conference. In the second stage, however, the Monetary Committee maintains its present composition, retaining formally its advisory functions. The reprentation of national central bank officials in the committee during this phase is crucially important because of the delicate policy mix in the run-up to monetary unification, the functioning of the EMS and the preparation of the final stage of EMU. Representatives of the European Monetary Institute were invited to attend the meetings from the start of the second stage.

In the aftermath of the signing of the Treaty on European Union there were attempts to infringe on the *competences* of the Monetary Committee in a study group of personal representatives of the ministers of foreign affairs, which was established to make proposals for streamlining the Council's machinery. In particular it was proposed to subordinate the committee to the Committee of Personal Representatives (Coreper), i.e. the national ambassadors, and transfer the secretariat to the General Secretariat of the Council. This drew indignant reactions of the Monetary Committee, which in a report to the ministers, identified five vital points for the unhampered functioning of the com-

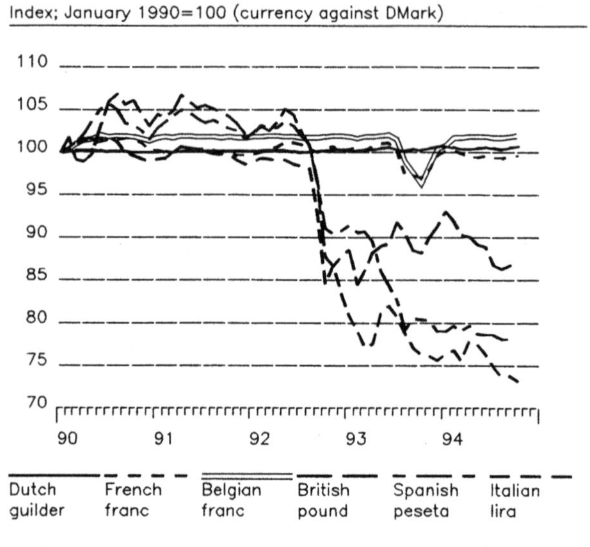

Fig. 21. Crises in the EMS.

mittee: it should retain all competences assigned to it by the Treaty; it reports directly to the Ecofin Council; it chooses its own chairman; the secretariat works on instructions of its chairman alone; and attendance would remain limited. These principles were confirmed in an informal Ecofin meeting in Oporto in May 1992 and indeed existing arrangements were maintained.

9.8 CRISES IN THE EUROPEAN MONETARY SYSTEM

The Treaty on European Union was adopted on 9 and 10 December 1991 in Maastricht and signed on 7 February 1992. Soon after the signing ceremony doubts started to arise whether the Treaty would be accepted in all 12 member states. In the run-up to Maastricht and in the first subsequent months the sentiment in the market had grown that the Exchange Rate Mechanism of the EMS in fact had developed into a *quasi monetary union*, in which the exchange rates need no longer be adjusted. Some of the authorities embraced such wishful thinking as well. They increasingly considered an exchange rate adjustment as an *ultimum remedium* which should be avoided at any cost, contrary to the Basle/Nyborg understandings. It was forgotten that economic developments in a number of countries had begun to diverge again and that the exchange rates no longer were based on the fundamentals. Investors considered the exchange risk to be minimal and invested capital in currencies with the highest interest rate. In this way a high-yielding, but fundamentally weak currency as the Italian lira traded at the upper end of the fluctuation band, whereas the Deutsche mark was trading at the lower end (see Figure 21).

9.8.1 The September 1992 Crisis

The sentiment causing this *inverse ranking* of ERM currencies *reversed* abruptly when the Danish population in a referendum on 2 June 1992 rejected the Treaty by a narrow margin. The euphoria which had surrounded the Maastricht Treaty quickly dissipated. In its slipstream the EMS no longer was viewed as a quasi-monetary union, but regained its original character as a system of fixed, but adjustable exchange rates. Strong pressures developed on the weak currencies, in particular on the Italian lira. But also outside the EMS, *Scandinavian countries* which had linked their currency to the ECU came under fire.

The perils in Scandinavia, leading to a devaluation and subsequent floating of the Finnish markka and extreme pressures on the Swedish krona, increased the awareness of an exchange risk within the EMS.

When speculative capital flows started to increase, the authorities were reluctant to increase interest rates because of a generally weak economic situation at home. On the contrary, the Deutsche Bundesbank was publicly called upon to lower its interest rates, which in the wake of German unification and its attendant inflationary consequences were kept relatively high. The Bundesbank refused to lower its interest rates out of fear that this would endanger further domestic price stability. In fact, the controversy which dominated European monetary arrangements ever since 1973, i.e. whether they should be operated in a symmetrical or an asymmetrical manner, had surfaced again. The financial markets could only deduct from this that countries were not prepared to accept the consequences of the maintenance of the exchange rate for domestic interest rates. Thus, a onesided exchange risk developed which made speculation highly attractive.

The principal weapon used by the authorities were large-scale *interventions* which, however, were not able to stem the tide. Finally, on 14 September 1992, a devaluation of the Italian lira was agreed, followed-up by a marginal decrease of interest rates in Germany. This was, however, not considered credible in the markets and attacks were resumed on the remaining candidates for devaluation: the British pound sterling and the Spanish peseta. On Black Wednesday, 16 September, ERM membership of sterling and of the lira, which had come under renewed attack, were suspended and the Spanish peseta was devalued. This unlucky episode was followed by repeated speculative attacks on most other currencies in the ERM. For some countries the pressure was such that temporary capital restrictions were reintroduced. Some critics of abolition of exchange controls felt vindicated by these developments.

Empirical evidence on the basis of the experiences of *Portugal and Spain* suggests that the effect of the reintroduced restrictions was limited and short-lived.[31] Both countries took measures to restrict lending in national currency to non-residents in order to forestall speculation against their currencies through the subsequent selling of these holdings in the foreign exchange markets. In the case of Portugal the domestic market was shielded to a certain extent from the subsequent sharp rise of the Euro escudo interest rate. Spain, which used the instrument of non-interest bearing cash reserves for incremental peseta lending to nonresidents, maintained the linkage between domestic and Euro markets. But in both cases the restrictions were, apart from a short-lived positive shock effect on the exchange rate, not effective in containing speculative pressures, and both currencies were devalued on 23 November 1992. The restrictions were soon lifted, also because of their negative indirect effects on other capital flows. Non-residents disposed of securities denominated in peseta and escudo, leading to a sharp drop in domestic bond and share prices. Both countries were confronted with sales of financial investments by fund managers who were unable to cover their positions and decided to bring down the peseta and escudo share in their portfolios. Within two weeks the Madrid stock exchange had fallen more than 15%, whereas long-term interest rates had risen substantially. The negative repercussions on long-term capital flows weighed heavily, because these countries were dependent on external finance for economic development. In view of these *negative confidence factors* the restrictions were abolished in both countries before the end of the year. The brief experimentation with controls had not been a success. Notwithstanding the severe pressures Spain and Portugal therefore did not renege on their commitment to liberalize. On 1 January 1993 Ireland was the last country to abolish exchange control. The deadline of the Internal Market had been adhered to. Only Greece, which was outside the ERM, maintained restrictions under its agreed derogation position.

9.8.2 The August 1993 Crisis

The discussion on free capital flows once more was opened in the aftermath of the second wave of speculation in the EMS in the summer of 1993. After repeated speculative attacks on the French franc and other weak currencies, and massive intervention by central banks, the Banque de France spending the equivalent of 3% of gdp on 29 July, the fluctuation bands in the Exchange Rate Mechanism were widened to 15% on 2 August 1993. This sparked off a host of comments. President Mitterrand commented that 'it was immoral that speculation could go unhampered, disturbing the lives of millions of powerless individuals'.[32] He called on a speeding-up of the introduction of EMU in order to fight the 'financial conspiracies'. Also Prime Minister Balladur rallied against 'the excesses of freedom' and said that there was 'an economic and moral duty' to find ways to curb such flows. Prime Minister

Dehaene of Belgium went one step further by speaking of an Anglo-Saxon plot and calling for immediate measures to protect against speculation.[33] Understandable as this Franco-Belgian call for measures was, it became quickly clear that there was little chance that controls would be reimposed. The Ministers of Finance of France and Belgium, Alphandery and Maystadt, quickly silenced suggestions of a reimposition of controls.[34]

The debate was reopened by Jacques *Delors* in a speech before the European Parliament on 15 September 1993.[35] It was an ironic turn of fate that the great proponent of freedom of capital movements now seemed to backtrack. Pointing to the sharply increased level of capital mobility and the size of turnover in the international markets, dwarfing the ammunition of central bank reserves, Delors proposed that capital movements should respond to certain rules of the game: 'Pour prendre un example routier, les voitures sont libres de circuler, mais il y a quand même des limites à la circulation.' He suggested that the Community take international *initiatives to regulate capital movements*. Moreover, he reminded that the monetary safeguard clause (Article 3 of the 1988 Directive) could still be invoked, permitting restrictive measures.

The reactions to the Commission's suggestions to think about the reimposition of exchange controls drew immediate and forceful rebuttals from the liberal countries. Bundesbank President Tietmeyer in numerous speeches forcefully opposed such a step back. In a typical reaction he said: 'There is a common understanding that freedom of capital movements is a major and indispensable achievement on the road to monetary integration. So, don't let us put this important achievement at stake as soon as we experience a surge of market reactions in the trial-and-error process which finally leads to sustainable equilibrium positions.'[36] Also the Governor of the Bank of England George held against those commentators who saw the remedy in the reintroduction of capital controls or other techniques inhibiting the freedom of capital movements that they 'mistook the symptom for the disease'.[37]

There were those who favoured a step back. There were also those who favoured the surge forward and argued that the exchange rate problem posed by the free movement of capital could only be solved by an early move to a European single currency. This was opposed by the same commentators. By the British because the underlying problem of diverging policy needs would not simply go away. By others, because the problem of diverging economic performance would not go away. The Maastricht convergence criteria were not adhered to and thus it was not possible to jump forward in a credible manner. The only feasible way seemed to be to continue to 'muddle through' and to turn the liability of a strained EMS into an asset which provided the opportunity to regain credibility, not by rules but by policy actions. Only by pursuing stable and sound economic policies the 'incompatible triangle' could be overcome. This was not to say that markets could not be destabilizing but by creating *two-way risks* in the exchange market and firm and consistent policies this should be overcome.

9.9 RESTRICTIONS REVISITED

The discussion on restrictions, sparked of by the currency turmoil in Europe, centered on two specific types: a tax on foreign exchange turnover, and reserve requirements on banks' foreign exchange transactions. The pros and cons will be briefly reviewed.

9.9.1 Taxation of Foreign Exchange Turnover

The fear for speculative capital movements combined with the drawbacks of capital controls have induced economists to come forward with alternative plans to shield the economy from undue external pressures. One old plan, which at the time had received particular attention from policy makers, had been forwarded by *James Tobin* as early as 1978, and now was unshelved by others. Tobin had proposed to 'throw some sand in the well-greased wheels' of the international money markets through the imposition of a uniform tax on all foreign exchange transactions. His proposal was launched at a time when many academics had become disappointed with the functioning of the floating rate regime. Flexible rates had not been 'the panacea' their more extravagant advocates, mostly academics as well, had hoped. Starting from the premise that goods and labor markets move much slower in response to price signals than the financial markets, Tobin argued that the foreign exchange markets are adrift without anchors and in the absence of any consensus on fundamentals. He was sceptical that 'the price signals these unanchored markets give are signals that will guide economies to their true comparative advantage, capital to its efficient international allocation, and governments to correct macroeconomic policies'. Tobin saw two ways which could be followed: one toward a common currency, the other toward financial segmentation between currency areas. The first route not being an immediately viable one, he 'regretfully' recommended the second one.

In the original plan of Tobin the tax would be applied *world-wide* in a uniform manner to all conversions of one currency into another in the spot market. By its nature it would discourage especially short-term flows, because then the interest differential would have to be relatively large in order to overcome the costs of the *conversion tax*. For longer-term portfolio investments or direct investment the cost would be small: in fact 'a permanent investment in another country or currency area, with regular repatriation of yield when earned, would need a 2% advantage over domestic investment'. Effectively it would also have to apply to cross-border trade involving currency exchange, because there would be no other way to prevent financial transactions to be disguised in the form of trade. The negative effects on international trade links could be mitigated by the creation of currency areas within which the tax would not apply, 'presumably the smaller EEC members and those LDCs which wished to tie their currency to a key currency'. Tobin hoped to restore to governments some fraction of the short-run autonomy they had lost with the increasing efficiency of financial markets.

It is not difficult to see why the proposal attracted attention of some policy makers, then and now again. The proposal seemed to promise that it would check financial flows which bore no relation to the real world, by raising their costs. The lure was that the policy-makers would be seen as doing something against those money-grubbing speculators who damaged and sometimes ruined their political reputation. At the same time, it was clear for most observers that such a proposal would not fly. The objections were manifold. The most important *drawback* was that it would damage normal legitimate financial and trade relations in quiet times, while its effects as to frightening-off speculation in turbulent times would be doubtful. The gains to be made by speculators in case of a devaluation of a pegged currency were a multiple of the tax and would not detract from the need to defend the currency by other means, including interest rate increases, as well. There was also the question as to how to reach European or even world-wide consensus and enforcement of such a tax, not to mention the question what to do with the proceeds.

As discussed in Chapter 8.2 the disadvantages of the 'traditional' direct restrictions were (a) the limited and decreasing effectiveness, (b) the high operational costs and (c) the efficiency losses because of suboptimal allocation. On the latter two disadvantages the Tobin tax if anything scores worse than direct restrictions. A tax of 1 or 2% implies a heavy cost with the increased level of capital flows and does not only harm these flows, but also potentially affects the underlying flows of trade and services. As postulated in Chapter 2 taxation is not less harmful to allocation than more direct forms of restrictions. The advantages of the Tobin tax therefore should lay in its allegedly easier practicability and greater effectiveness. But it is precisely at times of large disturbances that the tax has an insufficient deterrent effect. The proposal of a Tobin-tax therefore was quickly rejected in the late 1970s. When some politicians, among whom Jacques Delors, advocated a study of the merits of such tax in the aftermath of the EMS crises, the reception of the proposal was equally cool.

9.9.2 Reserve Requirements on Foreign Exchange Positions

Eichengreen and Wyplosz (1993) have advocated the temporary establishment of margin requirements on open foreign exchange positions of banks and other financial institutions. The costs of such non-interest bearing reserve requirements would raise the costs of speculation, even more so if interest rates were hiked as well to discourage speculation. The wish to control short-term capital movements, e.g. by such margin requirements, is based on the conviction that speculators use this route for taking short positions in currencies under attack. There are basically two methods of taking *short positions*. The first method is to sell the weak currency in the forward market. Forward sales ceteris paribus will cause downward pressure in the spot market and upward pressure on the interest rate. Under normal circumstances, this type of position-taking is relatively easy and cheap and does not involve great recourse to bank credit. However, in crisis situations the forward market can easily become illiquid. In that case investors have to sidestep to the second method of taking a short position: borrowing the weak currency and converting the proceeds into strong currency deposits.

In practice it is not easily determined whether both types of transactions are *outright speculation* or whether they are merely used to cover either outstanding debts in the strong currency or claims in the weak currency. However, if the underlying claim serves as collateral for the bank credit it can be assumed safely that the transaction is a *cover operation*. Fears of an imminent currency crisis also can be countered by the outright sale of claims denominated in the weak currency instead of undertaking hedging transactions. Also in this case a surge in (international) bank credit is likely to occur because market makers, who at the time of a crisis probably are the only buyers, wish to cover their own position in turn.[38]

In these circumstances attempts to try to counter speculative movements through the imposition of reserve requirements can be *counterproductive*. If institutional investors find the route for normal hedging operations closed because of sharply raised costs, it is likely that they will proceed to liquidate their assets as the only viable way of minimizing possible exchange losses.[39] Institutional investors characteristically try to diversify their risks. If the perception of an exchange risk is increasing, non-resident investors most likely will react stronger than the domestic investors. Institutional investors will be particularly concerned if there is concern that their assets could become trapped because of the reimposition of capital controls. In this way restrictions on short-term capital movements can work their way through in the long-term markets. Particularly if the country concerned has a history of switching on and off capital controls, as is implied in the proposals of Eichengreen and Wyplosz, this will tend to lessen the attractiveness of the currency for investors. Therefore, short-term capital controls meant to deter outright speculators in practice may frighten off long-term investors as well. Furthermore, they deter potential new foreign entrants on the domestic capital market.

As we have seen in this study the imposition of cash reserve requirements has had only fleeting success in warding off speculation. The experiences of Germany and France in the beginning of the 1970s were unsuccessful (see Chapters 6.6 and 6.7) as was the experiment in Spain in the end of 1992 (Chapter 9.8.1). More in general reserve requirements tend to dislocate financial activity to other financial centres. Reserve requirements for instance have contributed to the growth of Deutsche mark deposits in Luxembourg. For the instrument to be effective it would be necessary that it were applied on a European if not larger scale. There is no chance that such EC regime would come about, given the reservations of the monetary authorities in major financial centres. The risk would be too great that a 'Euromarket' in the EC currencies would develop in financial centres outside the Community.[40]

There are important practical obstacles as well with respect to the imposition of margin requirements. The magnitude of open foreign exchange positions by commercial banks is limited by prudential supervisory regulations. It is normally not the proprietary trading of banks themselves which generate large capital movements, but rather transactions on behalf of their clients or directly from other financial institutions. As to the latter it is not obvious that the authority exists which could impose requirements on those non-bank institutions. Moreover, to be effective a very frequent, if not daily reporting of exchange positions would be required, which in practice would impose high costs on the institutions and the administrative bodies which are supposed to monitor this. As elaborated before, it is not possible to develop an objective method which would distinguish between normal hedging transactions, which are directed precisely towards the closing of open positions, and the taking of speculative positions. Finally, margin requirements on open positions would seriously hamper normal uncovered portfolio diversification operations by institutional investors.

9.9.3 Liberalization in Greece

Freedom of capital movements was not to be obstructed by the exchange turmoil. When Greece on 16 May 1994 abolished its remaining restrictions, all member states had fully liberalized capital movements. The Greek move had been preceded by considerable speculation that the abolition of capital controls, which had to take place before end-June, would be combined with a substantial devaluation of the drachma. In defence of the exchange rate interest rates were hiked up and the abolition of exchange control was brought forward. The exchange crisis was withstood and the strengthening of confidence enabled a decrease in interest rates to lower levels than before the crisis. As other countries Greece embarked on a program of modernization of its money and capital markets. Combined with full freedom of capital movements this may help attract foreign investment on condition that budgetary discipline is restored. In any case the disincentive to place capital in Greece, stemming from uncertainty about the ability to repatriate, had been removed.

9.10 CONCLUSION

The 1988 directive which provided for the full liberalization of capital movements had been implemented in a satisfactory manner. Action by member states to remove restrictions well in advance of the formal deadline was generally regarded by the financial markets as a *sign of strength.* Capital liberalization, decreasing inflation differentials and satisfactory cyclical circumstances all provided a virtuous circle, mutually reinforcing each other. If member states which abolished restrictions experienced any problems, these were mainly caused by capital inflows attracted by relatively high interest rates, market participants being oblivious of the exchange rate risks involved. The large inflows pushed up the exchange rates of the former weak-currency countries in the band of the Exchange Rate Mechanism and thus gave an unusual sense of comfort to countries where the exchange rate normally would trade at the lower end of the fluctuation band. The inverse position of the participating currencies lured some market participants to the conclusion that Europe was already in a quasi-monetary union.

In this atmosphere of confidence there were no major obstacles to include the freedom of capital movements as a directly applicable obligation in the *Treaty on European Union.* Also other provisions were included in the Treaty, notably with respect to avoiding excessive budget deficits and banning their privileged financing, which made the liberalization of capital movements virtually irreversible. The real breakthrough having taken place with the adoption of the 1988 Directive, a traditional phenomenon surfaced with the codification in the Treaty: member states became very cautious when it came down to the actual drafting of legally binding texts. Thus the Treaty does not unequivocably embrace the erga omnes principle and leaves open the possibility for member states and, in the third stage, for the Union to take temporary safeguard measures in exceptional and serious circumstances. The wish to retain a margin to manoevre in this respect prevailed over the experience that precisely in those circumstances capital controls had proved to be of no avail.

The Treaty on European Union comprised a workable blueprint of a monetary union of which a truly integrated European capital market would form a constituent part. The transitional second stage of EMU would provide an opportunity to see whether in an environment of free capital movements member states would on their own conduct balanced macro-economic policies directed towards price and exchange rate stability. Thus the credibility of policies would be put to the test of the financial markets. As regards *monetary policy* central banks in many countries were endorsed with a larger degree of independence, in anticipation of the third stage of EMU, and a clearly-defined mandate to pursue domestic price stability in order to remove uncertainties in the financial markets.

Budgetary policies proved to be the Achilles heel of capital liberalization. When widened budget deficits in Germany, caused by the costs of unification, pushed up interest rates in Europe, doubts emerged whether other countries were prepared to follow suit in a rather subdued cyclical situation. Put to the test by the markets, countries hesitated to defend the exchange rate through a hike-up of interest rates. The EMS crises painfully demonstrated that the pursuit of exchange rate stability has to be underpinned not only by stability-oriented macro-economic policies, but also by the willingness to use the interest rate instrument in defence of the exchange rate, once more if a four-square track record of the authorities in this respect was lacking. Moreover, lax budgetary policies outside Germany, which no longer could be financed by having recourse to the central bank or to privileged access to domestic markets, added to the uncertainty.

There were nagging doubts about the wisdom of capital liberalization when the European Monetary System in a sharply changed environment came under severe pressure. Capital liberalization had increased market discipline, but this *disciplinary effect* came late and therefore with all the more force. Some countries which were still allowed to do so without calling in the monetary safeguard clause experimented briefly with a *reintroduction of exchange controls*. This however, proved to be counterproductive as international investors shied away from longer-term investments in these countries as well. Proposals to impose a Tobin-tax or take other measures to regulate capital flows were briefly discussed but they were quickly discarded, because their costs would be high and their effectiveness remained in doubt. It was recognized that toying with the idea of reintroducing capital controls could further undermine the confidence in the currency concerned and thus would be counterproductive. The episode left Europe sadder and hopefully, wiser. Just as exchange controls had not been able to shield the domestic currency, their abolition was not a cure which could avoid painful adjustment measures. The disciplinary effects, which proponents of capital liberalization had claimed, had come after all, only later than expected. Though painful, these disturbances had the beneficial effect of forcing authorities to put their house in order and pursue fiscal consolidation, which sooner or later would have become unavoidable in any case.

The progress made with respect to capital liberalization has been impressive. The contrast with the situation in the first half of the 1980s is remarkable. With the liberalization in Greece in May 1994 all EC member states have abolished all controls and there has been no recourse to the safeguard clauses. The main remaining obstacles now concern *domestic regulations* which, in conformity with Article 73c, have remained in place. Such obstacles relate intra alia to investment in financial services, where reciprocity requirements are applied, and to inward direct investment where in most countries governmental authorization is called for in specific sectors, such as communications, fishing and transport. These obstacles, however, are of minor importance in comparison with the earlier restrictions and are mainly taken for micro-economic reasons. Their abolition would bring a truly integrated European financial area closer, to be crowned by monetary unification.

NOTES

1. The remaining restrictions concerned the opening by residents of bank accounts abroad or of foreign currency deposits. ECU deposits, however, were no longer restricted, as a final testimony to European favouritism.
2. On 1 March 1989 a reserve requirement on incremental foreign exchange deposits was reintroduced in order to discourage credit taking in foreign currencies. The latter had surged under influence of relatively high Italian interest rates.
3. Ireland, which had a tradition of treating capital movements within the EC more liberally than with non-EC countries, did maintain certain restrictions on outward investment flows outside the Community.
4. Address by Minister Ray MacSharry to the Institute of Bankers, 11 November 1988.
5. The Irish decision to wait was mainly one of administrative convenience, since the powers under the Exchange Control Act lapsed at the end of 1992. Thus the simplest course of action was to let them run their course.
6. In June 1988 authorization requirements were tightened with respect to the taking-up by residents of credit abroad, and in 1989 a penal deposit requirement was introduced on foreign borrowing. Both restrictions were abolished in the first half of 1991.
7. Some minor restrictions were maintained on the export of bank notes and gold, as well as on the issuing of securities by non-residents in the domestic capital market.
8. Banco de Portugal, Annual Report 1991, p. 87.
9. The Banca d'Italia had warned after the full liberalization of capital movements: 'If we are to hold our own in the EC, however, there is still much to do (...) if we failed in this, we would risk ourselves in a position of inferiority in the very edifice we are helping to build. The urgent tasks facing us are to restore sound public finances and defeat inflation.' Annual Report 1989.
10. France requires authorization of direct investment by non-EC owned companies, the United Kingdom maintains powers to restrict direct investment in case of national interest.
11. Germany removed the remaining restriction on purchases of certain categories of government bonds by non-residents on 1 January 1991.
12. Memorandum of the Commission on The free movement of capital in the Community, dated 27 November 1990.
13. Meeting of the Ecofin Council on 12 December 1988.
14. Under the heading 'la délocalisation n'a pas eu lieu', Investir Magazine on 16 June 1992 wrote: 'C'était la grande peur de 1989. Accablée d'impôts, brimée par des contraintes qu'ignoraient nos voisins, l'épargne française sous pression allait s'envoler, aspirée par la brèche ouverte dans le contrôle des changes.' But interviews with commercial banks and the Banque de France confirmed that such deplacements had not occurred on a significant scale.
15. Solvency Ratio Directive (EEC/89/647). Earlier the Own Funds Directive (EEC/89/299) had been adopted in which the Basle definitions of Tier I and Tier II capital for the own funds of credit institutions were assumed.
16. In a lecture in Frankfurt on 2 July 1987 Minister Balladur stated: 'I do not believe that such a radical step forward as the establishment of the internal market in 1992 can be taken without parallel advances in the monetary domain. (...) The EMS has not been conceived as a simple agreement on fixed exchange rates. Its final objective indeed is an economic and monetary union equipped with a European currency, issued by a European Central

Bank'. It is significative that Balladur in this wide-ranging lecture did not one single time mention the ECU. Auszüge aus Presseartikeln, Deutsche Bundesbank, 3 July 1987, p. 4–8.

17. Hans-Dietrich Genscher (1988), Memorandum für die Schaffung eines europäischen Währungsraumes und einer europäischen Zentralbank (Note on the creation of a European monetary space and a European central bank), Bonn (26 February).
18. Admittedly the preamble of the Single European Act recalled that 'at their Conference in Paris from 19 to 21 October 1972 the Heads of State or of Government approved the objective of the progressive realization of economic and monetary union', but this was history as well, and there had been no meaningful follow-up.
19. Report on Economic and Monetary Union in the European Community, Luxembourg, 1989. The outside experts were Miguel Boyer, Alexandre Lamfalussy and Niels Thygesen. The European Commissioner for Economic and Monetary Affairs Frans Andriessen was also member of the committee. Günter Baer and Tommaso Padoa-Schioppa were rapporteurs.
20. As discussed in Ch. 7, p. 162 the Single European Act had not rendered inoperative the escape clause of Article 67.
21. The debates on the capital provisions in the Treaty were concentrated in the working group of the personal representatives. These representatives in the IGC normally were the same persons as the Treasury representatives in the Monetary Committee. Discussions in the Monetary Committee ensured that the view of central banks was heard as well, while the central bank representatives could liaise with the Committee of Governors.
22. Note by the Commission on EMU and capital liberalization, dated 5 February 1991.
23. Articles 68, 69 and 71 dealt with the progressive liberalization of capital movements and thus became redundant in the context of freedom of capital movements. Articles 70 and 73 contained exemptions and safeguard clauses to the freedom of capital movements which were considered undesirable. Article 72, which dealt with the collection of statistical information, became redundant because the ESCB would become responsible for this, cf Article 5 of the ESCB Statutes.
24. Proposal from the Netherlands delegation for Articles 67–73 (UEM/39/91), dated 2 April 1991.
25. Non-paper from the Luxembourg presidency (UEM/41/91), dated 3 April 1991, discussed in the meeting of the Intergovernmental Conference at ministerial level of 8 April 1991.
26. Articles 108 and 109 have been relabeled 109h and 109i in the Treaty on European Union. The imposition of capital controls on the basis of these articles would seem to be at odds with the principle of freedom of capital movements. Its actual use, therefore, will be very much a matter of interpretation. As regards the monetary safeguard clause, compare Chapter 8, note 36.
27. In the final Ministerial IGC under the Luxembourg presidency on 10 June 1991 the issue of capital liberalization was not touched upon at all. The respective non-papers of the presidency on the articles with respect to capital movements remained, apart from minor drafting amendments, unchanged from the April 3 text.
28. Even after the agreement reached in Maastricht on the text of the Treaty there still was a category added in the so-called nettoyage process, in which the texts were screened on small irregularities of a textual nature. At the request of Greece on 14 January 1992 it was specified that direct investment could include investment in real estate. Greece wished to have a legal basis to prevent that real estate in the North of Greece would be acquired by residents of Macedonia.
29. The Commission had an active hand in the promotion of this provision. The Dutch Presidency draft text had caused concerns in DG II since no longer a distinction was made between 'capital movements' and 'transfers in respect of capital movements'. Thus in the Commission's view the text could have undermined reciprocity conditions in existing financial services directives and could have abolished in one stroke the few remaining reservations by member states under the OECD Codes. The Commission felt that member

states were not fully aware of the implications the original text might have in areas other than direct exchange controls.

30. Where the balance will be struck between Articles 73d(1)a and 73(d)3 remains to be seen. The Commission, concerned about possible intra EU tax discrimination, tried, without success, to eliminate Article 73d(1)a, which was basically inserted by certain member states which were worried that they would be obliged to extend tax credits to companies in tax havens.
31. For a further elaboration see Sleijpen (1994) and Fieleke (1994). Ireland, too, took measures during the European currency turmoil. It suspended authorization of swap operations in order to ensure that these were not used to circumvent restrictions on short-term capital movements still in force.
32. Interview in Sud-Ouest, 16 August 1993.
33. Interview in Le Soir, 13 August 1993.
34. Interview with Reuters, 16 August 1993; respectively in Le libre Belgique, 16 August 1993.
35. Reprinted in Auszüge aus Presseartikelen, Deutsche Bundesbank, no. 64, 21 September 1993.
36. Hans Tietmeyer in a statement at the Frankfurt European Banking Congress on 19 November 1993, as reproduced in Deutsche Bundesbank, Auszüge aus Presseartikeln, 22 November 1993.
37. Eddy George in a statement at the Frankfurt European Banking Congress, see note 36.
38. According to a study of the IMF staff during the September 1992 crisis in the EMS institutional investors have used the three types of transaction – forward cover (hedging), 'short' sales against collateral and liquidation – roughly in equal proportions.
39. The experience of Ireland in the aftermath of the September 1992 crisis seems to vindicate the view that a clamp down on possibilities of hedging leads to a wholesale unloading of the basic instruments. German disinvestment of £1 billion accounted for 60% of the total disinvestment from Irish gilts in the second half of 1992.
40. See also William Lightfoot, Capital controls will only hurt, mr Delors, in: Wall Street Journal, 30 September 1993.

CHAPTER 10

Conclusion

10.1 GENERAL OVERVIEW

European countries have taken *diverging attitudes* vis-à-vis capital controls as an instrument of economic policy. In the first post-World War II years all countries had an extensive array of controls out of sheer necessity. Full exchange convertibility for trade-related payments was not restored until late 1958. Some countries, in particular Germany, soon liberalized most capital transactions as well, but the large majority retained exchange controls. In the Treaty of Rome a limited obligation to liberalize capital movements was agreed upon, confined by an escape clause providing that such liberalization should only take place to the extent necessary to ensure the proper functioning of the Common Market. In the first years of the Community of the Six common obligations were agreed upon requiring member states to refrain from restrictions on those transactions which were deemed to have the closest link to trade and direct investment and thus would contribute most to fostering economic growth in the Common Market. The improved economic performance in Europe and the building-up of a comfortable level of international reserves were conducive to this relaxation of controls. But soon the momentum was lost and after the adoption of the first two directives on capital liberalization all subsequent attempts on the part of the Commission to advance came to nothing. Member states were not willing to dismantle restrictions on short-term capital flows and some of them kept in place a number of controls on long-term capital flows as well, such as issues on domestic capital markets and cross-border transactions in shares of unit trusts. Also domestic regulations were maintained which de facto protected the domestic capital market by discriminating against non-residents. Ways parted as to what member states were prepared to do on an individual basis. Germany was close to full liberalization in the 1960s and France experienced a brief spell of near-freedom of capital movements. The latter was abruptly interrupted by the domestic unrest following 'les événements' in May 1968. Other member states kept control systems in place throughout the decade. Thus the attitude among the original six founding members of the European Community varied along the whole spectrum from a liberal to a dirigistic attitude.

At the beginning of the 1970s, in the changed international environment characterized by large speculative money flows fleeing out of the US dollar, there was a move in the opposite direction, culminating in the 1972 Directive aimed at regulating international capital flows. For some time the *regulation of capital flows* became even one of the proclaimed aims of monetary policy. The reintroduction and strengthening of capital controls which followed upon the oil crisis of 1973 was a major further step back. The different policy responses of the large European member states, now including the United Kingdom, resulted in large divergences in macro-economic performance. In this atmosphere the political willingness to work together towards European integration was lacking. In the transitional phase, following the switch to floating and preceding the establishment of the EMS, the Community more or less muddled through, combining a wide variety of exchange arrangements with capital controls of varying intensity. The newly acceded members, who lacked the institutional background of the EEC and the common determination to strive for closer integration, held extensive exchange control systems in place as well.

The only member states which in the course of the 1970s gradually dismantled controls were Germany and to a lesser extent the Netherlands. These countries had come to the conclusion that the drawbacks of control systems weighed heavier than the advantages. But these were *individual, uncoordinated actions,* where the EEC institutions stood at the sidelines. Within the Community the attention of the Commission and the Monetary Committee was diverted to other issues, which were considered to be of greater importance such as the enlargement of EEC credit facilities in order to support adjustment. The member states, however, were not very good in imposing conditions on these loans and in fact, the European economies still diverged to a considerable extent at the end of the decade. Capital liberalization in a Community framework was deadlocked for nearly twenty years.

The establishment of the European Monetary System in 1979 marked a *new beginning*, as did the switch to liberal policies in the Anglo-Saxon world under the Reagan and Thatcher administrations. The latter influenced economic thinking on the Continent. The abolition of exchange control in the United Kingdom in 1979, the deregulation of capital markets in the Anglo-Saxon world, together with other market-oriented policies aimed at strengthening the supply side, fostered economic growth. The rapid development and integration of financial markets increasingly began to nibble at the effectiveness of remaining capital controls. The erosion of regulatory powers contributed greatly to the shift in the balance between the pros and cons of capital controls over time. For the authorities the trade off between the need to protect the official reserves or the exchange rate against the dead weight efficiency costs of capital controls increasingly became in favour of abolishing them altogether.

Official thinking evolved, first in those countries which had steered a middle course, like the Netherlands and Denmark. They abolished nearly all restrictions. It was, however, not until the mid–1980s that a satisfactory degree of stability had been reached within the EMS, which enabled a resumption of common attempts towards financial integration and capital liberalization.

Increasingly, the focus of domestic monetary policies in Europe shifted from attaining internal objectives towards the maintenance of exchange rate stability vis-à-vis the anchor currency, the Deutsche mark. Especially after the change of policy direction in France in 1983, the EMS started to operate more and more as the zone of monetary stability it was intended to be. The fundamental reorientation of French policies implied a far-reaching modernization of the financial system and of the conduct of monetary policy as well. In this changed financial structure there was no place for exchange control.

The *changed vision of France* with respect to the freedom of capital movements had important implications for the Community as a whole. After Germany and the United Kingdom, France was the third major country to pursue such liberalization. This swayed the balance within the Community and other countries now had to follow suit. In the context of improved convergence the shielding of domestic financial markets became less important an objective, whereas the effectiveness of capital controls to safeguard the exchange rate from speculative pressures had greatly eroded, as experience had shown. When it was decided to forge ahead a dynamic process was set in motion which eventually would lead to a resumption of the discussions on economic and monetary union.

The initiative to resume the drive towards capital liberalization came from within the *Monetary Committee*. The initial reaction of the *Commission* had been hesitant, but at a later stage under the inspired leadership of Delors the initiative was vigorously reclaimed. The Commission persisted in its pursuit of full capital liberalization. It made the strategic decision to force the issue of full capital liberalization in the expectation that this would compel the member states to take the necessary adjustment measures in other areas. The Commission brushed aside objections of member states which claimed that tax harmonization should precede full capital liberalization out of fear of tax-evasion inspired outflows. If it would have surrendered to those demands, it would have gotten nowhere.

In 1988 a directive was agreed upon which provided for the *full liberalization* of capital movements within a given time schedule. When on 1 July 1990 the first stage of the Economic and Monetary Union started, capital restrictions had been effectively abolished in 8 out of 12 member states. The full freedom of capital movements was codified in the Treaty on European Union and therewith was made directly applicable. Although in the wake of the EMS crises of 1992 and 1993 suggestions were made to reinstate measures to regulate speculative capital flows, these were quickly discarded because of their ineffectiveness and their adverse effect on credibility. When in May 1994 Greece abolished its exchange control system, the liberalization of capital movements in Europe was completed.

10.2 AN ECONOMIC APPRAISAL OF THE ATTITUDES OF MEMBER STATES

Germany has been a driving force towards capital liberalization. Traditionally being inclined to liberal policies, Germany already had abolished a large part of its capital controls at a relatively early stage. The liberalization of capital movements fitted well in the Ordnungspolitik of the post-war German government. One of the ideological guiding principles was that there needed to be disciplinary mechanisms which would force the monetary authorities to stay on a stability-oriented track. In this view large-scale capital outflows had to be regarded as sign of unbalanced economic policies that called for adjustment.

The post-war economic institutional structure allowed the *independent Bundesbank* to raise interest rates in case of inflationary pressures without political interference. During the Bretton Woods period, the anti-inflationary objectives of the Bundesbank were time and again thwarted by inflows of foreign capital. Faced with monetary expansion at a rate which endangered price stability, the Bundesbank repeatedly advocated the revaluation of the domestic currency. Exchange rate policy being in the realm of government, these requests were frequently opposed, mainly on the ground that this would weaken the competitive position of German industry. With the demise of the Bretton Woods System in sight, the Bundesbank advocated the imposition of controls on capital inflows, but when these controls eventually were imposed, they could not stem the surge of foreign funds. With the transition to generalized floating their need vanished and they were soon abolished.

Germany became a more forceful and more vocal advocate of free capital movements in the 1980s. There was a strong wish on the part of the monetary authorities to *strengthen financial discipline* in the neighbouring EC countries. Their accommodative monetary policies and lax fiscal policies frequently caused tensions in the post-Bretton Woods European monetary arrangements. Capital controls in these countries were circumvented and Germany was both faced with liquidity inflows and with requests for financial assistance under the enlarged European financing mechanisms. Exchange tensions in these arrangements exerted pressure on the Bundesbank to lower interest rates more than it found desirable on domestic grounds. All along for Germany internal stability came first. But this was not to say that its domestic monetary policy was phrased without any consideration of the external repercussions. For Germany, as a relatively open economy the exchange rate was too important to be indifferent to developments in the exchange markets. In practice the Bundesbank was prepared to align its policies with a view to preserving stability within the EMS. However, in case of a conflict with demands of internal stability the latter would be given precedence. The decision whether such a conflict existed the Bundesbank wished to make on its own authority. Any common decision-making with respect to monetary policy in the Community was rejected. When the obligation to fully liberalize capital movements had been accepted in the Community Germany could be satisfied with the general outcome. It had not been necessary to make large concessions, especially not in the most crucial area of monetary policy. Full freedom of capital movements had been assured and when the Maastricht Treaty was ratified some years later it contained satisfactory provisions regarding the transitional and final stages of EMU.

France held the balance for a common stance towards capital liberalization in the 1980s. France traditionally had relied on tight control mechanisms, which mainly were inspired by exchange rate and monetary policy considerations. The monetary authorities were fearful of speculation against the national currency, especially by residents, and thus kept controls in place to check cross-border outflows. They also wished to follow a low-interest rate policy in order to promote domestic investment and did not want to see this policy jeopardized by the need to raise interest rates in case of speculation against the currency.

For France there was a further ideological, *protectionist argument* for capital controls. They fitted well in the post-war dirigistic approach to economic development, characterized by macro-economic planning, industrialization policy and sectoral differentiation. Monetary policy was geared to channel savings to prioritary industrial sectors, often at preferential interest rates. Such an economic environment called for protective shields at domestic borders, with respect to capital movements and, albeit at a lesser extent, to trade movements. After a brief experiment with nearly full capital freedom in 1967, which was to be accompanied by a switch to the use of more indirect instruments of monetary policy, the subsequent domestic and international disturbances made the government very apprehensive towards any relaxation of controls. Throughout this period the French franc remained a currency prone to speculative attacks. France changed strategy in a major shake-up of policies in 1983 after having become disillusioned about the possibility of following an independent course, partly because of the inability of exchange controls to prevent speculative attacks on the currency. Its switch to a hard currency policy (déflation compétitive) needed to be accompanied by a modernization of the domestic financial structure. The abolition of capital restrictions, through giving free rein to competitive forces, could contribute to the restructuring of the financial sector and the advancement of Paris as a financial centre.

The *Netherlands* in the 1960s stood midway between the liberally-oriented policies of Germany and the rather restrictive attitude of most other member states. The main motivation to hold on initially to certain restrictions on capital outflows was the wish to keep domestic savings for its own use. At the same time restrictions on inflows were deemed necessary in order to support the attainment of quantitative monetary targets. The restrictions were not related to exchange rate considerations, although there may have been a wish to avoid upward pressure on the exchange rate which could threaten the competitive position. Monetary policy was executed by means of direct instruments, i.e. credit ceilings for commercial banks. It was feared that these restrictions would be circumvented by residents taking up credit with commercial banks in third countries. Restrictions on inward capital movements thus were regarded as a necessary cap on this loophole. When the Netherlands after the demise of the Bretton Woods system increasingly aligned its policies with Germany, it gradually abolished capital controls. In the 1980s it became a forceful advocate of capital liberalization within the EC and, after an overhaul of its monetary instruments, deregulated its domestic financial markets in a decisive manner.

Belgium throughout the discussions did not actively participate. On the one hand it felt it was in the comfortable position of having de facto free capital movements, in any case as long as the divergence between the free and the commercial exchange rate was negligible. On the other hand the dual market still provided protection against speculative attacks. It came under repeated pressure to abandon the system because other countries did consider the dual market as a form of exchange control which would have to be abandoned. Its continued existence constituted a delaying factor in the move towards full capital freedom in Europe. A complicating factor from the Belgian standpoint was that their Luxembourg partners considered the existence of a dual market as a safeguard against more severe interventions against capital flows. In practice this meant that Belgium and Luxembourg kept to the sidelines in the debate and did not play an active role.

Although *Italy* in the first years of the Community had been an advocate of capital liberalization because of the contribution this could make to the financing of the economic development of Southern Italy, its own practice was one of elaborate controls. Protection of its relatively underdeveloped capital market and, increasingly, shielding the currency against speculative outflows were prime motives of the authorities. In the 1970s the economy was seriously destabilized and a battery of controls was established even with respect to trade. When in the 1980s the European drive towards capital liberalization gained momentum Italy, which was in favour of a gradual approach, tried to decelerate the process. With an overvalued currency and fiscal policies still out of line it remained vulnerable to speculation. But in the end Italy, too, came to the conclusion that exchange controls would not be effective to counter speculative outflows and that the gradualism which it advocated had as its logical conclusion full liberalization. This left Italy with no choice than to embark on a process of fiscal consolidation.

10.3 A POLITICAL APPRAISAL

The initiative in the early 1980s to take up again the issue of capital liberalization was mainly taken on political grounds. In the early years of the European

Monetary System the hard-currency countries as Germany and the Netherlands were constantly pushed on to the defence by French-inspired proposals for yearly packages to strengthen the EMS mechanisms. In practice these proposals aimed at shifting the burden of adjustment to the hard-currency countries, thus endangering their pursuit of price stability. They went on the counteroffensive and searched for constructive means of putting pressure on the other countries to adjust their policies. The nearly forgotten objective of capital liberalization satisfied this desire because it could be embraced by all countries as a precondition for whatever long-term ideal of monetary integration member states might cherish. Discussions on capital liberalization brought out into the open the initially diverging views as to the ultimate goal of the strengthening of the EMS and the promotion of the ECU. In the end all countries rallied around the ultimate goal of monetary unification. Thus the history of the liberalization of capital movements in Europe to a large extent coincides with the history of monetary cooperation in Europe.

The 1988 Directive, effectively freeing all capital movements, was a *landmark* in the process of European integration. Fundamental factors had been at work which heralded the abolition of controls: their effectiveness was in doubt, their operational costs were high, and they led to suboptimal allocation. Nevertheless, taking into consideration the endless discussions on their abolition at earlier instances the move towards full liberalization was quick. The favourable economic climate in the second half of the 1980s provided a *window of opportunity*. At previous occasions the authorities had shied away from undertaking common obligations in adverse cyclical circumstances. But also the political climate was favourable. Politicians were once again prepared to work together towards European integration, as evidenced by the acceptance of the White Book. The relatively stable situation in the European Monetary System was conducive to foster this feeling of political well-being.

The relative speed with which agreement was reached on the 1988 Directive merits further consideration. Some have advanced that capital liberalization was the *bargaining chip* needed to persuade Germany to make concessions with respect to progress towards monetary unification. It is true that Germany had made it abundantly clear that it did not wish to contemplate any further steps to strengthen or institutionalize the EMS and ECU mechanisms before capital movements would have been fully liberalized. It re-enforced its arguments by the unchallenged claim that freedom of capital movements constituted a sine qua non for European monetary integration. Both the 'economist' and 'monetarist' schools of thought agreed on this, although the monetarists would have liked to support the drive for liberalization by firmer commitments on monetary cooperation from the hard-currency countries. It was therefore not surprising that in the course of the negotiations attempts were made to extract monetary concessions from Germany. But these all fell short of further-reaching schemes for monetary unification and the capital directive finally was unconditionally approved. The French initiative to take up again the study of economic and monetary union, which received political support in Germany, fell in well-prepared ground because its precondition, freedom of capital movements, would be fulfilled and exchange rates in the EMS had stabilized. But the outcome of these negotiations at the time could not be predicted and even after adoption of the Treaty on European Union the establishment of EMU remains uncertain. Therefore this explanation does not suffice. Other forces have been at work as well.

This study shows that a more likely explanation for the abandonment of capital controls in Europe is that *France,* playing a *pivotal role* in Europe, considered for reasons of its own that it should do away with exchange controls, following the example of Germany and the United Kingdom. At the same time France aligned its policies to those of Germany. Other countries now had to follow suit, sometimes reluctantly, if they did not want to severe the political and economic links with the mainstream in Europe. France played a key role in the final steps towards full capital liberalization. Not only the transition to solid macro-economic policies in 1983, but even more so the rather radical reform of its financial system and its monetary policy instruments were important elements. The evolution in French thinking provides an important clue to the question why this attempt to liberalize succeeded where others had failed. But this success could not have been brought about without the active support of the Commission.

From the outset of the EEC the *Commission* had pleaded for capital liberalization. But in the course of the 1970s the Commission had lost its appetite in the face of large divergences between member states. It needed considerable prodding, especially from Germany and the Netherlands, to move on with its quest for capital liberalization. But when the Commission eventually did move on, it did so with great courage. By proposing full freedom of capital movements it removed exchange controls as what was considered by some participants in the Exchange Rate Mechanism as the ultimate line of defence in case of exchange unrest. The good functioning of this system had been instrumental in changing Eurosclerosis into Eurodynamism. With its proposals for full and unconditional capital liberalization, the Commission seized the window of opportunity provided by the favourable economic and political climate, and by the conversion of France. It made the strategic choice to give absolute priority to capital liberalization, in the end declining a direct conditional link to other areas, such as taxation, coordination procedures or the promotion of the ECU. The latter had been demanded as a quid pro quo in the first operational years of the EMS but these requests had run aground against stubborn resistance of Germany. The Commission deserves high marks for its persistence.

10.4 THE EFFECTIVENESS OF CONTROLS

In the *changing appraisal* on the part of the authorities of the pros and cons of capital liberalization an important consideration was that restrictions, once they were partially liberalized, were no longer effective. The experiences of the 1970s had already shown the limited effectiveness of capital controls. Faced with strong disturbances in the exchange markets they were powerless. For Germany this was sufficient reason to abolish them. Other countries, although they acknowledged the limited effectiveness, preferred to play it safe as long as controls were not considered to be very harmful either. They may have had some effect to shield domestic monetary policies at times of calm on the exchange markets. Effectiveness eroded further with the increasing sophistication of financial markets and the emergence of derivative financial products which blurred the traditional distinctions between market segments. The restrictions therefore resembled more and more playing cat and mouse: as the former president of the Nederlandsche Bank Zijlstra has said, it just is not possible to put a cat for every hole. This explains why countries, once they embarked on the process of liberalization, ultimately pushed for full liberalization.

If capital controls were increasingly considered to be ineffective with respect to their stated goals, why is it then that authorities have wished to implement or maintain them anyway? One reason is a factor which might be called the *placebo effect.* In the face of wide-spread speculation there is an imperative political wish for the authorities to be seen as doing something. They can, in their own view, not be seen as merely standing by. When images of greedy speculators, making huge fortunes, are displayed for the public eye, it is difficult to accept the free play of market forces. The imposition of capital controls can help, so it is hoped, in calming down the markets and the general public, although experts know they will in the end not achieve what they are intended for. To this end the authorities wished to keep capital controls available as an instrument to fall back upon. Therefore they were not willing to submit them to common EEC obligations even in cases where on an individual basis member states had liberalized more than was called for under the directives. More often than not the tightening of capital controls served as a subsitute for policy adjustments. When authorities in the face of market pressures and confidence crises repeatedly reached out for capital controls, the instrument of capital controls became blunt and the country concerned was likely to be worse off. The financial markets would conclude that the authorities were not willing to administer real medicine, i.e. adjustment measures, and would withdraw capital.

Capital controls bear fewer *political costs* than devaluations of the national currencies. Capital controls are perceived as being aimed at foreign speculators, wishing to bring about a change in the value of the national currency, or at disloyal tax-evading residents. The authorities may consider it important to be seen as taking decisive actions, even if they realize that the effectiveness of the measures is rather questionable. The impact of the measures on domestic market operators is normally not felt directly by the general public at large. Devaluations, on the other hand, are more visible and they shatter national pride. Political resistance against devaluations typically is strong. In this reasoning a political case can be construed for buying time through the imposition of capital controls. Over time it has increasingly been recognized that exchange control measures do not alter the fundamental causes of speculation. Evidence has shown that they do not change exchange rate expectations in a significant and durable way. Therefore they do not provide a durable relief for speculative pressures on the exchange rate.

The call for capital controls which came up in the wake of the *EMS crises* of 1992 and 1993 must be regarded in the same vein as a manifestation of the wish to do something about perceived speculation. Delors, who faced with the turbulence gave the Commission's hitherto firm position a disappointing twist, made the analogy with speed controls on highways, where capital controls should limit excessive movements in financial markets. This study shows that speed controls are the realm of supervision on financial institutions and on payment systems. Supervision takes care that financial transactions are carried out in a sound and transparent environment. Speed controls are not an instrument to control the flows themselves. Because of the interlinkages between the short and long segments of the financial market, the imposition of capital controls implies that sand is thrown not only in the speculative radar wheels but also in the transactions of bonafide institutional investors and companies which are deprived of making hedging operations. The interference in the functioning of the markets may give a serious blow to confidence and thus have a perverse effect.

10.5 THE OPPORTUNITY COSTS OF CAPITAL CONTROLS

To the extent that capital controls are effective in hindering capital outflows, the national currency becomes a *mousetrap-currency*. Investors can put assets in the trap, but there is no legal way to get them out. Moreover, in so far as controls are effective, commercial relations and investment decisions are influenced, increasing the cost of international trade financing. There is not an easy on-off switch with respect to capital controls. They cannot be restricted to a limited number of transactions, they have a tendency to spread unchecked and ultimately may lead to a loss of confidence in the currency concerned. They could not provide an alibi for not using the interest rate instrument or other means to defend the exchange rate.

Over time the opportunity costs of capital controls have increased. The growing advantages of *open financial markets* have been understood by the authorities. For France this provided an important motive to pursue liberalization. In the Internal Market it was essential for France to remove the constraints which capital restrictions imposed on its industrial and financial sector. These constraints risked to place French industry in an unfavourable competitive position vis-à-vis the industrial sector in other countries. The position of Paris as a financial centre was at stake as well. The authorities had already realized that the French currency never could reach the same status of global currency as the other major currencies – US dollar, Deutsche mark and Japanese yen – had reached. Therefore in discussions on the international monetary system it had always put its stakes on the furthering of the SDR, and in the European context, on the ECU and on monetary integration. These initiatives all had run aground. It did not prove possible to detract from the reserve currency status of the US dollar and the Deutsche mark through the promotion of artificial basket-type currencies. France had to accept that such a multilateralized system was not attainable and that the continuation of a multicurrency monetary system was likely. In order for France to play an influential role on its own, its financial centre had to be enabled to grow and to innovate. This was only possible in an open environment in which its financial institutions and its markets were exposed to the fresh wind of competition. France realized that national financial markets that are heavily regulated or restricted in their external transactions would lag behind and eventually would become less important. It recognized that liberalization, if need be unilaterally, would be to its own advantage.

It felt strengthened by the positive confidence factors in other countries. And it wished to try to regain some of the lost ground to London which as a financial centre had greatly gained from the deregulation and liberalization policies of the Thatcher administration. In fact London eclipsed other financial centres on the Continent, despite the fact that the pound sterling did not participate in the European monetary arrangements (apart from the interlude from 1990–92). Capital liberalization was the crown on the French efforts to strengthen and modernize its financial system and to switch to market-oriented instruments of monetary control.

These motives carried validity for other countries as well, but not always the same policy conclusions were drawn. Italy, for instance, came to another evaluation, weighing the costs against the perceived benefits of controls. Italy had a weaker economy, in particular because of its traditionally large fiscal deficits, whereas France with generally sound fiscal policies was better placed to liberalize, in conformity with the theory of sequencing. Moreover, France was more inclined to displaying international ambitions in the monetary field and letting its financial institutions play a global role than Italy with its fragmented financial system. In the end countries like Italy, however, had *no choice*. By not following the lead Italy risked to be relegated to the second plan. Italy could not afford that its strong industrial sector would be put at a financial disadvantage vis-à-vis other countries. In the framework of modern financial markets capital controls had become an illusion.

Some critics considered the currency crises which forced Italy out of the EMS as proving their case that free capital flows were not compatible with exchange rate stability. They are misreading the events and forgetting history. Full freedom of capital movements had been achieved four years earlier and had not stood in the way of exchange rate stability. Neither had it done so in other countries with a longer history of capital freedom. The EMS crises were caused by macro-economic imbalances and insufficient preparedness to adjust policies accordingly. Signaling out free capital movements is tantamount to mistaking the symptom for the cause. History shows that capital restrictions would have been powerless in the face of massive speculative flows. The case of France, which too, despite balanced macro-economic policies, was hit by speculative attacks in 1993, proves that once financial markets are disturbed the determinedness of the authorities to defend the exchange rate will be tested. In this they must stand firm, as the French authorities did, with success. In doing so, the preservation of exchange rate stability must rank above domestic considerations. In the end, a relatively low interest rate will provide ample reward for the domestic economy.

10.6 LINKAGES WITH OTHER POLICY DOMAINS

The proposals for capital liberalization have been attended by proposals in related policy domains. The most important linkages have been to:

(a) a strengthening of *coordination* procedures, in particular with respect to monetary policy;
(b) an increase of the *financing mechanisms* of the EEC, including the structural funds, and the European Monetary System;
(c) *taxation* issues.

As far as the first two linkages are concerned, the traditional opposite positions of the 'monetarists' and the 'economists' came to the fore, largely boiling down to the question of the distribution of the adjustment burden. The 'monetarist' recipe of relaxing the external constraints for the weak-currency countries and favouring collective decision-making with respect to monetary policy had for a while received some support of the Commission. Especially the promotion of the ECU, introducing symmetrical responses in the EMS, had been a popular theme. Capital liberalization could be seen as a crowbar to infringe upon the autonomy of the central bank of the EC's anchor currency, the Bundesbank. Against this 'monetarist' recipe the 'economist' recipe of letting work through the disciplinary effects of external constraints on domestic policies was advanced. The latter view prevailed when the Commission eventually decided to relinquish these linkages and so embark on a dynamic process. This forced policy adjustments on member states, by exposing the macro-economic policy stance more fully to the judgement of financial markets. This judgement will be based on the fundamental strength of the economy and the orientation of monetary policy, relative interest rate levels and inflation performance being the chief determinants of exchange rates. Thus capital liberalization increases the importance of sound monetary and fiscal policies.

Taxation, the third linkage, is a real issue. Differences in fiscal treatment can disturb the optimal allocation of scarce capital resources. In the negotiations fiscal issues proved to be of such immense political sensitivity that any demand for tax harmonization to precede capital liberalization would have boiled down to putting off indefinitely the latter. The opportunity costs of exchange control having increased, it was a right decision to first reap the advantages of capital liberalization and see which disturbances actually evolve because of tax divergences. In some cases, such as France, these proved to be less serious then initially was feared. If, however, tax arbitration and tax evasion were to become a real problem of significant proportions, undermining tax moral, this would provide an important political incentive to tackle tax divergences within the Community and seek agreement, setting aside national political sensitivities. The Commission's strategy to push through unconditionally capital liberalization thus may have the positive side-effect of initiating a dynamic process towards harmonization in the field of taxation.

10.7 WILL CAPITAL CONTROLS BE REINTRODUCED?

After having analysed the forces which have been behind the accomplishment of the full freedom of capital movements a tentative answer must be formulated as to the likelihood that this freedom will hold. Of course, any such answer is hazardous and, in the ebb and tide of economic history, ideologies, mechanisms and instruments may change. There are major arguments which would lead to impose the conclusion that reintroduction of capital controls in Europe in the foreseeable future is not likely. These arguments briefly can be listed under three headings: (a) formal constraints, (b) political considerations, and (c) economic considerations.

(A) Formal Constraints

In the Treaty on European Union formal steps are distinguished which will lead up to the establishment of EMU. In the final stage, which according to the Treaty, is to start in any case on 1 January 1999 with those countries which are considered to have fulfilled the relevant criteria, there will be no capital controls by definition among the participating countries. In the transitional phase which started on 1 January 1994 the possibilities to restrict intra-EC capital flows are severely limited. Derogations remain possible under Articles 109h and 109i, providing for emergency measures in case of severe balance-of-payments difficulties, but the Treaty's intentions would be rather stretched if such measures were to include capital restrictions. The possibility to do so is contradicted by the general obligations of Article 73b. The Commission, however, has the right to propose temporary restrictions vis-à-vis third countries (under Article 73f) 'in exceptional circumstances', and only if there are serious difficulties which could undermine the operation of EMU. The Treaty is clear that, if restrictions are allowed, they can only be temporarily imposed in case of severe disturbances. Experience has shown, as discussed in this study, that precisely in those circumstances they are least likely to be effective.

(B) Political Considerations

Reintroduction of capital controls in individual member states would form a serious if not unsurmountable set-back for the establishment of EMU. It would carry high political costs for the country concerned as well, by providing a signal that the country was not able to make it in the first group entering the final stage of EMU. The creditworthiness of the EMU process, which has already been damaged by the fragile degree of acceptance among the populations and the EMS crises, would receive another serious and possibly final blow, especially if one of the countries perceived to belong to the core group would set such steps. But also, the reintroduction of controls by countries which cannot be expected to soon join EMU, would further imprint the image of a two-speed Europe.

(C) Economic Considerations

The analysis in this book has shown that exchange controls or other disguised measures aimed at limiting cross-border capital flows have been rather unsuccessful as to the attainment of their goals. They have not been able to ward off downward or upward pressures on exchange rates in case of imbalances. They may have provided some protection for domestic capital markets and domestic monetary policies at quiet times in the early post-war decades of underdeveloped markets and direct instruments of monetary control. But in the modern financial environment of today they have become an anachronism, carrying significant opportunity costs. Reintroduction of capital controls would deal a blow to confidence in the currency concerned and most likely would result in higher domestic interest rates rather than in lower ones. In doing so, they would impose costs on normal commercial and financial transactions and thus hamper economic growth.

10.8 CONCLUDING OBSERVATIONS

In many respects the liberalization of capital movements in Europe can be judged as a vindication of the German body of economic thought. Its market-oriented ideology has been adopted in all other European countries. The necessary underpinning by sound macro-economic policies, viz. avoidance of excessive budget deficits and maintenance of domestic price stability, have become widely accepted, though not generally implemented. The German use of indirect instruments of monetary control has become the European standard. The dialectics of progress have left Germany, however, with some rigidities in its instruments, such as unremunerated cash reserves. The British swing to liberal policies in the early 1980s, too, greatly influenced thinking on the Continent. It has helped refocus attention on the real demands of the Common Market: open markets and freedom for economic decision-makers. When, however, the United Kingdom displayed disinterest in the further integration efforts such as EMU, its influence quickly waned.

France has made a remarkable turnaround, switching-over to a policy of competitive disinflation, supported by market-oriented monetary instruments, mainly in the form of open-market operations. What really moved the actual forces towards liberalization was an endogenous process in the financial markets and the real economy towards increased internationalization. This was grasped by the French authorities when they for domestic reasons came to the conclusion that only in a competitive, open environment French industry and financial institutions could continue to play a global role. The Commission grasped the window of opportunity provided by a favourable economic climate and a positive disposition of these large member states to push through a programme of full capital liberalization in Europe. Therewith it took a decision of high political and strategic dimension. Capital liberalization removed a major obstacle to economic and monetary union. It provided more impetus to the European integration process than many had foreseen, culminating in the adoption of the Treaty on European Union. Now it is up to the member states to attune their policies to the convergence needed for economic and monetary unification. If in doing so they will have irrevocably locked their currencies, and thus will have banned exchange rate uncertainty, they will have removed the main remaining obstacle for the free movement of capital in Europe.

Chronology

Chronology of major measures with respect to the regime of capital movements in the member states of the European Community
(Direction of measures: L – liberalization, T – tightening)

1958	16 January	L	Germany – Permission for residents to maintain foreign currency accounts abroad.
	21 June	L	France – Incorporation of the surcharge of 20% on the official exchange rate in a new reference rate for the US dollar.
	1 July	L	Germany – Liberalization of inward investment by non-residents.
	13 August	L	Germany – Liberalization of transactions in German bonds denominated in foreign currency.
	27 December	L	EEC – Liquidation of the European Payments Union; EEC currencies become externally convertible in current payment transactions.
1959	1 May	L	Germany – Abolition of all remaining restrictions on the import of capital.
	5 June	L	France – Abolition of requirement of a 50% deposit on foreign exchange purchases by importers.
	24 August	L	Italy – Easing of regulations concerning investment abroad by residents.
1960	1 January	L	France – Monetary reform: introduction of the 'new' franc, abolition of the Exchange Office.
	11 May	L	EEC – Adoption by the Council of the First Directive on capital movements.
	4 June	T	Germany – Prohibition to pay interest on Deutsche mark deposits held by non-residents and to sell money market paper to non-residents.
	16 July	L	The Netherlands – Issuance of general licences for a number of outward capital movements.

1961	1 September	L	Germany – Coming into effect of the new Foreign Trade and Payments Law, establishing a positive system of exchange regulation.
	1 October	L	The Netherlands – Further relaxation of exchange controls.
1962	2 January	L	Italy – Merger of the free market for capital transactions with the official exchange market.
	24 February	L	France – Easing of foreign exchange allowances for travel purposes and other transactions in the personal sphere.
	2 April	L	France – Abolition of the parallel devises-titres market for cross-border transactions by residents in foreign securities.
	24 April	L	The Netherlands – Opening-up of the Netherlands capital market for the issuance of foreign guilder loans up to a ceiling.
	18 December	L	EEC – Adoption by the Council of the Second Directive on capital movements (Directive 63/21/EEC).
	21 December	L	France – Further relaxation of exchange controls.
1963	28 March	L	Italy – Abolition of restrictions on investments in foreign securities by residents.
	10 April	T	France – Prohibition of payment of interest on French franc deposits held by non-residents.
	7 August	T	France – Curtailment of loans by non-residents to residents.
1965	25 March	T	Germany – Introduction of a withholding tax ('coupon tax') on interest income on assets held by non-residents.
	15 October	L	France – Abolition of restriction for commercial banks to engage in forward transacions.
1966	22 January	L	Italy – Extension of permission of outward direct investment to the OECD area (previously only EEC).
	1 October	L	The Netherlands – Abolition of the "free market" for cross-border transactions in securities.
1967	31 January	L	France – Introduction of a positive system of exchange regulation. Substantial relaxation of exchange controls. Abolition of the prohibition to pay interest on French franc deposits held by non-residents.

	10 November	L	Italy – Easing of limitations on export of bank notes and of settlement requirements.
1968	29 May	T	France – Reintroduction of temporary exchange control and of restrictions on allowances for foreign travel by residents.
	23 July	T	EEC – France is authorized by the Commission to invoke safeguard measures (Decision 68/301/EEC).
	4 September	L	France – Abolition of the exchange control measures introduced in May 1968.
	25 November	T	France – Reintroduction of essentially the same exchange control measures of May 1968.
	1 December	T	Germany – Imposition of a minimum reserve requirement on the growth of external bank liabilities.
1969	11 August	T	France – Reintroduction of the devises-titres market.
	31 October	L	Germany – Abolition of the minimum reserve requirement on the growth of external bank liabilities.
1970	1 April	T	Germany – Reintroduction of the minimum reserve requirement on the growth of external bank liabilities.
	4 August	L	France – Easing of restrictions on outward direct investment and abolition of the carnet de change for foreign travel allowances.
1971	1 April	T	France – Imposition of a minimum reserve requirement on external bank liabilities.
	10 May	T	Germany – Prohibition of payment of interest on bank deposits of non-residents and of purchases by non-residents of money market paper.
	11 May	T	Belgium – Complete separation of the official and the free exchange market.
	23 August	T	France – Establishment of a dual exchange market, comprising an official market for import and export transactions and trade-related invisibles, and a financial franc market for all other transactions.
	6 September	T	The Netherlands – Introduction of a free market for bond transactions ("0-circuit").

	20 October	T	France – Merger of the devises-titres market into the dual exchange market.
1972	1 March	T	Germany – Imposition of a cash reserve requirement ('Bardepot') for liabilities incurred vis-à-vis non-residents.
	9 March	T	The Netherlands – Prohibition of payment of interest on guilder deposits held by non-residents.
	21 March	T	EEC – Adoption by the Council of the Directive on regulating international capital flows and neutralizing their undesirable effects on domestic liquidity (Directive 72/156/EEC).
	27 June	T	Italy – Introduction of measures aimed at restricting capital outflows; ban on net external credit position of banks; suspension of external convertibility of Italian banknotes.
	1 July	T	Germany – Prohibition of sales of fixed interest securities to non-residents. Tightening of minimum reserve and Bardepot requirements.
	17 July	T	The Netherlands – Further tightening of exchange controls, affecting leads and lags and the taking up of foreign credit by residents.
1973	22 January	T	Italy – Establishment of a dual exchange market.
	1 February	T	Germany – Prohibition of sales of all credit instruments and of borrowing to non-residents.
	16 March	T	France – Prohibition of payment of interest on bank deposits of non-residents and raising of the minimum reserve requirement on the growth of external bank liabilities to 100%.
	19 March	L	Denmark – Liberalization of inward and outward portfolio and direct investment.
	22 June	T	Germany – Further tightening of the minimum reserve and Bardepot requirements.
	27 July	T	Italy – Introduction of a 50 per cent compulsory non-interest bearing deposit scheme with respect to most capital outflows.
	8 October	L	France – Abolition of the prohibition of payment of interest on bank deposits of non-residents and abolition of the minimum reserve requirement on the growth of external bank liabilities.

1974	1 January	L	Germany – Abolition of the minimum reserve requirement on the growth of external bank liabilities.
	19 January	T	France – Prohibition of French franc borrowing by non-residents, restriction of forward transactions by residents, relaxation of borrowing abroad by residents.
	1 February	L	The Netherlands – Abolition of the closed bond "0-circuit".
	1 February	L	Germany – Reduction of the Bardepot requirement and abolition of authorization requirements for sales to non-residents of credit instruments other than domestic fixed interest securities with a maturity of less than 4 years.
	21 March	T	France – Abolition of the dual exchange market. Severe tightening of controls on capital outflows and relaxation of controls on capital inflows.
	22 March	L	Italy – Abolition of the dual exchange market.
	7 May	T	Italy – Introduction of a temporary compulsory non-interest bearing deposit scheme with respect to imports, excluding raw materials, oil and investment goods. Italy is authorized by the Commission to invoke safeguard measures (Decision 74/287/EEC).
	15 September	L	Germany – Abolition of the Bardepot provisions.
1975	1 September	L	Germany – Abolition of the prohibition to pay interest on Deutsche mark deposits held by non-residents. Abolition of authorization requirements for sales to non-residents of securities with a maturity of 2 to 4 years.
1976	1 January	L	The Netherlands – Abolition of the prohibition to pay interest on guilder deposits held by non-residents.
	18 March	T	Italy – Reintroduction of compulsory bank financing in foreign exchange for advance settlement of imports.
	6 May	T	Italy – Reintroduction of the non-interest bearing import deposit scheme.

	1 October	T	Italy – Imposition of a temporary special tax on purchases of foreign currency and payments abroad. Extension of the compulsory import deposit scheme.
1977	18 February	L	Italy – Expiration of the special tax on foreign currency purchases.
	15 April	L	Italy – Abolition of the compulsory import deposit scheme.
	24 June	T	Ireland – Reimposition of reserve requirement (of 50%) on capital inflows with commercial banks.
	1 September	L	The Netherlands – Switch-over to a positive system of exchange control. Further easing of regulations concerning capital outflows.
	15 December	T	Germany – Reintroduction of authorization requirements for sales to non-residents of securities with a maturity less than 4 years.
1978	1 January	T	Germany – Reintroduction of a minimum reserve requirement on the growth of external bank liabilities.
	1 June	L	Germany – Abolition of the minimum reserve requirement on the growth of external bank liabilities.
	18 December	T	Ireland – In consequence of Ireland's decision to participate in the EMS exchange controls were extended to the United Kingdom. Abolition of the investment currency market.
1979	6 February	T	Denmark – Restriction of purchases by non-residents of Danish bonds. Denmark is authorized by the Commission to invoke safeguard measures.
	18 July	L	United Kingdom – All restrictions on outward direct investment are abolished and outward portfolio investment is significantly liberalized.
	4 September	L	Ireland – Easing of restrictions on acquirement of foreign securities.
	23 October	L	United Kingdom – The Exchange Control Act of 1947 is suspended and all remaining barriers to inward and outward flows of capital are removed.
1980	17 March	L	Germany – Relaxation of restrictions on the sale of short-term paper to non-residents.

	11 July	L	France – Restrictions on inward and outward direct investment are relaxed.
	3 December	T	EEC – Ireland is authorized by the Commission to invoke safeguard measures.
1981	12 March	L	Germany – All restrictions on the sale of short-term Deutsche mark paper to non-residents are abolished.
	1 May	L	The Netherlands – Coming into force of the External Financial Relations Act, which supersedes the Exchange Control Decree of 1945.
	21 May	T	France – Reintroduction of the devises-titres market. Limitations on leads and lags in trade settlements. Limitations on direct investment abroad.
	28 May	T	Italy – Reintroduction of the non-interest bearing deposit scheme with respect to purchases of foreign currency by residents.
1982	8 February	L	Italy – Abolition of the advance deposit scheme.
	25 March	T	France – Further restrictions on the surrender of export proceeds and on direct investment abroad.
1983	28 March	T	France – Further reduction of foreign travel allowances, a ban on the use of personal credit cards abroad and introduction of the 'carnet de change', a booklet in which foreign exchange purchases were recorded.
	1 May	L	Denmark – Easing of restrictions on purchases of foreign securities and direct investment. Abrogation of the safeguard measures.
	1 July	L	The Netherlands – Abolition of all remaining restrictions on capital inflows.
	17 December	L	Italy – Certain direct investment abroad is exempted from the 50 per cent non-interest-bearing deposit requirement.
	23 December	L	France – Some easing of limits on foreign travel allowances and foreign direct investment; abolition of the 'carnet de change'.
1984	1 January	L	Denmark – Abolition of restrictions on the purchase of foreign shares by residents.
	31 July	L	France – Abolition of the ban on use of personal credit cards abroad.

	1 August	L	Germany – Abolition of the coupon tax on interest income on assets held by non-residents.
	14 November	L	France – Easing of controls on direct investment.
	3 December	L	Italy – Reduction of compulsory zero-deposit requirements on portfolio investment abroad.
	19 December	L	EEC – The Commission sets an expiry date for the existing safeguard clauses for France (2 years), Italy and Ireland (3 years), and limits the safeguards to existing restrictions (Decisions 85/14, 15 and 16/EEC).
1985	25 February	L	France – Easing of inward direct investment orginating from non-EEC countries.
	3 April	L	France – Authorization of Eurobond issues denominated in French francs.
	11 June	L	Denmark – Further liberalization measures.
	1 September	L	France – Easing of financing rules for outward direct investment outside the EC.
	23 October	L	Italy – Abolition of the compulsory deposit requirement for direct investment abroad. Residents' foreign exchange deposits are freely convertible into other currencies and the ban on transfer of foreign securities and loans between residents is lifted. Reduction of compulsory deposit requirements on other transactions.
	22 November	T	EEC – Greece is authorized by the Commission to take certain safeguard measures for a period of three years (Decision 85/594/EEC).
	2 December	L	France – Easing of regulations for outward portfolio and direct investment.
	20 December	L	EEC – Adoption by the Council of the Directive (85/583/EEC) on Undertakings for collective investments in transferable securities (UCITS).
1986	26 January	L	France – Easing of foreign travel allowances.
	16 April	L	France – Elimination of requirement of prior authorization of direct foreign investment.
	22 May	L	France – Abolition of the devises-titres market; liberalization of purchases of secondary residences abroad; easing of forward foreign exchange operations; easing of authorization procedures for direct investment abroad.

	23 May	L	EEC – The Commission presents a Programme for the liberalization of capital movements in the Community.
	4 June	L	EEC – Abrogation of the safeguard clause with respect to France.
	27 June	L	Spain – Liberalization of inward direct investment and the right of establishment.
	8 August	L	Italy – Restoration of external convertibility of Italian banknotes.
	1 October	L	The Netherlands – Abolition of all remaining restrictions on capital outflows. Full liberalization of all capital transactions.
	7 November	L	Spain – Relaxation of controls on outward direct investment.
	17 November	L	EEC – Adoption by the Council of the Third Directive on capital movements (Directive 86/566/EEC).
	18 November	L	France – Partial liberalization of bank lending in French francs to non-residents; abolition of administrative control through the commercial banks of import and export settlements ('domiciliation' regime).
1987	25 February	L	EEC – Modification of the existing safeguard clauses with respect to Greece, Ireland and Italy in order to accommodate the extension of liberalization obligations under the 1986 Directive.
	20 March	T	Italy – Introduction of reserve requirement on bank deposits in foreign currency.
	13 May	L	Italy – Abolition of the non-interest-bearing deposit requirement for investment abroad in securities and real estate.
	21 May	L	France – Substantial easing of exchange controls for commercial enterprises; liberalization of trade in gold.
	1 June	L	Germany – German residents are allowed to incur ECU-denominated liabilities.
	1 July	L	EEC – Abrogation of the safeguard clause with respect to Italy.
	8 July	L	France – Abolition of limits on tourist travel allowances.
	13 September	T	Italy – Shortening of holding periods of foreign currencies.

	20 October	L	Spain – Relaxation of controls on foreign-currency operations by commercial banks.
	16 December	T	EEC – The safeguard clause for Ireland is extended with one year (Decision 88/12/EEC).
1988	1 January	L	Ireland – Easing of restrictions on long-term outflows.
	1 June	L	France – Permission for domestic enterprises to operate foreign currency accounts; abolition of restrictions on borrowing abroad.
	13 June	L	Italy – Restrictions on tourist spending are eased.
	24 June	L	EEC – Adoption by the Council of the Fourth Directive on capital movements (Directive 88/361/EEC).
	1 October	L	Italy – Introduction of a positive system of exchange control. Significant relaxation of controls.
	1 October	L	Denmark – Abolition of all remaining exchange control regulations.
	4 November	L	EEC – Abrogation of the safeguard clause for Ireland.
	29 November	T	EEC – The authorization for Greece to take safeguard measures is extended until end 1989 (Decision 88/600/EEC).
	22 December	L	Spain – Liberalization of outward direct investment and trade in medium and long-term foreign securities.
1989	1 January	L	Ireland – Liberalization of purchases of medium and long-term foreign securities by residents.
	31 January	T	Spain – Imposition of a non-remunerated reserve requirement on financial credits taken up abroad.
	9 March	L	France – Full liberalization of bank lending in French francs to non-residents.
	28 March	L	Portugal – Relaxation of foreign travel allowances.
	1 June	L	France – Liberalization of commercial banks' foreign exchange positions, from now on only to be regulated by prudential provisions; permission for all residents to open ECU-denominated accounts.

	20 September	L	Portugal – Relaxation of controls on purchases of foreign securities by residents.
	26 September	L	Spain – Permission for residents to open accounts denominated in ECUs.
	17 December	T	EEC – Further extension of the derogation enjoyed by Greece for six months (Decision 89/644/EEC).
	31 December	L	Portugal – Abolition of prior authorization requirement of inward direct investment.
1990	1 January	L	France – Abolition of all remaining exchange control regulations (Decree 89/938).
	19 January	L	Italy – Abolition of restrictions on purchases of foreign securities by residents.
	5 March	L	Belgium-Luxembourg – Abolition of the dual exchange market.
	28 March	L	Portugal – Easing of restrictions on acquirement of foreign securities.
	1 April	L	Ireland – Further relaxations and easing of administrative requirements.
	4 April	L	Spain – Further relaxation measures.
	14 May	L	Italy – Abolition of all remaining exchange control regulations.
1991	16 April	L	Spain – Abolition of restrictions on the opening of foreign-currency accounts.
	14 June	L	Portugal – Liberalization of direct and portfolio investment abroad.
1992	1 January	L	Ireland – Easing of restrictions on purchases of foreign securities, borrowing in foreign currency and extending loans to non-residents.
	1 February	L	Spain – Abolition of all remaining exchange control regulations.
	1 September	L	Portugal – Abolition of compulsory deposit requirement against foreign currency.
	24 September	T	Spain – Reintroduction of certain restrictions, mainly with respect to short-term financial credits.
	24 November	L	Spain – Abolition of all remaining exchange control regulations.
	16 December	L	Portugal – Abolition of all remaining exchange control regulations.

1993	1 January	L	Ireland – Abolition of all remaining exchange control regulations.
1994	16 May	L	Greece – Abolition of all remaining exchange control regulations.

Chronology

Chronology of the coordination of economic and monetary policies in Europe and major general events

1957	25 March	Signing of the Treaty of Rome.
1958	1 January	The Treaty on the European Economic Community becomes effective.
	4 June	Constituent meeting of the Monetary Committee.
1964	8 May	Establishment of the Committee of Governors (Decision 64/300/EEC). Obligation to consult the Monetary Committee with respect to international monetary issues (Decision 64/301/EEC).
1965	30 June	Empty chair policy of France until February 1966.
1969	1–2 December	The European Council in the Hague expresses the readiness to establish economic and monetary union.
1970	6 March	The Werner Committee is established by the Council with a view to prepare a report on the attainment of economic and monetary union.
1971	22 March	Adoption by the Council of a Resolution on the attainment of economic and monetary union in stages, of a Decision on the strengthening of the cooperation between the national central banks (71/142/EEC) and of a Decision on medium-term financial assistance (71/143/EEC).
1972	10 April	Establishment of the snake.
1973	1 January	Enlargement of the EEC with Denmark, Ireland and the United Kingdom.
	3 April	Establishment of the European Monetary Cooperation Fund (Regulation 907/73/EEC).

1974	18 February	Adoption of the Decision on the attainment of a high degree of convergence of the economic policies of member states (74/120/EEC). Establishment of the Economic Policy Committee (Decision 74/122/EEC).
1978	7 July	The European Council in Bremen agrees on the broad outlines of the European Monetary System.
	5 December	The European Council in Brussels agrees on the establishment of the European Monetary System.
1979	13 March	Establishment of the European Monetary System.
1981	1 January	Greece becomes the tenth member of the EEC.
1984	3 and 4 December	The European Council in Dublin agrees that steps should be taken to complete the Internal Market.
1985	28 June	Publication of the White Book on the Completion of the Internal Market.
1986	1 January	Portugal and Spain join the EEC.
	28 February	Signing of the Single European Act which provides for the completion of the Internal Market in 1992.
1987	1 July	The Single Europese Act becomes effective.
1988	24 June	Establishment of a single facility providing medium-term financial assistance for member states' balance of payments.
	28 June	The European Council in Hannover establishes the Delors Committee with a view to propose concrete stages leading to economic and monetary union.
1989	17 April	Presentation of the Delors Report on Economic and Monetary Union in the European Community.
1990	8 January	Adoption of the narrow fluctuation margin in the exchange rate mechanism of the EMS for the Italian lira.
	12 March	Adoption of the Decision on multilateral surveillance (90/141/EEC) and of the Decision on the Committee of Governors (90/142/EEC).
	1 July	Start of the first stage of the Economic and Monetary Union.

	8 October	Entry of the British pound sterling in the exchange rate mechanism of the EMS.
1991	10 December	Adoption of the Treaty on European Union in Maastricht.
1992	2 June	Rejection of the Treaty on European Union in a referendum in Denmark.
	17 September	Suspension of the participation of the British pound sterling and the Italian lira in the exchange rate mechanism of the EMS.
	20 September	Adoption by a narrow margin of the Treaty on European Union in a referendum in France.
1993	18 May	Ratification of the Treaty on European Union in Denmark.
	21 July	Adoption of the Treaty on European Union in the British House of Commons.
	1 August	Widening of the fluctuation bands in the exchange rate mechanism of the EMS to 15%.
	1 November	The Treaty on European Union becomes effective.
1994	1 January	Start of the second stage of the Economic and Monetary Union. Establishment of the European Monetary Institute.

Annex 1

Extracts from the Treaty establishing the European Communities concerning capital movements and the balance of payments

Capital

Article 67

1. During the transitional period and to the extent necessary to ensure the proper functioning of the common market, Member States shall progressively abolish between themselves all restrictions on the movement of capital belonging to persons resident in Member States and any discrimination based on the nationality or on the place of residence of the parties on the place where such capital is invested.

2. Current payments connected with the movement of capital between Member States shall be freed from all restrictions by the end of the first stage at the latest.

Article 68

1. Member States shall, as regards the matters dealt with in this Chapter, be as liberal as possible in granting such exchange authorizations as are still necessary after the entry into force of this Treaty.

2. Where a Member State applies to the movements of capital liberalized in accordance with the provisions of this Chapter the domestic rules governing the capital market and the credit system, it shall do so in a non-discriminatory manner.

3. Loans for the direct or indirect financing of a Member State or its regional or local authorities shall not be issued or placed in other Member States unless the States concerned have reached agreement thereon. This provision shall not preclude the application of Article 32 of the Protocol on the Statute of the European Investment Bank.

Article 69

The Council shall on a proposal from the Commission, which for this purpose shall consult the Monetary Committee provided for in Article 105, issue the necessary directives for the progressive implementation of the provisions of Article 67, acting unanimously during the first two stages and by a qualified majority thereafter.

Article 70

1. The Commission shall propose to the Council measures for the progressive coordination of the exchange policies of Member States in respect of the movement of capital between those States and third countries. For this purpose the Council shall issue directives, acting by a qualified majority. It shall endeavour to attain the highest possible degree of liberalization. Unanimity shall be required for measures which constitute a step back as regards the liberalization of capital movements.[1]

2. Where the measures taken in accordance with paragraph 1 do not permit the elimination of differences between the exchange rules of Member States and where such differences could lead persons resident in one of the Member States to use the freer transfer facilities within the Community which are provided for in Article 67 in order to evade the rules of one of the Member States concerning the movement of capital to or from third countries, that State may, after consulting the other Member States and the Commission, take appropriate measures to overcome these difficulties.

Should the Council find that these measures are restricting the free movement of capital within the Community to a greater extent than is required for the purpose of overcoming the difficulties, it may, acting by a qualified majority on a proposal from the Commission, decide that the State concerned shall amend or abolish these measures.

Article 71

Member States shall endeavour to avoid introducing within the Community any new exchange restrictions on the movement of capital and current payments connected with such movements, and shall endeavour not to make existing rules more restrictive.

They declare their readiness to go beyond the degree of liberalization of capital movements provided for in the preceding Articles in so far as their economic situation, in particular the situation of their balance of payments, so permits.

The Commission may, after consulting the Monetary Committee, make recommendations to Member States on this subject.

Article 72

Member States shall keep the Commission informed of any movements of capital to and from third countries which come to their knowledge. The Commission may deliver to Member States any opinions which it considers appropriate on this subject.

Article 73

1. If movements of capital lead to disturbances in the functioning of the capital market in any Member State, the Commission shall, after consulting the Monetary Committee, authorize that State to take protective measures

in the field of capital movements, the conditions and details of which the Commission shall determine.

The Council may, acting by a qualified majority, revoke this authorization or amend the conditions or details thereof.

2. A Member State which is in difficulties may, however, on grounds of secrecy or urgency, take the measures mentioned above, where this proves necessary, on its own initiative. The Commission and the other Member States shall be informed of such measures by the date of their entry into force at the latest. In this event the Commission may, after consulting the Monetary Committee, decide that the State concerned shall amend or abolish the measures.

Balance of payments

Article 104

Each Member State shall pursue the economic policy needed to ensure the equilibrium of its overall balance of payments and to maintain confidence in its currency, while taking care to ensure a high level of employment and a stable level of prices.

Article 105

1. In order to facilitate attainment of the objectives set out in Article 104, Member States shall coordinate their economic policies. They shall for this purpose provide for cooperation between their appropriate administrative departments and between their central banks.

The Commission shall submit to the Council recommendations on how to achieve such cooperation.

2. In order to promote coordination of the policies of Member States in the monetary field to the full extent needed for the functioning of the common market, a Monetary Committee with advisory status is hereby set up. It shall have the following tasks:

- to keep under review the monetary and financial situation of the Member States and of the Community and the general payments system of the Member States and to report regularly thereon to the Council and to the Commission;
- to deliver opinions at the request of the Council or of the Commission or on its own initiative, for submission to these institutions.

The Member States and the Commission shall each appoint two members of the Monetary Committee.

Article 106

1. Each Member State undertakes to authorize, in the currency of the Member State in which the creditor or the beneficiary resides, any payments connected with the movement of goods, services or capital, and any transfers of capital

and earnings, to the extent that the movement of goods, services, capital and persons between Member States has been liberalized pursuant to this Treaty.

The Member States declare their readiness to undertake the liberalization of payments beyond the extent provided in the preceding subparagraph, in so far as their economic situation in general and the state of their balance of payments in particular so permit.

2. In so far as movements of goods, services and capital are limited only by restrictions on payments connected therewith, these restrictions shall be progressively abolished by applying, mutatis mutandis, the provisions of the Chapters relating to the abolition of quantitative restrictions, to the liberalization of services and to the free movement of capital.

3. Member States undertake not to introduce between themselves any new restrictions on transfers connected with the invisible transactions listed in Annex III to this Treaty.

The progressive abolition of existing restrictions shall be effected in accordance with the provisions of Articles 63 to 65, in so far as such abolition is not governed by the provisions contained in paragraphs 1 and 2 or by the Chapter relating to the free movement of capital.[2]

4. If need be, Member States shall consult each other on the measures to be taken to enable the payments and transfers mentioned in this Article to be effected; such measures shall not prejudice the attainment of the objectives set out in this Chapter.

Article 107

1. Each Member State shall treat its policy with regard to rates of exchange as a matter of common concern.

2. If a Member State makes an alteration in its rate of exchange which is inconsistent with the objectives set out in Article 104 and which seriously distorts conditions of competition, the Commission may, after consulting the Monetary Committee, authorize other Member States to take for a strictly limited period the necessary measures, the conditions and details of which it shall determine, in order to counter the consequences of such alteration.

Article 108

1. Where a Member State is in difficulties or is seriosly threatened with difficulties as regards its balance of payments either as a result of an overall disequilibrium in its balance of payments, or as a result of the type of currency at its disposal, and where such difficulties are liable in particular to jeopardize the functioning of the common market or the progressive implementation of the common commercial policy, the Commission shall immediately investigate the position of the State in question and the action which, making use of all the means at its disposal, that State has taken or may take in accordance with the provisions of Article 104. The Commission shall state what measures it recommends the State concerned to take.

If the action taken by a Member State and the measures suggested by the Commission do not prove sufficient to overcome the difficulties which have arisen or which threaten, the Commission shall, after consulting the Monetary Committee, recommend to the Council the granting of mutual assistance and appropriate methods therefor.

The Commission shall keep the Council regularly informed of the situation and of how it is developing.

2. The Council, acting by a qualified majority, shall grant such mutual assistance; it shall adopt directives or decisions laying down the conditions and details of such assistance, which may take such forms as:

(a) a concerted approach to or within any other international organizations to which Member States may have recourse;
(b) measures needed to avoid deflection of trade where the State which is in difficulties maintains or reintroduces quantitative restrictions against third countries;
(c) the granting of limited credits by other Member States, subject to their agreement.

During the transitional period, mutual assistance may also take the form of special reductions in customs duties or enlargements of quotas in order to facilitate an increase in imports from the State which is in difficulties, subject to the agreement of the States by which such measures would have to be taken.

3. If the mutual assistance recommended by the Commission is not granted by the Council or if the mutual assistance granted and the measures taken are insufficient, the Commission shall authorize the State which is in difficulties to take protective measures, the conditions and details of which the Commission shall determine.

Such authorization may be revoked and such conditions and details may be changed by the Council acting by a qualified majority.

Article 109

1. Where a sudden crisis in the balance of payments occurs and a decision within the meaning of Article 108 (2) is not immediately taken, the Member State concerned may, as a precaution, take the necessary protective measures. Such measures must cause the least possible disturbance in the functioning of the common market and must not be wider in scope than is strictly necessary to remedy the sudden difficulties which have arisen.

2. The Commission and the other Member States shall be informed of such protective measures not later than when they enter into force. The Commission may recommend to the Council the granting of mutual assistance under Article 108.

3. After the Commission has delivered an opinion and the Monetary Committee has been consulted, the Council may, acting by a qualified majority,

decide that the State concerned shall amend, suspend or abolish the protective measures referred to above.

NOTES

1. Paragraph 1, as amended by Article 16(4) of the Single European Act. The original text of the Treaty establishing the European Economic Community provided after the first identical sentence: 'For this purpose the Council shall issue directives, acting unanimously. It shall endeavour to attain the highest possible degree of liberalization.'
2. Articles 63 to 65 refer to the liberalization of services.

Annex 2

Members of the Monetary Committee

Belgium		
1958–1968	Franz de Voghel	Bank
1958–1966	Maurice Williot	Finance
1966–1975	Marcel D'Haeze	Finance
1968–1975	Cecil de Strycker	Bank
1975–1988	Georges Janson	Bank
1975–1983	Jacques van Ypersele	Finance
1983–1984	Emiel Kestens	Finance
1985–1988	René Lauwerijns	Finance
1988	Louis Meulemans	Finance
1988–1989	Alfons Verplaetse	Bank
1988–1990	Edgard van de Pontsele	Finance
1989 –	Guy Quaden	Bank
1990 –	Grégoire Brouhns	Finance
France		
1958–1961	Jean Sadrin	Finance
1958–1964	Pierre Calvet	Bank
1962–1965	André de Lattre	Finance
1964–1973	Bernard Clappier	Bank
1965–1967	M. Perouse	Finance
1967–1971	Raymond Larre	Finance
1971–1973	C. Pierre-Brossolette	Finance
1973–1978	Jean-Yves Haberer	Finance
1974	André de Lattre	Bank
1974–1979	R. de la Genière	Bank
1978–1984	Michel Camdessus	Finance
1980	M. Théron	Bank
1980–1984	Alain Prate	Bank
1983–1984	Philippe Jurgensen	Finance
1984–1993	Philippe Lagayette	Bank
1984–1987	Daniel Lebègue	Finance
1987–1993	Jean-Claude Trichet	Finance
1992–1993	Ariane Obolensky	Finance

1993 –	Hervé Hannoun	Bank
1993 –	Christian Noyer	Finance

Germany

1958–1967	Rolf Gocht	Economic Affairs
1958–1977	Otmar Emminger	Bank
1967–1970	W. Hanemann	Economic Affairs
1970–1972	W. Henkel	Economic Affairs
1972–1973	D. Hiss	Finance
1974	H.H. Weber	Finance
1976–1979	Karl-Otto Pöhl	Finance/Bank
1980–1989	Leonhard Gleske	Bank
1980	M. Lahnstein	Finance
1980–1982	Horst Schulmann	Finance
1982–1993	Hans Tietmeyer	Finance/Bank
1982	K. Wesselkock	Finance
1985–1987	W. Müller-Enders	Finance
1989	Helmut Schlesinger	Bank
1990–1993	Horst Koehler	Finance
1993 –	Gert Haller	Finance
1993 –	Helmut Schieber	Bank

Italy

1958–1964	Amadeo Gambino	Finance
1958–1959	Paride Formentini	Bank
1959–1960	Guido Carli	Bank
1960–1963	Paolo Baffi	Bank
1963–1964	A. Vernucci	Bank
1964–1970	G. Stammati	Finance
1964–1975	Rinaldo Ossola	Bank
1970–1975	G. Miconi	Finance
1975–1980	G. Magnifico	Bank
1975–1980	S. Palumbo	Finance
1980–1981	F. Ruggiero	Finance
1980–1994	Lamberto Dini	Bank
1981–1982	L. Izzo	Finance
1982–1991	Mario Sarcinelli	Finance
1989–1991	Augusto Zodda	Finance
1991 –	Mario Draghi	Finance

Luxembourg

1958–1959	René Franck	Bank
1958–1969	Paul Bastian	Finance
1959–1966	J. Heinen	Economic Affairs

1966–1971	R. Weber	Bank
1969–1974	J. Schmitz	Finance
1971–1974	C. Lamboray	Bank
1975–1977	A. Dondelinger	Bank
1975–1989	R. Kirsch	Finance
1977–1990	Pierre Jaans	Bank
1989 –	Yves Mersch	Finance
1990 –	Jean Guill	Bank

The Netherlands

1958–1969	Emile van Lennep	Finance
1958–1964	S. Posthuma	Bank
1964–1968	J.H.O. graaf v.d. Bosch	Bank
1968–1972	A.W.R. baron Mackay	Bank
1969–1971	Willem Drees	Finance
1971–1976	Coen Oort	Finance
1973–1994	André Szász	Bank
1977–1981	Nout Wellink	Finance
1982–1986	Piet Korteweg	Finance
1986–1992	Cees Maas	Finance
1991–1992	Pieter Stek	Finance
1992 –	Henk Brouwer	Finance
1994 –	Nout Wellink	Bank

Denmark

1973–1982	Svend Andersen	Bank
1973–1979	Kurt Hansen	Economic Affairs
1979–1987	Niels Ussing	Economic Affairs
1982–1990	Richard Mikkelsen	Bank
1988 –	Jens Thomsen	Economic Affairs
1990 –	Bodil Andersen	Bank

Ireland

1973–1976	Bernard Breen	Bank
1973–1974	Seán Murray	Finance
1974–1976	Tomás O'Cofaigh	Finance
1976–1982	Michael Horgan	Finance
1976–1982	Timothy O'Grady-Walshe	Bank
1982–1983	David McCutcheon	Finance
1982–1985	Padraig McGowan	Bank
1983–1987	Maurice Doyle	Finance
1985 –	George Reynolds	Bank
1987–1990	Michael Somers	Finance
1991–1994	Maurice O'Connell	Finance

1994 –	Noël O'Gorman	Finance
United Kingdom		
1973–1975	Christopher Fogarty	Finance
1973–1974	Christopher McMahon	Bank
1974–1985	Michael Balfour	Bank
1976–1979	Nicolas Jordan-Moss	Finance
1980–1983	Sir Kenneth Couzens	Finance
1983–1988	Geoffrey Littler	Finance
1985–1989	Anthony Loehnis	Bank
1988	David Peretz	Finance
1989 –	Nigel Wicks	Finance
1989–1993	Andrew Crockett	Bank
1993–1994	Paul Gray	Finance
1994 –	Alastair Clark	Bank
1994 –	Gus O'Donnell	Finance
Greece		
1981	G. Drakos	Bank
1981–1982	C. Mavraganis	Finance
1981–1984	D. Chalikias	Bank
1982	T. Dimopoulos	Finance
1983–1984	S. Thomadakis	Finance
1984–1985	P. Korliras	Bank
1984–1985	L. Katseli	Finance
1987–1989	Jannis Papanikolaou	Finance
1989	D. Mavragannis	Finance
1985–1988	Lucas Papademos	Bank
1985–1987	Nicholas Garganas	Finance
1988	Papageorgiou	Bank
1989–1990	Sidiropoulos	Finance
1989–1990	Lucas Papademos	Bank
1990–1993	G. Provopoulos	Bank
1990–1992	I. Papadakis	Finance
1992–1993	Miranda Xafa	Finance
1993–1994	George Katiforis	Finance
1994 –	Nicholas Garganas	Bank
1994	Anastassios Giannitsis	Finance
1994 –	Ioannis Stournaras	Finance
Spain		
1986–1988	Juan Ruiz de Alda	Bank
1986	José Garcia Alonso	Finance
1986–1988	Pedro Martinez Mendez	Finance

1988–1992	L. Rojo	Bank
1988 –	Manuel Conthe	Finance
1992 –	Miguel Martin	Bank

Portugal

1986	Manuel de Melo	Finance
1986	Alexandre Pinto	Bank
1986–1987	Brito Da Silva Girao	Finance
1986–1989	V. Marques	Bank
1987–1989	Gomes Moreno	Finance
1990–1993	Antonio Borges	Bank
1990–1991	Carlos Tavares	Finance
1992–1993	José Braz	Finance
1993 –	Joao Costa Pinto	Bank
1994 –	Manuel Pinho	Finance

EEC

1958–1964	Leonhard Gleske
1958–1967	F. Bobba
1964–1968	Tom de Vries
1967–1979	U. Mosca
1968–1981	F. Boyer de la Giroday
1979–1983	Tomasso Padoa-Schioppa
1982–1989	J.P. Mingasson
1983–1987	Massimo Russo
1987–1990	Antonio Costa
1989–1994	Jean-François Pons
1990 –	Giovanni Ravasio
1994 –	Hervé Carré

Secretaries Monetary Committee

1958–1961	Alain Prate	France
1962–1969	R. de Kergorlay	France
1969–1978	Giampietro Morelli	Italy
1978–1993	Andreas Kees	Germany
1993 –	Günter Grosche	Germany

NOTE

For Italy members originating from the Ufficio dei Cambi have been registered as representatives of the central bank. For Luxembourg, where the Luxembourg Monetary Institute was only established later, members originating from the Contrôle des Banques or from the state-owned Caisse d'Epargne have been registered as Bank representatives.

Annex 3

Statutes of the Monetary Committee[1]

The Council

Having regard to Article 105(2) of the Treaty establishing the European Economic Community which sets up a Monetary Committee in order to promote coordination of the policies of Member States in the monetary field to the full extent needed for the functioning of the common market,

Having regard to Article 153 of the Treaty pursuant to which the Council determines the rules governing the committees provided for in the Treaty,

Having obtained the Opinion of the Commission,

has decided that the Rules governing the Monetary Committee shall be as follows:

Article 1

The Committee shall keep under review the monetary and financial situation of Member States and of the Community and also the general payments system of Member States, and shall report regularly to the Council and to the Commission thereon.

Article 2

When examining the monetary and financial situation of Member States, the Committee shall endeavour in particular to foresee any difficulties which may affect their balance of payments. It shall address to the Council and to the Commission any suggestions designed to avert these difficulties while at the same time preserving the internal and external financial stability of each Member State.

Article 3

In respect of the general payments system of Member States, the Committee shall, in particular, keep under review the implementation of the provisions of Article 106(1) to (3) of the Treaty. Where necessary, it shall address to the Council suggestions concerning measures to be taken by Member States in accordance with Article 106(4). It shall inform the Commission thereof.

Article 4

The Opinion of the Monetary Committee must be obtained either by the

Council or, in the cases provided for in Article 69, in the last subparagraph of Article 71, in the first subparagraph of paragraph 1 of Article 73 and in paragraph 2 thereof, in Article 107(2), in the second subparagraph of Article 108(1), and in Article 109(3), by the Commission.

The Opinion of the Committee may also be obtained in other cases by the Council or the Commission.

In any event, the Committee has the power and the obligation to draw up Opinions on its own initiative whenever it considers it necessary for the proper fulfilment of its task.

Article 5

Member States and the Commission shall each appoint two members of the Committee. They may also appoint two alternate members of the Committee. The members of the Committee and the alternates must be selected from among experts possessing outstanding competence in the monetary field. As a general rule, each Member State shall select one member from among senior officials of the administration and the other member on the proposal of the central bank; the alternates may be selected in the same way.

Members of the Committee and alternates shall be appointed in their personal capacity and shall, in the general interests of the Community, be completely independent in the performance of their duties.

The term of office of the members of the Committee and of the alternates shall be two years. It shall be renewable. It shall end on death, voluntary resignation, or compulsory retirement. In such cases the new member or alternate shall be appointed for the remainder of the term of office.

A member of the Committee or an alternate may be compulsorily retired against his wishes only by the authority which appointed him and then only if the member or alternate no longer fulfils the conditions required for the performance of his duties.

Article 6

Each member of the Committee shall have one vote.

Article 7

The Committee shall appoint from among its members a Chairman and three Vice-Chairmen to be elected by a majority of 11 votes for a period of two years. If a Chairman or Vice-Chairman ceases to hold office before his full term has expired, the vacancy thus caused shall be filled for the remainder of the term of office.

Article 8

Unless the Committee decides otherwise, alternates may attend meetings of the Committee. They shall not take part in the discussions and shall not vote.

A member who is unable to attend a meeting of the Committee may delegate his functions to one of the alternates; he may also delegate them to another member.

Article 9
The Committee shall meet not less than six times a year.

It shall be convened by the Chairman on his own initiative or at the request of the Council or of the Commission or of two members of the Committee.

Article 10
Opinions of the Committee, within the meaning of Article 4, shall be adopted by a majority of 11 votes. The minority may set out its views in a document attached to the Opinion of the Committee.

Where a majority within the meaning of the preceding subparagraph is not obtained, and in the case of any other decision, suggestion or communication intended for the Council or the Commission, the Committee shall submit a report setting out either the unanimous opinion of its members or the various opinions expressed in the course of the discussion.

Article 11
The Committee may propose to the Council or to the Commission that one or more of its members be attached to these institutions in order to comment orally on any document which may be addressed to them by the Committee.

Article 12
The Committee may entrust the study of specific questions to working parties composed of members of the Committee or alternates. The Committee and the working parties may call upon experts to assist them.

Article 13
In important cases the Committee may, before drawing up a report or delivering an Opinion on a specific country, request all necessary information.

Article 14
The Committee shall establish close cooperation with the Managing Board of the European Payments Union or, if the case should arise, with the Board of Management of the European Monetary Agreement, on all questions of common interest. To this end, the Committee may in particular invite the Managing Board of the European Payments Union or, if the case should arise, the Board of Management of the European Monetary Agreement, to be represented at its meetings, or may propose that joint meetings be arranged.

Article 15
Discussions of the Committee and of the working parties shall be confidential.

Article 16
The Committee shall be assisted by a secretariat. The staff needed for this shall be supplied by the Commission.

The expenses of the Committee shall be included in the estimates of the Commission.

Article 17
The Committee shall adopt its own rules of procedure.

Consultation of the Monetary Committee by the Council and the Commission

Translation of an extract from the minutes of the second meeting of the Council of the European Communities held in Brussels on 25 February 1958

With regard to Article 4 (of the Statutes of the Monetary Committee), the Council and the Commission declared that they propose, as a general rule, to consult the Monetary Committee before taking any of the decisions provided for in Article 70(2), paragraph 2; Article 73(1), paragraph 2; or Article 108(3) paragraphs 1 or 2; and before making any of the recommendations or proposals provided for in Article 70(1); Article 108(1), paragraph 1; or Article 109(2) of the Treaty establishing the EEC.

NOTE

1. Council Decision of 18 March 1958 amended by Council Decision of 2 April 1962, by Article 29 of the Act of Accession of 22 January 1972 and by Council Decision of 25 March 1976 (76/332/EEC).

Annex 4

First Council Directive of 11 May 1960 for the implementation of Article 67 of the Treaty[1]

The Council of the European Economic Community,

Having regard to the Treaty, and in particular Articles 5, 67(1), 69, 105(2) and 106(2) thereof,

Having regard to the proposal from the Commission, which consulted the Monetary Committee for this purpose,

Having regard to the Decision of 11 May 1960 on the application to Algeria and to the French overseas departments of the provisions of the Treaty concerning capital movements,

Whereas the attainment of the objectives of the Treaty establishing the European Economic Community requires the greatest possible freedom of movement of capital between Member States and therefore the widest and most speedy liberalization of capital movements,

Has adopted this Directive:

Article 1

1. Member States shall grant all foreign exchange authorizations required for the conclusion or performance of transactions or for transfers between residents of Member States in respect of the capital movements set out in List A of Annex I to this Directive.

2. Member States shall enable such transfers of capital to be made on the basis of the exchange rate ruling for payments relating to current transactions.

Where such transfers are made on a foreign exchange market on which the fluctuations of exchange rates are not officially restricted, this obligation shall be taken to mean that the exchange rates applied must not show any appreciable and lasting differences from those ruling for payments relating to current transactions.

The Monetary Committee shall watch closely the trend of exchange rates applied to such transfers of capital, and shall report thereon to the Commission. If the Commission finds that these rates show appreciable and lasting differences from those ruling for payments relating to current transactions, it shall initiate the procedure provided for in Article 169 of the Treaty.

Article 2
1. Member States shall grant general permission for the conclusion or performance of transactions and for transfers between residents of Member States in respect of the capital movements set out in List B of Annex I to this Directive.

2. Where such transfers of capital are made on a foreign exchange market on which the fluctuations of exchange rates are not officially restricted, Member States shall endeavour to ensure that transfers are made at rates which do not show appreciable and lasting differences from those ruling for payments relating to current transactions.

The Commission may, after consulting the Monetary Committee, make recommendations in this connection to Member States.

3. Where the transfers are made either on the same foreign exchange market as payments relating to current transactions, or on a market on which exchange rate fluctuations are kept within limits applicable to such market as aforesaid, the application of paragraph 1 of this Article may, as a temporary measure, be confined – as regards the acquisition of foreign securities by residents – to the financial institutions and to the undertakings which acquire securities of foreign companies established for a like purpose.

The Commission may, after consulting the Monetary Committee, make recommendations in this connection to the Member States.

Article 3
1. Subject to paragraph 2 of this Article, Member States shall grant all foreign exchange authorizations required for the conclusion or performance of transactions and for transfers between residents of Member States in respect of the capital movements set out in List C of Annex I to this Directive.

2. When such free movement of capital might form an obstacle to the achievement of the economic policy objective of a Member State, the latter may maintain or reintroduce the exchange restrictions on capital movement which were operative on the date of entry into force of this Directive (in the case of new Member States, the date of accession). It shall consult the Commission on the matter.

The Commission shall examine the measures for coordinating the economic policies of Member States which will enable these difficulties to be overcome and, after consulting the Monetary Committee, shall recommend their adoption by the Member States.

3. The Commission may recommend that the State in question abolish the exchange restrictions which are maintained or reintroduced.

Article 4
The Monetary Committee shall examine at least once a year the restrictions which are applied to the capital movements set out in the lists contained in Annex I to this Directive; it shall report to the Commission regarding restrictions which could be abolished.

Article 5

1. The provisions of this Directive shall not restrict the right of Member States to verify the nature and genuineness of transactions or transfers, or to take all requisite measures to prevent infringements of their laws and regulations.

2. The Member States shall simplify as far as possible the authorization and control formalities applicable to the conclusion or performance of transactions and transfers and shall where necessary consult one another with a view to such simplification.

3. The restrictions on capital movements under the rules for establishment in a Member State shall be abolished pursuant to this Directive only in so far as it is incumbent upon the Member States to grant freedom of establishment in implementation of Articles 52 to 58 of the Treaty.

Article 6

Member States shall endeavour not to introduce within the Community any new exchange restricion affecting the capital movements that were liberalized at the date of entry into force of this Directive (in the case of new Member States, the date of accession) nor to make existing provisions more restrictive.

Article 7

Member States shall make known to the Commission, not later than three months after the entry into force of this Directive (in the case of new Member States, three months after the date of accession):

(a) the provisions governing capital movements at the date of entry into force of this Directive which are laid down by law, regulation or administrative action;

(b) the provisions adopted in pursuance of the Directive;

(c) the procedures for implementing those provisions.

They shall also make known, not later than the time of entry into force thereof, any new measures going beyond the obligations of this Directive, and any amendment of the provisions governing the capital movements set out in List D of Annex I to this Directive.

Article 8

Deleted

Article 9

This Directive shall apply without prejudice to the provisions of Articles 67(2), 68(3) and 221 of the Treaty.

Article 10

List A, B, C and D contained in Annex I, together with the Nomenclature of Capital Movements and the Explanatory Notes in Annex II, form an integral part of this Directive.

ANNEX 1

LIST A

Capital movements referred to in Article 1 of the Directive

Direct investments

excluding purely financial investments made with a view only to giving the persons providing the capital indirect access to the money or capital market of another country, through the creation of an undertaking of participation in an existing undertaking in that country

Liquidation of direct investments

Investiments in real estate

Personal capital movements

Gifts and endowments

Dowries

Inheritances

Settlement of debts in their country of origin by immigrants

Transfers of capital belonging to residents who emigrate

Transfers of capital belonging to emigrants returning to their country of origin

Transfers of workers' savings during their period of stay

Transfers by instalment of blocked funds belonging to non-residents by the holders of such funds in case of special hardship

Annual transfers of blocked funds to another Member State by a non-resident account holder, up to an amount or a percentage of the total assets, fixed uniformly by the Member State concerned for all applicants

Transfers of minor amounts abroad

Granting and repayment of short and medium-term credits related to commercial transactions or to provision of services in which a resident is participating

Sureties, other guarantees and rights of pledge and transfers connected with them related to short and medium-term credits in respect of commercial transactions or provisions of services in which a resident is participating

related to long-term loans with a view to establishing or maintaining lasting economic links

Transfers in performance of insurance contracts

as and when freedom of movement in respect of services is extended to those contracts in implementation of Article 59 *et seq.* of the Treaty

Operation in securities

Acquisition by non-residents of domestic securities not dealt in on a stock exchange and repatriation of the proceeds of liquidation thereof

Acquisition by residents of foreign securities not dealt in on a stock exchange and use of the proceeds of liquidation thereof

Acquisition by non-residents of units in domestic unit trusts dealt in on a stock exchange and repatriation of the proceeds of liquidation thereof

Acquisition by residents of units in foreign unit trusts dealt in on a stock exchange and use of the proceeds of liquidation thereof

Acquisition by residents of foreign bonds dealt in on a stock exchange, issued on a foreign market and denominated in national currency

Physical movements of the securities mentioned above

Granting and repayment of long-term credits related to commercial transactions or to the provisions of services in which a resident is participating

Granting and repayment of medium and long-term credits related to commercial transactions or to the provision of services in which no resident is participating

Granting and repayment of medium and long-term loans and credits not related to commercial transactions or to the provisions of services

Sureties, other guarantees and rights of pledge and transfers connected with them and relating to:

long-term credits in respect of commercial transactions or provision of services in which a resident is participating

medium and long-term credits in respect of commercial transactions or provision of services in which no resident is participating medium and long-term loans and credits not related to commercial transactions or to provision of services

The use of the proceeds of liquidation of assets abroad belonging to residents must be permitted at least within the limits of the obligations as regard liberalization accepted by Member States.

Death duties

Damages (where these can be considered as capital)

Refunds in the case of cancellation of contracts and refunds of uncalled-for payments (where these can be considered as capital)

Authors' royalties
Patents, designs, trade marks and inventions (assignments and transfers arising out of such assignments)

Transfers of the moneys required for the provision of services

The use of the proceeds of liquidation of assets abroad belonging to residents must be permitted at least within the limits of the obligations as regards liberalization accepted by Member States.

LIST B

Capital movements referred to in Article 2 of the Directive Operations in securities

Acquisition by non-residents of domestic securities dealt in on a stock exchange (excluding units of unit trusts) and repatriation of the proceeds of liquidation thereof

Acquisition by residents of foreign securities dealt in on a stock exchange and use of the proceeds of liquidation thereof

(I) excluding the acquisition of bonds issued ona foreign market and denominated in national currency
(II) excluding units of unit trusts
Physical movements of the securities mentioned above

The use of the proceeds of liquidation of assets abroad belonging to residents must be permitted at least within the limits of the obligations as regards liberalization accepted by Member States.

LIST C

Capital movements referred to in Article 3 of the Directive

Issue and placing of securities of a deomestic undertaking on a foreign capital market

Issue and placing of securities of a foreign undertaking on the domestic capital market

LIST D

Capital movements referred to in Article 4 of the Directive

Short-term investments in Treasury bills and other securities normally dealt in on the money market

Opening and placing of funds on current or deposit accounts, repatriation or use of balances on current or deposit accounts with credit institutions

Granting and repayment of short-term credits related to commercial transactions or to provision of services in which no resident is participating

Granting and repayment of short-term loans and credits not related to commercial transactions or to provisions of services

Personal capital movements

loans

Sureties, other guarantees and rights of pledge and transfers connected with them

related to short-term credits in respect of commercial transactions or to provision of services in which no resident is participating

related to short-term loans and credits not connected with commercial transactions or to provision of services

related to private loans

Physical import and export of financial assets

Other capital movements: Miscellaneous

NOTE

1. Text incorporating the amendments contained in the Second Directive of 18 December 1962 (63/21/EEC) and in Article 29 of the Act of Accession of 12 January 1972.

Annex 5

Council Directive of 21 March 1972 on regulating international capital flows and neutralizing their undesirable effects on domestic liquidity (72/156/EEC)

The Council of the European Communities,
Having regard to the Treaty establishing the European Economic Community, and in particular Articles 70 and 103 thereof,

Having regard to the proposal from the Commission,

Whereas exceptionally large capital movements have caused serious disturbances in the monetary situation and in economic trends in Member States; whereas these disturbances may hinder the establishment by stages of an economic and monetary union; whereas the Council, in its resolution of 9 May 1971, agreed to discuss before 1 July 1971 the adoption of appropriate measures to deal with this situation;

Whereas, so that contingencies of comparable character and magnitude do not recur, the Member States should supplement the instruments that are available for regulating domestic liquidity;

Whereas to this end it is imperative that Member States adopt measures immediately in order to have available, should occasion arise, the appropriate instruments for the purpose of discouraging exceptionally large capital movements, in particular to and from third countries, and of neutralizing their effects on the domestic monetary situation, thereby creating the conditions required for concerted action on the part of the Member States in those fields in order to ensure smooth trading conditions within the Community and the achievement of economic and monetary union;

Whereas exceptionally large capital movements can produce serious stresses on the exchange markets of the Member States, the smooth operation of which constitutes the object of the policy with regard to rates of exchange which each Member State must, by virtue of Article 107(1), treat as a matter of common concern;

Whereas, in order to ensure the efficacy of the measures to be taken to prevent exceptionally large capital movements, the regulation of loans and credits not related to commercial transactions or to provision of services and granted by non-residents to residents must be extended to medium and long-term loans and credits; whereas for this purpose a derogation from Article

3(1) of the First Directive for the implementation of Article 67 of the Treaty, as amended by the Directive of 18 December 1962, should be permitted,

Has adopted this Directive:

Article 1

The Member States shall take all necessary steps to ensure that the monetary authorities have available the following instruments and are able, where necessary, to put them into operation immediately without further enabling measures:

(a) for effective regulation of international capital flows:

(i) rules governing investment on the money market and payment of interest on deposits by non-residents;

(ii) regulation of loans and credits which are not related to commercial transactions or to provision of services and are granted by non-residents to residents, if need be by derogating from Article 3(1) of the First Directive for the implementation of Article 67 of the Treaty;

(b) for the neutralization of those effects produced by international capital flows on domestic liquidity which are considered undesirable:

(i) regulation of the net external position of credit institutions;

(ii) fixing minimum reserve ratios, in particular for the holdings of non-residents.

Article 2

1. The Member States shall forthwith adopt the necessary measures to comply with this Directive.

2. Each Member State shall, where necessary, and taking account of the interests of the other Member States, apply all or some of the instruments mentioned in Article 1. To this end the Commission, in cooperation with the Monetary Committee and the Committee of Governors of Central Banks, shall ensure close coordination between the competent authorities of the Member States.

3. The Commission, after consulting the Monetary Committee and the Committee of Governors of Central Banks, shall keep the Council informed of the situation and its development.

Annex 6

Council Directive of 24 June 1988 for the implementation of Article 67 of the Treaty (88/361/EEC)

The Council of the European Communities,
Having regard to the Treaty establishing the European Economic Community, and in particular Articles 69 and 70(1) thereof,

Having regard to the proposal from the Commission, submitted following consultation with the Monetary Committee,

Having regard to the opinion of the European Parliament,

Whereas Article 8a of the Treaty stipulates that the internal market shall comprise an area without internal frontiers in which the free movement of capital is ensured, without prejudice to the other provisions of the Treaty;

Whereas Member States should be able to take the requisite measures to regulate bank liquidity; whereas these measures should be restricted to this purpose;

Whereas Member States should, if necessary, be able to take measures to restrict, temporarily and within the framework of appropriate Community procedures, short-term capital movements which even where there is no appreciable divergence in economic fundamentals, might seriously disrupt the conduct of their monetary and exchange-rate policies;

Whereas in the interests of transparency, it is advisable to indicate the scope in accordance with the arrangements laid down in this Directive, of the transitional measures adopted for the benefit of the Kingdom of Spain and the Portuguese Republic by the 1985 Act of Accession in the field of capital movements;

Whereas the Kingdom of Spain and the Portuguese Republic may, under the terms of Articles 61 to 66 and 222 to 232 respectively of the 1985 Act of Accession, postpone the liberalization of certain capital movements in derogation from the obligations set out in the First Council Directive of 11 May 1960 for the implementation of Article 67 of the Treaty, as last amended by Directive 86/566/EEC; whereas Directive 86/566/EEC also provides for transitional arrangements to be applied for the benefit of those two Member States in respect of their obligations to liberalize capital movements; whereas it is appropriate for those two Member States to be able to postpone the application of the new liberalization obligations resulting from this Directive;

Whereas the Hellenic Republic and Ireland are faced, albeit to differing degrees, with difficult balance-of-payments situations and high levels of external indebtedness; whereas the immediate and complete liberalization of capital movements by those two Member States would make it more difficult for them to continue to apply the measures they have taken to improve their external positions and to reinforce the capacity of their financial systems to adapt to the requirements of an integrated financial market in the Community; whereas it is appropriate, in accordance with Article 8 of the Treaty, to grant those two Member States, in the light of their specific circumstances, further time in which to comply with the obligations arising from this Directive;

Whereas, since the full liberalization of capital movements could in some Member States, and especially in border areas, contribute to difficulties in the market for secondary residences; whereas existing national legislation regulating these purchases should not be affected by the entry into effect of this Directive;

Whereas advantage should be taken of the period adopted for bringing this Directive into effect in order to enable the Commission to submit proposals designed to eliminate or reduce risks of distortion, tax evasion and tax avoidance resulting from the diversity of national systems for taxation and to permit the Council to take a position on such proposals;

Whereas, in accordance with Article 70(1) of the Treaty, the Community shall endeavour to attain the highest possible degree of liberalization in respect of the movement of capital between its residents and those of third countries;

Whereas large-scale short-term capital movements to or from third countries may seriously disturb the monetary or financial situation of Member States or cause serious stresses on the exchange markets; whereas such developments may prove harmful for the cohesion of the European Monetary System, for the smooth operation of the internal market and for the progressive achievement of economic and monetary union; whereas it is therefore appropriate to create the requisite conditions for concerted action by Member States should this prove necessary;

Whereas this Directive replaces Council Directive 72/156/EEC of 21 March 1972 on regulating international capital flows and neutralizing their undesirable effects on domestic liquidity; whereas Directive 72/156/EEC should accordingly be repealed,

Has adopted this Directive:

Article 1

1. Without prejudice to the following provisions, Member States shall abolish restrictions on movements of capital taking place between persons resident in Member States. To facilitate application of this Directive, capital movements shall be classified in accordance with the Nomenclature in Annex 1.

2. Transfers in respect of capital movements shall be made on the same exchange rate conditions as those governing payments relating to current

transactions.

Article 2
Member States shall notify the Committee of Governors of the Central Banks, the Monetary Committee and the Commission, by the date of their entry into force at the latest, of measures to regulate bank liquidity which have a specific impact on capital transactions carried out by credit institutions with non-residents.

Such measures shall be confined to what is necessary for the purpose of domestic monetary regulation. The Monetary Committee and the Committee of Governors of the Central Banks shall provide the Commission with opinions on this subject.

Article 3
1. Where short-term capital movements of exceptional magnitude impose severe strains on foreign-exchange markets and lead to serious disturbances in the conduct of a Member State's monetary and exchange rate policies, being reflected in particular in substantial variations in domestic liquidity, the Commission may, after consulting the Monetary Committee and the Committee of Governors of the Central Banks, authorize that Member State to take, in respect of the capital movements listed in Annex II, protective measures the conditions and details of which the Commission shall determine.

2. The Member State concerned may itself take the protective measures referred to above, on grounds of urgency, should these measures be necessary. The Commission and the other Member States shall be informed of such measures by the date of their entry into force at the latest. The Commission, after consulting the Monetary Committee and the Committe of Governors of the Central Banks, shall decide whether the Member State concerned may continue to apply these measures or whether it should amend or abolish them.

3. The decisions taken by the Commission under paragraphs 1 and 2 may be revoked or amended by the Council acting by a qualified majority.

4. The period of application of protective measures taken pursuant to this Article shall not exceed six months.

5. Before 31 December 1992, the Council shall examine, on the basis of a report from the Commission, after delivery of an opinion by the Monetary Committee and the Committee of Governors of the Central Banks, whether the provisions of this Article remain appropriate, as regards their principle and details, to the requirements which they were intended to satisfy.

Article 4
This Directive shall be without prejudice to the right of Member States to take all requisite measures to prevent infringements of their laws and regulations, inter alia in the field of taxation and prudential supervision of

financial institutions, or to lay down procedures for the declaration of capital movements for purposes of administrative or statistical information.

Application of those measures and procedures may not have the effect of impeding capital movements carried out in accordance with Community law.

Article 5

For the Kingdom of Spain and the Portuguese Republic, the scope, in accordance with the Nomenclature of capital movements contained in Annex I, of the provisions of the 1985 Act of Accession in the field of capital movements shall be as indicated in Annex III.

Article 6

1. Member States shall take the measures necessary to comply with this Directive no later than 1 July 1990. They shall forthwith inform the Commission thereof. They shall also make known, by the date of their entry into force at the latest, any new measures or any amendment made to the provisions governing the capital movements listed in Annex I.

2. The Kingdom of Spain and the Portuguese Republic, without prejudice for these two Member States to Article 61 to 66 and 222 to 232 of the 1985 Act of Accession, and the Hellenic Republic and Ireland may temporarily continue to apply restrictions to the capital movements listed in Annex V, subject to the conditions and time limits laid down in that Annex.

If, before expiry of the time limit set for the liberalization of the capital movements referred to in Lists III and IV of Annex IV, the Portuguese Republic or the Hellenic Republic considers that it is unable to proceed with liberalization, in particular because of difficulties as regards it balance of payments or because the national financial system is insufficiently adapted, the Commission, at the request of one or other of these Member States, shall in collaboration with the Monetary Committee, review the economic and financial situation of the Member State concerned. On the basis of the outcome of this review, the Commission shall propose to the Council an extension of the time limit set for liberalization of all or part of the capital movements referred to. This extension may not exceed three years. The Council shall act in accordance with the procedure laid down in Article 69 of the Treaty.

3. The Kingdom of Belgium and the Grand Duchy of Luxembourg may temporarily continue to operate the dual exchange market under the conditions and for the periods laid down in Annex V.

4. Existing national legislation regulating purchases of secondary residences may be upheld until the Council adopts further provisions in this area in accordance with Article 69 of the Treaty. This provision does not affect the applicability of other provisions of Community law.

5. The Commission shall submit to the Council, by 31 December 1988, proposals aimed at eliminating or reducing risks of distortion, tax evasion

and tax avoidance linked to the diversity of national systems for the taxation of savings and for controlling the application of these systems.

The Council shall take a postition on these Commission proposals by 30 June 1989. Any tax provisions of a Community nature shall, in accordance with the Treaty, be adopted unanimously.

Article 7

1. In their treatment of transfers in respect of movements of capital to or from third countries, the Member States shall edeavour to attain the same degree of liberalization as that which applies to operations with residents of other Member States, subject to the other provisions of this Directive.

The provisions of the preceding subparagraph shall not prejudice the application to third countries of domestic rules or Community law, particulary any reciprocal conditions, concerning operations involving establishment, the provisions of financial services and the admission of securities to capital markets.

2. Where large-scale short-term capital movements to or from third countries seriously disturb the domestic or external monetary or financial situation of the Member States, or of a number of them, or cause serious strains in exchange relations within the Community or between the Community and third countries, Member States shall consult with one another on any measure to be taken to counteract such difficulties. This consultation shall take place within the Committee of Governors of the Central Banks and the Monetary Committee on the initiative of the Commission or of any Member State.

Article 8

At least once a year the Monetary Committee shall examine the situation regarding free movement of capital as it results from the application of this Directive. The examination shall cover measures concerning the domestic regulation of credit and financial and monetary markets which could have a specific impact on international capital movements and on all other aspects of this Directive. The Committee shall report to the Commission on the outcome of this examination.

Article 9

The First Directive of 11 May 1960 and Directive 72/156/EEC shall be repealed with effect from 1 January 1990.

Annex 7

Extracts from the Treaty on European Union concerning capital movements

Capital and payments

Article 73a
As from 1 January 1994, Articles 67 to 73 shall be replaced by Articles 73b, c, d, e, f and g.

Article 73b
1. Within the framework of the provisions set out in this Chapter, all restrictions on the movement of capital between Member States and between Member States and third countries shall be prohibited.

2. Within the framework of the provisions set out in this Chapter, all restrictions on payments between Member States and between Member States and third countries shall be prohibited.

Article 73c
1. The provisions of Article 73b shall be without prejudice to the application to third countries of any restrictions which exist on 31 December 1993 under national or Community law adopted in repect of the movement of capital to or from third countries involving direct investment – including investment in real estate – establishment, the provision of financial services or the admission of securities to capital markets.

2. Whilst endeavouring to achieve the objective of free movement of capital between Member States and third countries to the greatest extent possible and without prejudice to the other Chapters of this Treaty, the Council may, acting by a qualified majority on a proposal from the Commission, adopt measures on the movement of capital to or from third countries involving direct investment – including investment in real estate – establishment, the provision of financial services or the admission of securities to capital markets. Unanimity shall be required for measures under this paragraph which constitute a step back in Community law as regards the liberalization of the movement of capital to or from third countries.

Article 73d

1. The provisions of Article 73b shall be without prejudice to the right of Member States:

(a) to apply the relevant provisions of their tax law which distinguish between tax-payers who are not in the same situation with regard to their place of residence or with regard to the place where their capital is invested;

(b) to take all requisite measures to prevent infringements of national law and regulations, in particular in the field of taxation and the prudential supervision of financial institutions, or to lay down procedures for the declaration of capital movements for purposes of administrative or statistical information, or to take measures which are justified on grounds of public policy or public security.

2. The provisions of this Chapter shall be without prejudice to the applicability of restrictions on the right of establishment which are compatible with this Treaty.

3. The measures and procedures referred to in paragraphs 1 and 2 shall not constitute a means of arbitrary discrimination or a disguised restriction on the free movement of capital and payments as defined in Article 73b.

Article 73e

By way of derogation from Article 73b, Member States which, on 31 December 1993, enjoy a derogation on the basis of existing Community law, shall be entitled to maintain, until 31 December 1995 at the latest, restrictions on movements of capital authorized by such derogations as exist on that date.

Article 73f

Where, in exceptional circumstances, movements of capital to or from third countries cause, or threaten to cause, serious difficulties for the operation of economic and monetary union, the Council, acting by a qualified majority on a proposal from the Commission and after consulting the ECB, may take safeguard measures with regard to third countries for a period not exceeding six months if such measures are strictly necessary.

Article 73g

1. If, in the cases envisaged in Article 228a, action by the Community is deemed necessary, the Council may, in accordance with the procedure provided for in Article 228a, take the necessary urgent measures on the movement of capital and on payments as regards the third countries concerned.[1]

2. Without prejudice to Article 224 and as long as the Council has not taken measures pursuant to paragraph 1, a Member State may, for serious political reasons and on grounds of urgency, take unilateral measures against a third country with regard to capital movements and payments.[2] The Commission

and the other Member States shall be informed of such measures by the date of their entry into force at the latest.

The Council may, acting by a qualified majority on a proposal from the Commission, decide that the Member States concerned shall amend or abolish such measures. The President of the Council shall inform the European Parliament of any such decision taken by the Council.

Article 73h

Until 1 January 1994, the following provisions shall be applicable:

(1) Each Member State undertakes to authorize, in the currency ot the Member State in which the creditor or the beneficiary resides, any payments connected with the movement of goods, services or capital, and any transfers of capital and earnings, to the extent that the movement of goods, services, capital and persons between Member States has been liberalized pursuant to this Treaty.
The Member States declare their readiness to undertake the liberalization of payments beyond the extent provided in the preceding subparagraph, in so far as their economic situation in general and the state of their balance of payments in particular so permit.

(2) In so far as movements of goods, services and capital are limited only by restrictions on payments connected therewith, these restrictions shall be progressively abolished by applying, mutatis mutandis, the provisions of this Chapter and the Chapters relating to the abolition of quantitative restrictions and to the liberalization of services.

(3) Member States undertake not to introduce between themselves any new restrictions on transfers connected with the invisible transactions listed in Annex III to this Treaty.
The progressive abolition of existing restrictions shall be effected in accordance with the provisions of Articles 63 to 65, in so far as such abolition is not governed by the provisions contained in paragraphs 1 and 2 or by the other provisions of this Chapter.[3]

(4) If need be, Member States shall consult each other on the measures to be taken to enable the payments and transfers mentioned in this Article to be effected: such measures shall not prejudice the attainment of the objectives set out in this Treaty.

Article 109c

1. In order to promote coordination of the policies of Member States to the full extent needed for the functioning of the internal market, a Monetary Committee with advisory status is hereby set up.

It shall have the following tasks:

– to keep under review the monetary and financial situation of the Member States and of the Community and the general payments system of the

Member States and to report regularly theron to the Council and to the Commission;
- to deliver opinions at the request of the Council or of the Commission, or on its own initiative for submission to those institutions;
- without prejudice to Article 151, to contribute to the preparation of the work of the Council referred to in Articles 73f, 73g, 103(2), (3), (4) and (5), 103a, 104a, 104b, 104c, 109e(2), 109f(6), 109h, 109i, 109j(2) and 109k(1);[4]
- to examine, at least once a year, the situation regarding the movement of capital and the freedom of payments, as they result from the application of this Treaty and of measures adopted by the Council; the examination shall cover all measures relating to capital movements and payments; the Committee shall report to the Commission and to the Council on the outcome of this examination.

The Member States and the Commission shall each appoint two members of the Monetary Committee.

2. At the start of the third stage, an Economic and Financial Committee shall be set up. The Monetary Committee provided for in paragraph 1 shall be dissolved.

The Economic and Financial Committee shall have the following tasks:
- to deliver opinions at the request of the Council or of the Commission, or on its own initiative for submission to those institutions;
- to keep under review the economic and financial situation of the Member States and of the Community and to report regularly thereon to the Council and to the Commission, in particular on financial relations with third countries and international institutions;
- without prejudice to Article 151, to contribute to the preparation of the work of the Council referred to in Articles 73f, 73g, 103(2), (3), (4) and (5), 103a, 104a, 104b, 104c, 105(6), 105a(2), 106(5) and (6), 109, 109h, 109i(2) and (3), 109k(2), 109l(4) and (5), and to carry out other advisory and preparatory tasks assigned to it by the Council;
- to examine, at least once a year, the situation regarding the movement of capital and freedom of payments, as they result from the application of this Treaty and of measures adopted by the Council; the examination shall cover all measures relating to capital movements and payments; the Committee shall report to the Commission and to the Council on the outcome of this examination.

The Member States, the Commission and the ECB shall each appoint no more than two members of the Committee.

3. The Council shall, acting by a qualified majority on a proposal from the Commission and after consulting the ECB and the Committee referred to in this Article, lay down detailed provisions concerning the composition of the Economic and Financial Committee. The President of the Council shall inform the European Parliament of such a decision.

4. In addition to the tasks set out in paragraph 2, if and as long as there are Member States with a derogation as referred to in Articles 109k and 109l, the Committee shall keep under review the monetary and financial situation and the general payments system of those Member States and report regularly thereon to the Council and to the Commission.

Article 109h

1. Where a Member State is in difficulties or is seriously threatened with difficulties as regards its balance of payments either as a result of an overall disequilibrium in its balance of payments, or as a result of the type of currency at its disposal, and where such difficulties are liable in particular to jeopardize the functioning of the common market or the progressive implementation of the common commercial policy, the Commisssion shall immediately investigate the position of the State in question and the action which, making use of all the means at its disposal, that State has taken or may take in accordance with the provisions of this Treaty. The Commission shall state what measures it recommends the State concerned to take.

If the action taken by a Member State and the measures suggested by the Commission do not prove sufficient to overcome the difficulties which have arisen or which threaten, the Commission shall, after consulting the Committee referred to in Article 109c, recommend to the Council the granting of mutual assistance and appropriate methods therefor.

The Commission shall keep the Council regularly informed of the situation and of how it is developing.

2. The Council, acting by a qualified majority, shall grant such mutual assistance; it shall adopt directives or decisions laying down the conditions and details of such assistance, which may take such forms as:

(a) a concerted approach to or within any other international organizations to which Member States may have recourse;
(b) measures needed to avoid deflection of trade where the State which is in difficulties maintains or reintroduces quantitative restictions against third countries;
(c) the granting of limited credits by other Member States, subject to their agreement.

3. If the mutual assistance recommended by the Commission is not granted by the Council or if the mutual assistance granted and the measures taken are insufficient, the Commission shall authorize the State which is in difficulties to take protective measures, the conditions and details of which the Commission shall determine.

Such authorization may be revoked and such conditions and details may be changed by the Council acting by a qualified majority.

4. Subject to Article 109k(6), this Article shall cease to apply from the beginning of the third stage.[5]

Article 109i

1. Where a sudden crisis in the balance of payments occurs and a decision within the meaning of Article 109h(2) is not immediately taken, the Member State concerned may, as a precaution, take the necessary protective measures. Such measures must cause the least possible disturbance in the functioning of the common market and must not be wider in scope than is strictly necessary to remedy the sudden difficulties which have arisen.

2. The Commission and the other Member States shall be informed of such protective measures not later than when they enter into force. The Commission may recommend to the Council the granting of mutual assistance under Article 109h.

3. After the Commission has delivered an opinion and the Committee referred to in Article 109c has been consulted, the Council may, acting by a qualified majority, decide that the State concerned shall amend, suspend or abolish the protective measures referred to above.

4. Subject to Article 109k(6), this Article shall cease to apply from the beginning of the third stage.

NOTES

1. Article 228a refers to the interruption or reduction of economic relations with third countries in the framework of the common foreign and security policy.
2. Article 224 refers to consultations among member states in order to prevent the functioning of the common market being affected by measures taken to cope with serious internal disturbances (law and order, (threat of) war, etc.).
3. Articles 63 to 65 refer to the liberalization of services.
4. Article 151 refers to the Committee of Permanent Representatives as being responsible for preparing the work of the Council.
5. Article 109k(6) provides that Articles 109h and 109i shall continue to apply to a member state with a derogation.

Literature

Charles Adams and Jeremy Greenwood (1985), Dual exchange rate systems and capital controls: an investigation, Journal of International Economics 18, 43–63.

Alberto Alesina, Vittorio Grilli and Gian Maria Milesi-Ferretti (1993), The political economy of capital controls, Discussion paper, Centre for Economic Policy Research, London.

J.S. Alworth (1993), The globalisation of financial markets and the implications for tax policy, OECD, Paris.

Michael J. Artis and Mark P. Taylor (1989), Abolishing exchange control: the UK experience, Greek Economic Review, Vol. 2, No. 1, 19–48.

Michael J. Artis and Mark P. Taylor (1990), International financial stability and the regulation of capital flows, in Bird (1990), 163–196.

Gunter D. Baer and Tommaso Padoa-Schioppa (1989), The Werner Report revisited, in Committee for the Study of Economic and Monetary Union (1989b).

A.F.P. Bakker (1995), The international financial institutions.

A.F.P. Bakker *et al.* (1994a), Monetary stability through international cooperation, Essays in honour of André Szász, Amsterdam.

A.F.P. Bakker (1994b), The Dutch attitude towards capital liberalization, in Bakker (1994a).

Bank of England (1967), The UK exchange control: a short history, Quarterly Bulletin, Vol. 7, No. 3, 245–260.

Bank of England (1976), The investment currency market, Quarterly Bulletin, Vol. 16, No. 3, 314–322.

Bank of England (1977), A guide to United Kingdom Exchange Control, February.

Bank of England (1981), The effects of exchange control abolition on capital flows, Quarterly Bulletin, Vol. 21, No. 3, 369–373.

Leonardo Bartolini and Gordon M. Bodnar (1992), An analysis of the process of capital liberalization in Italy, IMF Working Paper WP/92/27.

J.W. Beyen (1950), Over de Europese integratie, reproduced in Hommes (1980).

J.W. Beyen (1968), Het spel en de knikkers, Rotterdam.

Jagdish Bhagwati (1978), Anatomy and consequences of exchange control regimes, Cambridge, U.S.A.

Graham Bird (1990) (ed.), The international financial regime, London.

BIS (1986), Recent innovations in international banking, Basle.

Graham Bishop and Ann O'Kelly (1992), Capital liberalisation, The end of the ERM and the beginning of EMU, London.

H.J. Blommestein and A.F. Tulp (1987), Naar een geliberaliseerd internationaal verkeer van kapitaal en diensten, Bank- en Effectenbedrijf, 389–393.

Christian de Boissieu (1988), Financial liberalization and the evolution of the EMS, European Economy, No. 36, 53–70.

Christian de Boissieu (1988), The dynamics of the EMS in the light of European financial integration, Journal of Banking and Finance, Vol. 14, 889–908

Alec Cairncross (1973), Controls of long-term international capital movements, Brookings Staff Paper.

Commission of the European Communities (1959), La libération de mouvements de capitaux en application de l'Article 67,1 du Traité de Rome, No. 1106/59-F.

Commission of the European Communities (1985), Completing the Internal Market, White Paper from the Commission to the Council, Luxembourg.
Commission of the European Communities (1988), Creation of a European financial area, European Economy, No. 36.
Committee for the Study of Economic and Monetary Union (1989a), Report on Economic and Monetary Union in the European Community, Luxembourg.
Committee for the Study of Economic and Monetary Union (1989b), Collection of papers submitted to the Committee for the Study of Economic and Monetary Union, Luxembourg.
Deutsche Bundesbank (1979), Die D-Mark als internationale Anlagewährung, Monatsberichte, November.
Deutsche Bundesbank (1985), Zur Freizügigheit in Kapitalverkehr der Bundesrepublik mit dem Ausland, Monatsberichte, July.
Lamberto Dini (1988), The liberalization of capital and the strengthening of the EMS, Statement before the Committee on Economic and Monetary Affairs and Industrial Policy of the European Parliament (13 July).
Rudiger Dornbusch (1986), Special exchange rates for capital account transactions, The World Bank Economic Review 1, 3–33.
W.F. Duisenberg (1985), Steps towards international monetary order, Speech at a meeting of the Friedrich Ebert Foundation, Berlin, 24 January.
Sebastian Edwards (1984), The order of liberalization of the external sector in developing countries, Essays in International Finance, Princeton.
Barry Eichengreen (1993), Reconstructing Europe's trade and payments, The European Payments Union, Manchester.
Barry Eichengreen and Charles Wyplosz (1993), The unstable EMS, Brookings Papers on Economic Activity, Washington DC, 51–143.
Wietze Eizenga *et al.* (1988), The quest for national and global economic stability, Dordrecht.
Otmar Emminger (1986), D-Mark, Dollar, Währungskrisen, Erinnerungen eines ehemaligen Bundesbankpräsidenten, Stuttgart.
Donald E. Fair and Christian de Boissieu (1988), International monetary and financial integration, The European dimension, Dordrecht.
Donald E. Fair and Christian de Boissieu (1989), Financial institutions in Europe under new competitive conditions, Dordrecht.
Favier Pierre and Michel Martin-Roland (1990), La décennie Mitterand, Paris.
Norman S. Fieleke (1994), International capital transactions: should they be restricted?, New England Economic Review, March/April.
Carsten Freiberg-Jensen and Jens Hald (1986), Foreign exchange liberalization and capital movements, Monetary Review, Danmarks Nationalbank, Copenhagen (February).
Michel Galy (1986), La place du contrôle des mouvements de capitaux dans la politique économique française et les perspectives lieés à son allégement, in Fair and de Boissieu (1988).
Alberto Giovannini and Jae Won Park (1992), Capital controls and international trade finance, Journal of International Economics 33, 285–304.
Leonhard Gleske (1986), The liberalization of capital movements in the European Community, Translation of a speech for the Institut für Kapitalmarktforschung, Frankfurt.
Joseph Gold (1977), International capital movements under the law of the International Monetary Fund, IMF Pamphlet Series, no. 21, Washington D.C.
John B. Goodman (1992), Monetary sovereignty; the politics of central banking in Western Europe, Ithaca/London.
Vittorio Grilli (1989), Europe 1992: issues and prospects for the financial markets, Economic Policy, 388–421.
Hans von der Groeben (1991), Kommentar zur EWG Vertrag, Baden Baden.

Daniel Gros (1988), Dual exchange rates in the presence of incomplete market separation, Long-run effectiveness and policy implications, Staff Papers, International Monetary Fund, Vol. 35, 437–60.
Daniel Gros and Niels Thygesen (1992), European monetary integration, From the European Monetary System to the European Monetary Union, London.
Daniel Gros and Niels Thygesen (1992), Capital controls and foreign exchange market crises in the EMS, European Economic Review 36, 1533–1544.
Noud Gruijters (1995), Financiële integratie en monetair beleid, Amsterdam.
Gottfried Haberler (1976), The case against capital controls for balance of payments reasons, in Swoboda (1976).
V.A. Halberstadt *et al.* (1974), Economie in overleg, Leiden.
John Hewson and Eisuke Sakakibara (1977), The effectiveness of German controls on capital inflow, Weltwirtschaftliches Archiv, Band 113, Heft 4, 645–666.
M.W. Holtrop (1956), Monetaire aspecten van de economische integratie, De Economist (104), reprinted as Monetary aspects of economic integration, in M.W. Holtrop (1972), Money in an open economy, Leiden.
M.W. Holtrop (1968), Het tot stand brengen van een Europese kapitaalmarkt, recensie van het Rapport van een door de Commissie van de EEG ingestelde groep deskundigen, De Economist, 752–758.
P.M. Hommes (1980), Nederland en de Europese eenwording, Den Haag.
J. Keith Horsefield (1969), The International Monetary Fund 1945–1965, Washington, DC.
André Icard (1994), The experience gained with monetary policy instruments in France, speech held in Frankfurt, reproduced in Deutsche Bundesbank, Auszüge aus Presseartikeln, June.
International Monetary Fund (1978), Articles of Agreement, Washington DC.
International Monetary Fund, Annual Reports on Exchange arrangements and exchange restrictions, Washington DC.
H. Jager (1987), Financial integration, exchange-rate regimes and macro-economic performance, An empirical optimisation approach, Research memorandum, University of Amsterdam.
H. Jager and E. de Jong (1990), Internationale financiering; de theorie en de Nederlandse praktijk, Leiden/Antwerpen.
P.J.G. Kapteyn and P. Verloren van Themaat (1987), Inleiding tot het recht van de Europese Gemeenschappen, Deventer.
Andreas Kees (1984), The Monetary Committee; monetary integration through a committee, translation of a contribution to the Jahrbuch der Europäischen Integration 1981, Institut für Europäische Politik, Bonn.
Andreas Kees (1987), The Monetary Committee of the European Community, Kredit und Kapital (20), Heft 2, 258–267.
Andreas Kees (1994), The Monetary Committee as a promoter of European integration, in Bakker (1994a).
Reiner Koenig and Michael Ledig (1989), Capital transactions, exchange rates and external adjustment, An analysis from the standpoint of the Federal Republic of Germany, mimeo, Deutsche Bundesbank, Frankfurt.
Alexandre Lamfalussy (1981), Changing attitudes towards capital movements, in F. Cairncross (ed.), Changing perceptions of economic policy, London.
Nigel Lawson (1992), The view from No. 11, Memoirs of a Tory radical, London.
Emile van Lennep (1991), Emile van Lennep in de wereldeconomie, Herinneringen van een internationale Nederlander, Leiden.
Jean-Victor Louis (1988), 'Monetary capacity' in the Single European Act, Common Market Law Review, No. 25, 9–34.
Peter Ludlow (1982), The making of the European Monetary System, A case study of the politics of the European Community, London.

Nancy P. Marion (1994), Dual exchange rates in Europe and Latin America, The World Bank Economic Review 8, 213–245.
Robert Marjolin (1989), Architect of European Unity: Memoirs 1911–1986, London.
William Marois (1980), La réglementation des mouvements de capitaux à court terme depuis 1959, Banque, Nos. 401 and 402.
Donald J. Matthieson and Liliana Rojas-Suárez (1993), Liberalization of the capital account, Experiences and issues, International Monetary Fund, Occasional paper, Washington DC.
Ronald I. McKinnon (1991), The order of economic liberalization, Financial control in the transition to a market economy, Baltimore/London.
Paul van de Meerssche (1971), De Europese integratie 1945–70, Antwerpen/Rotterdam.
Jacques Mertens de Wilmars (1963), Währungsperspektiven des Gemeinsamen Marktes, in: Weltwirtschaftliches Archiv (90), 350–376.
Monetary Committee (1958), Statutes of the Monetary Committee, Brussels.
Monetary Committee (1978), Twenty years of the Monetary Committee, 1958–78, Brussels.
Monetary Committee (1979), Compendium of Community monetary texts, Brussels.
Monetary Committee (1979), Annual activity reports, 1958–1987, Brussels/Luxembourg.
Nationale Bank van België (1992), The operation of the two-tier foreign exchange market, The experience and its lessons, mimeo, Brussels.
Colette Neme (1986), Les possibilités d'abolition du contrôle des changes français, Revue d'Economie Politique, No 2, 177–194.
Conrad J. Oort (1988), Freedom of capital movements in the European Community, in Eizenga (1988).
Organisation for Economic Co-operation and Development (1982), Controls on international capital movements, The experience with controls on international financial credits, loans and deposits, Financial Markets Trends, 1–13, Paris.
Organisation for Economic Co-operation and Development (1990), Liberalisation of capital movements and financial services in the OECD area, Paris.
Organisation for Economic Co-operation and Development (1992), Banks under stress, Paris.
Organisation for Economic Co-operation and Development (1993), Exchange control policy, Paris.
Tommaso Padoa-Schioppa (1987), Efficiency, stability and equity: a strategy for the evolution of the economic system of the European Community, Brussels.
S. Posthuma (1959), Some monetary aspects of the Rome Treaty, reprinted in Analyses en beschouwingen in retrospect, Leiden/Antwerpen, 1982.
H.O.C.R. Ruding (1969), Naar één geïntegreerde Europese kapitaalmarkt?, Leiden.
H.O.C.R. Ruding (1986), Speech for the International Capital Market Conference, London.
A.A. Scholten (1990), Liberalisatie van de financiële markten, in: Jager and de Jong (1990).
Olaf Sleijpen (1994), Kapitaalrestricties: Portugese en Spaanse ervaringen, ESB, 19 January.
Anthony D. Smith (1992), International financial markets: the performance of Britain and its rivals, National Institute of Economic and Social Research, Cambridge.
René Smits (1991), Commentary on Article 105 in: von der Groeben *et al.*, 3026–3039.
Pieter Stek (1994), The OECD and international economic cooperation, in Bakker (1994a).
Alfred Steinherr (1989), Financial innovation, internationalization, deregulation and market integration in Europe: Why does it all happen now?, in: Fair and de Boissieu (1989), 49–63.
Alfred Steinherr and Geoffrey de Schrevel (1988), Liberalization of financial transactions in the Community with particular reference to Belgium, Denmark and the Netherlands, European Economy, No. 36, 117–147.
Alexander Swoboda (1976), Capital movements and their control, Proceedings of the second conference of the International Center for Monetary and Banking Studies, Leiden/Genève.
A. Szász (1974), De rol van deviezenrestricties bij de regulering van het internationale kapitaalverkeer, in V.A. Halberstadt (1974).
A. Szász (1988), Monetaire diplomatie, Nederlands internationale monetaire politiek 1958–1987, Leiden.

Guiseppe Tesauro (1985), The exchange control in Italy and itspossible reform, mimeo, Maastricht.

Louis-Georges Teyssier (1973), Le contrôle des changes en France de 1932 à 1972, Paris.

Margaret Thatcher (1993), The Downing Street years, London.

Niels Thygesen (1985), The phasing-out of exchange controls in Denmark, Skandinaviska Enskilda Banken, Quarterly Review, No. 3, 59–65.

Jan Tinbergen (1952), On the theory of economic policy, Amsterdam.

James Tobin (1978), A proposal for international monetary reform, The Eastern Economic Journal, Vol. 4, No. 3/4, 153–159.

W.F.V. Vanthoor (1993), Een oog op Holtrop, Grondlegger van de Nederlandse monetaire analyse, Amsterdam.

Alan Walters (1986), Britain's economic renaissance: Margaret Thatcher's reforms 1979–1984, Oxford.

H.R. Warris (1992), Het Monetair Comité en de liberalisatie van het kapitaalverkeer binnen de EG, doctoraalscriptie Universiteit van Groningen.

A.H.E.M. Wellink (1990), Mogelijkheden van het monetaire beleid na de liberalisering: de visie van de Nederlandsche Bank, in: De mogelijkheden voor het monetaire beleid na de liberalisatie, Preadviezen, NIBE, Amsterdam.

Charles Wyplosz (1986), Capital controls and balance of payments crises, Journal of International Money and Finance 5, 167–179.

Charles Wyplosz (1988), Capital flow liberalization and the EMS: A French perspective, European Economy, No. 36, 87–103.

Jelle Zijlstra (1985), A central banker's view, Selected speeches and articles, ed. by C. Goedhart, *et al.*, Dordrecht.

Subjects

Persons

FINANCIAL AND MONETARY POLICY STUDIES

* * 1. J.S.G. Wilson and C.F. Scheffer (eds.): *Multinational Enterprises.* Financial and Monitary Aspects. 1974 ISBN 90-286-0124-4
* * 2. H. Fournier and J.E. Wadsworth (eds.): *Floating Exchange Rates.* The Lessons of Recent Experience. 1976 ISBN 90-286-0565-7
* * 3. J.E. Wadsworth, J.S.G. Wilson and H. Fournier (eds.): *The Development of Financial Institutions in Europe, 1956–1976.* 1977 ISBN 90-286-0337-9
* * 4. J.E. Wadsworth and F.L. de Juvigny (eds.): *New Approaches in Monetary Policy.* 1979 ISBN 90-286-0848-6
* * 5. J.R. Sargent (ed.), R. Bertrand, J.S.G. Wilson and T.M. Rybczynski (ass. eds.): *Europe and the Dollar in the World-Wide Disequilibrium.* 1981 ISBN 90-286-0700-5
* * 6. D.E. Fair and F.L. de Juvigny (eds.): *Bank Management in a Changing Domestic and International Environment.* The Challenges of the Eighties. 1982 ISBN 90-247-2606-9
* * 7. D.E. Fair (ed.) in cooperation with R. Bertrand: *International Lending in a Fragile World Economy.* 1983 ISBN 90-247-2809-6
* 8. P. Salin (ed.): *Currency Competition and Monetary Union.* 1984 ISBN 90-247-2817-7
* * 9. D.E. Fair (ed.) in cooperation with F.L. de Juvigny: *Government Policies and the Working of Financial Systems in Industrialized Countries.* 1984 ISBN 90-247-3076-7
* 10. C. Goedhart, G.A. Kessler, J. Kymmell and F. de Roos (eds.): *Jelle Zijlstra, A Central Banker's View.* Selected Speeches and Articles. 1985 ISBN 90-247-3184-4
* 11. C. van Ewijk and J.J. Klant (eds.): *Monetary Conditions for Economic Recovery.* 1985 ISBN 90-247-3219-0
* * 12. D.E. Fair (ed.): *Shifting Frontiers in Financial Markets.* 1986 ISBN 90-247-3225-5
* 13. E.F. Toma and M. Toma (eds.): *Central Bankers, Bureaucratic Incentives, and Monetary Policy.* 1986 ISBN 90-247-3366-9
* * 14. D.E. Fair and C. de Boissieu (eds.): *International Monetary and Financial Integration.* The European Dimension. 1988 ISBN 90-247-3563-7
* 15. J. Cohen: *The Flow of Funds in Theory and Practice.* A Flow-Constrained Approach to Monetary Theory and Policy. 1987 ISBN 90-247-3601-3
* 16. W. Eizenga, E.F. Limburg and J.J. Polak (eds.): *The Quest for National and Global Economic Stability.* In Honor of Hendrikus Johannes Witteveen. 1988 ISBN 90-247-3653-6
* * 17. D.E. Fair and C. de Boissieu (eds.): *The International Adjustment Process.* New Perspectives, Recent Experience and Future Challenges for the Financial System. 1989 ISBN 0-7923-0013-0
* 18. J.J. Sijben (ed.): *Financing the World Economy in the Nineties.* 1989 ISBN 0-7923-0090-4

FINANCIAL AND MONETARY POLICY STUDIES

19. I. Rizzo: *The 'Hidden' Debt.* With a Foreword by A.T. Peacock. 1990 ISBN 0-7923-0610-4
*20. D.E. Fair and C. de Boissieu (eds.): *Financial Institutions in Europe under New Competitive Conditions.* 1990 ISBN 0-7923-0673-2
21. R. Yazdipour (ed.): *Advances in Small Business Finance.* 1991 ISBN 0-7923-1135-3
*22. D.E. Fair and C. de Boissieu (eds.): *Fiscal Policy, Taxation and the Financial System in an Increasingly Integrated Europe.* 1992 ISBN 0-7923-1451-4
23. W.C. Boeschoten: *Currency Use and Payment Patterns.* 1992 ISBN 0-7923-1710-6
24. H.A. Benink: *Financial Integration in Europe.* 1993 ISBN 0-7923-1849-8
25. G. Galeotti and M. Marrelli (eds.): *Design and Reform of Taxation Policy.* 1992 ISBN 0-7923-2016-6
*26. D.E. Fair and R. Raymond (eds.): *The New Europe: Evolving Economic and Financial Systems in East and West.* 1993 ISBN 0-7923-2159-6
27. J.O. de Beaufort Wijnholds, S.C.W. Eijffinger and L.H. Hoogduin (eds.): *A Framework for Monetary Stability.* Papers and Proceedings of an International Conference (Amsterdam, The Netherlands, 1993). 1994 ISBN 0-7923-2667-9
*28. D.E. Fair and R. Raymond (eds.): *The Competitiveness of Financial Institutions and Centres in Europe.* 1994 ISBN 0-7923-3131-1
29. A.F.P. Bakker: *The Liberalization of Capital Movements in Europe.* The Monetary Committee and Financial Integration, 1958–1994. 1996 ISBN 0-7923-3591-0
30. H.A. Benink: *Coping with Financial Fragility and Systemic Risk.* 1995 ISBN 0-7923-9612-X

*Published on behalf of the *Société Universitaire Européenne de Recherches Financières* (SUERF), consisting the lectures given at Colloquia, organized and directed by SUERF.

Kluwer Academic Publishers – Dordrecht / Boston / London

MIX
Papier aus verantwortungsvollen Quellen
Paper from responsible sources
FSC® C105338

If you have any concerns about our products,
you can contact us on
ProductSafety@springernature.com

In case Publisher is established outside the EU,
the EU authorized representative is:
Springer Nature Customer Service Center GmbH
Europaplatz 3, 69115 Heidelberg, Germany

Printed by Libri Plureos GmbH
in Hamburg, Germany